C. F. Martin
& His Guitars,
1796-1873

C.F. Martin & His Guitars, 1796-1873

Philip F. Gura

THE UNIVERSITY OF NORTH CAROLINA PRESS   CHAPEL HILL & LONDON

© 2003
The University of North Carolina Press
All rights reserved
Designed by Richard Hendel
Set in Monotype Walbaum, Rosewood, Monotype Clarendon
by Eric M. Brooks
Manufactured in the United States of America
Color section manufactured in China

This book was published with the assistance of the
H. Eugene and Lillian Youngs Lehman Fund of the University of
North Carolina Press. A complete list of books published with the
assistance of the Lehman Fund appears at the end of the book.

Library of Congress Cataloging-in-Publication Data
Gura, Philip F., 1950–
C. F. Martin and his guitars, 1796–1873 / Philip F. Gura.
    p. cm. — (H. Eugene and Lillian Youngs Lehman series)
Includes bibliographical references (p.) and index.
ISBN 0-8078-2801-7 (cloth: alk. paper)
1. C. F. Martin & Co. 2. Martin, C. F. (Christian Frederick),
1796–1873. 3. Guitar makers—United States. I. Title. II. Series.
ML424.M275 G8   2003
787.87'1973—dc21   2003004079

cloth   07 06 05 04 03   5 4 3 2 1

FOR JIM BOLLMAN:

connoisseur, bon vivant, roustabout, good friend

The time was, and that not many years hence, when we regarded the guitar as an instrument of about as much importance as a good corn-stalk fiddle, a pumpion [pumpkin] trumpet, or a two-penny jews-harp; and in about the same company, as we are aware, it is still ranked by thousands who estimate its merits by the tones produced on the wretched catchpenny instruments so common in this country. . . . To fix a just estimate of the guitar one should listen to the tone produced on a good instrument, by a competent guitarist.
—Family Magazine, *1838*

I think and know Martin Guitars are the best made and feel so shur of it that I could nearly Preach it.
—E. A. Coldridge, Demopolis, Alabama, October 8, *1867*

In your father the world has lost—not only a good man, but an ingenious and truly great artist in his line, for who has not heard of the world-renowned "Martin Guitar"?
—N. Marache, New York City, October 28, *1873*

CONTENTS

Selections of color illustrations follow pages 12, 44, 108, 140, and 172.

PREFACE

"An institution," Ralph Waldo Emerson reminds us, "is the lengthened shadow of one man." So it is with C. F. Martin & Company, maker of what are generally considered the finest acoustic guitars in the world. Remarkably, the company has held this distinction for over one hundred fifty years, testament to the uncompromising devotion to craftsmanship of its founder, Christian Frederick Martin. *C. F. Martin and His Guitars, 1796–1873*, based in a myriad of hitherto unexamined primary sources — scores of account books, hundreds of letters, and other unique archival materials (see Appendix A) — made available by C. F. Martin & Company, traces the history of this firm from 1833 to 1873, through Martin's career in America. Not strictly a biography, this book uses Martin to offer both a touchstone to the nineteenth-century music trade and a unique tutorial in the evolution of America's burgeoning nineteenth-century economy.

Martin's initial success as a guitar maker depended on the culturewide interest in the guitar and its music that had begun in Europe about 1800 and reached the United States a few decades later. By these years the instrument had acquired its modern, six-stringed form, and widely published "tutors" for the guitar promulgated a sophisticated technique congruent to the music of the European classical tradition. Eventually, the instrument even drew its own composers, Hector Berlioz and Joseph Kreutzer among them, and its own virtuosos, solo performers such as Fernando Sor and Niccolò Paganini (better remembered for his violin playing), who filled large concert halls. One Frenchman even coined a term for the European infatuation with the guitar. He called it *la guitaromanie* — guitarmania.

By the 1820s the guitar, like European classical music in general, had become à la mode in the United States as well, but on terms different from those across the Atlantic. Not many of the great virtuosos, for example, performed on these shores, and concertgoers outside New York and other large cities had fewer opportunities to hear the instrument on the stage. Instead, Americans stricken by the transatlantic strain of "la guitaromanie" adapted it to their own needs and interests. Less expensive and more portable than the piano, requiring different facility than wind instruments, the guitar proved a welcome accompaniment to the parlor songs, ballads, and popular operatic music that proliferated in Victorian America. By the 1840s the guitar, like the piano, violin, and flute, was a fixture in homes in which the performance of music marked a family's engagement with emergent middle-class culture.

This was the setting to which Christian Frederick Martin (1796–1873) brought his skills as craftsman and entrepreneur and in which his instruments eventually were judged the finest available. His story begins in Saxony, the son of a member of the cabinetmakers' guild. The young Martin followed in his father's footsteps but also wished to learn to make musical instruments, a craft he eventually mastered in Vienna under the tutelage of the renowned guitar maker Johann Georg Stauffer. After rising to foreman in Stauffer's shop, Martin returned to his home in Neukirchen to practice his craft. But in 1833 he followed the lead of many of his compatriots and immigrated to the United States, settling in New York City and quickly establishing himself in its vibrant musical life. In addition to producing a small number of guitars on the designs he had learned in Vienna, Martin imported large numbers of European instruments for both professional and amateur musicians and developed an extensive business in instrument repair.

In 1839, at the instigation of Heinrich Schatz, also from Saxony and an instrument maker, Martin moved ninety miles to the southwest, to Nazareth, Pennsylvania, near the large Moravian settlement at Bethlehem. This rural area had reminded Schatz of his native country, and Martin obviously concurred. By the late 1840s he was making guitars, now of his own design, on a full-time basis and marketing them throughout the United States. He showed remarkable initiative in developing new business contacts throughout the Midwest and South as well as in the Northeast. Handling his own advertising and correspondence, Martin capitalized on the nation's rapid geographic and economic expansion in the antebellum years. By 1860 his had become the country's premier guitar, eclipsing those of such rivals as James Ashborn of Wolcottville, Connecticut, and William B. Tilton of New York City, his main competitors for market share.

After 1865, spurred by the rapid expansion of capital initiated by the North's mobilization during the Civil War, Martin changed his business plan to accord with the supercharged economic climate. To expedite marketing and shipping, he established a close relationship with the New York musical instrument dealer and importer C. A. Zoebisch, to whom he sent almost all his instruments. In addition, in 1867, as his age dictated a gradual withdrawal from the more demanding aspects of his business, he formed a legal partnership with his son C. F. Martin Jr. and his nephew, C. F. Hartmann. C. F. Martin and Company, as the firm now was called, continued its relationship with Zoebisch, who worked tirelessly to keep Martin's guitars in the public eye, as well as to crush other competitors. At his death in 1873, Martin was widely eulogized as the country's most notable guitar maker, a reputation that his company maintained and extended over the next decades.

The archive of C. F. Martin's forty-year career is unsurpassed in its depth and richness. It consists of scores of accounting daybooks, ledgers, and other financial record books, and a great volume of business correspondence, both letters and bills. This archive documents various decades differently. For Martin's years in New York City (1833–39), for example, several large account books record in great detail his importation and resale of European musical instruments and his extensive musical instrument repair business. In addition, these accounts document Martin's first attempts to make guitars, though this was not yet his major business. Another record book reveals Martin's complex business arrangements with Charles Bruno, whom he took in as a partner in the mid-1830s. Another describes Martin's entire inventory in 1839, when he was about to move to Pennsylvania and contracted to sell his business to another New York firm. This document and other related ones provide an invaluable index of wholesale pricing in the music trade in the late 1830s.

For some unknown reason, though, the period from 1839 to 1850, covering Martin's first decade in Nazareth, is almost wholly undocumented. No accounting journal is extant, and only from the late 1840s are there any letters. Beginning about 1850, however, the documentation becomes remarkably full from both account books and, for the first time, business correspondence. The following decade was particularly important for Martin. During this period he refined his guitars' construction, settling on a new way to brace his instruments' tops which marks his lasting contribution to modern guitar design. The 1850s also saw the standardization of his guitars' dimensions and appointments, documented in one of the manuscript daybooks from this decade which lists hundreds of his instruments, with their sizes and ornamentation recorded in great detail. By this point Martin was almost exclusively a guitar maker, no longer importing instruments, and repairing only those of his own manufacture if returned for that purpose.

The remarkable archive of business correspondence with firms all over the eastern United States, hundreds of letters and bills, records the story of Martin's embrace of the "market revolution" that transformed the American economy from a regional to a national entity. At this time a revolution in transportation that permitted the relatively inexpensive and dependable transfer of goods west to the Mississippi River, south to the Gulf Coast, and, soon thereafter, across the continent, opened important new markets for savvy entrepreneurs. The letters detail how Martin brokered his own instruments through scores of middlemen in these regions with whom he kept in almost weekly contact and who received his goods via the new "express" agencies that expedited shipment over long distances. Virtually on a daily basis, he personally addressed the needs of anyone interested in music: owners of large urban music houses, well-known performers, music instructors at private academies and in city studios, even amateur players who wrote of their special needs in instruments. Supplemented by detailed account books and records of his transactions with local banks, Martin's correspondence demonstrates how the "American system" of canals, railroads, steamboats, and banks, along with the express companies that linked them all, enabled an entrepreneur to cultivate a national market for his goods.

In the 1850s Martin battled for supremacy in the guitar world with two other makers, James Ashborn and William Tilton. We are fortunate to be able to compare Martin's business with Ashborn's, for one of Ashorn's account books, for the early 1850s, is extant and documents his highly mechanized factory in rural Connecticut. There he built instruments of one standard size and adapted their manufacture to the strict division of labor that marked the earliest phase of the industrial revolution. Ashborn also chose to market all his instruments to only two firms, large New York wholesalers who advertised his guitars as their own. Martin's other competitor, Tilton, patented several important innovations in guitar design and eventually sold his rights to them to other large music houses, which then had the instruments manufactured under their names. Unlike Ashborn, however, whose instruments rarely carried his name, Tilton insisted on having his prominently displayed on them, alongside the music house's stamp.

Martin's own records during this period show that he, like Ashborn, took steps to streamline work in his factory. He welcomed the greater publicity for his instruments that came through his agents' advertisements and the endorsements from prominent teachers and artists. But when some of the same kinds of large firms that had signed Ashborn and bought the rights to Tilton's patents approached him, Martin maintained his independence. Thus, although through the 1860s Ashborn produced many more guitars per annum than Martin (we have no records of Tilton's output), the unexcelled quality of Martin's guitars allowed him to maintain supremacy in the trade.

After the Civil War, Martin began to change his way of doing business. In particular, he moved more and more of his instruments through one wholesaler, C. A. Zoebisch & Sons, which worked with him in various ways to manipulate the market in favor of his instruments. By 1864 he and Zoebisch carried on an extensive correspondence regarding orders for guitars that Zoebisch & Sons had acquired in and beyond the city. Concomitantly, the extensive correspondence with other houses and clients around the country which had characterized Martin's business in the 1850s now greatly decreased. Instead, most inquiries and comments came via Zoebisch & Sons, which, while not claiming Martin's guitars as its own, clearly had become essential to Martin's success in the market.

In 1867 Martin implicitly acknowledged his advancing age through the formation of a partnership with his son (known as Frederick or Fritz) and his nephew, both of whom had long worked for him. From this point, he stamped his guitars "C. F. Martin & Co." rather than "C. F. Martin." This new arrangement, which required the two junior partners to invest in the firm, ensured the financial future of the company that Martin had labored to build over three decades. Daybooks and ledgers from this period indicate Frederick's growing involvement in and control over business decisions in the firm.

These accounts also record the first orders from Lyon & Healy, a Chicago-based music wholesaler that, in the 1870s, began to challenge other houses for preeminence in the American music trade. Martin's difficulties in supplying Lyon & Healy with the numbers of guitars it sought, and at the discount prices it wanted, caused much friction and eventually contributed to the Chicago firm's decision to manufacture its own instruments. By the 1880s Lyon & Healy had become one of the largest musical instrument makers in the nation. Even as C. F. Martin & Company struggled to meet this challenge, however, it rejected the large-scale factory production that eventually defined Lyon & Healy's operation. Instead, it continued to handcraft its guitars, even as it allowed Zoebisch & Sons to try every trick to keep Martin guitars, and its own firm, on top of the market.

For four decades C. F. Martin adapted to a constantly expanding and evolving market economy. Indeed, his career epitomizes the early history of manufacturing. He began his trade in Europe in a medieval guild system of handcraftsmanship based in the tutorial relationship of master and apprentice. Frustrated by the restrictions this placed on his enterprise, he immigrated to New York City, where he rightly gauged the new nation's obsession with music. He capitalized on his European connections and seized the opportunity to establish himself as a middleman in the transatlantic importation of goods. After he moved to Nazareth, he constructed a small steam-powered workshop and reorganized his labor force according to each worker's specific skills, both actions characteristic of the early industrial revolution. By the post–Civil War era he had confronted the challenge of competitors that produced goods in huge factories like Lyon & Healy's, where much of the labor was carried on by steam-powered machinery and which spent large sums of money on national advertising. He responded by consolidating his relationship with a major New York wholesaler that could better sell his goods in the new markets these upstarts had begun to serve.

To be sure, Martin's success in the early American music trade was unique. But his career is equally significant for its typicality. His is an inside narrative of American business during the decades when thousands of other nineteenth-century craftspeople, immigrant and native-born, similarly embraced the promise of American enterprise. And, like many of these entrepreneurs, Martin, too, succeeded financially through his cultivation of a new class of consumers who viewed the goods they acquired as markers of their social position. His story opens new windows on our view of nineteenth-century American business.

In many ways, this has been an unusual book to write. For one thing, it was a bit like trying to discuss *Hamlet* without the prince, for although the book has C. F. Martin at its center, we know very little about his personal life. Almost none of his own letters survive, and thus I have had to reconstruct large portions of his story through the correspondence of those who wrote to him. Further, very few of these letters concern personal matters but instead are devoted to the manufacture and marketing of guitars. Only a handful are from family members, and these missives do not provide enough information to give rich texture to Martin's biography. Ironically, however, we are compensated for this paucity of sources about Martin's personal life by the sheer depth of the archive for his career in the music trade. With the exception of the mysterious 1840s, documentation of Martin's business career, from his several activities in New York in the 1830s to his death in 1873, is unprecedented for the history of early American music.[1]

I first became aware of these materials after I had published an essay on James Ashborn's Wolcottville, Connecticut, guitar factory and had begun, with James F. Bollman, to write *America's Instrument: The Banjo in the Nineteenth Century* (1999). Perusing Jim Washburn and Richard Johnston's *Martin Guitars* (1997), I noticed a photograph and description of scores of the company's account books, dating back to Martin's immigration to New York. For Ashborn I had had only one such source—a single record book—yet had been able to reconstruct a detailed picture of his guitar-making business in the mid-1850s. The magnitude of the Martin archive stunned me. If each record book was as rich as the single one for Ashborn's business, I could, I believed, study and present the early American musical trade from an entirely new vantage point.

In the midst of the banjo project I wrote to C. F. Martin IV to indicate my interest and ask if I might have access to the archive. After a few letters back and forth, Chris Martin consented to let me look at the materials. I had intended to do so in the course of a family trip through Pennsylvania to New England in 1998 but was unable to fit the visit into my schedule. There things lay until the summer of 2000, when I renewed the overture and was put in contact with Dick Boak, director of artist relations at C. F. Martin & Company. Dick and I finalized plans, and in July my older son, David, and I drove to Bethlehem, Pennsylvania, where we stayed overnight before driving the last ten miles to Nazareth.

None of this work would have been possible without the generosity of Chris Martin, but in particular Dick Boak's full cooperation expedited my project. After giving us a Cook's tour of the entire Martin operation, an unforgettable experience, Dick brought us to a large, old-fashioned locked filing cabinet and a sturdy vault. Personal papers and photographs of family members were in this latter storage. And then, in the locked cabinet, there they were: scores of leather-bound record books of all sizes.

When I entered the company that day, I had wanted to make an inventory and assess the books' contents, to learn what was there and what period the records covered. Within minutes I was overwhelmed. There were no fewer than three account books and ledgers from the 1830s. There was a volume that described in detail every guitar made for several years in the 1850s, as well as other accounts for that decade. There were records with the Easton Bank in nearby Easton, Pennsylvania. There were several more ledgers for the period from the Civil War through Martin's death in 1873. And there were scores more record books, and even detailed inventories of equipment, into the early twentieth century, when Martin's son, and then his grandson, ran the firm. Although this material was not unknown — some of it had been used by Mike Longworth, Walter Carter, and Jim Washburn and Richard Johnston, in different books they had done about the company — no professional historian had ever inventoried and systematically worked with it. The trove was beyond my wildest expectations.

I was so stunned that I did not know how to proceed. Properly to assess these materials would take months. Microfilming was one possibility, though costly. Photocopying on the Martin premises was an option but would still take much time and inconvenience the staff. Working at Nazareth from the originals was, for family reasons, impractical for me. I called Dick into the room where he had brought the materials and tried to give him a sense of their value to historians of nineteenth-century America. I then asked if he knew of any other materials in other parts of the factory. He spoke of *boxes* with *hundreds* of nineteenth-century letters in the attic of the "old" factory building on North Main Street! I talked with him about options for the proper organization and preservation of all these materials. And then I asked a question so preposterous that I still marvel at my presumption.

Could I take the account books, if I promised to deposit them in my home institution's rare books library immediately upon arrival and use them only therein? I didn't want an immediate answer. I wanted Dick to talk to Chris Martin, to explain the value of the materials to historians, the kind of history one could write from the archive, and how such work could be expedited if I had everyday access to the materials. We continued our family vacation, and as planned, the day before we headed south I called Dick. He gave me the go-ahead to keep them for a year.

The next day we drove virtually nonstop from Rockport, Massachusetts, to Nazareth to try to get to the factory before closing. We made it, but the individual who had recently installed new locks on the cabinet had mistakenly retained the keys and was not at work that day. Dick called him, and he drove in from his home several miles away, but with the wrong keys! Rather than send him back, Dick finally decided to call a maintenance worker to break open the lock. We sorted the books I wanted, those which covered the years of C. F. Martin Sr.'s life (for I had decided that he would be the focus of my project), packed them in one large box, placed them behind the front seat of the van, and started for North Carolina. Somewhere on Interstate 95 I realized that I had in my hands nothing less than the entire history of an American institution. I instructed my children to throw the box from the vehicle in case of any accident, but we fortunately arrived home after midnight without incident. At 8 A.M. the next morning I deposited all the materials in the rare books library, where eventually I photocopied or transcribed them. A year later, on another trip to New England, I brought these items home to Nazareth, relieved of a charge that had been both exhilarating in the work it made possible yet frightening in the responsibility it had placed on me as custodian of such a treasure.

And there still were all those boxes of letters and other ephemeral materials that lay unprotected in the attic of the "old" Martin building, on North Main Street. A century earlier someone had sorted them into bundles by year, each year tied with what had become old string, packets now suffused with the aroma of rosewood dust that had settled into them. Dick decided to send me one box of letters at a time by overnight express delivery. These bundles provided as many thrills as the account books. When one box arrived, I would open it carefully, like a child savoring a present, not knowing what it would hold. I unfolded hundreds of letters — many of which had not been read since C. F. Martin himself opened them — photocopied them, and returned the batch, eagerly to await another.

In addition to the rich correspondence from the 1850s with dealers and customers west to the Mississippi River and the immense run of letters from C. A. Zoebisch & Sons, I found hundreds of bills from the companies from which Martin ordered his supplies and raw materials, each piece of paper pierced in the middle as it was stuck down on the spike of an old-fashioned bill holder. Confronted with all these remarkable materials, as well as other family artifacts the company had graciously provided for my inspection, I began to fashion a narrative. This book is the result, the story of C. F. Martin, a life in the early American music trade.

In this work I have had the assistance of many individuals and institutions. As I have already indicated, the cooperation of C. F. Martin & Company was indispensable. The American Antiquarian Society (AAS) awarded me a Peterson Fellowship for this project, and the society's incomparable collections allowed me to fill in important gaps in my knowledge of early American music and nineteenth-century history generally. At this institution I would particularly like to thank Carolyn Sloat and Joanne Chaison, who expedited my work. The University of North Carolina at Chapel Hill provided a research leave at a critical juncture, as well as funding for illustrations and travel through an endowed professorship. At the Library Company of Philadelphia my friend James Green was always quick to answer questions when I had them, and Dale Cockrell at Vanderbilt University was equally generous with his knowledge. Robert Fraker, dealer in rare books and aficionado of music, found rare items for me, including James Ballard's guitar tutor and Charles de Marescot's *La Guitaromanie*.

Laurence Libin, of the Metropolitan Museum of Art, has always been a strong supporter of my work. On this project he was an indispensable resource as I tried to piece together the intricacies of the transatlantic trade in musical instruments. Paul Wells, at the Center for Popular Music, Murfreesboro, Tennessee, graciously responded to my inquiries, as did the music historian Lloyd Farrar. Frank Ford generously allowed access to his photographs of early guitars. Tony Creamer, owner of the Fretted Instrument Workshop in Amherst, Massachusetts, made available some of his splendid instruments for illustrations, as did Stan Werbin at Elderly Instruments in Lansing, Michigan; André P. Larson, at America's Shrine to Music; Fred Oster, of Vintage Instruments in Philadelphia; and Cathy Chinery, the Chinery Collection. David LaPlante shared his great knowledge of the construction of Martin guitars and gave me a free hand to pick from his important collection of slides that illustrate the restoration work he has performed. Bailey Adams and Bill Capell, two enthusiastic collectors of early guitars, shared photographs and pointed out many important things to me. Greg French, John and Rosalie Jacobs, Keith Davis of the Hallmark Photographic Collection, and Grant Romer at the George Eastman House generously loaned rare and beautiful images from their collections for illustrations. Fred Stipe of Photographic Services at the University of North Carolina at Chapel Hill did yeoman's work in preparing the black-and-white photographs and some of the color. John and Cheryl Conron again graciously hosted my stay in Worcester when I was at AAS.

As always, I thank my wife, Leslie, and my children, David, Katherine, and Daniel, for their love, their understanding of how much time it takes to write a book, and their toleration of my idiosyncrasies. Finally, Jim Bollman, my coauthor on *America's Instrument: The Banjo in the Nineteenth Century*, supported this project as enthusiastically as he did our earlier collaboration. Elsewhere in this book I have put on record my respect for his knowledge of and dedication to the world of early American stringed instruments, and my thanks for his years of friendship. I never would have begun writing about nineteenth-century music without him, for it was he who, in the early 1990s, sold me the guitar maker James Ashborn's remarkable financial record book and got me started in new endeavors.

Chapel Hill, North Carolina
2002

Guitarmania

PIERRE, ISABEL, AND THE GUITAR

"Bring me the guitar!" cries Isabel, the heroine of Herman Melville's novel *Pierre; or, The Ambiguities*, published in 1852. "Now listen to the guitar; and the guitar shall sing to thee the sequel of my story; for not in words can it be spoken."[1] Thus begins one of the most memorable passages in the novel through which Melville tried to win back a readership that a year earlier had been puzzled or disappointed by his *Moby-Dick*.

Unlike his five previous books, *Pierre* was set on land: rather than the "salt water" of his previous tales, in this story he promised "a rural bowl of milk."[2] Like other works in what literary historians identify as the sentimental tradition, *Pierre* centers on a romantic plot. But Melville was unable to shake off the wild philosophical speculation that many reviewers believed had marred his recent tale of the whaling industry. He thus gave his own peculiar twist to the story of young Pierre Glendinning's rejection of his wealthy fiancée, Lucy Tartan, for the mysterious, attractive, and desperately poor Isabel Banford, about whom he knew virtually nothing.

Although Melville intended finally to mock and subvert the sentimental genre, he could do so because he had read enough popular fiction to know how to manipulate its conventions. Thus, when he described Pierre's first interview with the magnetic and sensual Isabel, he put a quintessential romantic icon in her hands. As a child, Isabel explained, she had gotten her guitar, its strings broken, from a peddler who had bought it from a servant at some grand house. For some reason she then could not fathom, Isabel immediately identified with the instrument. After the peddler had restrung and tuned it for her, she took it home, laid it on her bed, and plucked different strings. Finally, she explained to Pierre, she realized that "the guitar was speaking to me; the dear guitar was singing to me; murmuring and singing to me." "Then I sang and murmured to it with a still different modulation," she continued, "and once more it answered me from a different string." This imaginary conversation, Isabel told her entranced guest, continued until she came to believe that the guitar was human.

"So listen to the guitar," she now commanded him. "Instantly," Melville wrote, "the room was populous with sounds of melodiousness, and mournfulness, and wonderfulness; the room swarmed with the unintelligible but delicious sounds." They "seemed waltzing in the room," he continued. They "hung pendulous like glittering icicles from the corners of the room; and fell upon [Pierre] with a ringing silveryness." "Among the waltzings," Melville noted in his typically rapturous way, "and the droppings, and the swarmings of the sounds," Pierre now also heard Isabel sing her own mysteries, her "tones above deftly stealing and winding amid the myriad serpentinings of the other melody."

At their next interview this almost supernatural counterpoint of voice and instrument resumed, when Isabel again relied on the guitar to speak for her. She swiftly drew the magical instrument "beneath her dark tent of hair," and as she played, Pierre was "almost deprived of consciousness by the spell flung over him." In this conversation Isabel dispelled some of the guitar's mystery. Among other things, she believed it had been owned by the mother whom she never had known, a French woman romantically connected to the man (quite possibly Pierre's father) from whose estate the peddler had purchased the instrument. Isabel proved this to Pierre by slowly breathing the words "mother, mother, mother" into the sound hole of the instrument, which, after a short time, untouched by human hand, "responded with a quick spark of melody" that "long vibrated and subsidingly tingled in the room" (plate 1-1).

At this point, with Pierre hopelessly infatuated by the young woman who might have been his half sister, Melville dropped the guitar from his story and worked other literary conventions. But the instrument had done its office. What Melville had to say about the seductive beauty and melancholy of the guitar's sounds and their preternatural identification with the human voice was a staple of mid-nineteenth-century popular culture. Isabel's guitar signaled Melville's audience in cultural codes that most of them immediately recognized and understood.

THE PHYSICAL DEVELOPMENT OF THE GUITAR

Melville used the instrument with such effect because his readers partook in a culturewide fascination with the guitar and its music (figs. 1-1 and 1-2).[3] In turn, the instrument's great popularity in Europe was directly related to its continuing physical evolution, in the late eighteenth and early nineteenth centuries, toward its modern six-string form.[4] By the 1780s, for example, six-string guitars, tuned in the modern way (E-A-D-G-B-E) and thus allowing a range of two octaves between the first and sixth strings, circulated in France and Italy and, shortly thereafter, in Spain. In that country some instruments

Figure 1-1. *This lovely engraving, published a year before Melville's* Pierre, *captures the American public's infatuation with the beauty and mystery of the guitar and its players. The long veil suggests the European origins of the instrument and its repertoire. (From* The Ladies Repository: A Monthly Periodical Devoted to Literature and Religion *[1851])*

appeared with fan strutting to reinforce the soundboard, an important new structural component often identified with the instruments of José Pagés of Cádiz. Hitherto, soundboards had been braced with bars perpendicular to the grain, a system that reduced the flexibility of the top and thus inhibited the guitar's sound. The fan strutting, with braces radiating from the sound hole

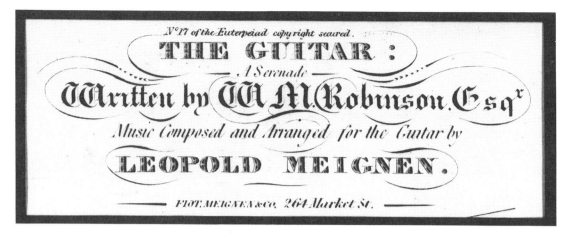

Figure 1-2. *Title page of* The Guitar: A Serenade *(ca. 1830), set to music by Leopold Meignen, who has many works for the instrument to his credit. Even by this early date in the United States the instrument and its romantic associations were widely known. (Collection of the author)*

in a fan- or star-shaped pattern, freed the soundboard's vibrations while strengthening it even more than earlier ladder bracing. This new bracing pattern, one historian of the instrument has written, marked the guitar's final "emancipation" from the lute.[5] Makers of these guitars, however, still followed tradition in positioning the bridge fairly low on the body and securing the strings by tying them through slots or holes in the bridge.

In the final transition to the early-nineteenth-century "Spanish" guitar, makers enlarged the lower bout and centered the bridge on it, a change that moved the bridge closer to the sound hole. In addition, they replaced the intricately carved rose with an open sound hole and extended the fingerboard, which now met the body at the twelfth fret, over the body right up to the hole, increasing the range of available octaves. All vestiges of a rounded, ribbed back now disappeared, and a new kind of bridge became common. Rather than tying off the strings through slots in it, makers drilled holes through the bridge and the soundboard and wedged in pins against the strings to secure them. The strings also now passed over an ivory saddle mounted on top of the bridge, a refinement that allowed one to define the lower vibrating end of the string more precisely and thus to make one's fret scale more accurate.

By the second decade of the nineteenth century this type of guitar had become standard, increasingly popular, and widely manufactured in Europe. Very quickly, a few makers began to dominate the high end of the market by virtue of their overall craftsmanship as well as their further refinement of the instrument's design. In England, foremost among these was Louis Panormo (1784–1862), patriarch of a family of instrument makers, who enjoyed the patronage of important performers. He is remembered particularly for building thin and light instruments braced by seven rather than five fan struts.[6]

On the Continent, Panormo's competition came from René-François La-cote, a celebrated French maker whose guitars, like others in the French school, had particularly narrow waists. In addition, Lacote's instruments often featured scalloped fingerboards. Johann Georg Stauffer, a Viennese maker who raised or "floated" the fingerboard above the soundboard, a struc-tural change that improved an instrument's tone, was equally influential and highly regarded.[7] London-Paris-Vienna thus marked the chief axis of the guitar trade, although makers in certain regions in Spain, particularly around Cádiz, and in Mirecourt in France also contributed significantly to the trade.

THE VIRTUOSOS

As important as they were, however, these makers and the structural changes they initiated did not alone account for the instrument's soaring popularity. Rather, craftsmen such as Panormo, Lacote, and Stauffer rose to fame along-side European performers and composers who tirelessly brought the guitar and its music before an increasingly entranced public and thus helped to cre-ate a larger market for the instruments. As one historian has noted, these gui-tarists/composers saw the need to bring the newly versatile instrument into appropriate relationship with the European musical world and thus con-stantly thought about, and composed for, the guitar in relation to other in-struments. "For the first time in musical history," A. P. Sharpe writes, "gui-tarists were looking outward at the repertoire of pianoforte, violin and symphony orchestra, instead of comparing their efforts at composition with the tradition of the lute and other fretted instruments." Because these new performers' and composers' virtuosity and pedagogy were totally comple-mentary, they "dazzled the public with their brilliance and prepared the way for amateur interest in the guitar with methods, divertissements, minuets, waltzes and studies which catered to the need of the raw novice."[8]

Foremost among these virtuosos was Fernando Sor (1778–1839), who be-stowed his blessing on Panormo's and Lacote's instruments in particular (fig. 1-3).[9] Born in Barcelona, as a composer and performer Sor early on received considerable patronage in his home country, as he later did in Paris and Lon-don. He wrote operas, symphonies, string quartets, and a number of songs, an oeuvre so important that one enthusiastic contemporary declared, "We ought to consider Sor as the inventor of a new method of *composing*."[10] Sor's most important contribution to the emergent culture of the guitar, however, resided in his five books of "studies," the first of which he published in 1827, and his influential *Methode pour la guitare*, issued in Paris in 1830.

Sor was equally praised as a performer, entertaining audiences from Lon-don to Moscow and many venues in between. Widely known and appreciated, he was particularly associated with introduction of the Spanish guitar to Eng-land, and while in London between 1815 and 1823 he had become something of a celebrity. He had the honor, for example, of a solo performance of his own

Figure 1-3. *Engraving of Fernando Sor, ca. 1820, one of the foremost virtuosos who popularized the guitar in the early nineteenth century. His instruction method and various studies, primarily composed in the 1820s and early 1830s, retain their significance today.*

work at a London Philharmonic concert and was even elected an honorary member of the Royal Academy of Music. An article in the *Harmonicon*, a periodical devoted to music, testified to his significance in English music circles. The guitar's new popularity, the writer declared, was attributable directly to "the exquisite and wonderful performances of M. Sor," for he stood "at a vast distance from all other guitarists, both as a performer and a composer." His command over an instrument, the writer concluded, "which in other hands is so limited in its means, is not only astonishing but—what is far more important—always pleasing."[11] While basking in such praise, Sor also found the time to contribute to the instrument's physical evolution, working with Panormo to refine the style of his guitars. In particular, Sor counseled him to make the soundboard, back, and sides of very light and thin woods, a feature that became a hallmark of Panormo's guitars and improved their tone.[12]

The only contemporary mentioned in the same breath with Sor, as a performer, was the Italian Mauro Giuliani (1781–1829). He had begun his illustrious musical career in Vienna, arguably the musical capital of Europe, and in 1808 played before an audience that included Beethoven.[13] Giuliani toured the continent and eventually settled in Italy, in whose cities he frequently gave concerts. Like Sor, he composed for the instrument (most successfully in duets for piano and guitar), and through his compositions he, too, became widely known in England.

People most often noted Giuliani's manner of playing, particularly his right-hand technique. As one reviewer in *Giulianiad* (an English journal named in his honor) observed, "The tone of Giuliani was brought to the greatest possible perfection." In his hands, the admirer continued (in words that Melville could have borrowed to describe Isabel's playing), "the guitar became gifted with a power of expression at once pure, thrilling and exquisite." "*In a word,*" this writer concluded, Giuliani "*made the instrument sing.*"[14] Like Sor, Giuliani was interested in refining the instrument and adapting it to new modes of expression. In some of his performances, for example, he used a smaller "terz" guitar, which he is credited with introducing into the concert repertoire. The instrument's shorter string length allowed one to tune it to a higher pitch, a third (hence, terz) above standard guitar tuning.

Dionisio Aguado (1784–1849), another Spanish guitarist, was a great admirer and eventually a good friend of Sor, with whom he spent much time in Paris toward the end of Sor's life. Like Sor, Aguado attained prominence not only through his performances but also through publishing a guitar method (1824) and several influential studies in which he advocated and exemplified a style of playing very different from that counseled by his peers. In particular, Aguado urged the use of the fingernails when plucking, a method which was rejected by Sor but which later found its greatest champion in Andrés Segovia. Aguado also introduced the "tripodion," a three-legged stand on which he rested the guitar when playing, freeing him to concentrate more fully on the tone he wished to derive from the instrument.[15]

Although Europe abounded with other talented guitarists during the first two decades of the nineteenth century, two more Italians deserve mention here, Ferdinando Carulli (1770–1841) and Matteo Carcassi (1792–1853). From Naples and Florence, respectively, these two also were highly regarded performers. Like Sor, Carulli was interested in perfecting the physical form of the instrument and toward that end advised Lacote. In addition, as early as 1810 the Neapolitan published an influential method and, more important, in

1825 a treatise titled *L'harmonie appliquée a la guitare*, the first method to focus on the instrument as accompaniment and in which he explored the relationships among both chords and arpeggios.[16]

His younger compatriot Carcassi toured widely, including to England in the early 1820s, and is best remembered for his various studies, which went through many editions and were favorites of amateur players. As Carcassi put it in the preface to one of his works, he did not intend his tutorial as a scientific treatise but rather wrote "to facilitate the study of the Guitar by adopting a system that in the most clear, simple and precise manner, might offer a thorough knowledge of this instrument." Thus, he took "the greatest care to dispose on a progressive plan each lesson in order that a pupil totally ignorant of this instrument might learn by degrees to play from the first to the last exercise without meeting any of those difficulties which through their aridity are too often the cause of his getting discouraged."[17] His method's frequent republication on both sides of the Atlantic speaks to the clarity and usefulness of Carcassi's presentation, and his own brilliant technique as a performer naturally made him more significant to a rising generation of players, many of whom were Americans.

Through these and other compelling personalities, the guitar and its music spread rapidly in the first three decades of the nineteenth century, the instrument's dizzying rise aided by the fact that some of the age's greatest composers found inspiration in and through it. The guitar was a favorite of Carl Maria von Weber and Gioacchio Antonio Rossini, for example, both of whom used it to compose the songs for which they are so well known, and was loved as well by Franz Schubert. Earlier, Luigi Boccherini had written for it, as had Joseph Kreutzer, the composer and brother of the violinist Rodolphe, his well-received trio for flute, clarinet, and guitar being particularly memorable. Even the great Niccolò Paganini wrote many solo and ensemble pieces for the instrument, an example, one historian writes, "of a musical genius of the highest order giving himself to the whole-hearted study of the guitar's mysteries."[18]

The guitar was important enough to Hector Berlioz, for whom it was a primary instrument, for him to devote several pages to it in his famous *Treatise on Instrumentation and Orchestration* (1856), where he observed that "it is almost impossible to write well for [it] without being a player." The guitar's "melancholy and dreamy character," he continued, are most distinctive and give the instrument "a real charm of its own."[19] Berlioz's training on it undeniably influenced his finest work. With the *Symphonie Fantastique* in mind, for example, one historian writes that the way Berlioz "spaces out orchestral chords, the way his phrases are shaped and his rhythms change reveal a fresh, flexible mind that has been trained in the school of the guitar rather than in the boxed-in formula of keyboard harmony."[20]

But even more than the virtuosos or the great composers, countless amateur musicians contributed to the guitar's meteoric rise (fig. 1-4). As a contributor to *Giulianiad* noted, for example, "No instrument in fifteen years [had] attained such decided success and extensive circulation," for its music and power of expression spoke to people in new and profound ways.[21] Another writer for that same journal observed that the guitar's very accessibility was a key to its popularity, for there was "something so social, so friendly, in the instrument." "It can be taken up or laid aside with so much ease," he continued, "and with its means, in a circle of friends, whether in town or country, may be had the power of dispensing . . . such quiet and full enjoyment as, taken together, belongs to no other instrument."[22] And always there was what Melville recognized, the guitar's seemingly uncanny ability to imitate human speech, for the guitar could, a writer for the *Westminster Review* noted, "warble, or articulate, or sign, or wail, or tremble, like the human voice under emotion."[23] As more and more individuals attended the performances of memorable players, and as more and more amateurs played for their own pleasure, serenading friends and lovers, the instrument and its music permeated European society.

The French guitarist and composer Charles de Marescot dubbed this rage *la guitaromanie* (guitarmania), the title of his collection of original pieces for beginning players.[24] Lithographs that depict various venues for the guitar charmingly illustrate his book (plates 1-2, 1-3, 1-4). One of these images is itself titled "La Guitaromanie." It shows a drawing room where a few guitarists entertain friends, but bursting through the door is a rush of additional players, instruments in hand, eager to join the moment. Humorously, yet accurately, this image captures the contagious excitement engendered by the six-string guitar.

MUSIC IN ANTEBELLUM CULTURE

By the 1830s, germs of guitarmania had spread across the Atlantic, where the instrument was just as eagerly embraced and, given America's unique social and economic conditions, further democratized. Again, Melville's invocation of the guitar is instructive, for we recall that Isabel was no wealthy virtuosa but a poor working girl, self-taught on the instrument. Yet she, like those European performers who dazzled audiences with their guitars' ability to evoke a range of human emotions, also used it to express otherwise unutterable truths, to give form and substance to her inner life (fig. 1-5). A guitar—unlike, say, a piano—was as accessible to people like Isabel as to the upper class Glendinnings.

Nor was Isabel unusual in her attraction to its melodies for in Jacksonian America music was omnipresent, and divisions between high and popular culture were not yet as strictly demarcated as in Europe. In particular, in the United States music functioned as a great common denominator. The historian Nicholas Tawa evokes this memorably when he writes:

Figure 1-4. *Quarter-plate ambrotype, ca. late 1850s. With the method books of Sor, Aguado, Carcassi, and others to guide them, amateur players like this striking gentleman devoted themselves to the guitar's mastery. The ribbons on his lapel perhaps indicate some sort of award for his musical skill. Also note the crude backdrop, indicative of a traveling photographer's studio. (Collection of the author)*

Figure 1-5. *Sixth-plate daguerreotype, ca. 1850. The plain clothes worn by this guitarist indicate her moderate means and thus the instrument's presence at many levels of society. Her guitar has a mustache-shaped bridge indicative of European makers. Also note the stenciled wall behind her, which suggests that the daguerreotypist took this in the woman's home. (Collection of the author)*

Everywhere the traveler went in antebellum America, he heard music of a kind and to an extent unknown in later times. He would often be awakened in a hotel at night to the guitars and voices of serenaders or to the warbling of people returning home from a concert or theater presentation. He explored city and town streets to the sounds of vendors' musical cries, street boys' whistling, street musicians' and organ grinders' performances, ballad hawkers singing their aires, and military and club-sponsored bands continually on the march, ceaselessly tooting. As he journeyed from town to town, he listened to the inveterate singing of fellow passengers in coaches, on trains, and on ships. Roaming through the countryside, on foot or horseback, he frequently caroled to himself as he went along and occasionally came upon music-making picnickers. Stopping overnight at an inn, he joined other travelers to provide the evening's entertainment, which included vocalizing, usually around a piano, in the inn's common room. If he was fortunate, someone contributed the sound of a violin, flute, or guitar, since many Americans traveled with musical instruments and ached to play them.

"In short," Tawa concludes, in antebellum America "music was likely to be heard anywhere and at any time."[25]

In New York City and Philadelphia, for example, and only to a slightly lesser extent in Boston and Charleston, the gentry and emergent middle class sought to replicate the experience of European concerts and salons, subscribing to the performances of European virtuosos or multi-instrument ensembles and inviting in their neighbors to hear the better amateur musicians among them.[26] Attempts were made to start indigenous orchestras. Teachers, often aspiring concert musicians themselves, offered lessons to those who could afford them, and method books for all manner of instruments—flute, banjo, melodeon, guitar, violin, and pianoforte, among others—gave those without as much time, money, or discipline a chance to participate in musical culture (fig. 1-6).

But such formal occasions accounted for only a tiny part of the musical activity that flourished in the new republic, for, as Tawa indicates, the sheer range of music was truly extraordinary. With the spread of labor-saving technology, for example, and the concomitant extension of leisure even in rural communities, Americans not only flocked to concerts and musical theater but to minstrel shows and burlesque opera. What most marked the culture, however, was amateur music making in the home. An editorial in the *American Musical Journal* made this connection explicit. "Music is cultivated privately to a great extent," it was noted, and "almost all parents consider it a necessary accomplishment for their children" (fig. 1-7). "Every house of respectability," the editorial continued, "has its piano, guitar, or harp, and music is the chief source of amusement at our social meetings."[27]

As the music historian Richard Crawford puts it, this phenomenon "was a business from the start," for "producers [of musical goods] taught Americans that they could have music in their homes if they made it themselves," and "their customers, sparked by aesthetic interest and special aspiration, learned how to become active participating musical consumers." And the center of it

Plate 1-1. *Sixth-plate daguerreotype, ca. 1850, of bewitching young woman seated in a simple country chair. If she let down her braided hair, she could represent the hypnotic "Isabel" who mysteriously communicates with her guitar in Herman Melville's novel* Pierre *(1852). (Collection of John and Rosalie Jacobs)*

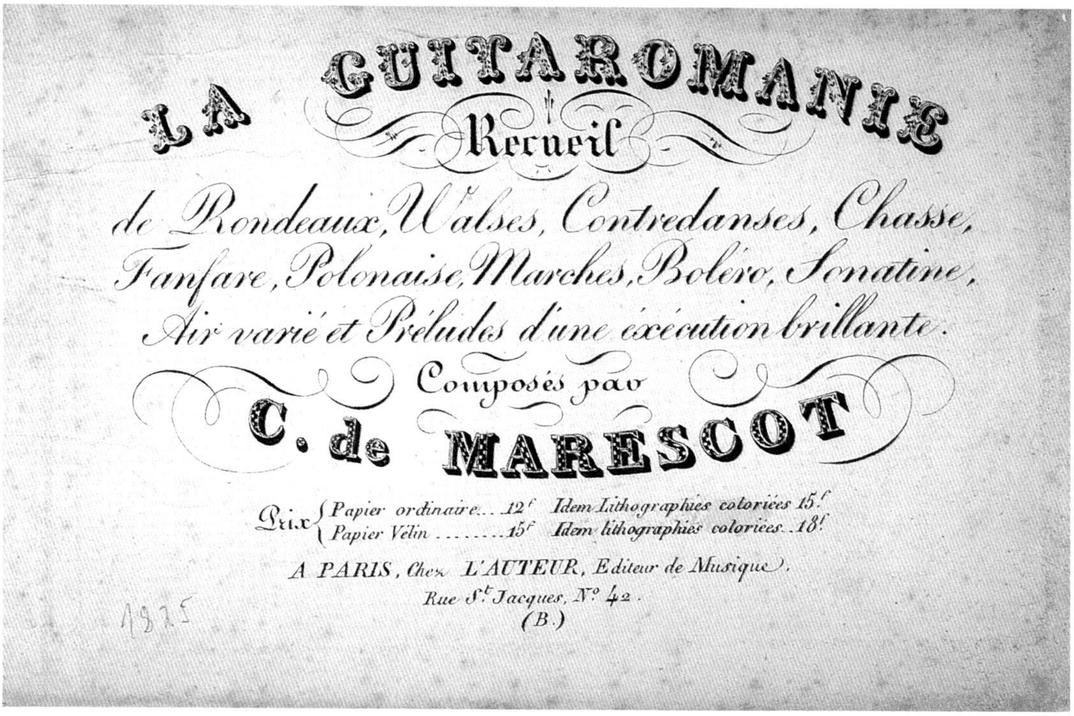

LA GUITAROMANIE

Recueil

de Rondeaux, Walses, Contredanses, Chasse, Fanfare, Polonaise, Marches, Boléro, Sonatine, Air varié et Préludes d'une exécution brillante.

Composés par

C. de MARESCOT

Prix { Papier ordinaire... 12f Idem Lithographies coloriées 15f
Papier Vélin .... 15f Idem lithographies coloriées .. 18f

A PARIS, Chez L'AUTEUR, Editeur de Musique.
Rue St. Jacques, N° 42.
(B.)

1825

Plate 1-2. *Title page of Charles de Marescot's* La Guitaromanie *(ca. 1830), a collection of pieces for guitar, illustrated with six amusing lithographs that show various advanced stages of "guitarmania" in Europe at the time that C. F. Martin left for the United States. (Collection of the author)*

Plate 1-3. *"La Guitaromanie," the title illustration from Marescot's* La Guitaromanie, *shows a formal performance of guitar music interrupted by many more players bursting through the door. Note the small child with instrument next to the player in the center of the image. (Collection of the author)*

Plate 1-4. *"La Contredanse," from Marescot's* La Guitaromanie, *shows an elegant evening entertainment with dance music provided by guitarists. One of the earliest American guitar instruction books points out that the instrument is ideal for accompaniment to such music. (Collection of the author)*

Plate 1-5. *Sixth-plate daguerreotype, ca. 1850s. This large group of musicians, including one flutist, appears to be rehearsing for a choral concert. Or perhaps they were friends gathering for an evening's entertainment. Whatever their purpose, they exemplify the importance of music to antebellum Americans. (Collection of Greg French)*

Plate 1-6. *Half-plate daguerreotype, ca. 1850. By the 1850s Americans considered playing the guitar an accomplishment that marked cultural sophistication, clearly the case in this striking image of the upper-class woman depicted in a large daguerrean format. Martin had several such New York customers who purchased expensive instruments. (Courtesy of Hallmark Photographic Collection, Hallmark Cards, Inc., Kansas City, Missouri)*

Plate 1-7. *Quarter-plate tintype, ca. 1865. By the 1840s the guitar was being played by African Americans as well as by whites. In his diary, for example, William Johnson, a free African American in antebellum Natchez, Mississippi, noted that he was taking guitar lessons. This rare image depicts a group of African American musicians, including a guitarist, posed before the photographer's backdrop. Their dress suggests that they are performers. (Collection of Greg French)*

Plate 1-8. *Quarter-plate daguerreotype, ca. 1855. These two young women, obviously from wealthy families, knew that the guitar, as well as their elegant clothes, signaled their social status. The instrument, with both bouts about the same size, probably is European. Note as well the extraordinarily long hair of the woman on the left. (Collection of Greg French)*

all was the sheet music industry, which provided an inexpensive product, "tailored to the skills and tastes of buyers, and hence an ideal artifact for a democracy." Thus the sheet music trade, Crawford concludes, "was the economic agent that, more than any other, turned the American home into a marketplace for music."[28] Writing their music to be accessible, composers of popular songs and tunes turned out hundreds of thousands of pieces of sheet music intended for performance in the parlor, the center of the new domestic sphere (fig. 1-8). Familiarity with such folios, songs meant to be accompanied by piano or, with increasing frequency, the guitar, as well as purely instrumental music, marked those who aspired to middle-class respectability (fig. 1-9). Such immensely popular performers as the Huthchinson Family singers and Jenny Lind, "the Swedish Nightingale," whose American tour was promoted by P. T. Barnum, and such composers as Stephen Foster and George Root, whose song sheets were eagerly purchased by their admirers, signaled the nation's embrace of music.[29]

Such amateur music making, deeply connected to the culture's values, was thus most significant for the subsequent development of the American musical instrument trade. An instrument and the music one played on it signaled one's social values. Vera Brodsky Lawrence, for example, one of the most astute chroniclers of the history of American music, has observed that in this period an instrument in the parlor was "more than a mere prideful status symbol," for it "provided the very foundation on which rested a pivotal nineteenth-century social institution—music in the home." "The American parlor," she continues, "rang with home-generated music: keyboard performances (often four-handed) of popular overtures, marches, and dance music (often arrangements of popular tunes from popular operas), and amateur warblings—solo and ensemble—of sentimental ballads, hit tunes from the

Figure 1-6. *Carte-de-visite, ca. late 1850s. This musician plays a melodeon, an early keyboard instrument worked by foot-operated bellows. Along with the flute, violin, and guitar, melodeons and pianos were commonly found in the Victorian home. A proliferation of instruction books put musical competence within the reach of budding musicians on all such instruments. (Collection of the author)*

Figure 1-8. *Carte-de-visite, ca. 1860. This impressively dressed musician may have been a professional performer. At his feet lies a piece of popular sheet music, "Miss Lucy Long," a tune which was initially performed on the American minstrel stage but which subsequently spread throughout Victorian culture. (Collection of the author)*

Figure 1-9. *Sixth-plate daguerreotype, ca. 1850, copy of earlier daguerreotype, ca. 1840s. This prosperous woman dressed in her finest to have her portrait taken with her guitar, indicating how much she considered it part of her self-image. Although it is difficult to tell for sure, this may be a Martin guitar. (Collection of the author)*

ing room, the African American man stroking dance tunes on his gourd banjo: these and countless other examples illuminate the variety of music making in antebellum culture. Even so unlikely a person as Henry David Thoreau, whom we usually associate with solitude in his beloved Nature, played the flute and loved to sing. "Please remember me to your family," he wrote his good friend Daniel Ricketson in 1857, "and say that I have at length learned to sing Tom Bowlin [a popular ballad] according to notes."[33] This range of amateur musical activity, one historian writes, led to nothing less than "a dramatic proliferation of instrument makers, music teachers, and music publishers," a vast subculture whose economic success centered on how they might best capitalize on this democratization of sound.[34]

THE GUITAR AND AMERICAN MUSIC

Where did the guitar fit in the hierarchy of antebellum instruments? Judging from extant sheet music and tune collections, in the 1820s the violin, flute, and piano were most common. But beginning in the 1830s, as more and more Americans learned of the new "Spanish" guitar and heard its music, it, too, became widely popular and permeated popular culture (fig. 1-10). In 1838, for example, a writer for the *New York Sunday Morning News* observed that he had "experienced much gratification from observing that the guitar [was] fast rising in the estimation of the public" and would not be surprised "if it were soon found to rival the pianoforte in popular favor." By 1854, when John Weeks Moore issued his *Complete Encyclopaedia of Music*, the most ambitious book of its kind yet published in the United States, he wrote in his entry for the "guitar" that the demand for this beautiful and graceful instrument had greatly increased until it had come into "very general use." In the same year, in one of its advertisements, the large New York music house William Hall & Son noted the "almost unparalleled demand for this beautiful and graceful instrument." The popularity of the guitar had spread so much "that there is now scarcely a family of any musical pretension but at least one of its members number [*sic*] among their accomplishments, that of playing the Guitar."[35]

Part of the guitar's growing appeal was related to its reasonable cost, for a fine instrument could be had for $25 and a serviceable one for half that, while a piano might cost several hundred dollars.[36] Portability and convenience also were factors, for, like the violin and flute, the guitar could easily be carried to wherever a musician was asked to perform and, compared, say, to a piano or harp, was no trouble to tune or maintain. Then, too, with the continued immigration of European musicians, particularly Germans, to America's cities, instruction on it (as on many other instruments) was more readily available. Finally, as Melville's use of the guitar in his fiction suggests, the instrument's association with the romantic era—and in particular its preternatural association with the human voice—also contributed greatly to its popularity.

As Hall & Son's advertisement indicates, by the 1850s the guitar had long been identified particularly with young women, and many viewed the ability to play it as one of a lady's necessary accomplishments (plate 1-6). This was, of course, true about music in general; as Tawa puts it, women "were expected to include music as part of their education. If a private teacher did not come to their homes or they to a music studio, then attendance at a private academy or seminary afforded the desired study."[37] Many instrument makers depended on such teachers for business from the young ladies in their neigh-

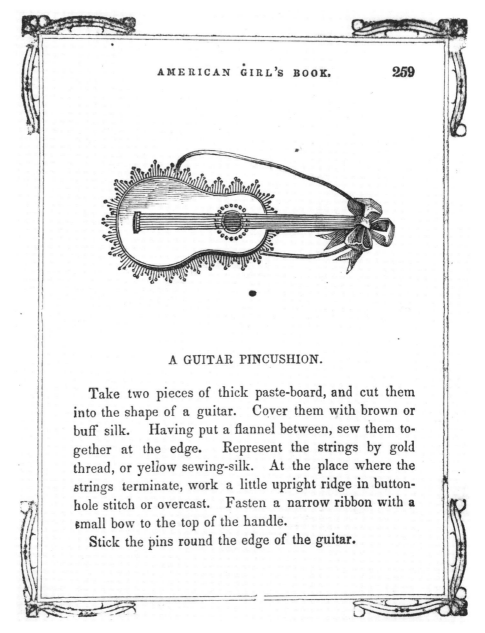

A GUITAR PINCUSHION.

Take two pieces of thick paste-board, and cut them into the shape of a guitar. Cover them with brown or buff silk. Having put a flannel between, sew them together at the edge. Represent the strings by gold thread, or yellow sewing-silk. At the place where the strings terminate, work a little upright ridge in button-hole stitch or overcast. Fasten a narrow ribbon with a small bow to the top of the handle.

Stick the pins round the edge of the guitar.

Figure 1-10. *Page from Eliza Leslie,* The American Girl's Book; or, Occupations for Play Hours *(1831; reprint, 1859). This pattern for a pincushion in the shape of a guitar indicates how deeply, even by 1831, the instrument had permeated American culture.*

borhoods, and the published descriptions of women's academies testify to the prevalence of courses of study in piano or guitar, as well as in needlework, singing, painting, and other "female" accomplishments in such institutions (fig. 1-11). As early as 1843, for example, the Albany Female Academy in New York offered instruction on the guitar as well as on the piano, as did the Columbia Female Institute in Tennessee. Indeed, this latter institution was so committed to music that it numbered among its instruments one church organ, three harps, ten pianos, and "an ample supply of guitars."[38]

Such facility particularly marked young women of quality and social ambition. Reviewing a new instruction book, for example, a writer for the *New-York Mirror* observed that "the guitar is now becoming every day a greater favourite as its capabilities are better known, especially among the ladies, who esteem it for the elegance of its form and the facilities it affords for accompanying the voice in singing."[39] The Charleston, South Carolina, writer William Gilmore Simms exemplified such commentary when he wrote a friend that the Miss Roach whom he had just met (and whom he eventually married) was "young—just 18—a pale, pleasing girl." She was "very gentle and amiable," he continued, "with dark eyes and hair," and she "sings sweetly and plays upon piano and guitar." Another author, William Wirt, away on business, wrote his daughter in Baltimore and asked, "Shall I bring you a Spanish guitar . . . what say you?," no doubt knowing that such a gift would delight a teenager who knew what was expected of her socially. And in *Annie Grayson*, a novel about life in the nation's capital, Mrs. N. P. Lasalle captured many people's sentiments when she had a character explain that he had bought a guitar for Ella, a young lady, because music was "one of life's best gifts." "It makes the heart more joyous in its hours of mirth, and it soothes it when oppressed with sorrows."[40]

Lasalle's description of the power of guitar music points to another reason for the guitar's popularity in antebellum culture: its potentially beneficial effect on character. As I have noted, people commonly associated the guitar with the parlor and the domestic scene, unlike, say, the banjo, which most often evoked the rowdiness of the minstrel stage or the dance hall (fig. 1-12).[41] The guitar's use and music thus contributed positively to one's moral development. One writer for a New York paper, for example, opined that he was glad to see the guitar better appreciated, for he looked upon the instrument "as one of the best means for diffusing through the whole mass of our variously constituted population the softening and elevating influences of music."[42] So powerful was this aspiration that it even crossed long-established racial boundaries. William Johnson, a free African American in Natchez, Mississippi, who, as a barber, had achieved considerable financial means, surrounded himself with musical instruments. In his diary for 1841 he noted that he was "taking a Lesson the Guitarr," even though he already played the piano and violin (plate 1-7).[43]

Speaking about another instrument—the accordion—whose popularity soared at the same time as the guitar's and that similarly was accessible to the masses, David Ritter praised the still-novel free reed instrument for its promotion "in children and people generally, [of] a taste for music as a source for enjoyment, and as a wonderful preservative from debasing pleasures and associates" (fig. 1-13). Such an instrument, he maintained, made "the domestic fireside pleasant for children and youth" so that, "instead of spending their time at all places where they will learn much of evil, and contract habits of

Figure 1-11.
Half-plate ambrotype, ca. 1857. This group of young, fashionably dressed women, probably a class at a "female academy," display a guitar as well as a book, perhaps to indicate that music is part of their course of study, as it was at many such institutions. Some of Martin's clients, for example, resided at "Mrs. O'Kill's Boarding School" in New York City. (Collection of the author)

Figure 1-12. *Sixth-plate daguerreotype, ca. 1855. Between 1840 and 1860 the banjo became very popular but, unlike the guitar, was associated primarily with the minstrel and dance hall stages. Only after the Civil War did it enter the Victorian parlor as an instrument worthy of study by amateurs. This banjoist's elegant dress suggests that he may have been a popular stage performer. (Courtesy James F. Bollman)*

being absent from home to find pleasure and amusement," they would absorb the beauty and discipline that accompanied music.[44] The culture presumed amateur music making in the home, be it on an accordion or a guitar, to have just such a wholesome effect.

Finally, the guitar's advocates presented it to Americans as an ideal instrument because one could use and enjoy it with a minimum of instruction and

Figure 1-13. *Sixth-plate daguerreotype, ca. 1850s. These sisters, dressed for the daguerreotypist, hold their precious belongings: one a book; the other, a small accordion, a free-reed instrument (related to the harmonica) that had a vogue in the 1840s, in part because it is easier to play than a piano or guitar but still contributed to a child's social and moral development. Note the delicate mesh gloves each child wears. (Collection of the author)*

without necessarily devoting great amounts of time or money to its mastery. In 1847, for example, the author of a guide for young ladies, probably having in mind performance on the piano, complained, "A fondness for music is so universal, that the danger is, that young ladies will devote too much time to its acquisition." Those who have no genius for it, she continued, "must sacrifice years, and, after all, give a little pleasure by their mechanical performance."[45]

The basis for this complaint did not escape one of the first American authors of a guitar tutor. "There are many persons, who, having a taste for music, would be induced to learn to accompany themselves," James Ballard wrote in 1838, "and to play a few pleasing pieces, if they thought they could do so without any serious encroachment upon the time devoted to every-day life." To such individuals, the guitar offered "peculiar facilities, since from no other instrument can be produced so much music in so short a time." A reviewer of his book concurred, noting that it supplied an important need because "many who want neither inclination nor ability to learn to accompany themselves, are deterred from making the attempt, by a consideration of the time and expense demanded for the study of the pianoforte." Well suited to busy and industrious people—in other words, to Americans—the guitar offered a way, Ballard himself wrote, to "contribute that share toward the amusements of the social circle which it is almost the duty of every one of its members to furnish."[46]

THE AMERICAN "METHODS"

Ballard introduced his tutorial method, which took into account the busyness of the American people, in his *Elements of Guitar-Playing* (1838), the first substantial instruction book for the guitar published in the United States. The earliest effort in this line had been *New Instructions for the Spanish Guitar . . . by a Professor*, published in Philadelphia by George Willig about 1816. In his preface, this anonymous "professor" celebrated the Spanish guitar as an instrument with a tone "more proper to Accompany a Voice in a Room than even the Harp or the Piano-Forte." He also urged the guitar on performers who played at "Country Dances," for it joined very well with other instruments to "fill up the Harmony." Finally, this early American advocate praised the guitar's sheer handiness. "Besides all these other Advantages," he wrote, "It has that of being so light and handy and portable that it suits all purposes of Amusement either in the House or Garden."[47]

The Philadelphia professor also recorded his surprise that the guitar was not yet as fashionable in the United States as it was abroad, "particularly among the Ladies, to whom it adds so much grace and Elegance, being (the Piano excepted), the Instrument the most adapted to them." Less than two decades later, however, in his *New and Improved Method for the Spanish Guitar*, Otto Torp noted that the "beauties of the instrument" needed no "eulogy," for by that time the guitar had become widely regarded as "an accompaniment to the voice" and, more specifically, "a means of enhancing its perfection and concealing its defects." Torp, who had offered a guitar tutor as early as 1829, thereupon contributed sections on the rudiments of music, instructions on how to hold and finger the instrument, and "easy, progressive lessons, from favorite operas with German, Italian, and English words" (fig. 1-14).[48]

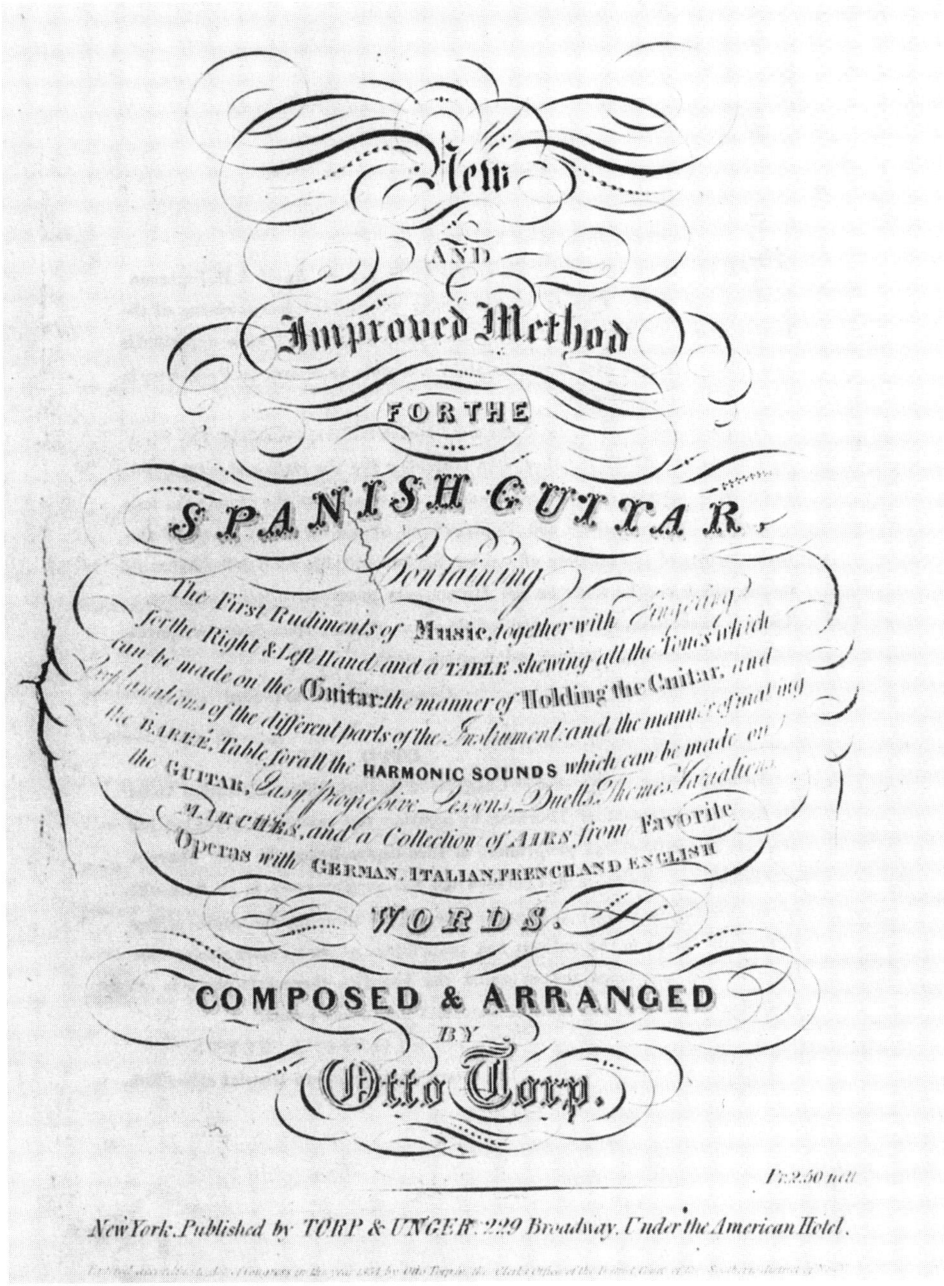

Figure 1-14. *Otto Torp,* New and Improved Method for the Spanish Guitar *(1834). One of the earliest American instruction books devoted exclusively to the six-string "Spanish" guitar, Torp's also included its author's strictures on using the guitar to accompany singing. (From the collections of the Center for Popular Music, Middle Tennessee State University)*

Ballard, however, was the first American to produce a method comparable in sophistication with those of the great European players and composers (fig. 1-15). Before its publication, teachers usually counseled their students to secure copies of the European books, particularly Carcassi's, available in an edition prepared first by Leopold Meignen (fig. 1-16). An elegant sixty-eight page folio production consisting of a beautiful lithographed frontispiece,

THE ELEMENTS

OF

GUITAR-PLAYING:

INCLUDING

A COMPLETE SYSTEM OF FINGERING,

FOUNDED ON

CHORD POSITIONS;

TOGETHER WITH

A GENERAL VIEW OF THE RUDIMENTS OF HARMONY,

ADAPTED TO THE FORMATION OF

Guitar Accompaniments.

BY JAMES BALLARD.

NEW YORK:

PUBLISHED BY GEIB AND WALKER, 23 MAIDEN LANE.

Price $3 00 nett.

A NEW EDITION OF

CARCASSI'S

Celebrated Instructions for the

GUITAR

Comprising a new Text. French & English; a uniform System of Fingering; a number of new Lessons in all the Keys; a collection of Popular Songs, Operatic Airs &c. the whole arranged.

Revised and corrected.

BY

Leopold Meignen.

WM HALL & SON. New York.

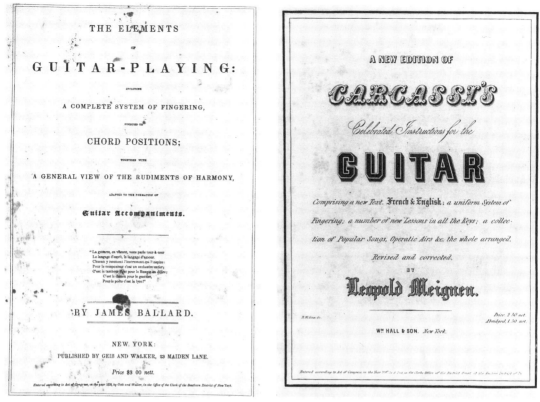

left:

Figure 1-15. *James Ballard,* The Elements of Guitar-Playing *(1838). One of the earliest American guitar methods, Ballard's* Elements *was also one of the largest and most sophisticated. He also wrote an early history of the guitar, for the New York guitar maker William B. Tilton. In the 1830s, however, Ballard purchased an instrument from C. F. Martin. (Collection of the author)*

right:

Figure 1-16. *Leopold Meignen,* A New Edition of Carcassi's Celebrated Instructions for the Guitar *(1847). Meignen, who composed and arranged guitar music (see fig. 1-2), also served the American guitar world by making available his redaction of Carcassi's famous method. (From the collections of the Center for Popular Music, Middle Tennessee State University)*

forty-five pages of instructional text, chord charts, and musical examples, and, in the remaining pages, engraved musical examples from the European tradition, Ballard's *Elements of Guitar-Playing* offers a benchmark of guitar culture at the same time that C. F. Martin moved to Nazareth, Pennsylvania, to devote his career to guitar making (fig. 1-17).

Brought out by the well-regarded music-publishing firm of Geib and Walker at $3.00 per copy, Ballard's book is prefaced by several endorsements and laudatory reviews that tell us what little we know of him beyond his listings as a music teacher in the New York City directories. W. Penson, for example, "the leader and conductor of music at the National Theater," observed that the author was "a disciple of the far-famed Sor—the Paganini of the Spanish guitar." A writer for *Family Magazine* added that Ballard was "a

Endicott   New York.

Figure 1-17. *Frontispiece to James Ballard's* Elements of Guitar-Playing *(1838). This beautiful engraving depicts a teacher and his young pupil. Note the opulent surroundings, including the view through the entryway to formal gardens, all signaling the wealth of the aspiring guitarist. (Courtesy of American Antiquarian Society)*

thorough musician, a perfect master of the instrument, and a most successful teacher."[49] Penson's word "disciple," rather than "student," suggests that Ballard was not personally acquainted with the great man but had devoted himself to his method and studies, to which he alludes on several occasions.

These prefatory "Critical Remarks" also indicate how important Ballard's contemporaries considered his work. The book's endorsers agreed, for example, on how necessary the book was, particularly to the amateur musician. At this date, Sor's method was the only European one that had been fully translated into English, but in the opinion of one writer, who preferred Ballard's work, the translation had been "miserably executed" (fig. 1-18).[50] "Until the publication of this work of Mr. Ballard," another writer noted, "there was no good instruction book or method to assist the pupil or amateur." "We are happy to say," he continued, "that this objection exists no longer." Another added that Ballard's was quite simply "the best work hitherto published on this side of the Atlantic," for it was "*lucid, concise*, and very *original*." The reviewer for the *Sunday Morning News* agreed. He thanked Ballard for placing "a fundamental knowledge of music within the easy attainment of all."[51]

In his introductory comments, Ballard spoke to his book's (and his method's) uniqueness. Finding that the guitar was becoming more popular "and that the altered and superior style of modern guitar music required a suitable instruction book," he wished to furnish a work combining "a reasonable brevity of description" with a reference to all of the fundamental principles necessary to learn the unique system of harmony offered by the guitar. As far as he knew, there was then no treatise published in the country "whose claims to patronage rest[ed] upon any thing like the development of a system of teaching worthy of the improved character" of the instrument. And sensitive to criticism that he might have given too much space to "theoretical details," he pointed out that "in a country where scientific knowledge is brought within the reach of all," most readers would welcome such information.[52]

In support of what I have discussed about the omnipresence of music in the American home, Ballard also prophesied that in a country where vocal music had become such a decided preference, the guitar, "considered merely as an instrument of accompaniment, must eventually become even more extensively used than it is at present." But he also acknowledged that, though now very fashionable, the guitar long had labored "under a slight difference of sentiment with regard to its uses and merits." Hitherto, it had been thought of as "*only* fit for an accompaniment to the voice," but he also wished it to be recognized for "the performance of instrumental pieces."[53]

Ballard admitted without self-consciousness that he was indebted to Sor. Several times he quotes directly from Sor's method—when he describes the proper position in which to sit, for example—and he includes as well a long excerpt about Sor from the *Giulianiad*, which suggests the depth of his interest in guitar culture. The second part of Ballard's book, the lessons and exercises, is similarly indebted to the great Spanish composer and performer but also includes pieces by Kreutzer, Giuliani, Aguado, and Johann Strauss. Ballard's own contribution to the text is copious and, to judge from the blurbs, was well received. As one of the book's reviewers noted, the author's prose was clear and helpful, making the tutor a pleasure to read.[54] Ballard also indicated his intention, shortly, to publish "in the form of an Appendix to the present work, a Series of Lessons, Exercises, and pleasing pieces, accompanied by Remarks on topics interesting to the Guitarist."[55] If issued, however, this work has not come to light.

More tutors followed in the 1840s and 1850s, but none were as ambitious as, nor reached the level of sophistication of, Ballard's. In 1846, for example, Elias Howe, a prolific author and publisher of method books for all sorts of instruments, issued *Howe's Instructor for the Guitar*, a title subsequently acquired by the large music house of Oliver Ditson, who reissued it in 1851.[56] Like most of Howe's productions from this period, however, the instructions specific to the given instrument are minimal, though he did include Ferdinand Carulli's celebrated exercises. The same year that Ditson published Howe's tutor, the music house also issued Richard Culver's *Guitar Instructor*. Perhaps with the cost of Ballard's large book in mind, Culver explained that he wanted to meet the demand for a "really good book of Instruction for the Guitar, of a moderate size, and sold at a moderate price." To accomplish this he made "suitable selections from several of the best works, with some slight alterations and additions" of his own in the "explanatory part" of the text. He also appended some "Popular Airs" and "Duetts [*sic*] for Two Guitars."[57]

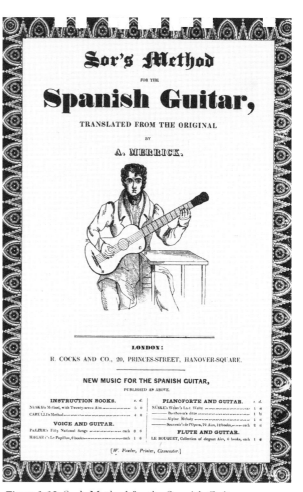

Figure 1-18. Sor's Method for the Spanish Guitar, Translated from the Original by A. Merrick *(ca. 1830)*. *Critics unhappy with this translation of Sor's important work praised the American James Ballard's instruction book because it made Sor's methods more accessible.*

In 1855 Charles C. Converse, brother of Frank, a well-known banjo player on the minstrel stage and author of method books for that instrument, brought out his *New Method for the Guitar, Containing Elementary Instructions in Music, Designed for Those Who Study without a Master* (fig. 1-19; see also fig. 4-5). Herein he contributed to the growing number of instruction books aimed at those who, lacking time or money, did not hire a teacher for lessons—hence, "without a master"—thus further democratizing the instrument. As he put it in his preface, he had written in "catechetical form, not so much to aid the teacher, as to impress those who pursue a course of self-instruction with that which they most need to know." Further, in presenting his work to the American public, he "sought to adapt it to the wants of those whose taste and leisure lead them to learn this graceful instrument." He observed that few persons who studied the guitar went on to become solo per-

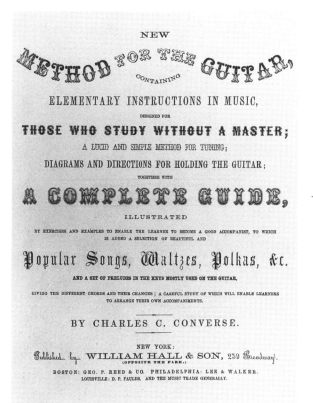

formers, yet all the instruction books that he had inspected had had "as their leading object the development of its [the guitar's] capacities for that purpose." Thus, he offered his tutor to a different constituency, to that far greater number who studied the instrument "on account of its charming quality for accompaniment to the Voice." By thus "smooth[ing] the path of the learner," he observed, he aimed to "add to the number of admirers of this elegant and convenient instrument."[58] As Converse's tutor suggests, by the Civil War guitars were in the hands of people of all classes and occupations (plate 1-8).

GUITAR MAKING IN AMERICA, 1833

Ballard noted one other drawback to the guitar's popularity in the United States: the poor quality of available instruments. He observed, for example, that the low opinion some people held of the guitar's capabilities stemmed from their experience with instruments that were either "originally bad or temporarily out of repair," for many guitars seemed little better than toys. But it was quite simply unjust, he argued, "to class together the sounds from such instruments with the rich and mellow harp tones of a good guitar, as it would be to confound the different effects obtained by an accomplished performer from a Dutch toy fiddle and a Cremona."[59]

Ballard had put his finger on a real problem, for before the mid-1830s there were very few guitar makers in the United States and none who con-

6788X

E. N. Sherr,

Guitar,

Patented Oct. 6, 1831.

Figure 1-20. *Patent drawing for E. N. Scherr's "harp guitar," 1831. Scherr is one of the few documented early American guitar makers. The instrument's patentable feature was its great size, which enabled one to play it standing up rather than on one's lap.*

tributed significantly to the instrument's development. The first United States patent for an "improvement" to the guitar, for example, registered in 1831 by E. N. Scherr of Philadelphia, was for a "harp guitar" (figs. 1-20 and 1-21). Essentially a huge guitar (four feet ten inches long, by the patentee's description), it was played upright, like a bass violin or a harp, hence the name. Scherr's patentable feature, he claimed, was the enlargement and adaptation of the instrument so that it could be rested on the floor. In 1832 Scherr's novel instrument garnered a premium at the exhibition of the Franklin Institute in Philadelphia, but his idea did not catch on. One commentator attributed this particularly to the fact that "having to be supported between the knees of the player, its appearance was not considered graceful." Moreover, "the elevated position of the left hand was inimical to rapid execution" of the notes.[60]

Apart from Scherr's patent, little evidence exists of other American guitar makers before the mid-1830s. Indeed, most instruments were imported. A price list from the New York firm of Vallotte and Lété, ca. 1819–20, for examples, notes "Spanish guitars of all description" from six dollars to thirty

MANNER OF HOLDING THE HARP GUITAR.

For Torp's Improved Method

Figure 1-21. *Illustration from Otto Torp's* New and Improved Method for the Spanish Guitar *(1834). Although never widely popular, Scherr's harp guitar obviously was enough of a novelty for Torp to puff it in his early tutor, which he did both verbally and with this splendid illustration. (Courtesy of American Antiquarian Society)*

Figure 1-22. *This printed price sheet from the New York music firm of Vallotte and Lété, ca. 1819–20, has a handwritten addition, noting that Spanish guitars "of all description" could be had at a cost of six to thirty dollars. (Collection of the author)*

dollars (fig. 1-22). As late as 1837 an advertisement for Samuel C. Jollie & Company, another large New York music wholesaler, noted an "elegant assortment of French and German guitars, with Plain and Patent Heads, of the latest Pattern," but none by American makers.[61] Many of these imports were of such poor quality, however, that the public had reason to wonder what the fuss over guitars was all about. In his *Complete Encyclopaedia of Music*, Moore echoed this assessment. Until very recently, he wrote, most guitars had been imported from France or Germany, "and some few from Spain." Those from the first two countries, "though very pretty in outward appearance, were, many of them, weak in tone, and would not stand the severity" of the American climate. And the Spanish models, though very much superior in tone to the French and German, were of "but little use here, as they soon went to pieces." In 1854, however, Moore could happily report that this finally had been remedied, for interest in the instrument had so increased "that several American houses had commenced the manufacture of them."[62]

Moore had in mind, among others, a handful of German craftsmen who, beginning in the 1830s, had established the guitar trade in the United States. Indeed, when Ballard himself needed an instrument, he patronized one of these, C. F. Martin, in New York City.[63] The remainder of this book tells Martin's story. For forty years he, more than any other, was at the center of the instrument's design, production, and promulgation, and his guitars contributed immeasurably to the American public's embrace of the instrument. C. F. Martin's career as a guitar maker touches amateur and professional musicians, composers and teachers, business partners, music wholesalers in both local and national arenas, other musical instrument makers—in short, participants along the entire spectrum of "guitarmania" discussed in this chapter. Through him we can understand in new ways not only America's love affair with this instrument but also the complex interplay of craftsmanship, business, and advertising that by the 1870s made possible his kind of national recognition and success. Making guitars for all America, he left an unparalleled record of a life in the American music trade.

C. F. Martin in
New York City,
1833–1839

EARLY YEARS IN SAXONY

The guitar maker Christian Frederick Martin arrived in New York City in the autumn of 1833, when the United States was in the throes of "guitarmania." He already was thirty-seven years old, married, and the father of two young children. In the late summer Martin and his family had embarked from the North Sea port of Bremen to join the large German-speaking population—among them his friend Heinrich Schatz, another instrument maker—in lower Manhattan. Like many of his compatriots, Martin had heard much about the promise of America. Surely New York, a city of some two hundred thousand people and the center of the young nation's music trade, would reward his skills with economic success.[1]

Martin was born in Neukirchen, Saxony, on January 31, 1796, the son of Johann Georg Martin (1765–1832) and Eva Regina Paulus. We know little of his parents, except that his father was a member of the cabinetmaker's guild and had been interested in guitar making. Nor do we know much about Christian Frederick's early years, save that, like many other children whose fathers belonged to guilds, he decided to follow in his parent's footsteps. Like his father, too, the boy developed an interest in guitar making, a skill in demand in the early nineteenth century because of the instrument's popularity. Willing to encourage his son in such work, his father sent the fifteen-year-old Christian Frederick to Vienna as an apprentice to Johann Georg Stauffer.[2]

The elder Martin had high standards for his son, for Stauffer's guitars were among the few mentioned in the same breath with those of the great French and English makers, René-François Lacote and Louis Panormo.[3] In addition to producing high-quality instruments, Stauffer also "improved" them in various ways. He extended the fingerboard over the sounding board of the instrument, for example, and developed a detachable neck that tightened to the body by a key mechanism, allowing the player to adjust the neck angle and hence the height of the strings above the fingerboard (plate 2-1).[4] Working as he did in one of the great European music capitals, Stauffer catered to a sophisticated clientele, and a young man who trained in his shop could expect a lucrative career if he started his own business. Over the fourteen years the young Martin spent in Stauffer's workshop, he rose to the important position of foreman. He left Stauffer in 1824, but before taking the final step to independence waited one more year, during which he worked for another Viennese maker, Karl Kühle. His new position paid off in unexpected ways, for in 1825 he married Kühle's daughter, Ottilie Lucia. Shortly after the birth of their son, Christian Frederick Jr., on October 2, 1825, Martin moved his young family back to Neukirchen, where their second child, Rosalie Ottilie, was born on May 4, 1832.[5]

Having spent fifteen years in Vienna in the guitar-making trade, Martin presumably had returned home to continue this work, for the region around Neukirchen (now called Markneukirchen) was well known as an instrument-making center.[6] But he stepped into a hornet's nest that had been periodically stirred since before he had left for Vienna, an ongoing quarrel between the violin makers' and cabinetmakers' guilds over who had the right to make guitars. In the guild economy that still prevailed in some crafts in Europe, violin makers held a monopoly on the manufacture of stringed instruments, a privilege that governments had granted for the regulation of the quality and cost of goods. Because the guitar outwardly resembled other stringed instruments, the Markneukirchen violin makers considered its manufacture under their control.

Because of the instrument's newfound popularity, however, as early as 1800 some cabinetmakers had begun to make guitars. In 1807 the violin makers formally complained to the government about this usurpation of what they regarded as their prerogative. In response, the cabinetmakers argued that the guitar, a "newer" instrument, was not explicitly named in the violin makers' guild's charter and thus not under its control. The issue was not resolved and simmered for two more decades. Then, shortly after, and perhaps in good measure because of, Martin's return to the area, in petitions in the spring and summer of 1826 the violin makers lodged another complaint against the upstarts, again seeking to halt their manufacture of guitars.

These documents reveal how deeply the guild system remained embedded in a pre-capitalist economy in which tradition and craftsmanship took precedence over the innovation and entrepreneurship that marked the emergent industrial age. The violin makers, for example, asked the authorities to consider the difference in training and skill between members of the two guilds. They self-servingly called themselves artists whose work "presupposed not simple skill, but a specific study, an art," in contrast to the cabinetmakers, whose only skill lay in making furniture and who thus were "nothing more than other mechanics." "Who doesn't recognize on first glance," the violin makers haughtily asked, "that a grandfather chair or a night stool isn't a guitar?" Further, because about 40 of the 120 violin makers in Markneukirchen were already engaged in the guitar trade, they worried about what the unregulated manufacture of guitars would mean for their own livelihoods, particularly because the cabinetmakers recently had begun taking in foreign apprentices. As a result, the cabinetmakers argued, there was a danger that the fledgling guitar-making industry they had worked so hard to develop would be "dragged into foreign lands," a somewhat specious argument given that the guitar had been made in Spain and elsewhere long before the Markneukirchen violin makers registered their initial complaint.[7]

The petition again was rejected, no doubt because by the 1820s many viewed a guild's control of such an emergent industry an impediment to rapid economic growth. But five years later the uncompromising violin makers renewed their objection. They renewed their claim to the exclusive production of guitars by citing their instrument's similarity to other stringed instruments whose manufacture their guild historically had controlled. What finally distinguished their work from that of the cabinetmakers, they insisted, was their requirement of a masterpiece before a journeyman rose to master of his craft, something not required of a cabinetmaker crossing into the guitar trade. Further, to allow poorly trained cabinetmakers to make inferior guitars only hurt the reputation of all local instruments in the wider European market. Hurling a final insult, the violin makers observed that their rivals should rest satisfied with the profits they already could make in the guitar trade, from their manufacture of "the many boxes and cases necessary for packaging and shipping the instruments."

The cabinetmakers' lengthy response to this petition indicates the Martin family's prominent role in this controversy. Before travelers had brought guitars into the region about "thirty to thirty-five years ago" (i.e., in the 1790s), the guild pointed out, no one, including the violin makers, had made them. And once the instrument had been introduced, not the violin makers but the cabinetmakers—they singled out "Georg Martin" (that is, Martin's father)—had greatly improved it. Most prominent of all these craftsmen, though, was Johann Georg's son, Christian Frederick, "for many years employed as foreman in the factory of the famous violin maker and guitar manufacturer Johann Georg Stauffer." The young Martin, his colleagues reported, had made instruments "which in consideration of quality and beauty left nothing more to be desired and marked him as a craftsman."

Such arguments sufficiently impressed the regional government that controlled the guilds, for they allowed the cabinetmakers to continue to make guitars, but bad feelings between the two guilds continued into the early 1830s. In the midst of this simmering anger, Christian Frederick Martin, perhaps prompted by his father's recent death or his disgust at the violin makers' recalcitrance, decided to move to the United States. His erstwhile neighbor and fellow guitar maker, Heinrich Schatz, had already settled in New York City and encouraged him. Schatz, like Martin and his father, had been deeply stung by the violin makers' charges. Emigration had offered the opportunity to establish a business without the animosity or potential economic restrictions that Martin encountered in Saxony, for in the United States competition in the market was not feared but encouraged. When Martin boarded the ship for America, then, he left a medieval economic order for a modern one defined most distinctively by expansive, free-market capitalism. As with so many thousands of other immigrants in the antebellum period, the ocean journey changed his life (fig. 2-1).[8]

Figure 2-1. *Photograph of pencil sketch depicting C. F. Martin, ca. 1830. The original sketch has disappeared, but this copy remains important as the second known image of the guitar maker. (Courtesy of C. F. Martin & Company Archives)*

COMING TO AMERICA

If the Martin family's experience was typical of that of others sailing from the North Sea ports, it was not overly pleasant.[9] Like many other German emigrants, they traveled to Bremen to find passage, in their case, on the ship *Columbia*. In addition to Martin, his wife, and their two children, their party (as noted on the ship's manifest) consisted of five others: John W. Hartman, fifty-three, Johann Georg Martin's brother-in-law and a "professor"; Francis Kühle, presumably a member of Ottilie's family (perhaps her brother), thirty-one, a "merchant"; and another merchant, a dentist, and a farmer. Martin himself was designated as a "mechanic," the same term used by the violin makers to describe a member of the cabinetmakers' guild.[10]

If the group's experience was typical, they waited from a few days up to as much as a month for the right weather for the transatlantic crossing. The *Columbia* was a large vessel and carried, in addition to its crew, almost two hundred other passengers from various parts of Germany, all bound for the United States. Like other such vessels, it probably had left the United States laden with cotton, tobacco, and other staples, and returned with passengers and ballast. Local agents procured passengers room in the steerage of such a vessel. The emigrants' baggage and sea chests stowed in the hold below them, they selected narrow wooden berths, their only personal space, from the hundreds provided in steerage. Access to this part of the vessel was through the deck, and ventilation was minimal, particularly during storms when the crew had to secure the hatches. Sanitation, too, was primitive, and outbreaks of disease among the crowded travelers a constant concern. Under the best of conditions, the voyage was trying, the more so with small children in one's care. The Martins finally arrived in New York's harbor on November 6, 1833.[11]

Their destination was a huge, bustling port, its wharves filled on any given day with several hundred merchant vessels. In large measure from a constant influx of immigrants, New York City grew steadily through the 1830s. Like other immigrants, the Martins probably contracted for rooms—at rates from fifty cents to three dollars per week—in some boardinghouse along the East River docks or on Greenwich Street on the West Side, or perhaps they stayed for a while with Schatz. Martin also would have paid some cartman fifty cents for hauling his family's good to the temporary quarters.[12]

In his search for permanent housing, Martin found Manhattan already divided into distinct neighborhoods defined by wealth. By 1833, for example, Broadway had emerged as a prestigious commercial and, in its upper reaches, residential thoroughfare. Particularly after the disastrous fire of 1835 claimed thirteen acres of buildings, most of them businesses, in lower Manhattan, even more people began to move uptown. One especially attractive area was on Broadway between Canal and Fourteenth Streets, where large, elegant dwellings began to spring up (fig. 2-2). In contrast, the areas around Five Points and the Bowery had even then become bywords for a poverty only exacerbated in the next two decades with the arrival of tens of thousands of destitute Irish immigrants (fig. 2-3).[13] Along this economically defined axis, newly arrived crafts- and tradespeople congregated primarily in two areas: near the Hudson River due north from Chambers Street, along Greenwich Street as far as Canal Street, and along the East River, on an axis parallel to Water Street, north toward Houston Street. This latter area was particularly popular among recent German immigrants.[14]

Newcomers with contacts in the city were wise to use them, and Martin probably followed suit. Perhaps on the advice of Schatz (or of the German Society of the City of New York, an organization devoted to the socialization of recent emigrants), he and his young family eventually settled on the west side, at 196 Hudson Street, just east of Greenwich Street, in a house he rented for $112.50 per quarter (three months) from one Mr. McVicker.[15] This residence probably resembled those of other craftsmen in that area: a small two- or three-story building with a workshop on the ground floor. As one historian observes, this left the basement, kitchen, and upper floors for living space. If an individual's craft required the use of larger tools, for sawing or planing wood, for example, he undertook such work in outbuildings behind the dwelling. If, as in Martin's case, he also sold goods or provided services from his dwelling, he did so in whatever front room opened onto the street.[16]

Figure 2-2. *Lithograph,"Mansion House (Bunker's), Broadway, New-York, 1831," for* Valentine's Manual of New York *(1855). This image shows the neighborhood that, even by the early 1830s, had become the most fashionable part of New York and where many of Martin's customers resided. (Courtesy of Robert Fraker)*

As early as 1834 Martin established his business at the same address.[17] He not only began to make guitars for customers in the city but also to serve the music trade variously as importer, merchant, and repairman. As he found his way in his newly adopted country, he conducted this business on a very personal level. Music teachers, amateur and professional musicians, wholesalers, and other craftspeople—often German-speaking compatriots—constantly visited his busy storefront to pay for goods or services or, in the case of other individuals in the music trade, for Martin to pay them for work he had brought to them. Early on, he also began to ship musical goods to merchants in other cities, primarily in Boston and Philadelphia. His activities during this period thus document in great detail the important years shortly before the consolidation of New York's—and, by extension, the nation's—music trade in large wholesale houses that eventually squeezed out or absorbed many independent craftsmen and shopkeepers.[18]

MARTIN'S INVENTORY IN THE 1830S

Martin's initial business in New York consisted largely of his importation and resale of a variety of European musical goods, acquired primarily through German firms or obtained from New Yorkers already established in the music trade. This activity was particularly lucrative because, even at this early date, New York City was the undisputed center of America's musical

Figure 2-3. *Lithograph, "Five Points, 1827," for* Valentine's Manual of New York *(1855). The region around Five Points was the destination of many poorer immigrants during the 1830s. This image provides a good sense of the sheer numbers of people and activities one could encounter in New York City around the time of Martin's arrival there. (Courtesy of Robert Fraker)*

world. And although American craftsmen had begun to make flutes, violins, and brass and woodwind instruments to supply amateur and professional musicians, demand for most instruments was so great that the majority still had to be imported. From Martin's accounts we learn much about what stock crossed the Atlantic and what he procured locally, as well as how these goods were resold in and through New York.

Martin's focus on such business had its parallel among other German immigrants recently arrived in America. A decade or so earlier, for example, Heinrich Christian Eisenbrandt (1790–1860) established a similar trade in instruments in Baltimore. Eisenbrandt, whose father was a well-known maker of woodwinds in Göttingen, followed his craft and, after a couple of brief stays, settled permanently in the United States in 1819. Like Martin, he cultivated business contacts with family and friends across the Atlantic and soon was at the center of a group of musical instrument importers, including the drum and banjo maker William Boucher in Baltimore. Although a guild-trained craftsman, Eisenbrandt clearly found the moment ripe for the importation of musical goods and put much of his energy in that direction.[19]

So, too, did Martin. By May 1834, Martin was storekeeping at his Hudson Street address, and at first his business was small and local. One of his first and most frequent customers was a German music instructor, Edward Fehrman, at 76 Walker Street, who regularly bought strings and also sent many of his students to Martin's shop. Another early client was William Rönnberg, a well-known wind instrument maker who purchased, among other things, a terz guitar of the sort introduced on the European concert stage by the virtuoso Giuliani (fig. 2-4).[20]

Sometime within the next year, however, Martin's business began to grow, as he received large shipments of goods from across the Atlantic, specifically from contacts in Neukirchen. From this point, his trade both within and outside New York increased significantly. One page in his daybook from this period, for example, summarizes shipping and customs charges totaling $368.16 for three different transactions for goods forwarded by both Wilhelm Schatz, perhaps Heinrich's relative, and August Hartmann of Neukirchen, who may have been related to the Hartman who traveled across the Atlantic with the Martins. Between June 1835 and May 1837, Hartmann became Martin's main contact, in one case for goods that totaled $200.41 before customs charges.[21]

Martin's meticulously kept journal for 1836 provides more details of his business arrangements with such overseas suppliers, primarily with August Hartmann and F. T. Merz, an important wholesaler who had been in business in Markneukirchen since 1827. In April 1836, for example, Martin sent to Hartmann at Neukirchen a bill of exchange in the amount of "200 Risdollars Bremen Gold" and debited his own accounts $160.00, an indication of the rate of exchange. The same day he forwarded a similar kind of note, for the same amount and payable the same way, to Merz and within a month repeated the transaction.[22]

From this point, Merz became Martin's supplier.[23] Every few months this merchant shipped Martin one or two crates of goods, the arrival of which he recorded by number. On September 23, 1836, for example, Martin noted that box "No. 19" had arrived safely from Merz.[24] When such an overseas shipment arrived in New York, Martin had other financial obligations, namely, freight charges due on delivery and tariff duties, which during this period averaged about 30 percent of the value of the goods.[25] One shipment from Merz in 1836, for example, cost Martin an additional sixty dollars in duty. Occasionally, evaluation and payment of these tariffs required the intervention of third parties especially skilled in this line. Thus, early in 1837 Martin paid eight dollars to one Mr. Gutman "for Custom-House business" that he had undertaken through January 1 and on several occasions before that had paid him two dollars per order to expedite deliveries of individual shipments.[26] Martin sometimes recorded specifically what transatlantic shipping companies—usually, Caspar Meyer and Company or D. H. Schmidt & Son—had carried such land and sea freight. More often, however, he did not record the purveyor, only the shipping costs.[27] Finally, Martin also had to pay one of the city's ubiquitous cartmen for carriage of these large crates of instruments

Figure 2-4. *Carte de visite by S. L. Buser, Warren, Illinois, December 20, 1868 (identified on back). This musician plays a small terz guitar, popularized in Europe by Giuliani. It is tuned a third higher than standard guitar tuning; hence, the name "terz," or "third." One of Martin's first recorded transactions, in the spring of 1834, was for the sale of such an instrument. (Collection of the author)*

from the pier to Hudson Street. In each entry for the receipt of transatlantic goods, he always duly noted a payment, usually fifty cents but up to $1.75 (for a piano), to a "cartman" for "the carrying of the box" to his store.[28]

What precisely was in these shipments? We can infer their contents from instruments and supplies that he began to sell shortly after the arrival of a large order. It is clear that the crates contained European guitars (plates 2-2, 2-3). But stringed instruments—violoncellos and double bass, as well as violins of several grades—and bows, also graded, accounted for the largest part of his imported stock (plate 2-4). On Martin's walls and shelves customers also found quantities of brass instruments such as trumpets, keyed bugles, trombones, French horns, and the occasional ophicleide, as well as woodwind instruments such as flutes, flageolets, and clarinets (plate 2-5).

Martin sometimes stocked more unusual or expensive items, harps from France, for example, or bassoons, bass horns, and the occasional pianoforte. At the lower end of the price scale, he also did a lively trade in accordions, novel and fairly inexpensive free-reed instruments (usually from France) then in considerable vogue; and replacement parts (tailpieces, bridges, and pegs) and instrument strings (most of which also came from his overseas suppliers) for all members of the violin family as well as for guitars (fig. 2-5). Walk-in customers also purchased tuning forks, instruction books for the various instruments he carried, rules "for drawing music lines," and even imported novelties called "musical fruit," in the form of apples, pears, melons, and lemons that probably had bells in them and cost but a few cents each.[29]

To augment his supply of imported goods, Martin stocked some instruments and goods of local or American manufacture, when he could acquire them, or that others in his circle imported. From 1836 on, for example, he regularly purchased large quantities of guitar strings from Heinrich Gottlob Gütter, another German instrument maker and dealer, who had settled in Bethlehem, Pennsylvania.[30] From him Martin also received stringed instruments, including violins and at least one violoncello and two guitars. Some orders with Gütter were quite large. On one account in the summer of 1836, for example, Martin paid $95.40 for unspecified goods, and on another, $92.25 for a box of violins. Many of these instruments may have come from Europe, for Gütter's family in Markneukirchen wholesaled shipments directly to Bethlehem. Such goods then found their way to Martin along with items that Gütter manufactured or procured from local craftsmen. In return, Martin sent Gütter various goods, particularly brass instruments (always in demand in Bethlehem, a Moravian community where such instruments were popular) but also household staples, like the "16 yds. Cotton" Martin once noted.[31]

Gütter, as the main music dealer in the region, might have procured some of the violins and guitars that he sent Martin from other craftsmen in and around Bethlehem. The most prominent of these was Martin's old friend

Plate 2-1.

Guitar attributed to Johann Georg Stauffer, Vienna, ca. 1820–30. Stauffer, with whom Martin trained, was one of the best-regarded European guitar makers. In this beautiful example of work in his style, note the mustache-shaped bridge, the clock-key adjustment for the neck, and the six-in-a-row metal tuning machines commonly associated with the Vienna school of makers. The angled cut at the end of the fingerboard and the pearl sound hole rosette are also distinctive. Compare with the Martin guitar in plate 2-25. (Photograph courtesy of the Chinery Collection)

left

Plate 2-2. *"Vienna-style" guitar, probably made in Germany, ca. 1830. Note the elaborate decoration around the edges of the top and the sound hole. When Martin first arrived in New York City and began to import musical instruments from Europe, he offered such instruments to a public increasingly eager for them, and his early guitars have the same style of peg head. (Courtesy of Tony Creamer)*

top

Plate 2-3. *Close-up of "Vienna-style" peg head and tuners on guitar illustrated in plate 2-2. Note the unusual mythological creatures and the musical theme. (Courtesy of Tony Creamer)*

Plate 2-4. *Sixth-plate daguerreotype, ca. 1850s. Early in his New York career Martin imported and sold large numbers of violins of different grades, and when in partnership with Schatz he even listed the two of them as violin makers. Among Martin's customers for violins were folk musicians as well as performers of the classical repertoire. These boys, most likely recent Irish immigrants, play a bodhran and a fiddle, probably to accompany traditional Irish dance tunes. (Collection of Greg French)*

Plate 2-5. *Sixth-plate daguerreotype, ca. 1840s. This musician proudly displays his keyed bugle. In his New York store Martin carried large numbers of brass instruments, particularly trumpets and bugles, but also the occasional ophicleide, used primarily by professional musicians. Note that this man also holds sheet music. (Collection of Greg French)*

Plate 2-6. *Sixth-plate daguerreotype, ca. 1850s. Martin imported and sold flutes of all sorts, from single-keyed instruments to much more elaborate and sophisticated ones, often trimmed with ivory. He also carried those of several New York makers, fellow German immigrants. (Collection of Greg French)*

Plate 2-7. *Sixth-plate tintype, ca. 1860s. Martin had a large clientele for violins and violin repair, among them a Mr. Wiesner, a "blackman," who brought in his instrument several times between 1835 and 1838. African Americans constituted an important part of New York City's musical scene and leavened European music with their own culture's rhythms and tunes. (Collection of Greg French)*

Plate 2-8. *Quarter-plate daguerreotpye, ca. 1850s. "The Knoodles Band from Fairplay, Maryland." This rare image shows a full marching band, with a number of brass instruments of the sort that Martin imported and sold, on a wooden sidewalk. Among Martin's clients for brass were several such groups, including military bands. (Collection of Greg French)*

Plate 2-9. *Sixth-plate daguerreotype, ca. 1845. In his music store Martin carried all sorts of musical supplies, from bass violins to accordions and harmonicas. Customers could even purchase such important accessories as tuning forks, one of which is proudly brandished by this man, probably a music teacher. (Collection of Greg French)*

opposite, bottom
Plate 2-11. *Pages from one of Martin's business journals, from 1838. Virtually all the extant records are in a very readable hand, in this case, that of Charles Bruno, Martin's employee and, for a short time, partner. (C. F. Martin & Company Archives)*

Plate 2-10.

Grouping of Martin's journals, from the early 1830s through the turn of the twentieth century. In addition, C. F. Martin & Company holds the family's entire business correspondence from this same period. (C. F. Martin & Company Archives)

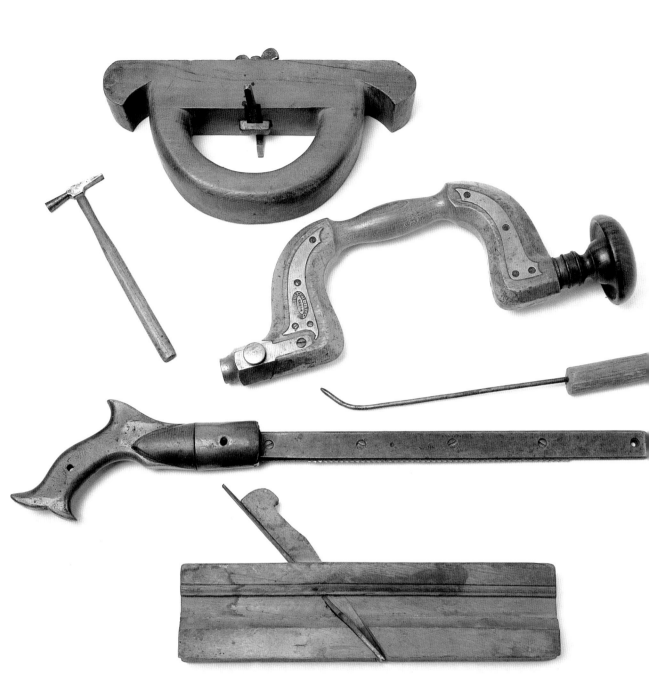

Plate 2-12. *A grouping of C. F. Martin's tools from his years in New York City and Nazareth. Martin purchased equipment and supplies from various purveyors in New York City but may have brought some of his equipment from Europe. On the brass part of the drill is a stamp that reads "Manchester Sheffield Works." (C. F. Martin & Company Archives)*

Plate 2-13. *Martin made some of his necessary equipment, including this guitar mold (to bend the instrument's sides to shape) from the antebellum period. (C. F. Martin & Company Archives)*

Plate 2-14.

Front view of C. F. Martin guitar, ca. late 1830s or 1840s. Labels of both Martin & Schatz and Martin & Coupa. Such double-labeled instruments were probably made in the 1830s, when Martin had teamed with Schatz, and then sold through Coupa, a New York music teacher. The body is rosewood veneer over mahogany. (Courtesy of Tony Creamer)

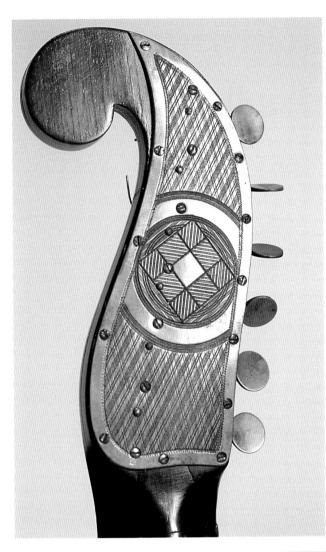

Plate 2-15. *Close-up of "Vienna-style" peg head and tuning machines on the guitar in plate 2-14. Martin imported such tuners at considerable expense. Compare this with the tuning machines in plate 2-3. (Courtesy of Tony Creamer)*

Plate 2-16. *Close-up of the "ice cream cone"– shaped heel of the guitar in plate 2-14. This design was typical of Martin's early guitars and should be compared with the heel construction (see plates 2-32, 2-33) typical of Spanish makers. (Courtesy of Tony Creamer)*

Plate 2-17.

Front view of Martin guitar, ca. 1830s. This beautiful instrument shows Martin's use of ivory, which he bought from a member of the Phyfe family in New York City, for both the bridge and angled fingerboard. This guitar also has the distinctive Stauffer-style or "Vienna" peg head. (Photograph courtesy of the Chinery Collection)

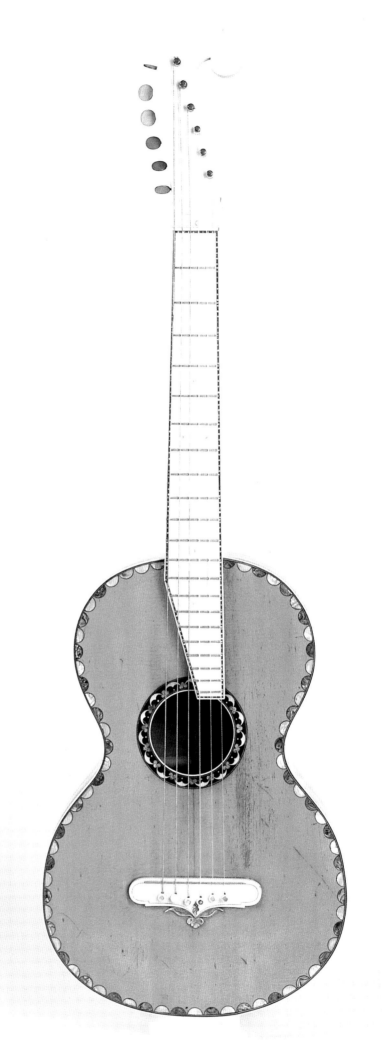

Plate 2-18. *Close-up of the ivory bridge on the instrument in plate 2-17.*

Note the mother-of-pearl insets in the bridge pins and the beautiful abalone fleur-de-lis.

(Photograph courtesty of the Chinery Collection)

Plate 2-19.

*Front view of Martin
& Coupa guitar,
ca. 1840. Compare with
the instruments in
plates 2-17 and 2-27.
Note that the ivory
fingerboard is not cut
away and that the
peg head is ebony, in
striking contrast to
the ivory beneath it.
(Courtesy of Fred
Oster)*

opposite
Plate 2-20. *Front view of Martin guitar, ca. 1830s. This Stauffer-style Martin, with
its striking abalone and pearl decoration around the top and sound hole, and its
decoration beneath the bridge, recalls the instruments in plates 2-17, 2-19, and 2-27.
Note, however, the different type of bridge and plain ebony fingerboard and peg
head. (Photograph courtesy of the Chinery Collection)*

Plate 2-21. *Label of C. Frederick Martin at 196 Hudson Street, his first New York City address, ca. mid-1830s. Payment to lithographers or engravers and printers for such work constituted a small but important expense. Note that Martin describes himself as both a guitar and violin manufacturer as well as an importer of other musical instruments. (C. F. Martin & Company Archives)*

Plate 2-22.
C. F. Martin guitar, ca. 1840. In his early years Martin made instruments of various sizes and shapes, but none more unusual than this one, its general contour derived from French guitars of the Renaissance period. But note the similarity of the body shape to that of the harp guitar in plate 5-1. This guitar also is unusual in having a screwed-down metal bridge, apparently contemporary to the instrument. (C. F. Martin & Company Archives)

Plate 2-23.

*Cittern-shaped guitar
built by C. F. Martin,
ca. 1830s. By the early
nineteenth century
the cittern, an earlier
relative of the guitar,
had become rare,
but for some reason
(perhaps at a customer's
request) Martin built
a six-stringed guitar
with its body shape.
The neck inlays on this
instrument were added
later, and the bridge
is not original, though
probably of correct
outline. (Courtesy of
Fred Oster)*

top

Plate 2-24. *Martin & Schatz guitar, ca. 1830s.*
Close-up of the clock key adjustment in the heel
of the instrument shown in plate 2-25. With such
a mechanism a player could adjust the pitch of
the neck and thus the playing "action" (the
height of the strings above the fingerboard).
(C. F. Martin & Company Archives)

right

Plate 2-25. *Front view of Martin guitar,*
ca. 1830s. This instrument carries only Martin's
label, from the early 196 Hudson Street address.
Its "mustache" bridge, the sound hole decoration,
and the way the fingerboard is cut away from
the base to the treble side recalls the guitars of
Stauffer of Vienna, under whom Martin trained
before coming to the United States. Compare this
with the guitar in plate 2-1. (C. F. Martin &
Company Archives)

Plate 2-26.

Close-up of neck of Martin guitar, ca. 1830s. The neck of this instrument (plate 2-25) is made of ebony and ivory, an appointment found only on his most expensive models. The instrument's clock-key mechanism (also shown in plate 2-24) is clearly visible. (C. F. Martin & Company Archives)

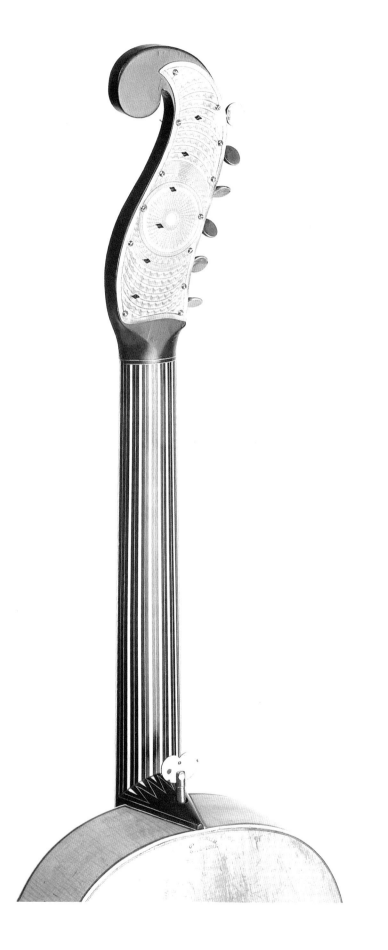

Plate 2-27.

Front view of Martin and Schatz guitar, ca. 1830s. Very similar to the guitar in plate 2-17, this instrument has an ivory fingerboard and bridge. The decoration around the sound hole and the binding, however, are different. In 1837 Martin sold a similar instrument for $63.00 to Nunns, Clark & Company, indicating that such instruments were among his most expensive. (C. F. Martin & Company Archives)

Plate 2-28. *Front, side, and rear views of Martin terz guitar, ca. 1830s. James Ballard, a guitar teacher, bought such an instrument from Martin in 1838, the same year he published an important guitar tutor. This guitar has a bird's-eye maple back veneered over rosewood, and solid bird's-eye sides, a feature of many contemporary European guitars. The unusual body shape, again similar to European designs, also suggests an early date. The instrument is fan braced and has only three back braces. The stamp, on the back, near the top, reads "C F Martin / New York." Note the unusual bridge and the decorative "dot" beneath it, made from the top of an end pin, with a mother-of-pearl center. The guitar also has black whalebone binding. (Collection of Bill Capell)*

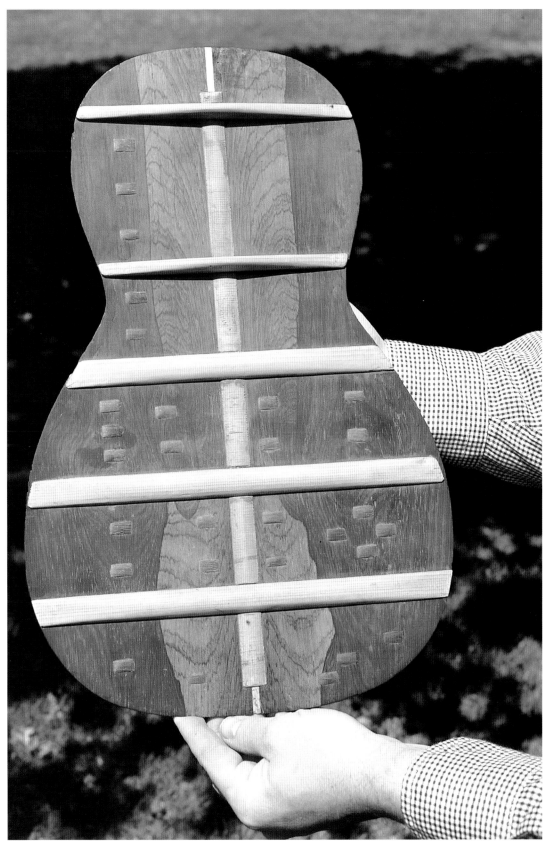

Plate 2-29. *Five-brace back typical on mid- to later 1800s Martin guitars. Some early Martin instruments have only three such braces, others four. (Courtesy of David LaPlante)*

Plate 2-30. *Martin & Coupa guitar, early 1840s with simple fan bracing. By the 1850s such bracing was the hallmark of guitars made by Antonio de Torres and other Spanish makers. (Courtesy of David LaPlante)*

Plate 2-31. *Martin & Coupa 3-24 or (23?), ca. 1845. Detail of tie bridge (as opposed to one with pins), with ivory or bone inset, common on Spanish guitars. (Courtesy of David LaPlante)*

Plate 2-32. *Martin & Coupa guitar, 1840s. Close-up of neck block with Spanish heel construction that by the 1840s was becoming more popular. (Courtesy of David LaPlante)*

Plate 2-33. *Martin & Coupa guitar, 1840s. Close-up of Spanish style heel (laminated) and heel cap. (Courtesy of David LaPlante)*

Plate 2-34. *Quarter plate ambrotype, January 1859. Another example of how special the guitar was to young women in the antebellum period. This daughter of well-to-do parents is dressed in all her finery, including a striking bonnet and ribbons, but she obviously felt that to capture her perfectly the ambrotypist would have to allow her to hold her prized instrument. Inside the case is written, in French, "V. Hall, seventeen years of age" and "taken by Mons. Dugal, given by Mons. F. Coffin in January 1859." This image shows a guitar probably manufactured in Europe. (Collection of the author)*

Plate 2-35. *Label for Martin & Coupa, 1840s or early 1850s. Coupa was a New York City performer and guitar instructor to whose studio Martin sent his instruments after he moved to Pennsylvania. Coupa had been his customer as early as the late 1830s, however, and it is unclear exactly when they established a special relationship. This label lists the address at which Coupa had his studio ca. 1850. (Courtesy of David LaPlante)*

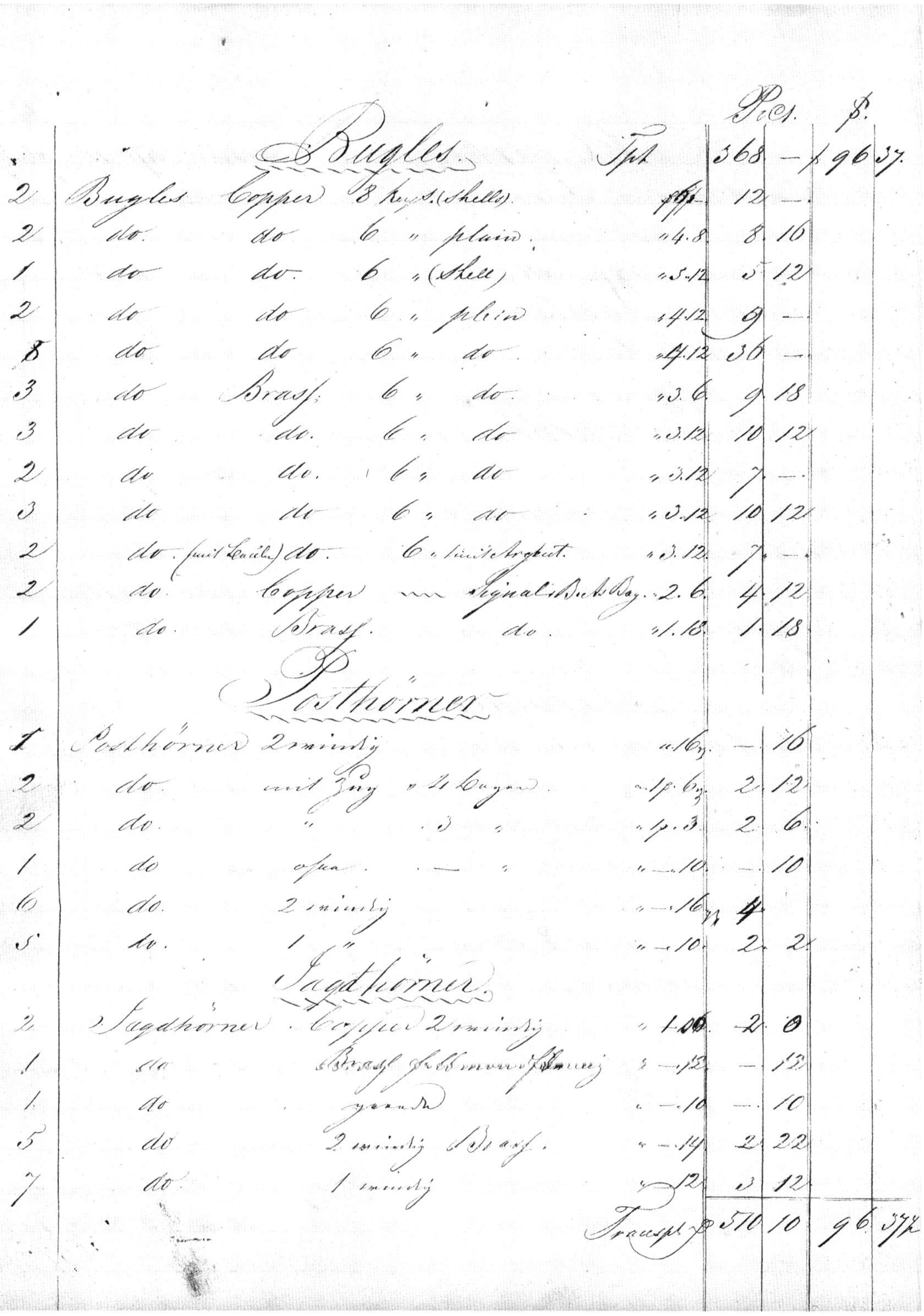

	Bugles				Tpt	568	–	96 37
2	Bugles	Copper	8 keys	(Shells)		12	–	
2	do.	do	6 "	plain	4.8	8	16	
1	do	do.	6 "	(Shell)	5.12	5	12	
2	do	do	6 "	plain	4.12	9	–	
8	do	do	6 "	do	4.12	36	–	
3	do	Brass	6 "	do	3.6	9	18	
3	do	do.	6 "	do	3.12	10	12	
2	do	do.	6 "	do	3.12	7	–	
3	do	do.	6 "	do	3.12	10	12	
2	do (mit Cadr) do.		6 "	mit Arbeit	3.12	7	–	
2	do	Copper		Signal Buk Boy	2.6	4	12	
1	do	Brass		do	1.18	1	18	

	Posthörner							
1	Posthörner	2 windig			16	–	16	
2	do	mit Zug u. 4 Bogen			1p.6	2	12	
2	do.	"			1p.3	2	6	
1	do	ofen			10	–	10	
6	do.	2 windig			16	4		
5	do.	1 "			10	2	2	

	Jagdhörner							
2	Jagdhörner	Copper 2 windig			1.00	2	0	
1	do	Brass			15	–	15	
1	do	ganz			10	–	10	
5	do	2 windig Brass.			14	2	22	
7	do.	1 windig			12	3	12	
				Transp.	510	10	96 37	

Plate 2-36. *Page from Martin's inventory of musical stock upon the sale of his business to Ludecus & Wolter in 1839. This document indicates that in his New York years Martin was as much an importer of musical instruments as a guitar maker. (C. F. Martin & Company Archives)*

Plate 2-37. *Half-plate daguerreotype, ca. 1860. By the time Martin moved to Nazareth in 1839, he had clients up and down the Atlantic seaboard who bought his guitars at different music emporiums in the larger cities. Thus, although a woman like this one might still play an inferior European instrument, more and more frequently she had the opportunity to purchase a guitar by the nation's premier maker. (Courtesy of George Eastman House)*

Figure 2-5. *Sixth-plate ambrotype, ca. 1857–60. Obviously dressed for the stage, these two musicians teamed up in a not very common duet of guitar and violin. In the 1830s Martin served such a clientele by offering strings and other accessories as well as instrument repair, particularly new violin bridges. (Collection of the author)*

Heinrich Schatz, who had worked with him in New York through 1835 but had moved to Millgrove, Pennsylvania, near Bethlehem, the following year. Whatever Schatz's arrangement with Gütter, he also traded with Martin directly. In the spring of 1836, for example, even as Martin himself began to make instruments, Schatz sent him six guitars and twelve guitar cases and, around the first of the year, shipped eight more instruments. In turn, Martin often sent his friend much needed supplies for his instrument making. On January 10, 1837, a day after Martin had received a shipment of Schatz's guitars, he forwarded a gallon of alcohol, an ounce of copal (for varnish), a quire of sandpaper, and seventeen ounces of German silver wire (presumably for frets or for string winding).[32] Further, Martin's notation of postage for a letter sent in 1838 to "Mssrs. Schatz and Stumcke" indicates that another German instrument maker, Charles Stumcke, had joined Schatz. Soon thereafter Martin sent him a sizable order of parts and strings (including guitar pegs in rosewood, ebony, and "softwood," and bridge and end pins). In the early 1840s Stumcke, like Schatz, relocated to Boston, where he continued to make guitars before moving, one final time, to California.[33]

Martin also stocked some instruments, particularly brass and wind, manufactured in New York. Occasionally, for example, he traded with Charles Christman, one of the city's best-known wind instrument makers. A native of Danzig in Prussia, Christman had been in New York since the early 1820s. From his operation on Pearl Street he supplied Martin with, among other things, flageolet mouthpieces and instruction books for bugles and trombones.[34] On one occasion, Martin sold him an ophicleide and six "Tyrolean" (that is, from Austria or northern Italy) violins, obviously part of a recent transatlantic shipment.[35] Richard Schroeder was another local wind instrument maker, at 163 Mott Street in 1836 and 191 Mulberry a year later. From him Martin purchased single keyed flutes with ivory trim (plate 2-6). If Martin needed fifes, he went to Heinrich Eduard Baack, originally from Hamburg, to whom he also occasionally brought flutes for repair.[36]

Although Martin frequently received shipments of imported guitar and viol strings, he also procured these necessities from other dealers right in the city, among them Charles F. Hoyer at 301 Broadway and Westlar and Company, 7 William Street. From this last firm he once bought five bundles of "third" (i.e., "D") strings and ten of "second" ("A") strings, paying five dollars in cash. (Unfortunately, we do not know how many strings constituted a bundle.) He also patronized Geib & Walker, with large stores in both New York and Philadelphia.[37]

Finally, a small portion of Martin's inventory came from customers who sold old instruments outright or who wished to barter for other goods in Martin's store. In the winter of 1836, for example, Miss Ann Eliza Wheeler of 231 Hudson Street ordered a new guitar that cost $24.00. She paid $20.00 in cash and the rest through the trade of an old guitar. Six days later, Frederick Schnepf, another German music teacher, brought in a cocuswood flute with eight silver keys and left with a new guitar worth $20.00. Violins also were commonly traded, for they were instruments that Martin could resell quickly, given their popularity. For one such instrument he paid $2.50 cash and, on another occasion, exchanged a violin bow for twelve bottles of white wine. Guitars taken in trade quickly found new owners. In May 1836, for example, Martin sent Julius Freygang of Bridgeport, Connecticut, a secondhand guitar worth $3.75; another that he got earlier that year he resold for $8.00.[38]

THE RETAIL TRADE AND INSTRUMENT REPAIR

Martin's daily business consisted primarily of retail sales both in and outside New York. In addition, he placed some instruments, particularly his guitars, on commission to music teachers throughout the city and augmented his income from retail customers by instrument repair. A closer look at some of these transactions provides information about the wholesale cost and retail markup of instruments, the various arrangements through which they were sold, and the significance of instrument repair to Martin's music business.

Sales to Martin's walk-in customers ranged from a few cents for a violin string to sixty dollars for a double bass with metal, geared tuning machines.[39] Neither the kinds nor costs of the musical instruments and accessories Martin handled fluctuated greatly during the six years he was in New York. From 1836 on, for example, after his business had become well established, violins constituted the largest part of his sales (plate 2-7). Because the customers for these instruments varied in talent and sophistication, his European contacts supplied him with goods of differing quality and, hence, price. One day, for example, Martin sold, for $8.50, a "fine Violin inlaid with Pearl and bow"; on another day, a "Tyrolean violin with a bow," for only $5.00, and a second, not described, for only $3.00. Violin bows, another common item in the accounts, ranged from fifty cents to a dollar, and he also supplied parts and accessories for his violins: boxwood mutes (at $.04 each); boxwood pegs ($.50 the dozen); and ebony tailpieces ($.43 to $.62 each).[40] On a daily basis, Martin sold many violin strings as well.

His trade in other members of the violin family was smaller. In the fall of 1836, for example, he sold a violoncello for $55.00, taking another in trade for $15.00 toward the purchase (fig. 2-6). Bows for this instrument also were expensive, retailing for as much as $3.50. In one transaction, a Mr. Barber traded a cello bow for "2 small Violin bows at $3[.00], 1 Tuning fork at 62½ cents, and 1 Violin string at 31½ cents." At the upper end of the violin family in terms of size, a double bass cost from $50.00 to $60.00. Even strings for this large instrument were costly, a dollar each, and a case for it was $12.00, as much as Martin charged for some guitars.[41]

Wind instruments, particularly flutes and fifes, also quickly moved through his store. Martin usually priced the latter at $.62½, but flutes varied according to their number of keys. One with six keys sold for $10.00, for example, but a four-keyed version (with case) cost only $5.00. A simple black instrument, perhaps without keys, sold for only $1.00. Flageolets, too, varied in price according to their sophistication. A "double flageolet" cost $9.00, but a single, ivory-tipped one only $2.50. Bassoons were unusual but available. Martin priced this item at $12.00 and carried reeds for it at $.15 each. For clarinets, reeds were a few pennies cheaper, but for some reason this was an instrument that he did not commonly sell. On the one occasion when he took in one in trade, he allowed $6.00 for it.

Both amateur and professional musicians purchased wind instruments, but most of Martin's customers for brass were professionals who demanded work of high quality. To a member of a group called the Prague Musicians, for example, he sold a trumpet with three valves for $21.00, and to Peter Abel of 333 Water Street a fine French horn with a case for $30.00.[42] A brass bugle

Figure 2-6.

Sixth-plate ambrotype, ca. 1860. This unusual image shows what well may be a minstrel troupe, whose members later that day would darken their faces and play in the public meetinghouse visible behind them. Their instrumentation also is remarkable, for in addition to violin, tambourine, and bones, we also see a triangle, an accordion, and, most oddly, a cello. This last was an expensive instrument, usually procured in the city. Martin often sold cellos at fifty dollars or more. (Collection of the author)

with six keys sold for $7.00, and bugle mouthpieces, $.37½ each. Very unusual was a brass serpent with three keys sent to one Schulz on August 8, 1838, and valued at $15.00. It accompanied a large order that included two tenor trombones and a bugle.[43] Martin also had clients for brass at West Point, presumably those with connections to its military bands, and he numbered among his customers as well similar military groups in the city. In 1838, for example, he sold two French horns to the "U.S. Music Band at Bedlow's Island and gave a $5.00 commission to Mr. Ballo, the musicmaster" (plate 2-8).[44]

Martin occasionally carried more unusual or larger instruments that were quite expensive. He once purchased a pianoforte on credit for $250.00, obviously with the thought of reselling it at a profit.[45] Such keyboard instruments, though increasingly common, varied in quality. To a client in New Haven he sent another piano at the wholesale price of $70.00 and a seraphine (a smaller keyboard instrument) at $80.00.[46] Martin also stocked the occasional harp. B. Bauclair, for example, paid $75.00 cash for what Martin described as a "French" harp (not to be confused with a harmonica, later so termed). At the opposite end of the spectrum, a customer could purchase a twelve-key accordion at from $3.50 to $6.50, or a "mouth harmonika, flat," for $.25. If someone needed a tuning fork, Martin had one for $.62½ (plate 2-9). A simple "capo d'astro" (that is, a capo, placed over the strings at a certain fret to raise the guitar's pitch) was $.09, but a more elegant one, of ivory, cost $2.00.[47]

Martin also stocked instruction books for various instruments. He commonly sold guitar tutors, and his selection provided students with English editions of the best European titles. In the summer of 1838, for example, he sold the Spanish guitar instructor John Coupa eight copies of Matteo Carcassi's *Complete Method for the Guitar* (translated from the French) for ten dollars (see fig. 1-16).[48] Mr. Bromberger paid a dollar for Giuliani's method, the work of a performer second in fame only to the great Fernando Sor.[49] The tutor that Martin sold most commonly by name, though, was Otto Torp's *New and Improved Method for the Spanish Guitar*, usually priced at $1.50 (see fig. 1-14). On the shelf with these guitar tutors were instruction books for accordion, flute, and other instruments and as well as music scores, often purchased by music instructors. Early in 1836, for example, Martin had on hand works by Haydn and Mendelssohn, Beethoven's Fifth and Sixth Symphonies, an overture by Vincenzo Bellini, and Louis-Joseph-Ferdinand Hérold's *Zampa*.

Instrument repair, particularly of guitars, constituted an important part of Martin's daily retail business. Unfortunately, he rarely specified what work he did on the instruments, and his charges varied widely, depending on its difficulty. On January 16, 1836, for example, he repaired two guitars, one for $6.00 and the other for $8.00, but for a smaller repair, he charged only a dollar or two. A customer paid $2.00 for varnishing a guitar's top, and for putting on a new one Martin asked $4.00. Another time Martin replaced the finger-

Figure 2-7. *Sixth-plate ambrotype, ca. 1858. A close look at this guitar reveals that there are only five white bridge pins. Presumably, the other was lost and replaced with a darker one. In the 1830s one could buy even such tiny and seemingly insignificant accessories at Martin's New York store. (Collection of the author)*

board and "ivory edges" (binding) on a client's instrument for $4.00. Often he simply installed new bridge pins and strings, work for which he charged $.75 or less (fig. 2-7).

Given the popularity of the violin and other instruments in that family, repair of such stringed instruments occupied much of Martin's time in these years. He frequently fit a sound post and a bridge to a violin at a standard rate of $.18¾. If he replaced the ebony fingerboard as well as a bridge, he charged the customer a little over a dollar. If he had to take off the back of an instrument to do internal repairs, the price was more, as it was when he worked on larger instruments. On one occasion he repaired a double bass and put two new strings on it, for $7.00.[50] Sometimes he sent out such work to others. Martin paid a Mr. Stark $1.50 for rehairing three cello bows, for example, and then charged his customer $2.25 for the job. He often called on Stark for such bow repair and even for work on simple wind instruments.[51]

From a record of Martin's orders received in 1838, appended to his journal for 1836–37, we also have a good idea of how long customers had to wait for such work. The usual turnaround time for minor repair work on guitars or violins was about one week. If there was a larger repair, as on June 7, 1838, when Miss Norma Lipkowsky, 109 Pearl Street, brought in a guitar "to put a new soundboard and new Frets on, & varnish the back," work that cost $7.25, it took longer.[52] Martin did not return Miss Lipkowsky's guitar for a month. For other repairs some customers waited up to six weeks.

Martin also took in brass and wind instruments, though he rarely performed this repair work himself. Instead, he subcontracted the job to others, often German craftsmen, who specialized in such trade. It is unclear, though, precisely how Martin determined the cost of such work. When Schroeder repaired a clarinet for him, for example, he charged Martin $.25, and Martin took $.37½ from the client. But for work on a flute, for which Martin charged his customer $.62½, Schroeder again received only $.25.[53] Martin and Schroeder must have had some understanding about these rates because Martin regularly bought wind instruments from his fellow craftsman, and Schroeder reciprocated by sending Martin customers who needed guitar repair.

Other wind repair work went to Christman, another craftsman who occasionally sold instruments through Martin's shop, or to William Paulus, 28 Cherry Street, a well-known maker who in 1837 went into partnership with Heinrich Eduard Baack.[54] On one occasion, Martin paid Paulus $.75 for work on a flute and charged the client $1.12.[55] If the repair work was on brass instruments, Jacob Hartman usually got the call. He charged Martin seventy-five cents for such work on June 27, 1836, and fifty-six cents on November 10.[56] As these examples indicate, Martin regularly referred instrument repair to others, often relying on his contacts with German craftsmen who had become part of his circle in New York City's music trade.

DEALER IN WHOLESALE AND COMMISSION GOODS

As important as walk-in customers for retail and repair were to Martin's growing business, his largest and most significant sales were to other music dealers in New York and other major American cities. In his first years of operation, through 1835, he supplied only a few firms, the most prominent of which was Joseph Atwill of New York, to whom Martin had sold instruments, including a guitar, as early as April 1835. About the same time, he also regularly began to send goods by steam packet to Charles H. Keith of Boston and by land to S. G. Miller of Philadelphia. Initially, these firms accounted for Martin's greatest volume of sales, but by 1837–38 he had further enlarged his circle of wholesale customers. Using coastal vessels for transport, Martin began to trade on a regular basis with firms in Philadelphia, Richmond, and Petersburg, Virginia; New Haven, Hartford, and Bridgeport, Connecticut; and even Quebec in Canada. On November 17, 1838, for example, he sent goods, via "the Tow boat Tracy," to Mr. Andrae, his customer in Quebec, "Lower Canada."[57]

Martin's first shipment beyond the city had come in the spring of 1835 when Keith in Boston received a large order of goods, including violins, bows, and post horns, invoiced at $122.24. A few months later a smaller order followed, with a dozen violins and bows, two trombones "without moveable tops," and one "to move both ways." (This also was the first entry in Martin's ledger in English rather than in German, which suggests that by this date he had become comfortable with his second language.) In the early fall Martin sent another large shipment, including a French horn with six crooks, five trombones (including one bass and one soprano), two keyed bugles, six violins, two dozen violin tailpieces, twenty-five violin bridges at $.18¾ each, a dozen tuning forks, and other goods, for a total of $155.31. Keith gave him a note for the total, payable in six months.[58] As was his custom, Martin carried forward these balances, and Keith eventually paid the total with $75.00 cash and a note for the remainder (see Chapter 3). Shipments to Miller in Philadelphia began at about the same time, were of comparable size, and were paid by note or cash or both every few months.[59] Occasionally, as with the account with Andrae in Quebec, Martin took payment in foreign currency and redeemed it for U.S. money at the current rate of exchange.[60]

A complete ledger of Martin's accounts does not exist until the spring of 1837, but a daybook begun at the new year in 1836 shows him sending goods to Miller and as well to new clients such as George Coe of New Haven, Nunns, Clark & Company in Philadelphia, and E. P. Nash in Petersburg, Virginia, all of which became long-term customers.[61] By June 10 Martin had added another client, P. H. Taylor of Richmond, Virginia, who thereafter regularly bought violins and bows, flutes, guitar and violin appointments, clarinet reeds, and other items. Taylor's first order was for about fifty dollars' worth of goods.

In this early period Martin also supplied other dealers and instructors in the city, particularly with imported strings and parts but also with instruments. Prominent among these new clients was William Pease, a piano dealer at 329 Broadway. In the winter of 1837 Pease received from Martin an order for $131.58 worth of instruments and accessories, most of them imported. Another shipment went to Bromberg and Company, which a week after this purchase bought more goods, worth $126.93.[62] Martin also sent goods on a commission basis to some of these clients and in his records duly noted any instruments returned unsold. On April 23, 1837, for example, Pease returned a serpent worth $22.00, a bass horn valued at $20.00, and a cello at $19.00.

A complete ledger exists for Martin's accounts beginning in the spring of 1837 until he liquidated his New York business in 1839 (plate 2-10).[63] This source, coupled with equally well kept journal entries for this period, provides a remarkably detailed view of Martin's business activities (plate 2-11). These records show him extending credit to sixty-two parties and also indicate that, while Martin sold more and more of his stock in New York, such out-of-state firms as P. H. Taylor in Richmond and Nunns, Clark & Company, now in Baltimore as well as Philadelphia, had become important customers in terms of the volume, particularly of imported instruments, they purchased (see Appendix B).[64] Nunns, Clark & Company's individual purchases, for example, often were in the hundreds of dollars.

From 1837 on, though, as Martin's guitar making began to bring in more income, he sold more of his general stock in New York and its environs, as Atwill's account in the city and Scheitz's at West Point (where Martin continued to do brisk business because of the military bands) indicate. He also continued to nurture his relationships with other instrument makers in the city. He sold them all manner of goods, subcontracted more repair work on brass and woodwinds, and paid commissions on the sale of his own guitars through their establishments. He similarly cultivated prominent music instructors, providing quantities of such basic supplies as strings, bridges, and tuners for their own simple maintenance or repair work. At their request, he also received all types of instruments for repair (even if he had to subcontract the work to others) and paid commissions when teachers referred students to him for guitars.

Atwill's account, one of Martin's earliest in the city, is typical in the amount and kinds of goods and services he provided local music dealers in these years. Indeed, in the spring of 1835, when Martin began to sell guitars with some regularity, his was the first firm through which Martin sold them. On January 23, 1836, for example, he noted that Atwill "remained in Commission 6 Guitars and 1 Aeolian harp to the amount of $85." Martin also regularly supplied this customer with guitar cases, guitar strings, and wind instrument reeds and was usually paid in cash. By the autumn of 1837, he had come to depend on Atwill for other income too. Virtually every week he brought Martin instruments, mostly guitars but some brass, for repair.[65]

Unlike Atwill, Christman, the wind instrument maker, chose to pay his bills in goods, with a "clarinet piece" worth $2.50, say, or with fifes, violin and guitar cases, or instrument strings, for which he obviously had his own sources. But with Hartman, the brass maker, the pattern was different. Because of Hartman's particular expertise, Martin brought *him* many brass instruments for repair and usually paid in cash, though once Hartman took some credit through a "German pipe" his associate wanted. Also, Martin sometimes took these craftsmen's instruments on commission for sale in his own shop. On May 8, 1838, for example, Eduard Baack brought to Martin's store "2 boxwood D Flutes, ivory tips, 6 German keys," worth $8.00 each, which he wanted Martin to sell.[66]

One of Martin's busiest New York accounts was with the well-known guitar instructor John Coupa, with whom he later contracted to sell guitars under the label "Martin and Coupa" (see Chapter 3). In 1837 Martin moved a large volume of strings, cases, and guitars through Coupa's studio at 195, and later 385, Broadway. In return, Coupa provided his associate with frequent guitar repair work. From July 1837 through September 1838, Martin did $271.51 of business with Coupa, who each month paid some part, though never the entire balance, of his bill in cash.

Two other guitar instructors, Schnepf and Fehrman, also frequently procured strings from Martin and sent many of their students as potential customers. If Martin sold them guitars, these teachers profited handsomely. Martin usually paid Schnepf, for example, a commission in the neighborhood of 20 percent. Fehrman, who often procured instruments for girls at "Mrs. Okill's Boarding School," was paid similarly, usually from 20 to 25 percent of the retail cost of the guitar.[67] Occasionally, some of these instructors' students or other professionals also rented guitars or other instruments from Martin, usually at the rate of one dollar per month. In 1838 Mr. Boucher, of 38 John Street, a violinist who regularly bought strings from Martin, rented a cello for "44 days, $1 month." On another occasion, Martin let a customer take a piano for two months, for three dollars, and even rented someone a flute for only one evening, for twelve and one-half cents.[68]

THE BUSINESS OF GUITAR MAKING

Martin did not keep business records for 1834 and 1835 as accurately as he did beginning in 1836. Thus, it is difficult to date precisely when he began to make guitars in New York City. A page of entries from May 9, 1834, for example, lists several guitars sold to Atwill, one to Fehrman, and a few to other individuals; a ledger-style entry records "Mr. Rönneberg" taking a terz guitar on June 16. While we cannot be sure that Martin himself made these instruments, no entry from 1834 records the arrival of imported goods. Stronger evidence for when Martin commenced his work, however, comes from accounts in March 1835 when he records a sizable purchase of wood—specifically, white pine, maple, and cherry—and other supplies, such as copal for varnish, that a guitar maker would use. By May he also had bought some bird's-eye maple veneer and "whitewood" (tulip). Thus we can say with some confidence that by the summer of 1835, if not before, Martin had resumed the trade he had spent so many years learning in Vienna under Stauffer.[69]

What did it take to establish a guitar-making business in New York in the mid-1830s? First, there had to be demand, and given the interest in the instrument generated by the great European virtuosos, we know that guitars were becoming more popular. Moreover, Martin could tap into this market through his contacts with other German instrument makers and teachers with whom he already did business. He also had the space to establish the kind of woodworking shop necessary to build such sophisticated instruments, as well as a prime business location. Indeed, by the spring of 1838 Martin signaled his formal entry into the trade by contracting with a Mr. Berger at ten dollars for painting a sign for his shop.[70] That summer Martin was also enough concerned with the appearance of his storefront that on several occasions he paid for "street wetting" to keep down the dust.[71]

He also needed a good number of hand tools, some of which he probably brought over with him from Germany but others that he acquired in or through his adopted city. A journal entry in the autumn of 1836 suggests that at this point Martin expanded his operations considerably. On October 13 he debited his account for the following: "1 stove for the Store — $20.00, 1 stove for cooking — $23.00, 2 Store lamps — $6.00, 1 large double plane — $1.65½, 1 large single plane — $.87½, 1 tooth plane — $1.00, 1 sash saw — $1.25, 1 hatchet — $1.65½, 1 large chisel — $.43¾, 1 hammer — $.43½, 1 machine for saw-setting — $2.00." A year later he purchased a few more tools: two files and handles for them and "1 pack blades" (plates 2-12, 2-13). On a regular basis now he also bought glue; copal, shellac, and "spirits" (usually from Bromberger) for varnishing the instruments; and flannel, presumably for polishing them or perhaps to line cases.[72]

Every couple of months beginning in 1835, Martin also bought wood, critically important in the construction of high-quality instruments. He used a lot of "whitewood" or tulip, for example, perhaps to line the interior of the guitar body underneath the rosewood or other exterior wood, for lining blocks (the small blocks in the interior of the guitar that hold together the back, sides, and top), or for cases. He needed spruce for the tops or sounding boards of his instruments. He bought pine for making instrument cases and also purchased maple and holly veneers to decorate the bodies and necks of his instruments. Like other guitar makers of this period, he was particularly fond of bird's-eye maple for such veneer work, as the 1835 order discussed above indicates.[73]

Martin also purchased exotic woods from wholesalers who specialized in such imported stock. For the backs and sides of his guitars, for example, he regularly used rosewood brought from the Caribbean or from Central or South America, and he occasionally used this same wood for the necks on his high-grade guitars. In 1837 he bought fifty dollars' worth of this wood from a Mr. Balzer and paid the bill at the Chemical Bank. Occasionally, he substituted mahogany for rosewood. On April 28, 1837, Brower, Ogden & Company of 392 Washington Street sold him "2 mahogani boards 21 feet" for $1.68 and another ten-foot board for $.70. Through dealers in African wood Martin procured ebony, either by the plank or already veneered, for the fingerboards of his guitars. In 1836, fifteen feet in the latter form cost him $1.87.[74]

Martin also needed metal tuning machines; bridge pins; ivory, bone, or shell for decorative inlay; and strings. In the 1830s, for example, he offered customers three options for tuning mechanisms: "plain heads" or "pegs," that is, regular violin-style friction pegs made from ebony, bone, or ivory; "patent screws," straight three-in-a-line metal geared tuning machines for slot-headed instruments; and "one-sided machines" (also known as "Vienna machines" or "Vienna side screws"), six-in-a-line metal geared tuners in an S shape, the kind that Stauffer regularly used on his guitars (plates 2-14, 2-15, 2-16).[75] Examples of Martin guitars with each style are extant from the 1830s, those with simple violin pegs or the Stauffer style being most characteristic of his work in this decade. Martin easily adapted violin pegs for his "plain heads." He regularly imported the two types of metal tuners that he needed. In the late spring of 1838, for example, he paid D. H. Schmidt & Son a freight charge on the delivery of "one case of Guitar screws from Vienna," presumably Stauffer style. Unfortunately, he did not record the price of the tuners themselves, but in the 1850s they cost him $2.00 a set.[76]

In this period Martin ornamented his instruments primarily with ivory and shell (plates 2-17, 2-18, 2-19). We find little information about these items save for the purchase of ivory (at considerable expense) on two occasions from John M. Phyfe, an "ivory turner" who dealt specifically in this item and whose main customers seemed to be the city's piano makers, who used the commodity for their instruments' keys (fig. 2-8). The going rate was four dollars per "set," though we do not know what constituted a set.[77] Even less information is available on the abalone or mother-of-pearl used for decoration on his most expensive instruments (plate 2-20). There is, however, one unusual (and unique) account, with Keith of Boston in December 1835, for the purchase of a pound of shells that may relate to these items, though why he would have to acquire these from Boston is unclear.[78]

Martin had two final business expenses, one large and one small. The value of his supplies and equipment—and of his inventory of instruments—was considerable, and he had to purchase insurance for it. He assessed the value of his goods at $3,500.00, the amount of an insurance policy he took out on May 21, 1838, from the North River Insurance Company, for which he paid a premium of $34.50.[79] In purchasing such protection he joined thousands of other New Yorkers who, particularly after the disastrous fire of 1835 a few blocks east of his location on Hudson Street, greatly feared such destruction of their means of livelihood as well as of their homes.

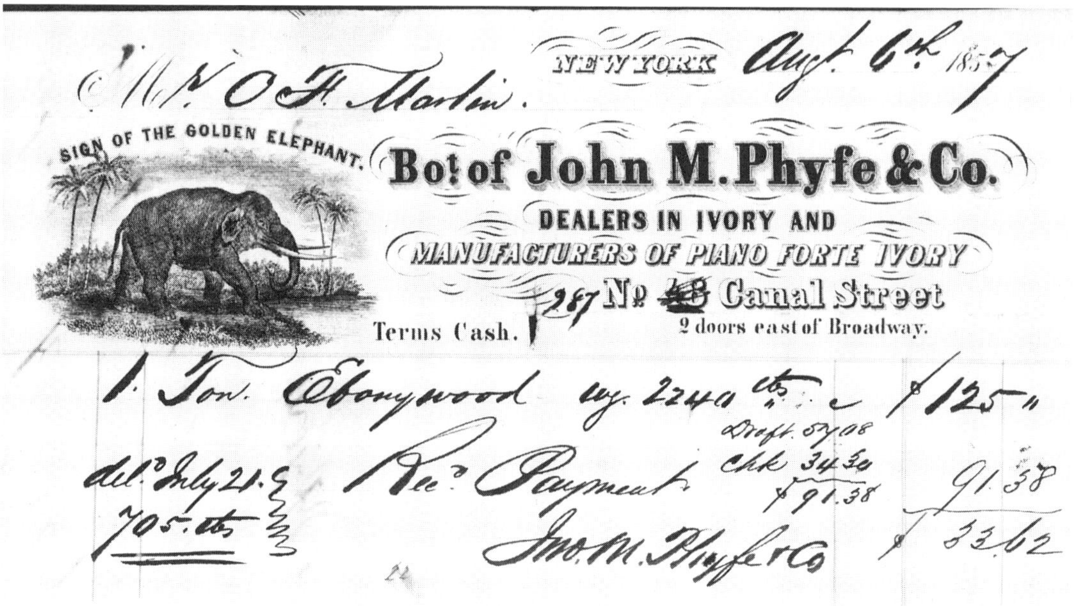

Figure 2-8. *Billhead from John M. Phyfe & Company, from whom Martin bought ivory while he was in New York and after he moved to Nazareth. Phyfe, who may have been related to the famous furniture maker, Duncan Phyfe, was listed in city directories as an "ivory turner." (Courtesy of C. F. Martin & Company Archives)*

Second and much more mundane, at least twice Martin availed himself of the services of local craftsmen to make the paper labels that identify his New York guitars (plate 2-21). In April 1835, for example, he paid a lithographer $7.00 for this work ("*Stein zu graviren*—$2.00" and "500 *cards zu drucken*—$5.00"). On March 21, 1837, when he needed a new supply, he went instead to Mr. Harris, an engraver, to have material scribed and printed. He paid $12.00 for the copper plate, that is, the engraving itself; $2.00 for two-hundred "papers"; and $6.00 more for three hundred "cards."[80]

MARTIN'S NEW YORK GUITARS

What kinds of guitars did Martin make and sell in the mid-1830s? Many of the instruments were what today we would term custom or special-order models, built after consultation with customers about the kinds of wood and appointments they wanted. Thus, one cannot speak of any standard model that Martin offered, a fact borne out by substantial differences in what he charged for instruments and as well by the variety among extant guitars from this decade (plates 2-22, 2-23).[81] Martin's business records thus provide important information about the types of guitars that he manufactured. In addition, they allow us to estimate both how long it took him to produce these instruments and his total output of guitars between 1836 and 1839.

When a customer ordered from him, Martin presented the individual with several important choices. First, as I have noted, he or she might select from three different styles of tuning mechanisms—"plain heads" with wooden friction pegs, "patent screws" for an instrument with a slotted peg head, and "one-sided" or "Vienna" machines, fit to a scroll or modified S-shaped peg head. Next, the customer chose a type of neck, for Martin offered either one with a fixed "ice-cream-cone"–shaped heel or, following Stauffer's innovation, one that was adjusted by means of a clock-key mechanism located where the neck met the body (plate 2-24). By inserting a key into a socket in the neck to adjust its pitch, a player could change the playing action of the strings.

The customer also could select the type of wood for the body of the guitar, the level of ornamentation, and the instrument's size. Martin always made his guitars' tops or sounding boards from spruce, and his necks usually from indigenous hardwoods such as birch or maple, stained black, or occasionally rosewood. For the guitar's sides and back, one could choose from maple, mahogany, rosewood, or, more rarely, zebra wood. Martin even made one instrument from brazilwood at the fairly high cost of thirty-two dollars.[82] Ornamentation most commonly consisted of ivory or (less commonly in Martin's early years) pearl decoration around the sound hole or the edges of the body or neck (a binding).

Occasionally, on higher-grade instruments, Martin used ivory for the bridge, or to decorate the fingerboard or even the back of the neck (plates 2-25, 2-26; see plate 2-17 as well). Such work could be quite intricate and added considerably to the price of the instrument. On July 15, 1837, for example, Martin sent Nunns, Clark & Company in Philadelphia a "ff [very fine] rosewood Guitar, ivory-plated fingerboard & ivory bridge with a mahogani case," for sixty-three dollars. Another, one of his first expensive instruments, finished in the summer of 1836, had an ivory inlaid neck and sold for sixty dollars (plate 2-27). Finally, although in this period Martin did not designate standard dimensions for body size, some customers ordered smaller-bodied terz guitars, popularized by Giuliani (see fig. 2-4). On January 26, 1838, for twelve dollars, Martin sold one of these (which he called a "third") to "Prof. Ballard," that is, to the guitar teacher James Ballard, who that very year brought out the first important American guitar tutor (plate 2-28).[83]

We can glean more about the construction of Martin's early guitars from extant instruments. As noted above, many guitars, particularly those of rosewood, were lined on the interior with spruce, while others have solid maple backs and sides. Such veneered backs, common as well to such European makers as Pagés, Lacote, and Panormo, suggest that during this period rosewood was used primarily for its attractiveness rather than for its acoustic properties.[84] Most of the earlier instruments also feature maple or birch necks made from three pieces—the cone-shaped heel and the peg head fit to the main length of the neck. Finally, during the 1830s Martin still braced the tops of his instruments as he had learned to do in Stauffer's shop and as was still done by the majority of European guitar makers, with five longitudinal strips strengthening the top, a system called ladder bracing (plate 2-29).[85] Although Martin occasionally described an order for a "Spanish" guitar, a term that in the 1850s connoted instruments that had the fan bracing associated with Antonio de Torres and other Spanish makers, what precisely he then meant by this designation is not clear (plate 2-30).[86] One hint comes in a record of a repair done for Coupa, who, in addition to having his sounding board polished, asked for "a new Spanish bridge and a set of strings."[87] This suggests a bridge through which the strings are tied off, rather than being held through the bridge and top with pins (plate 2-31). Such an instrument also might have had what came to be known as a Spanish-style heel, fit into the body differently from that on a guitar of the Vienna school, and internal blocks and brackets different from the kerfed linings commonly found on German and other makers' guitars (plates 2-32, 2-33).

As one might expect, a customer who chose a plain-headed model sought a fairly inexpensive instrument. Martin sold these as cheaply as twelve dollars, as he did in the spring of 1836 to his regular customer Schnepf. These guitars, affordable by students, occupied the bottom shelf of his stock, just above inexpensive "German" guitars, with pegs or patent tuners (never the Vienna style), which he imported and sold at from seven to twelve dollars each. On one occasion Martin traded one of these inexpensive models, priced at twelve dollars, for a lyre guitar (presumably European) which he valued at fifteen dollars and later sold for a dollar more.[88]

The price for one of Martin's guitars made with comparable woods and with patent tuning machines or one-sided machines was about the same, twelve dollars. More often than not, however, customers who chose the one-sided "Vienna" option had fancy European guitars in mind and thus opted as well for a significant amount of decoration. Early in 1836, for example, Martin sent Miller in Philadelphia such a guitar, of bird's-eye maple and with ivory edging, for $22.00. A few weeks later Ann Eliza Wheeler, who lived near Martin on Hudson Street, took an instrument of "maple wood, patent screws and some ornament," for $24.00. Instruments of zebrawood were more expensive. In May 1836, Martin sent Atwill on commission "one fine Guitar of zebrawood with Vienna machines + polished sounding board, a case to it," for $32.00. Another of that same exotic wood, built that fall, with Vienna tuners, ivory binding, a polished sounding board, and the adjustable neck, cost $26.00.[89]

Martin regularly sold such guitars in the thirty- to forty-dollar range, but other customers wanted yet more striking ones. The high end of his work is represented by instruments such as that sent to Miss L. R. June at White Plains, New York, late in the summer of 1836, "a ff [very fine] Guitar of rosewood + ivory neck, with a mahogoni case." He priced it at $85.00. Another, sold through Fehrman to Mr. Wells at 17 Washington Place but not described, cost $110.00. Fehrman commonly brought in such high-priced orders, perhaps an indication of the economic status of his pupils (plate 2-34). In the autumn of 1838, for example, he brokered a guitar sold for $80.00 to Mr. Haas at no. 126, Astor House.[90]

Fehrman's order also suggests how long it took Martin to make instruments of this sophistication, for his client had placed the order on October 26 and received the instrument on November 18. This information comes from Martin's list of "Orders Received" for the spring and summer of 1838, a trove of information about his production in these months. On May 22, for example, the music dealers Brauns & Focke in Baltimore ordered a "third [terz] guitar, of superior tone & touch, with ivory pegs, the face polished, to be made in the very best manner—Black painted case," for fifty dollars, for which they received a 10 percent commission. Martin was able to send it to their customer, Miss N. A. McEvers, care of the firm, on July 21.

On May 23 he received another order from Baltimore. Dr. H. Palmer knew exactly what he wanted: "*Body* of the largest size—*Neck* of strong, resisting wood, solid (not veneered) as thin as it can be without danger of warping, to suit a short, thick hand, of the usual breadth—*Frets* of good thickness, well rounded at the edges—*Patent screws three on a side*, are greatly preferred both to the scroll head where they are all on one side, and the pegs which are sometimes used." The instrument cost forty dollars when finished. Martin worked on Dr. Palmer's and Miss McEvers's orders simultaneously and sent them to Baltimore within a day of each other, via the "Philadelphia Transportation line."[91]

Thus, a customer usually waited one to two months for one of Martin's guitars, particularly for an instrument with elaborate decoration. Early in 1838, for example, Felix Stravinski at 156 Fulton Street ordered a guitar "like that one for Mr. Kruges but with a smaller neck." Martin promised to deliver it in two months.[92] In the autumn, Miss Rosa Macnevens, No. 4 Broadway, ordered a Spanish guitar and was told that it would be ready in three to four weeks. Just two weeks later Mr. E. Weston, 409 Fourth Street, ordered the same kind of instrument, but by then the wait had increased to from four to six weeks. Dr. Wheat of New Haven, Connecticut, got the quickest turnaround, a forty dollar instrument, to be done in ten to twelve days. At the other end, Mr. Retter, 48 West Street, waited the longest, and for a guitar that cost only twenty-two dollars. He ordered it on November 17, 1838, but did not receive it until the following February 12. If a customer was inconvenienced by such a wait, Martin might loan him an instrument. He did this with a Mrs. Edwards, no. 28 Varick Street, in the summer of 1830. He let her use a guitar "for a few days, til finished a new one."[93]

Finally, what can we say about Martin's guitar production in these years? Because in his financial records Martin indicates what guitars he *sold*, not necessarily those that he *made* and sold, it is difficult to arrive at precise numbers. For example, there are frequent records of very inexpensive guitars, retailed for under ten dollars. These were probably what he termed "German" guitars, that is, those which arrived in his shipments of other instruments from Europe. Furthermore, we know that he received some guitars from Schatz in Pennsylvania, but we do not know if Martin regularly carried out any finish work on these instruments or whether he sold them unlabeled or with the Martin & Schatz identification.

Evidence from the earliest records, though not complete, indicates that between May 9 and September 28, 1835, he sold eleven guitars, most through Atwill. The more complete accounts, beginning January 1, 1836, show that in 1836 he sold forty-six guitars; in 1837, thirty-three; and in 1838, thirty-nine. In terms of monthly sales, he sold as many as eight guitars in March 1836 and nine in March 1838 and, at the other end, none in November 1836. The records from 1836 also indicate that it was not until late August that he began to sell guitars of markedly higher price. On August 22, for example, he sold one at $40.00, shortly thereafter another went for $60.00, and on September 10 he sold the very expensive one, noted above, at $125.00, all, presumably, of his own manufacture.[94] From this point, although Martin continued to sell some inexpensive instruments, he clearly turned out a good number of guitars to customers' specific orders. He did so while managing an import business, retail sales, and considerable trade in instrument repair. To free time to devote to his guitar making, Martin had to employ others to help him.

EMPLOYEES AND PARTNERS

Martin's accounts indicate that he did so from an early date. In 1834 and 1835, for example, under the heading of "expenses for Wood, etc.," he lists twenty-five dollars in "wages for Louis from April 4th through May 1 [1835]." Other entries under "Accounts" for that year record "Louis" again and add "Heinrich" and "Jacob." On July 27 Martin paid the three $5.60, $1.00, and $4.00, respectively, with Heinrich also receiving another dollar on a few other occasions.[95]

Who Jacob was is unclear, although it may have been Jacob Hartman, who worked on wind instruments and perhaps was related to the August Hartmann in Markneukirchen, from whom Martin received shipments of European instruments; to John W. Hartman, who had traveled across the Atlantic with the Martin family; or to C. F. Hartmann, who worked with Martin after his move to Pennsylvania. Heinrich is almost certainly Heinrich Schatz, instrumental in having brought Martin to New York and with whom he formed a partnership before Schatz left for Pennsylvania in 1836.[96] Another ledger page in this same book, for "Louis Schmidt," suggests that Louis was the guitar maker who in 1836 established his own business at 92 Chatham Street. Later, in 1839, the year that Martin left New York City, Schmidt formed a long-lasting partnership with another maker, George Maul.[97] Schmidt was in Martin's employ as early as June 1834, at $4.00 a week, and for a while Martin provided him room and board. He continued to work for Martin through 1835 and settled his account early the next year, when he started his own business. The parting evidently was amicable, for subsequently Martin included him in his expanding circle of trade. On June 21, 1838, for example, when Schmidt was at his Chatham Street address, Martin sold him a bundle of "E" strings.

There is also evidence, though less conclusive, that Martin employed Schmidt's eventual partner, Maul. In the summer of 1838, for example, Martin made several large payments, from twenty to fifty dollars, to "Mr. Maul, no. 190 Canal Street," the amounts of which, without further notation, suggest that they may have been for guitar work performed, or even for guitars made, by Maul.[98] From what we know of the closely knit German musical instrument–making community in this period, it is logical that Maul might have worked for Martin, perhaps not long after his own arrival in New York. Such connections among all the German guitar makers, however, make it difficult to know who was making (or at least contributing to the construction of) exactly which instruments that carried Martin's name on the labels.

From the journal and ledger we know that in 1838 Martin employed Frederick William Rasche, of 212 Fulton Street, to attend to retail business at the store and to inlay pearl or abalone on the higher-grade instruments that Martin produced. On October 12 of that year, for example, Martin paid $7.00 "to Mr. Rasche the whole balance for attending the Store til Sept. 17" and, immediately following, added, "and the whole balance for Pearl work—$9.75." The entries in the concurrent ledger offer more detail. There under Rasche's name the entry reads, "By salary for attending the Store from May the 21st till Sept. the 17th, at $2 [per week]—$37.00." That day he also was credited for $12.75 for "425 Pieces Pearlwork, 3 cents a piece." Around the same time, Martin also paid a "Mr. Kretchmann" for "polishing a Guitar" and repairing other stringed instruments, including a double bass. Unlike Rasche, though, Kretchmann is not recorded in Martin's ledger and thus may only have been someone to whom Martin occasionally put out work, perhaps when he did not have time to complete it himself. One other significant, if brief, entry comes on April 21, 1838. That day Martin paid $.75 "to a man for Turning the string machine," the only evidence from this period we have of Martin winding his own instrument strings.[99]

Martin's earliest formal collaboration was with Schatz. As we have seen, in 1835 Martin made some payments to him and continued to trade with him after he left for Pennsylvania the next year. We also know that after he left New York, Schatz regularly sent guitars back to Martin via the "Easton [Pennsylvania] transportation line."[100] On January 9, 1837, for example, he shipped his friend six guitars with pegs, one with patent tuners, and, most interesting, "1 without a head, with ivory corners and ornamen[ted] sounding hole + polished sounding board." This last notation suggests that some instruments with a Martin & Schatz label in fact may be the result of this kind of collaboration, in this case with Martin fitting a peg head or, at the least, tuning machines, to the instrument Schatz had made. Further, the number of guitars Schatz forwarded on this occasion was not atypical. In the late winter of 1837, for example, Martin received "7 plain Guitars with pegs and 7 Guitar cases." Schatz regularly supplied Martin with these latter items. One shipment of cases, for example, consisted of a dozen of "whitewood" and two of cherry, forwarded with six more guitars.[101] Such transactions with Schatz cease, however, after March 1837 and perhaps indicate his move to Boston.

The Martin and Schatz labels add a little more information about this collaboration. One reads, "C. F. Martin & Schatz, Manufacturers of the celebrated Spanish and Vienna warranted Guitars, Violins, and Violincellos, and Double Bass. Made in the Best Italian Style." A variant notes, "Martin & Schatz, / from Vienna, Pupils of the Celebrated Stauffer. / Guitar & Violin Manufacturers / Importers of / Musical Instruments," and carries Martin's Hudson Street address (fig. 2-9). Thus Schatz, like Martin, had trained in Vienna, though it is unclear what precisely "Italian style" means. Furthermore, while one label identifies Martin and Schatz as "Guitar & Violin Manufacturers," another calls them "Manufacturers of the celebrated Spanish and Vienna warranted Guitars, Violins, and Violincellos, and Double Bass." Schatz thus may have made these other stringed instruments and sold them through Martin's shop. In any event, from the extant evidence, guitars that carry the Martin & Schatz labels probably date to the mid- to late 1830s and not beyond, unless they were instruments made by Schatz in Bethlehem and then either finished and labeled, or just labeled, by Martin upon their arrival in New York.

Martin's long-standing employee in the New York years was Charles Bruno, with whom he eventually entered into a formal (though short-lived) partnership, as he had done with Schatz. Although a city directory in 1837 lists Bruno as a bookseller, by that year he had entered Martin's employ and may have done so as early as 1836.[102] In the ledger that commences in April 1837, for example, Bruno's entry begins with a credit of $16.30 "Brought over from Page 12, ledger for 1836." The record also indicates regular monthly salary payments of $30.00 (comparable with those to Schmidt and Maul, a not inconsiderable amount) through November 20, 1838, with a final settlement on November 24, perhaps the date when he and Martin dissolved their partnership.

Bruno seems to have left the New York area around the same time that Martin did — he is not listed in city directories from 1840 to 1848 — and then reappears as a merchant and musical instrument dealer. He was listed as a musical instrument maker only for one year, in 1854, otherwise appearing

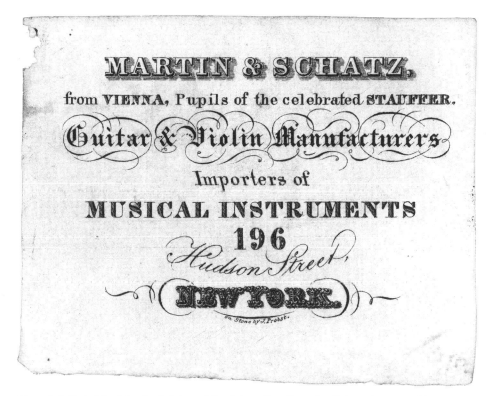

Figure 2-9. *Label for Martin & Schatz. Martin's earliest formal collaboration was with Heinrich Schatz, who had preceded Martin from Germany. In this, one of two known labels they issued, the partners make much of their training under the great Viennese maker, Stauffer. (Courtesy of C. F. Martin & Company Archives)*

under "musical instruments" or "importer musical instruments."[103] Whatever his responsibilities, in the 1830s he worked for Martin for at least two years.

The terms of their partnership are difficult to assess, but this much is clear: between May 1, 1837, and some date in 1839 (probably when Martin sold his entire stock just prior to his departure for Pennsylvania), they were legally partners. They formally notified the public of this on May 3, 1837, with a "Copartnership Insertion" in the *Courier & New York Enquirer* that cost $2.00. Then, on May 21, they paid $2.50 to Mr. Ludwig "for Label bills," presumably to identify the instruments they now sold together.[104] But, as noted above, Martin had employed Bruno at least since 1836 and perhaps longer. Further, as we have seen, a city directory for 1837 lists Bruno only as a bookseller, not as a musical instrument maker, and city registers do not record him as a musical instrument dealer until 1850. Given that he was neither a musical instrument maker nor a music teacher (as was John Coupa, another of Martin's associates), why would Martin want him as a partner?

It appears that Bruno functioned primarily as Martin's bookkeeper, with Martin using him to organize the financial records of an increasingly complex business. In Martin's journal for 1837–38, for example, between the pages ending with April 30 and May 1, 1838, one finds, in German, a notice to the effect that, while the pages before consisted of Martin's records, from that point on the accounts were those of Martin & Bruno. But this announcement, as well as all the accounts previous to it and through November 15, 1838, the last day covered by the book, are in the *same* hand, Bruno's. One entry offers incontrovertible proof of this fact. On February 10, 1838, next to a sixty-dollar credit, the bookkeeper writes: "Mr. Martin got from Mr. Prentiss at Boston for 1 Guitar & case, sent to him the 5th inst. #27 and for Mr. Wm Schubert $33 on account, & handed it to me, C. Bruno."

More surprising yet, the two other extant record books from the 1830s, back to 1835, also are in this hand, while accounts before that date, in the earliest book, are in a very different penmanship (presumably Martin's) and are primarily in German.[105] Finally, as I have noted, the earliest extant records of Martin's payments to Bruno date to 1836. All this suggests that Bruno worked for Martin—keeping his books—from an earlier date than we have supposed, even though, lacking the earlier ledger to which Bruno's own entry refers ("Brought over from Page 12, ledger for 1836"), this remains speculative.

Other internal evidence supports Bruno as the bookkeeper. Many of the entries, for example, show money credited specifically to "C. F. Martin on account" or read "Delivered to C. F. Martin." Repair work, too, was frequently entered in reference to Martin. On May 22, 1838, for example, there is an entry for guitar repair for Miss Collins, with $1.25 charged to her, and of that amount, $.75 credited to Martin. Another repair, for a Miss Bard, cost $7.00, with Martin credited for $5.00 of it. Presumably, in both cases the remainder went to Bruno as partner, whose records these were (hence, there was no need to name to whom the remainder of the profits went).

Further, the scribe often did errands for Martin. On July 7, 1838, for example, Bruno (for now we can name him) "Bought for Mr. C. F. M. 2 breads, meat, and beans," for one dollar. Another day Bruno listed an eight-cent expense for "passage to Brooklyn (to collect a debt from Mr. Baa[c]k for Mr. Martin)" and recorded the same expense two months later with "Passage to Brooklyn in Mr. C. F. Martins concerns." Finally, when Bruno balanced the accounts, as he did at the end of September 1837, he paid himself ($137.97 on this occasion) but not Martin. In contrast, throughout any given week Martin received regular payments, presumably for retail sales, repair work, and instruments manufactured and sold. No record shows Bruno making or repairing instruments.

Bruno also offered Martin a second business location, at 212 Fulton Street, in a building that he rented from a Mrs. Morris at $116.43 per quarter and which also housed Rasche, Martin's other employee in these years.[106] From 1837, Bruno sold books at this address, but from an early date he also carried Martin's musical merchandise. An entry for April 6, 1837, for example, has guitar and violin strings "delivered to the Store in Fulton Street," with no expense noted. Bruno also recorded a payment, for $3.75, to "Elise on acct. of Wages," quite possibly to someone (his wife?) tending shop at Fulton Street. Also significant in this regard is that, beginning on the first day of their partnership, Bruno recorded an inventory number for many of the instruments or accessories sold, something that never had appeared previously. These numbers may have been keyed to an inventory that he and Martin had prepared before their partnership went into effect, to enable them to determine Martin's original investment in the merchandise. After July, items so designated become fewer, perhaps because the partners now sold more goods in which they both had invested. Eventually, such entries virtually cease, perhaps indicating joint ownership of the remaining stock after a certain point.

Other details of the partnership remain murky, however. It is not clear, for example, if Bruno actually had invested in the firm monetarily or was paying through his labor. And it is difficult to say precisely what changed when Martin formally adopted him as a partner. Throughout this relationship, for example, Bruno continued to draw the same salary, $30.00 per month, which he had in the months before. The ledger in which Martin lists Bruno's accounts (again, in Bruno's own hand) shows that between April 1837 and the end of November 1838 he was paid $766.70 in salary—that is, without the kinds of balanced settlements noted above. Thus, for his own work Bruno evidently took a significant share of the profits from the general business, after Martin was paid.

Another individual associated with Martin in this decade was the professional guitarist and teacher John Coupa, a native of Spain who may have settled in Boston in the 1820s. Martin's earliest mention of him was in May 1837, when Martin charged him $12.00 for a guitar. That summer, with his increasing visibility on the concert stage, Coupa began to take in more pupils, which in turn led to more business with Martin. First listed in Martin's ledger at 198 Broadway, he frequently bought guitars (one for $50.00), cases, strings, instruction books (he favored Carcassi), and other supplies, presumably for resale to his tutees. He also regularly brought in instruments for repair. Between July 13, 1837, and December 1838, this amounted to $389.25 in business for Martin, on which Coupa paid about $50.00 a month. When Martin was about to leave the city in the spring of 1839, Coupa closed out most of his regular account by paying a large portion of the outstanding balance with two guitars and carrying forward $5.26 to Martin's "new book."[107]

Evidently Martin thought highly of Coupa, for as he was about to leave New York for Pennsylvania, he enlisted Coupa as his agent. City directories for 1840–41 thus list Martin & Coupa at 385 Broadway, a location that Martin used as a depot in the early 1850s (plate 3 33). Whether Martin retained him in this capacity throughout the decade is unclear, however, for the firm does not appear in subsequent directories, nor do we have Martin's records for these years. In any event, in 1849, when the records recommence, Coupa again serves this function (see Chapter 3).[108] Their label noted that Coupa and he "have always in hand the largest assortment of guitars that can be had in the United States."

Martin teamed as he did with Schatz, Bruno, and Coupa for different reasons. Schatz, also German, offered an entrée to the city and the comfort of familiarity. For the short span they worked together in New York, Schatz assuredly built instruments with Martin, who put Schatz's name on his labels and gave him a commission on instruments sold through his recommendation. Martin also purchased guitars from him after he moved to Pennsylvania, though it is not clear if he labeled these as "Martin & Coupa." Bruno offered Martin business acumen, which enabled him to spend more time building guitars rather than tending to his increasingly complex accounts. The patronage of Coupa, a well-known figure in New York's musical world, gave Martin's guitars an imprimatur that made them desirable to many amateur and professional musicians. He also served as his agent in the city after Martin moved to Pennsylvania.

MOVING ON

By the late 1830s Martin had established himself among America's musical instrument makers in the city that was the center of the nation's musical life. But he also had begun to consider relocating outside New York. Martin was aware, for example, that the young nation's expanding transportation system made such relocation economically feasible. As I noted, he had friends and clients in Bethlehem, Pennsylvania, ninety miles southwest of New York City and one of the centers of the Moravian Church in the United States. Most important of these individuals was Schatz, who in 1836, having heard of the beauty of the area from other Germans who recommended it as a rural alternative — much like Markneukirchen — to New York City, had moved to the Millgrove township, near Nazareth. Martin or his wife visited there on at least two occasions in the summer of 1838. They evidently liked what they saw.[109]

By November, Martin & Bruno's accounts show many fewer transactions than in the previous months, and the abrupt termination of the journal on November 29 indicates the date when Martin began to settle his accounts with Bruno. He paid Bruno through November 20, and on November 23 and 24 the latter was allowed to withdraw small amounts of cash as though reaching final agreement on what was due him. This is the only indication of any formal settlement with him as Martin wound down his New York career.

The ledger, however, also records other business conducted into 1839. On May 5, for example, Coupa received $40.00 credit on his account by giving Martin two guitars, leaving a balance due of $389.25 on new account. Similarly, Scheitz of West Point, one of Martin's more lucrative accounts for brass instruments, continued to buy goods, including a French horn, through April

1839. Other accounts show the same pattern, with the last business done in May.

Among the final entries for these long-time clients is a new name, Ludecus & Wolter, at 320 Broadway, overseen by Edward Ludecus and John Frederick Wolter. In November 1839 Martin transferred some of his regular customers' debits or credits to this firm. Martin's ledger book has a page for Edward Ludecus of New York, with no street address listed, and on May 14, 1839, a credit from Ludecus & Wolter to Martin of $25.00 "cash at Cherry Hill" (where he had settled in Pennsylvania) and another about the same time of $5.00. Aside from this, we know little of this firm, except that Martin sold them his entire stock of musical merchandise shortly after he moved to Nazareth, a transaction recorded in a detailed inventory prepared for the sale.[110]

This document, dated May 14, 1839, provides a unique record of a musical instrument seller's stock in the late 1830s (plate 2-36). The sheer numbers of goods that Martin had in his shop was extraordinary. Flutes constituted the largest volume, for Martin had over 150 in stock, instruments that he distinguished by the kinds of wood of which they were made and the number of keys each had. The next most common instruments were violins. Of these he had over 100, listed by grade and size (12 three-quarter-size and 10 one-half-size instruments, for example). Clarinets came next, numbering 36, and then 24 trumpets. Many other woodwind, brass, and stringed instruments were represented, from two tiny piccolos to one contrabass, a serpent, a tuba, and a glockenspiel. Martin had, among other brass instruments, 31 bugles, 12 trombones, 17 post horns, and 16 hunting horns. There were, however, only 7 guitars in the lot, perhaps European imports, for one of them was a "shield guitar," a model identified with the Mirecourt region of France (fig. 2-10).

A large part of the inventory consisted of accessories and parts for instrument repair. Ludecus & Wolter, for example, acquired sixty-seven violin bows (but only two for the cello and one for the double bass). They also took close to four hundred violin bridges, ninety for cellos, and seventeen for the double bass. The sale also included pegs for all members of the bowed instrument family and for guitars, and mouthpieces for the different brass and wind instruments. More unusual were handfuls of unfinished necks for violins, violas, and cellos, as well as three bass fingerboards, which suggest that Martin, or someone in his employ, made such instruments. There were also bassoon reeds, bundles of horsehair and "violin bow hair," large quantities of strings for the violin family as well as for the guitar, and smaller items like capos d'astro and violin mutes. Music instruction books and music completed the inventory.

After Martin factored in bank charges, interest, and overhead, Ludecus & Wolter acquired the goods for $2,576.90 in Prussian currency (Reichsthalers). They also promised that this sum, and any interest (at "5% from 1 October of

Figure 2-10. *Ninth-plate daguerreotype, ca. 1855. This unusual image shows what is known as a "shield guitar," a type of instrument identified particularly with the Mirecourt region of France but also produced elsewhere. When Martin liquidated his inventory in 1839 prior to leaving for Pennsylvania, he listed one of these in his sale. (Collection of the author)*

this year"), had to be settled with F. T. Merz in Neukirchen in the "shortest possible time." This, as well as the manner of settlement in Prussian currency, suggests that Martin himself had many of these European goods on commission through Merz or, at the least, had not yet paid in full for them.

His stock liquidated, Martin packed up his furniture, tools, and family and moved to Pennsylvania, where he began a new phase of his career. In his six years in New York he had established himself as one of the country's best-known guitar makers, his instruments found in music emporiums from Boston to Richmond and many smaller cities in between (plate 2-37). In good measure his success had been expedited by the close network of musical instrument makers and dealers, many of them German, with whom he exchanged goods and services. Like Martin, most of these individuals—his friend Schatz, his employee Louis Schmidt, the wind instrument makers Christman and Jacob Hartman, among others—had been raised in the same guild system that had marked Martin's early years in Saxony. In the United States such craftsmen flourished in a much less restrictive economy, one that encouraged precisely the kinds of openness to the market that characterized Martin's various ventures in the music trade.

We do not know precisely what prompted Martin's move to the Pennsylvania countryside, but it is likely that the aftermath of the panic of 1837—it was six years before the economy began to recover—had something to do with it.[111] Even though Martin's business did not seem to suffer, for example, conditions for city artisans and laborers were dire, with over half of New York City's craft workers out of work and violence over labor issues common. Martin had worked hard for his success and was an astute businessman with a significant number of clients, in and out of New York City. Like his friends Schatz and Stumcke and his client Gütter, he realized that one could live in the Lehigh Valley and easily move goods to New York (or to Philadelphia, for that matter), and through it to other cities. Furthermore, by this point Martin had decided to become primarily a guitar maker and thus to leave behind his import and retail business. In Cherry Hill, outside Nazareth, he could devote himself full-time to his chosen craft and still market his goods in and through the city.

The effects of the panic lasted through 1843, but with the country's economic recovery he soon had new opportunities to expand his business, for the world around him was changing in ways that redefined a craftsman's relation to the market. Railroads and steamboats opened immense new markets for trade, particularly in the interior of the country, and new "express" companies expedited transport to these areas. Moreover, the U.S. mails that traveled these same routes enabled businesspeople hundreds of miles apart to communicate with startling ease and speed. Moving to Nazareth, Martin positioned himself to take advantage of the next stage in the American economy's expansion. In this new market, however, impersonal business relations began to supersede the informal ethnic and cultural networks that had defined Martin's New York years and on which he had depended for his initial success. Who Martin would deal with and on what terms—in his phrase, who would have his guitars' "agency"—loomed as a central question. In its way, the challenge of beginning anew in Nazareth was as great as that which Martin had faced when he moved from Germany to New York. Once again, he seized the opportunity.

3 Nazareth, Pennsylvania, 1839–1855

SETTLING IN

On December 21, 1839, Martin bought eight acres at Cherry Hill, in the infant Bushkill Township outside Nazareth, in Northampton County, Pennsylvania.[1] Set against the Blue Ridge Mountains to the north and west, Nazareth, along the banks of Monocacy Creek, was a satellite to the larger community of Bethlehem, on the Lehigh River. Moravian missionaries and settlers, most of them from Germany, who a century earlier had ventured from Philadelphia, fifty-five miles away, had founded the two towns at about the same time.[2] Twelve miles downstream from Bethlehem, at the important commercial town of Easton, the Lehigh joined the majestic Delaware River, which divided Pennsylvania from New Jersey and formed one of nineteenth-century America's chief waterways. By the 1830s an impressive six-hundred-foot bridge spanned the river and connected Easton with Phillipsburg on the New Jersey side. At Easton and Phillipsburg both the Morris Canal, which linked commerce from Newark to the Delaware River valley, and the Lehigh Canal opened markets to the north and west, respectively, and stage roads and turnpikes linked the region to New Jersey's other commercial centers and to New York City.

When the Martin family moved to the Lehigh Valley, their friend and coworker Heinrich Schatz had already been living in the area, in the Millgrove Township, for three years. There is no evidence that Martin had made prior arrangements to purchase land, so he probably again depended on Schatz to orient and settle his family. Nazareth proper was still a deeply religious community owned and operated by the Moravian Church. It still restricted land sales, preferring instead to rent parcels to newcomers who shared the Moravians' faith. Thus, the Martins settled at Cherry Hill, just outside Nazareth proper, and worshiped with the Moravian congregation at what was known as Schoeneck.[3]

Long before 1840, Bethlehem and its smaller neighbor to the north marked the center of the Moravian Church in the New World. The larger community boasted Moravian College as well as a female academy, and Nazareth claimed Nazareth Hall, a well-regarded school for boys (fig. 3-1). Both communities were deeply immersed in music. As one early historian put it (speaking of Bethlehem), "Music was one of the institutions, which gave character to the town [and] afforded intellectual amusement and pleasure, both to the performers and hearers," amusement and pleasure that was varied.[4] In addition to the anthems and hymns sung by the Moravians at their services, they also enjoyed a concert life rich in chamber and orchestral music of the most prominent European composers and those from their own ranks.[5]

Famous for their "choirs" of trombones, the local musicians were equally adept on other brass and wind instruments, as well as on strings. One early-nineteenth-century visitor from New England, for example, recalled that in Bethlehem she came upon an ensemble of organ, two bass viols, four violins, two flutes, two French horns, two clarinets, and a bassoon, as well as some instrument that she had never heard before. She also noted that virtually every home contained a pianoforte.[6] Local crafts workers produced some of these instruments, but such a demand necessitated the importation of others, primarily from Germany through New York and Philadelphia. We recall that shortly after Martin's arrival in New York he began to trade with Gütter, Schatz, Stumcke, and other musical instrument makers and dealers around Bethlehem. By 1839 he had heard enough good about the area to move his thriving business to rural Pennsylvania.

JOHN COUPA AND THE NEW YORK CONNECTION

Inexplicably, the entirety of C. F. Martin's American career is profusely documented, save for his first decade in Pennsylvania. No accounts and only a few letters survive from between 1840 and 1849.[7] In the detailed ledger book in which Martin listed out his New York accounts (Ledger, 1837–40), for example, only two accounts continue into 1840 (that is, after the sale of Martin's inventory to Ludecus & Wolter), both for music teachers. One was of "Professor" D. Drucke, then of New York but later at Spring Garden Street in Philadelphia.[8] The other continuing account, for John Coupa, is more significant. As I have discussed, before Martin left for Pennsylvania he had done much business with this instructor, who between 1838 and early 1840 had bought nine guitars from Martin, who used him as his city agent in 1840–41.[9] When the records pick up again in 1849, in business correspondence, Coupa clearly was again (or still) functioning as Martin's main contact in New York City. The first in a line of people who worked as Martin's designated agents, through the 1840s until his death late in 1850 or 1851 Coupa handled the majority of guitars that Martin sent to New York, his most lucrative market.

Figure 3-1. *Advertisement for Nazareth Hall, a Moravian boarding school for boys near the community in which Martin settled after he left New York in 1839. The school offered instruction in piano, flute, and violin, as well as in singing. Martin occasionally repaired violin family instruments for faculty and students at the institution.*

The two men clearly had done business long enough to become friends and to speak openly about both business and personal matters. In 1849, for example, Coupa expressed displeasure that Martin had not forwarded a terz guitar that he needed immediately, for the delay had cost him the sale. Ordering four more guitars, Coupa directed Martin to send this batch the same week without fail. "I do not treat you as you do me," he complained. He reminded Martin that he always paid cash for his orders and, in return, only wished that Martin would tell him whether he could supply an order on time. "It is so bad," Coupa complained, "to disappoint people."[10]

Such frank talk did not estrange the two friends, who even shared family intimacies. A little later, for example, Coupa ordered seven more guitars, but not before he sympathized with Martin for having a toothache.[11] And he soon had his own bad news to share, much worse than a mere toothache. "I have been in great trouble," he confided to Martin a few weeks later. His daughter "Petite" had been very sick, evidently with measles, and the girl could hardly walk. Coupa's wife was so fatigued from nursing the child that she could hardly stand, and to make things even worse, the family had recently relocated, and his house was still "all upside down with moving."[12]

Fortunately, the Coupa family's crises passed without tragedy. In another letter, sent from New York City when he had briefly returned from his country home, Coupa did not even mention Petite but wrote that his wife was recovering her health. By that autumn, as people returned to the city from their summer away from its heat, his business as a musical instructor began to pick up, as did his orders to Martin. Coupa's letters from this period are particularly important because prior to 1850 Martin evidently had few other outlets for his instruments. The firms of Jonathan Mellon of Pittsburgh, for example, and Thayer and Collins in Albany were the only two others to whom he shipped guitars at this time.[13] Thus, from Coupa's correspondence we can piece together some details about Martin's guitar making before he greatly increased his customer base. With clients returning to the city in the fall, for example, Coupa urged Martin to send him three hundred dollars' worth of guitars because his showroom did "not look so well empty." "I will pay half cash and the other half when sold," he told Martin, and he added that he wanted instruments in the twenty-dollar range, at the lower end of Martin's price scale.[14]

Coupa could be much more specific in his requests. In October, for example, he ordered two "small Degoni" at twenty dollars each, two "large" ones with pegs, and one "Ferranti." The "Degoni" was a model named after Delores Nevares de Goni, a well-known performer who occasionally appeared on the stage with Coupa. When she came to the United States in 1843 she brought a large patterned Spanish guitar, copied by both Martin and Schmidt & Maul, which thus may have provided Martin with the incentive for producing some guitars in what was termed the "Spanish style." The "Ferranti" was named for another well-known player, Marc Aurelio de Ferranti, guitarist to the king of Belgium (fig. 3-2). His instrument was also described as large, of a more "circular" form—that is, with both bouts about the same width.[15] Coupa also inquired again for a terz guitar and added that it "must be [of] first rate tone." "I do not know which is the best model for brilliancy in a terz Guitar, either the Spanish or the Ferranti model," he continued, "but I think myself, that the one you made for [S. de la] Cova, was the best Terz I have ever heard." De la Cova was another well-known performer to whom Martin had sold guitars and whom Coupa knew. Indicating his familiarity with such celebrities, Coupa also gossiped that the renowned "Mrs. DeGoni has gone to Mexico" and had left behind her children, including a four-month-old baby.[16]

In addition to orders for guitars, Coupa sent Martin other business. On one occasion he forwarded, via the piano maker John C. Malthaner, a violoncello, presumably for repair, and thirteen bundles of guitar strings, which Martin had requested.[17] Coupa also had taken in a guitar with a broken neck and asked if Martin could repair it when he next came to the city. A month later he wrote Martin that if he were not visiting New York that week, he wanted his most recent order, for three guitars, shipped quickly. He testified to the close friendship between the two families by adding that if Martin did not come soon, he thought he might "take a trip to Easton, and make a nice New Year call at Cherry Hill."[18]

The repair work that Coupa forwarded was considerable and suggests that Martin was not yet occupied full-time as a guitar maker. In February 1850, for example, Coupa ordered three more guitars and sent three others, only one of which Martin had made, for repair.[19] One needed extensive work on the neck and was to be fixed so that it looked like one of Martin's. On this instrument the customer also wanted a Spanish bridge. Another, the guitar that Martin had made, now needed a new sounding board and was to be returned in two weeks at the most because the owner was em-

Figure 3-2. *Marc Aurelio de Ferranti, a well-known guitar player after whom Martin named one of his early instrument models, the "Ferranti."*

barking on a trip. Coupa also told Martin to make him two "large" guitars, with pegs, at nineteen dollars. Although earlier Coupa had ordered guitars by model number, as I will discuss, Martin obviously knew what he meant by such shorthand descriptions, whether of guitars described by a player's name ("degoni" or "Ferranti"), by price, or by size ("large" or "small"). Rarely did Coupa specify any ornament. Most commonly, he simply asked for a "yellow" sounding board instead of a lighter one, and he continued to order instruments at twenty dollars or under, with little decoration.

Coupa's last letter to Martin is dated February 4, 1850, and sometime within the next two years he died. Correspondence from his wife, Susan, sheds the only other light on the family. In the late winter of 1852 she told Martin that she would leave for England in a couple of weeks, "on the same ship that [her] sister came over in," and thus hoped that Martin could bring his wife to see her before she left the country permanently. But she also wanted him to settle a note to her deceased husband, for eighty-one dollars, due the first of that month.[20]

Martin answered quickly to say that he would pay his debt through William Raddé, a friend in the city who imported and sold German books and works on homeopathic medicine.[21] Martin also reported that Schatz had asked him to mention to Mrs. Coupa an outstanding debt of her husband's. She knew nothing about Schatz's claim on her husband's estate and found it strange that he had not made the demand during Coupa's lifetime, for Schatz "knew [him] to be very particular in his payments." Obviously, at this point Susan Coupa was settling her husband's affairs before going to England to make a new life. The Martins, unfortunately, were not able to see her before she sailed, and after this date the Coupa family drops from the Martin archives.[22]

CHARLES DE JANON

Even after he had moved to Nazareth, Martin sometimes returned to New York on business, staying with Coupa while he was alive. "I shall go next Friday to the country to remain until Monday next," Coupa had written him on one occasion. "If I knew certain that you would come on Friday, I would remain here untill Saturday." Because Martin could not offer this assurance, Coupa planned to "leave the keys with Maul, and [to] get ready a bed for you in the small room next to the parlour," another testament to the deep familiarity between Coupa and Martin.[23] This missive also indicates that George Maul, the guitar maker who had worked for Martin in 1834 and now lived at 388 Broadway, still remained part of this tight circle of guitar craftsmen and musicians.[24]

After Coupa's death, Martin continued these trips with some frequency, no doubt to attend to business that Coupa previously had handled for him.[25] Quite likely, too, he was trying to locate someone to replace Coupa as his chief contact and to oversee the city property that he either owned or rented, part of which he sublet to other parties.[26] During this same period, Martin's son also frequently visited the city and stayed for months at a time.[27] In his midtwenties, Frederick had begun to assume a larger role in his father's business, including the oversight of Martin's depot in New York after Coupa's death. Among the family documents from this period, for example, is a receipt for fire insurance dated June 26, 1850, that indicates the extent of Martin's investment in the city. He took out a policy for $225.00 on household goods and wearing apparel, as well as "plate, plate ware, and printed books," in a "three-story brick and slated building, occupied as a dwelling and music store, No. 385 Broadway." In addition, he insured twenty guitars, "none to be valued at over $25.00." He paid a full year's premium of $7.25 for $725.00 worth of insurance against loss or damage by fire of his property and goods.[28]

That summer Frederick sold or took orders for a total of twenty instruments, some for clients in the city and others for such now-regular customers as Balmer & Weber in St. Louis and F. I. Ilsley at Albany. He calculated the worth of these sales at $877.00 and paid himself $21.35 in commission.[29] He frequently sent money back to Nazareth (more often to his mother than to his father), and he purchased rosewood veneer and planks for the family business. These New York accounts continue through October 1851.

Martin and his son probably tired of such prolonged visits to the city and

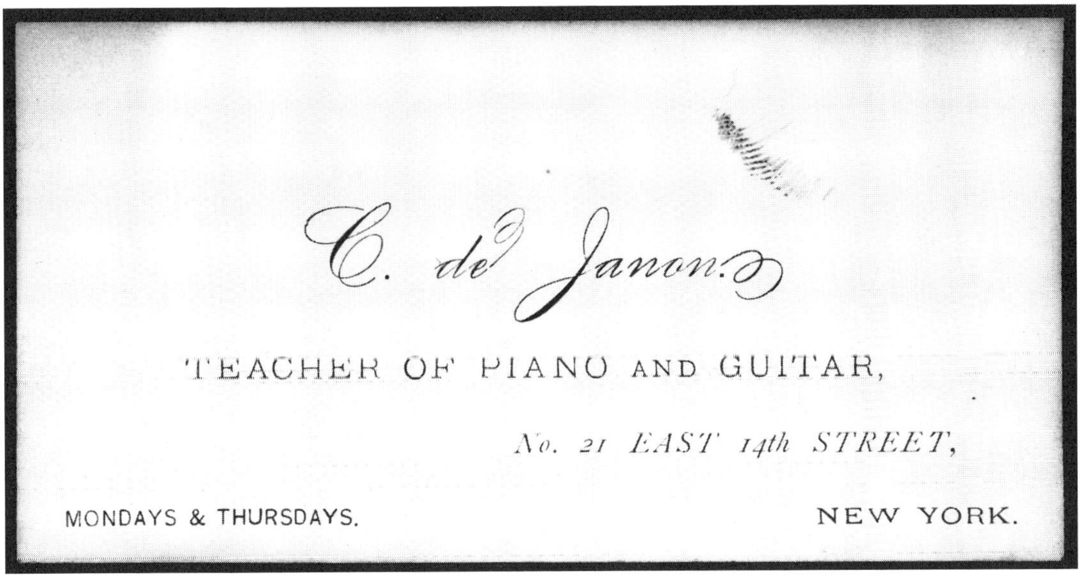

Figure 3-3. *Business card of Charles de Janon, a performer and teacher who served as Martin's agent in New York in 1851 after John Coupa's death. (Courtesy of C. F. Martin & Company Archives)*

thus were pleased to sign as an agent Charles de Janon, a "Professor of Music" with whom Martin had signed an agreement regarding Janon's agency for him (fig. 3-3). He very likely was related to Leopold de Janon, a concert musician who had first appeared on the New York stage in 1841 (the same year as Coupa) and through whom Martin probably met Charles.[30] The date of Martin's agreement with him—January 1, 1851—suggests that Coupa had died sometime after early February 1850, the time of his last communication with Martin, and the following New Year.

The three-page agreement that Martin and Janon signed on New Year's Day 1851 made him Martin's "sole and only agent in the City and County of New York" through February 1, 1852. On his part, Martin provided a suitable sales room for his instruments—a space that Janon also was allowed to use, rent free, for his guitar instruction—and carried the insurance on the premises, the building at 385 Broadway indicated in the insurance policy.[31] On his part, Janon was to keep Martin's instruments "in as good a state and condition as reasonable use will admit." More important, he was to market them and would receive a commission of 33 percent on each guitar he disposed of at retail. If he sold any of this stock through other parties and had promised them commission, however, he had to pay it from that percentage.

Martin gave Janon different terms, though, for wholesale orders that he procured and forwarded to Nazareth. If a customer was not already Martin's patron, Janon received 5 percent of the amount of his first order. Subsequently, however, this wholesale customer became Martin's own, without compensation to Janon. Finally, he was to provide Martin or his agent with the proceeds of every instrument so sold by him whenever Martin requested it or when some third party to whom Martin had become indebted demanded payment.

When Martin returned to Nazareth in February 1851, he and Janon corresponded regularly. From these missives it is clear that Martin also expected him to attend to a range of other matters, particularly the management of his city property at 385 Broadway, which Martin had retained after Coupa's death and in which he sublet space that he did not need either for his showroom or his agent's teaching studio.[32] By this time, such use of an agent to collect rent and otherwise supervise property was not unusual, for as landlords acquired more and larger rental properties, they supported a new group of individuals who made their living as property managers.[33]

Martin's headaches with his own renters indicate why many landlords preferred to hire such individuals rather than worrying about matters themselves. At one point, for example, one of his tenants, Mrs. Harriet Wilson, a milliner, was not willing to pay her rent or to "sell her furniture to the lady upstair[s]" to help pay for what she owed.[34] Janon sought Martin's direction with the uncooperative woman. Whatever he counseled, after two weeks Mrs. Wilson still was recalcitrant and had not given Janon the furniture, which itself had been mortgaged. As a consequence, Janon wanted to order her to leave the premises that week or to face an eviction warrant, provided that Martin gave him permission to do so. But Martin already had the matter in hand. In a postscript Janon added that he had just learned from the lady upstairs (though how *she* knew he did not say) of Martin's directive to his lawyer to put out Mrs. Wilson. "Mrs. Bertha" (perhaps the landlady), he added, was very disappointed by all this and wanted to have the room as soon as possible because "she cannot do Business until she have [it]."[35] On March 20 the warrant was served and the tenant put out, presumably freeing Mrs. Bertha to rent the room to another.[36]

Over the next few months, Janon devoted himself to other of Martin's affairs. As requested, for example, he frequently reported on payments he had received for Martin. At one point he mentioned that he had ninety dollars at Martin's disposition and would gladly send it to Nazareth when Martin needed it. He also told his employer that he had recently seen an agent of Nunns, Clark & Company of Philadelphia and had collected a draft for $134.15 from them. He continued to do other work for Martin too. He procured strings and patent tuners for him, for example, paying Joseph Rohé (over the decade one of Martin's chief suppliers for tuners) $75.00 and sending both items to Martin by Hope's Express, which Martin regularly employed for carriage between New York and Nazareth.[37] Janon also brought in lucrative orders from new retail customers. One of his first sales, for example, was a $50.00 instrument, with "Ivory E[d]ges, fine finish." Then, in June 1851, a "professor of the Guitar, Mr. Dongelli," ordered a "Ladies Guitar." He wanted, Janon wrote, "a *Beautifull* Guitar[,] fine ornamentation[,] No. 2½ with patent head — A Guitar that I can sell for $65."[38] Janon also secured new wholesale customers. In December he wrote Martin that he had received an order for six guitars from Mr. Christman (the wind instrument maker) for his son, now in business in New Orleans: "2 large Spanish with pegs, 2 Ladies No. 2½ and [2] small degoni."[39]

But whether or not it was Janon's fault, business eventually slowed. As early as October he lamented that he had sold but one guitar the prior month. "Business has been so bad," he told Martin, that he "had not the courage to write before." He attributed this downturn in part to his not having on hand a very large assortment of musical instruments. "I think if you can spare [a] few more it will be to your Advantage," he wrote, "as this is the principal Agency[,] it is well to have a good assortment in case of a demand."[40] In late January, though, just before their agreement expired, Janon reported business was again very dull, with no guitars sold since Martin had been in the city a week earlier. This time Janon blamed the slackness on very cold weather and snow a foot deep.[41]

No doubt due in part to such an economic downturn, Martin did not renew their agreement and soon wished to settle their account.[42] Janon was indebted to Martin for the considerable sum of $212.27, and Frederick Martin urged him to pay soon because the guitar maker was getting "no money from the western Cities & other places." "We have the note to pay yet to Mr. Rohé & the rent to Mr. Raddé," Martin Jr. continued, "who will settle the rent [for 385 Broadway] for us in the future." This detailed accounting, like nothing that hitherto had passed between the two parties, suggests that Martin had indeed terminated Janon's services. The parting, however, seemed amicable. In a postscript Martin Jr. asked Janon to "please take care of the dog" until he sent for it, a reference to his father's prized Newfoundland.[43]

Unfortunately, Janon could not make good on his debt for some years, and five years later Martin still had to remind him of his outstanding obligations.[44] Janon hoped to be able to send him some money soon and noted that whoever had told Martin that his (Janon's) business prospects recently had improved had been mistaken, for "I never had such hard times as I had this month." But he made clear that he did not want to disappoint his old patron. "I have not forgotten you as you may think," he continued, "and as soon as I get some of my bills collected I will forward to you some on account."[45]

THE BUSINESS OF "AGENCY"

As Martin's complex relations with Coupa and Janon indicate, in the late 1840s and early 1850s he still conducted much of his business in a very personal way, with knowledge of and trust in individuals handpicked to represent his interests. This was feasible when most of his orders continued to go through only a few central locations, as they did before 1852. Around 1850, for example, in addition to his New York connections, Martin's only other close business relationships were with several music teachers in Philadelphia. One was Edward Pique, who also arranged popular songs for guitar. Wishing to supply his students with fine-quality guitars, Pique provided Martin detailed instructions for special instruments, occasionally even sketching them so that there would be no misunderstanding of the client's wishes. One order is typical. It was "for a *young lady*, with a small hand, therefore the fingerboard pretty small, the head with good *patent machine screws*, a *yellow face*, little pegs to put the knots of the strings in." "She does not want any screw in the neck," Pique continued, and "the guitar shall be of the very best quality."[46]

Martin also had the patronage of William Schubert, whom another customer described as "a gentleman, a good Guitar Player[,] and a man to your Interest." "He speaks highly of your Instruments," the merchant William Peters told Martin, "and says he makes all his Pupils buy a Martin Guitar."[47] Schubert was proud of his association with Martin. In an advertisement he placed in a Philadelphia paper in 1848, for example, he informed the public that he had "on hand a large assortment of GUITARS, from the celebrated manufactory of C. F. Martin." Those who sought a "very superior instrument," he added, "both in tone and finish," should call on him at his rooms at no. 108 Walnut Street.[48]

The owner of a Philadelphia music store and publisher of sheet music Augustus Fiot was on similarly good terms with Martin.[49] When he sold his business to J. E. Gould & Company in 1853, the firm wrote Martin to see if he would continue Fiot's arrangements with it. Martin balked because he lacked acquaintance with the firm, but the partners were so eager for the privilege that they offered always to pay cash on delivery for his shipments.[50] This anecdote suggests that, as Martin's reputation grew and other customers and dealers sought his guitars, it was increasingly difficult for him to operate in the highly personal way to which he was accustomed, for such relationships took years to develop. At the same time, more and more individuals and firms sought, if not to become Martin's legal partners or agents in the formal ways that Coupa and Janon had been, to offer his guitars on the most advantageous terms by having the sole agency of them in certain cities or regions. In other words, rather than buying their stock through other New York houses or ordering directly from Martin, firms sought special arrangements (and discounts) that would allow them to maximize their profit on a very marketable commodity. Martin thus had to decide on whom to bestow trust that he hitherto had reserved for only a few individuals. Put another way, he had to learn how to operate in a national market economy that placed less and less emphasis on one-to-one relationships.

As early as 1849, for example, Martin had begun to sell instruments to Thayer and Collins, music dealers in Albany, New York. "You may be assured that we shall sell a good number of your guitars, if you put them to us at such a price that we can induce people to buy them," they wrote. "We hope that you can give us what advantages you can, with the confident expectation that it will result in your benefit as well as ours." A few months later they again pressed the point of discounts. "We have heard that you used to sell your guitars some cheaper to Mr. Newland," they observed. They wanted Martin to sell just as cheaply to them, for they always paid promptly, a promise that those who sought special arrangements commonly made.[51]

Thayer and Collins's request for special terms (and for a list of the prices and descriptions of his guitars) was a common refrain among Martin's customers in the early 1850s. George Hilbus, a Washington, D.C., music store owner, for example, had heard of Martin's guitars and asked for a list of wholesale prices and whether there was any inducement (that is, discount terms) for him to keep them in stock.[52] Others were less presumptuous. A. W. Penniman of Columbus, Ohio, wrote that he recently had embarked in the music business and sought to carry Martin's instruments. He offered several references, including "Mr. Capin[,] Superintendent of the Pennsylvania Institution for the Blind," and Gould & Berry, who had taken over Fiot's business. Worried about a markup from wholesalers, Penniman also wanted to know where he might fill orders "at the same rates as at your manufactory."[53]

In particular, firms that were located in the West sought to convince Martin that they were best suited to sell his guitars in their new and expanding markets. Truax and Baldwin of Cincinnati, for example, claimed that Martin's instruments "would meet with a trebly and perhaps larger increased sale were they more generally introduced here in the West." Their firm's facilities for introducing his guitars, they crowed, were unquestionably larger than those of any house in the West. But because as yet they had no special arrangements with him, they made a greater profit by the sale of "the best French Instruments." Should Martin choose to offer them a good discount, they were ready to reciprocate however they could.[54]

In the early 1850s, as Martin sought to expand his customer base, more often than not he granted such privileges, even though such arrangements could cause difficulties for one of the parties. This was particularly true when a firm learned that his instruments sold for less through another dealer in the same area. Alonso Brainard of Cleveland, Ohio, for example, wrote Martin asking for exclusive agency for his guitars in his home city; hitherto he had obtained them through New York. He also complained that in Cleveland Martin's instruments were kept "in this market by another house, and [were] sold at ruinous prices," instruments probably obtained, he speculated, "through some New York house like Rohé" that already had special arrangements with Martin. Brainard, who recently had started a music journal in the area, hoped for sole agency in Cleveland and to "advertise to that effect," but there is no indication that Martin granted the privilege.[55]

Things in Memphis were even more problematic. In July 1854 Churchill &

Company asked for agency in the area, remarking that Martin's instruments sold well in that part of the country. But the company reported that, although he might find it strange, he had been "most grossly imposed upon" there of late by someone "branding spurious Instruments with the name 'Martin' and selling them as genuine." Moreover, Churchill added, this same individual (whom he did not name) had been crass enough to have made "endeavours through his *St. Louis* friends" (perhaps Balmer & Weber) to obtain sole agency of Martin's guitars in Memphis.[56] Churchill & Company's implication was obvious: Martin should immediately declare the firm his agent in the city so that it could expose such counterfeits. A month later, when Churchill was in New York on business, he tried to see Martin personally about this matter, even though he had been told by someone else that *he* had obtained the exclusive agency for the South and the West. Churchill had not been willing to take this other party's word for it and prevailed on Martin to send him a shipment.

When he received his guitars, Churchill disposed of them easily because his competitor, E. H. Benson (very likely the one passing spurious instruments), had run into his own problems with genuine Martin guitars. In November of the same year he complained to Martin about a shipment of instruments that evidently had been lost en route. "This has been a great damage to me," Benson wrote, because the few other Martin guitars he had bought, through Zoebisch & Sons in New York, "all got sunk in the Mississippi River," presumably in a steamboat disaster. To make things worse, Benson continued, Churchill, who kept the other music store in Memphis, recently had received a dozen of Martin's guitars and had sold them to Benson's own customers, stating that he was the only agent for them, which he was not.[57] Obviously, if Benson was indeed responsible for selling the spurious instruments, it had brought a good deal of trouble on him.

Most customers, however, were quite satisfied with their relationships to Martin. James Mellon in Wheeling, Virginia, had sold Martin's guitars for several years, acquiring them through his son, John, in Pittsburgh, who already had an account in Nazareth. But Mellon had been in the "music and Variety business" for over sixteen years and now wanted sole agency in his town. Wheeling "improves in Population and wealth," he observed, and as a result the demand for high-priced guitars had increased. Martin thought his case compelling and granted his request, shipping him instruments by rail through his son.[58] That same year Edward Hopkins of Troy, New York, requested "exclusive sale" in his community and offered as references Rohé & Leavitt and Firth, Pond & Company in New York.[59] Martin obviously found the references convincing, for he granted the request.

Some parties did not even mind if their special terms with Martin remained sub rosa. Early in 1853, for example, M. Chambers of New York wrote and enclosed a circular to show Martin how he advertised his guitars.

Chambers continually circulated such announcements in the city's best hotels, he assured Martin, and mentioned the instruments conspicuously in other places, too, specifically, on his "Standard Frame Cards" and in his newspaper advertisements. After thus demonstrating his commitment to Martin's instruments, he asked for a more direct line to his goods.

He saw a problem, however, because of Martin's arrangement with the firm of Horace Waters, an influential New York music house to whom he sold large orders of guitars and which received a commission of two dollars on each instrument sold.[60] "Not knowing your arrangement with Mr. Waters," Chambers suggested, "if any difficulty is in the way[,] I can procure [the guitars] from you thro' the medium of a friend or I will pay you for them Cash." Further, if Martin wanted to supply him "directly or indirectly," it would be "*confidential* + no one need know you send them to me." He added that he had "made no decided arrangements with Mr. Maul" about any of this, which suggests that the guitar maker George Maul was the "friend" who would be part of the collusion. Chambers's ploy was even more convoluted because it included Martin's old associate Charles de Janon. If Martin agreed to this arrangement, Chambers wrote, Janon would "be able to exert his influence which he cannot do with propriety now," perhaps an allusion to this individual's abrogated contract with Martin. "Please reply in Confidence," Chambers concluded.[61] This situation suggests the considerable pressure Martin was under to please potential clients as he sought to evaluate their worth to him in the expanding marketplace.

TEACHERS AND PERFORMERS

Agents who proselytized Martin's instruments were a boon to his sales. So, too, were teachers and professional musicians who procured new customers for him. Coupa and Janon, of course, fit this category, but because Martin saw them so often and knew them so well, their relationships to him were of a different order than those of instructors or traveling musicians who had appreciated Martin's guitars and eagerly recommended them to their tutees or audiences. Fiot, Pique, and Schubert in Philadelphia were three other such individuals, bringing Martin much business in the late 1840s and early 1850s. But once the railroad lines opened up new markets, new instructors—some known to Martin, others not—in more far-flung places began to solicit favors for themselves and their students.

In the fall of 1853, for example, Franz Sulzner, an old acquaintance of Martin's and now a music teacher in Huntsville, Alabama, at the far end, geographically, of Martin's customer base, renewed his friendship. A published composer of parlor songs as well as a music teacher, over the years Sulzner had owned several of Martin's instruments but had sold or given his students all but one. Now he had another good student, a "young poor girl who plays well but has a miserable instrument." He wanted her to play with him in public at one of his concerts and requested one or two instruments of good tone and of a certain form, sketching in his letter a guitar with a little arrow pointing at where the neck joined the body.[62] Martin complied with his request.

Given Martin's growing reputation, however, more and more often instructors unknown to him contacted him about instruments (fig. 3-4). In the summer of 1852, for example, John Harvie, headmaster at an academy in Port Gibson, Mississippi, asked for two guitars for the young ladies at his school. Harvie reminded Martin that two years earlier he had shipped some instruments to Lewin G. Hartze, instructor in music (now deceased) at Harvie's school and who had considered Martin one of the best guitar manufacturers. Martin sent the new instruments, via New Orleans as requested by Harvie, who wrote again in early June to thank him. The guitars, he explained, had been for two teachers at the school taking music lessons. The "Musical professor" who taught them was so pleased that she wanted two more instruments, including a superior model, for herself. Harvie hoped that he might have the order by October, when the new session commenced.[63]

This relationship continued to bear fruit, for soon Harvie wrote again, to introduce Francis Funck, who had taken Hartze's place. Funck was, Harvie testified, a sober, industrious, and, he believed, honorable man. Funck's own letter of introduction followed. "About to enter into a new teaching situation as Music Teacher," he explained, he intended to "pay some attention to selling Musical Instruments." Allaying Martin's fears about how he would pay for his order, he detailed his connections to New York, where he claimed he could settle his bills as soon as the guitars were delivered. Given his assurance of payment through channels Martin knew, Funck naturally hoped that Martin would price the instruments as cheaply as possible.[64]

D. Drucke of Philadelphia was another tutor who brought Martin good business. In the winter of 1853 he wrote that recently he had commenced teaching and had frequently been called on to purchase guitars for his pupils. Thus, he wanted to know the prices of lower-end instruments appropriate to his new clientele. He was so confident of the merits of Martin's guitars, he opined, that, if the prices were in the right range (by which, like Funck, he probably meant inexpensive and thus appropriate for his students), he could forward the payment immediately and await the instruments.[65]

Some instructors could be more presumptuous. In 1853 Anson Tucker wrote from Lafayette, Indiana, that the principal at his institution "would be glad to obtain one of [Martin's] *best* Guitars" but was "not in condition to do so at present." Tucker thought that Martin still might be willing to place one of his best instruments at the school if the principal took pains to recommend them to others. If this were not enticement enough, the superintendent also was willing (in the institution's next catalog) "to recommend pupils assigned to take lessons on the Guitar, to purchase instruments of your manufacture." No further correspondence is extant between Martin and this party, however,

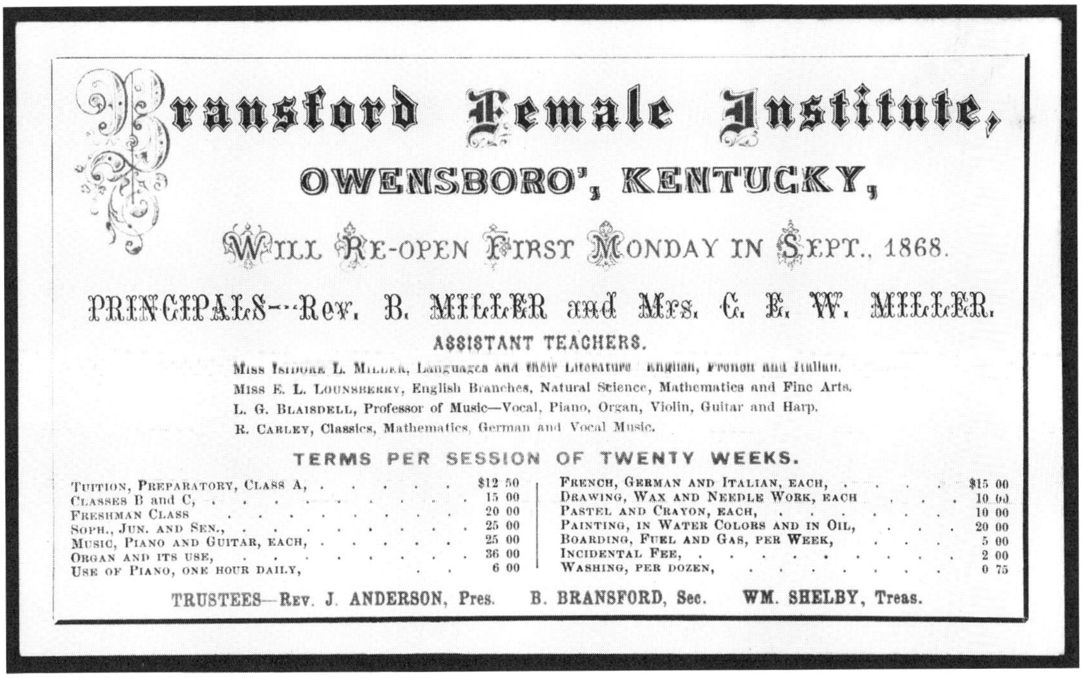

Figure 3-4. *Advertisement for Bransford Female Institute, Owensboro, Kentucky. Throughout the 1850s and 1860s instructors at such academies and other private schools wrote Martin in Nazareth to inquire about obtaining instruments for their pupils. Some even asked Martin if they might become his agents in their particular area. On this card, music, piano, or guitar classes were offered at twenty-five dollars for a twenty-week session. (Courtesy of C. F. Martin & Company Archives)*

and we can assume that Martin thought it foolhardy to send such an expensive instrument on such terms.[66]

Because of the high quality of his work, Martin also had as regular clients many prominent performers (fig. 3-5). H. Worrall of Cincinnati, for example, knew Martin personally, for when he wrote, on August 21, 1856, to report on his summer rambles, he singled out a recent "pleasant little visit to Cherry Hill." He also mentioned many mutual acquaintances, including William Schubert, the performer and teacher in Philadelphia, and C. F. Hartmann, then in Boston. Moreover, since his return to Ohio, Worrall had played with a Mr. Fossi, another of Martin's clients. Worrall had recently purchased an expensive guitar from Martin and now ordered a similar one for a Miss Babbs, precisely the kind of commission Martin hoped to receive through such contacts.[67]

Another player whom Martin knew well was S. de la Cova, a Spanish virtuoso who in the mid-1850s carried on a regular correspondence with Nazareth. De la Cova often bought strings from Martin and sent his instruments for repair. In March 1853, for example, he wrote Martin from his home in Panama City, Panama, to say that he was sending two guitars to Martin at his music store in Fulton Street (that is, to *Bruno's* address, where Martin had not kept guitars since leaving New York in 1839). De la Cova al-

Figure 3-5. *Carte-de-visite, ca. 1860. This striking photograph shows the kind of professional performer to whom Martin often sold instruments. Inside his traveling trunk, against which leans his guitar, are a violin and sheet music. His traveling clothes hang behind him. (Collection of the author)*

ways was very specific about the nature of the repairs and this time wanted one of the instruments refinished. He even knew Martin well enough to ask him to dine with him, "at the same old place where your son met me, Judson's Hotel[,] 61 Broadway" and reminded him that they had not seen each other in a decade. He sent Martin yet another repair, a guitar "which has been so much admired in Europe by every one who has seen it and heard it, even in Spain."[68]

We do not know if the two met again, but over the next two years as de la Cova toured he continued to order strings and to consult about problems with his instruments.[69] His last extant letter, in autumn 1855, shows how presumptuous such long-term clients might become. De la Cova detailed how Martin should alter a small guitar he had made for him the previous June (probably the terz mentioned by Coupa). Specifically, he wanted the twelfth fret lower, "near the mouth of the guitar," and the bridge lower down the body by an inch. "This would afford us more room to make the frets a little wider and easier to the left hand besides making the handle a little wider," he observed. He also suggested that, "if the body of the Guitar or the sounding box, was a little higher than it is now, it would sound better." Speaking candidly, he told Martin, the guitar was now "perfectly useless" to him and playing on it was "utterly out of the question." But he also reported that a friend in Lima, Peru, had decided to buy a Martin guitar that de la Cova had been urging on him.[70] Although Martin probably found de la Cova's eccentricity demanding, it was a small price to pay for the free advertising, literally on three continents, provided by this Spaniard.

OSSIAN DODGE AND THE CRYSTAL PALACE GUITAR

When de la Cova wrote Martin in the late fall of 1853, he reported that he had not yet had time "to see the Christall Palace + that beauty (I suppose) of your own manufactory."[71] He was referring to a very special instrument that Martin had made for display at the New York Exhibition of the Industry of All Nations, better known as the Crystal Palace Exhibition. Modeled on the highly successful Great Exhibition of the Works of Industry of All Nations in London two years earlier, the Crystal Palace show was the culmination on the national level of manufacturers' fairs that large cities had sponsored since the 1820s. Essentially what we now would call world's fairs, the London and New York exhibitions were major tourist attractions where visitors saw inventions and goods made by new or improved processes. Premiums or prizes were awarded in scores of different categories in manufacturing and the fine arts. Held in an immense glass building around what is now Bryant Park (Sixth Avenue between 41st and 42nd Streets), the Crystal Palace Exhibition opened on July 4, 1853 (fig. 3-6). It drew so many visitors that it remained open (though with less success as time passed) until destroyed by fire five years later.[72]

Figure 3-6. *Lithograph, ca. 1851, of the "New York Crystal Place," where the "Exhibition of the Industry of All Nations" was held. Martin sent an extraordinarily appointed guitar, one that cost $160.00, to this display and showed it at other venues as well.*

In New York, over fifty manufacturers or makers exhibited in the category of "Musical Instruments," and "C. F. Marten [*sic*], manu[facturer], Nazareth, Pennsylvania," entered two guitars, for which the jury awarded him a Bronze Medal, the highest for guitars, over the entries of William Tilton, a New York maker, who received only honorable mention (see Chapter 4). In its *Report of the Jury on Musical Instruments*, the judges of this category felt obligated to add that, while many of the other guitars were "of exquisite workmanship," most were judged inferior because of their "bad tone."[73] Presumably, Martin's excelled in both categories. One of his customers, George Hilbus of Washington, D.C., wrote him that while in New York he had "had the pleasure of seeing some of your fine instruments in the Christal Palace and did not think that they could be surpassed."[74]

We do not know exactly what this guitar looked like, but it might have been similar to another special instrument Martin made around the same time. In October 1852 the Cincinnati music dealer William C. Peters had ordered a very fine guitar. "The Patent head [is] to be plated Gold," he requested, "and ends of screws to be Pearl tip[p]ed." The frets, too, were to be gold, "18 carats," and the fingerboard covered with pearl instead of ebony. Over the next month Peters continued to refine his description of the instrument, for the client who wanted it was not particular about the price. He simply wanted an elegant guitar as a gift for a lady who was about to be married. Peters wrote that the instrument had to have a "black neck veneered with ebony" and a "pale yellow" sounding board. "It must not cost us [that is, wholesale] more than $110 but the frets must be gold."[75] Very few Martin instruments in this period approached this price, and we may presume that ornamentation of this sort also adorned his submission to the Crystal Palace Exhibition.

Another person who saw Martin's entries at the exhibition was the eccentric performer, author, and publisher Ossian E. Dodge, so taken with one of the instruments that he insisted on buying it or a comparable one (fig. 3-7). The Cayuga, New York, native pestered Martin about this prospect for months. By his own account, in addition to publishing a weekly paper called the *Literary Museum*, devoted to literature and music, Dodge was a guitarist and singer who gave concerts "nine months of the twelve in the cities and larger villages in the Union."[76] But other reports were more sanguine. One writer, for example, termed Dodge "a singer of comic songs and a giver of entertainments in which he was the sole performer," as well as the leader of a group called Ossian's Band. "His comic power," one of his auditors recalled, "consisted largely in grotesque grimaces, and feats of a voice that could go down and down into the very sepulchres and catacombs of basso profundo, until the hearer wondered in what ventriloqual caverns it would lose itself and become a ghost of sound."[77] This faint praise notwithstanding, Dodge and his troupe were undeniably popular, and he was well enough known even to share the stage with some members of the famous Hutchinson Family singers. During the last few weeks, he proudly told Martin in the fall of 1853, Ossian's Band had had to turn away over seven thousand people who wanted to hear their show and now were booked to perform at Boston's large "Music Hall," one of the city's chief venues.[78]

Dodge also wrote and published his own songs, although the author John Townsend Trowbridge, who knew him well, complained that most of these compositions "bore the unveracious description, 'Words and Music by Ossian E. Dodge.'" Trowbridge himself had provided the words to one, he reported, to which yet another acquaintance had supplied the music. "I had reason to believe," Trowbridge tartly observed in his reminiscences, "that all the songs he [Dodge] claimed as his own were produced in this vicarious manner."[79]

There was indeed something of the charlatan and the self-promoter in Dodge. Thus, it is appropriate that, for his ostentation, he is forever linked to the greatest showman of the age, P. T. Barnum. As a publicity stunt Barnum had auctioned prime tickets to hear the Swedish singer Jenny Lind (whose American tour Barnum managed) at her first Boston performance, and Dodge was the high bidder at the outrageous sum of six hundred dollars, a story that became national news. In true Barnum-esque fashion, Dodge commissioned a lithographed cover for a new song, "Ossian's Serenade," an illus-

Figure 3-7. *Woodcut of Ossian E. Dodge, from a concert program, January 17, 1849. This depicts the music periodical publisher and itinerant musician who pursued Martin to sell him the instrument exhibited at the Crystal Palace or to make him another, comparable one. (Courtesy of American Antiquarian Society)*

tration that shows Barnum introducing him to an elegantly attired Lind.[80] In addition to appearing on sheet music, this picture, Trowbridge recalled, "was exhibited in shop windows all over the city and in the suburbs, and it preceded the comic singer whenever his concerts were announced." Dodge's extravagance did exactly what he wished: it made him an object of great public interest, so much so that after he bought the ticket for Lind's performance, attendance at his own concerts increased significantly. In his next appearance, for example, he filled Boston's Tremont Temple, "at quadruple the old rates of admission." Thus, Trowbridge wryly recalled, Dodge was reimbursed "in a single night for the cost of the ticket." Dodge's biographer similarly noted the musician's success after the Lind affair. In the nine months after her concert, he observed, Dodge netted eleven thousand dollars in New England, "accompanying himself on the guitar."[81]

Dodge's wish to own Martin's Crystal Palace guitar undoubtedly stemmed from his insatiable desire for celebrity. He indicated his interest in obtaining the very instrument on exhibit but could "wait with pleasure until the close of the Fair." Not that Dodge did not already have fine instruments, for he owned the best guitar that Schatz ever made, he boasted to that maker's old friend. But even though it "speaks full and deep," he complained, its upper notes were imperfect and not loud enough for large concert rooms.[82] Dodge hoped that Martin's beautiful guitar would provide the tonal quality he sought.

Through the fall of 1853 he pestered Martin about the Crystal Place instrument. Having heard that the exhibition would continue through the spring, he again asked if Martin could remove the instrument from the exhibit and forward it to him, immediately. In particular, he wished to use it at his upcoming show at the Music Hall, where he would "display *Martin's best*, before an audience of *thirty five hundred*." Moreover, in the program to his performance he promised to state that "the guitar used on this occasion is the one exhibited at the Fair, N.Y. by C. F. Martin, the world renowned guitar manufacturer, now residing at Nazareth, Pa." "Let me hear from you when convenient," he concluded.[83]

In March he still worried the subject. Now in Brandon, Vermont, he was anxious to know when Martin would complete "the splendid maple guitar" he evidently had agreed to make in place of the one on exhibit. He also reported that in the next issue of the *Literary Museum*, Martin would see a puff for his guitars, a notice that Dodge believed would please him and do his business good. He closed this self-serving missive by reminding Martin that whenever guitarists asked him where to buy instruments, he always told them "to go to the music stores in New York, and be sure to get one of *Martin's*."[84]

At this point, Dodge disappears from Martin's records for a few years, to resurface three years later in Cleveland as the proprietor of a piano and music store. As we might expect, he wanted to know if he could obtain Martin's guitars and, if so, how and at what price.[85] Martin evidently was not eager to grant a special arrangement to this eccentric, but Dodge pressed the issue. He inquired if it were true that in Cleveland only Brainard's firm received Martin's guitars at wholesale prices. "If so," he continued presumptuously, "you did wrong not to let me know it, as I am an *old customer*, and *editor* of the *only Musical Paper in the United States*, and have the *largest music store in Ohio*!!" His store was sixty by one hundred feet, he explained, and through it he sold, he claimed, twice as many instruments as anybody else in Cleveland. Dodge sought a "fair, open, honorable, cash trade" for Martin's instruments in the price range of twelve to thirty dollars. Cocky as ever, he told Martin that unless he dealt with him "as fair" as he knew him to do with his agents in New York (that is, with a discount), he would get his guitars elsewhere.[86] Martin did not comply, and one suspects that he was glad to be done with such presumption and particularity.

Martin continued to show the famed Crystal Palace guitar at other prominent mechanics' fairs along the East Coast. In November 1854, for example, the Washington, D.C., firm of Hilbus and Heitz wrote to say that several days earlier the instrument itself—described in Martin's daybook on May 10, 1854, as "Crystal Palace Guitar[,] Rosewood Polished Case[,] $160.00"—had been forwarded to them through the Adams & Company express service. Was this indeed the same guitar, returned to Martin before he forwarded it to them, or was it another like it? A few days later, presumably at Martin's direction, Hilbus and Heitz wrote that they had shipped this valuable instrument to Weber in Philadelphia, adding that there had been "no mention of it made by the judges of the Baltimore fair, owing probably to [their] being unable to give it [their] personal attention." Hilbus and Heitz, however, asked Martin for the privilege of exhibiting it the following February at the Metropolitan Fair at the Smithsonian Institution, where the previous year Hilbus had shown an entire case of instruments, among them a fine guitar, at the first such exhibit held in Washington.[87]

AN EXPANDING WEB OF COMMERCE

By the early 1850s, customers for Martin's guitars learned of and could acquire them in a variety of ways. Industrial exhibitions and mechanics' fairs, for example, did as much as prominent artists such as de la Cova or Dodge to bring them to a larger public. Some clients were introduced to them through their music instructors, others through Martin's specially designated agents. Others bought them at such large music emporiums as that of Horace Waters in New York or Gould & Company in Philadelphia. Still others wrote to Martin directly at Nazareth. Although he was not making many more guitars than he had in the 1830s, between 1852 and 1856 his business expanded geographically, to cities throughout the East Coast and Ohio River valley, and even into the South, as the frequent requests for his agency suggest.

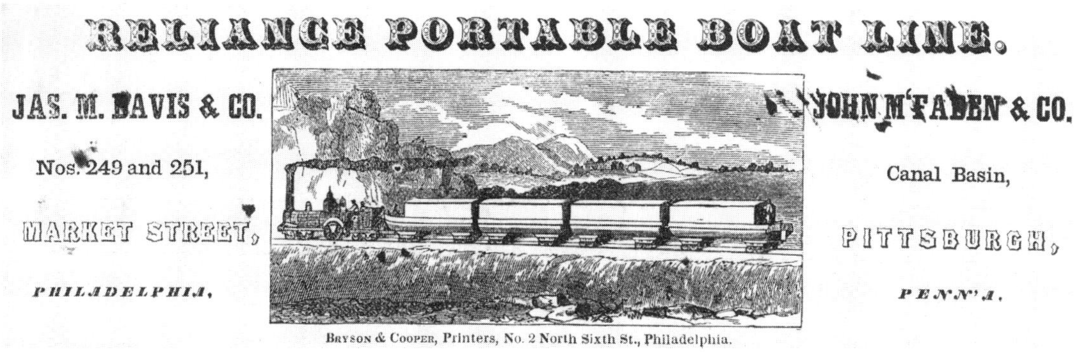

RELIANCE PORTABLE BOAT LINE.

JAS. M. DAVIS & CO.

Nos. 249 and 251,

MARKET STREET,

PHILADELPHIA,

JOHN M'FADEN & CO.

Canal Basin,

PITTSBURGH,

PENN'A.

BRYSON & COOPER, Printers, No. 2 North Sixth St., Philadelphia.

Figure 3-8. *Billhead for Reliance Portable Boat Line, Philadelphia and Pittsburgh. Before railroad lines were completed across states, businessmen often had to send goods via a combination of road, canal, and rail. From the woodcut, this company designed canal boats that would load easily on flat train cars, thus moving orders by both land and water without reloading them. In 1847 Martin used its services to send two boxes of guitars to Pittsburgh. (Courtesy of C. F. Martin & Company Archives)*

In the early 1850s the nation's rapidly expanding transportation system, particularly its railroads and proliferating "express" services that expedited transfer of goods across different rail lines, redefined Martin's business.[88] These express agencies had "forwarding agents" in all major and budding cities and specialized in the transport of high-value freight. In addition, they also offered the option of collecting the bills for it—what we now call collect on delivery, or COD—and returning the money to the seller. Although in their earliest incarnations they moved goods by stage, canal, and steamboat, by the 1850s such companies worked primarily by railroad and sometimes even purchased and outfitted their own freight cars (fig. 3-8).

Martin most often used Kasson's Dispatch, with its exclusive contract with the New York Central Railroad, for his long-distance shipping needs. He also patronized the well-regarded Adams Express Company, which by mid-decade got his nod for goods sent to Meyer in Lexington, Kentucky, and through the Ohio and Mississippi River valleys generally.[89] The company's advertisement spelled out their arrangements in some detail. They offered services for the "*daily transportation*, in their Express cars, of Cases of Goods, Packages, Parcels, Specie, Bank Notes, &c. &c. between all the principal Cities and Towns of the United States." Moreover, they offered "perfect security with the utmost dispatch" because they had secured messengers of "energy and trust." They also pointed out that notes, bills, and drafts—the heart of the new commerce—would receive particular attention for only a small commission.[90]

By 1855 Martin had other options for his shipping needs. He might use, for example, the Baltimore & Ohio Railroad, which ran from Baltimore through Wheeling, Virginia, and on to Cincinnati. Although it seems out of the way for Martin to have had to send his shipments to Philadelphia or Baltimore before they could go west, the express companies made this sort of interrail and interregion transport relatively easy, even supplying their own cars on some lines.[91] Martin even shipped some of his goods to the Northeast in such circuitous ways to take advantage of the express companies' services. In 1853, for example, J. E. Gould of Philadelphia placed an order for Oliver Ditson in Boston. "Be good enough to make inquiry," the company wrote, "whether the goods from your place, destined for the East, will reach New York and Boston sooner and at less expense, any other way than by the way of Philadelphia."[92]

In these years, Martin also still focused on markets where he long had had a presence. Above all, this meant New York City, where by 1853 the firm of Horace Waters was purchasing large numbers of his guitars, shipped to it by Hope's Express, but where other firms also vied for his patronage, and Philadelphia, where such steady clients as Lee & Walker and Gould & Company continued to place sizable orders.[93] Martin shipped goods to these two cities via long-established stage lines, canals, and, increasingly, the new express services, via railroads. In the early 1850s, for example, Lee & Walker regularly had its shipments sent by canal but by mid-decade preferred to receive goods by Howard's Express. Clients to the south, in Baltimore and Washington, were serviced conveniently by the Adams Express Company or by coastal steamers, as were customers in Richmond, Petersburg, and Norfolk, Virginia.[94] Nash in Petersburg had his goods shipped by canal to Philadelphia and then by steamer to Richmond, where he called for them. But the Ohio and Mississippi River valleys represented Martin's most important new market. His ledger for the early 1850s, for example, shows a great expansion of business, first through such new commercial centers as Louisville, Cincinnati, and St. Louis, and then, by the middle and later 1850s, north to Columbus and Cleveland, Ohio, and Chicago, and south to Nashville, Memphis, and New Orleans, all areas served by Adams Express.

If the client so requested, Martin still sent goods by other means. In the spring of 1852, for example, Lee & Walker of Philadelphia had gone to the stagecoach office but had not found its shipment of guitars. After it arrived the next day by canal boat, the company reminded Martin to indicate how he was sending their goods so that they would know when to expect them.[95] Similarly, when George Dutch in Marietta, Ohio (not yet served by rail), ordered a guitar for one of his customers, he wanted it sent by express (i.e., a combination of rail, stage, and canal) to Pittsburgh, care of D. G. Morgan & Company, where he or his customer would call for it.[96]

Martin also relied on coastal vessels. In 1856, for example, E. P. Nash of Petersburg, Virginia, wrote Martin that he did not want his next shipment sent by Adams Express but by "Penn[sylvania] Steamer from Philadelphia." When in 1857 he ordered nine more instruments, he directed Martin to send the shipment to Philadelphia, care of Lippincott, Grambo & Company, from where it could be sent on to Richmond (not Petersburg) "buy [*sic*] one of the *Steamers* running from that place."[97] On another occasion, Nunns, Clark &

Company, an important Philadelphia client, ordered six guitars for one of their New Orleans customers. The company wanted Martin to send them by packet; it would forward them by ship to Louisiana.[98] In Port Gibson, Mississippi, a new customer asked Martin to ship two guitars "by Steam to New Orleans, to the care of *George Connelly, and W. P. Holloway* [in] Grand Gulf, and [then to the] *Academy[,] Port Gibson*," the guitars' destination. When the goods arrived in Louisiana in June, he directed his agent in New Orleans to forward Martin "a draft on N.Y. on sight" for the amount owed.[99]

Forwarded over long distances, some shipments inevitably fell through cracks in the system, particularly if one did not use an express agency to expedite their routing. On one occasion James Demarest, an employee for the "Central Railroad" in New York, reported to Martin that he had a box in his storehouse for another of Martin's Mississippi customers, John Harvie of Port Gibson, sent in care of H. Smith at 25 Nassau Street in New York. But Demarest could not find this Smith anywhere in the city and wanted to know what to do with the shipment. It finally arrived in Mississippi three weeks later.[100] T. C. Loud's letter from Holly Springs, Mississippi, provides some notion of how complex it was to move such freight when many hands were involved. Loud told Martin he should forward his guitars to Mississippi via the Pennsylvania Railroad, care of Sprigmain Brown in Cincinnati and then care of E. M. Apperson & Company in Memphis.[101]

Although, as these examples indicate, there were alternative modes of transportation by the mid-1850s, the rails had become the most efficient. James Mellon of Wheeling, Virginia, for example, wanted Martin to send his next shipment by way of the Baltimore and Ohio Railroad. If Martin sent the guitars by way of Pittsburgh, they might be detained all winter because the Ohio River was closed by ice. But because the Baltimore and Ohio terminated in Wheeling, he reminded Martin, Mellon would get his order "direct and soon."[102] Even though such arrangements took Martin's guitars hundreds of miles out of the way, the rail system now guaranteed delivery through all seasons. And, overall, rail transport was safer than that by steamboat, given Benson's experience of having lost a shipment of guitars, bound for his store in Memphis, because the boat had sunk in the Mississippi.

A look at the total number of guitars sold to steady clients in the early and mid-1850s (see Appendix C) shows that music houses in the western regions now dominated Martin's accounts, eclipsing the New York market that, only a year or two earlier, had defined his business. In 1853, for example, Martin sold twenty-six guitars to Horace Waters, in that decade one of the most prominent of the city's music emporiums. But in the same year he shipped thirty-two to Peters & Sons and twenty-four to Colburn & Field, both in Cincinnati; eighteen to Jonathan Miller in Pittsburgh; sixteen to Brainard in Cleveland; and twelve to Balmer & Weber in St. Louis. The next year the story was similar. Waters took thirty-four, while Peters & Sons got twenty-three; Colburn, twenty-six; Balmer & Weber, eighteen; and Peters, Webb, in Louisville, twenty. Philadelphia was the only other market as strong; in 1853 and 1854 Gould & Company took thirty-four and fourteen, respectively. Indeed, because Martin moved most of his guitars through Philadelphia to their final destinations, for several years in this decade this city eclipsed New York as Martin's most important East Coast entrepôt.

Martin's orders from clients in more distant cities were not quite as large but still accounted for significant numbers of his guitars. In 1853, for example, Parsons in New Orleans took a dozen, and West in Nashville, eight. And by 1854 Martin was selling lots of six a year to B. K. Mould & Robert G. Greene in Chicago. The southeastern coastal city markets also were significant. In 1853, Nash in Petersburg, Virginia, took seventeen instruments, and in Baltimore, Benteen always took a dozen to eighteen per year. As we have seen, as early as 1852 Martin's guitars even reached Holly Springs and Port Gibson, Mississippi, and in 1854 a dealer in Natchez in that same state received six guitars.[103]

MEETING OBLIGATIONS IN THE MARKET ECONOMY

Martin's customers financed their purchases in a variety of ways that exemplified the expansion of the nation's system of commercial exchange. By the 1850s his clients were settling their accounts in person through cash or, more commonly, through some sort of credit arrangement.[104] The latter was the nation's preferred modus operandi, for, as one historian has written, "the antebellum economy was structured as much around borrowed money and promises of payment as it was around the routes of rivers, canals, and . . . railroads."[105] Improved mail delivery throughout the country at very reasonable rates expedited this elaborate system of credit, as did the proliferating express companies, which also collected payment for goods shipped. Beginning in 1851, for example, one could send a letter up to three thousand miles—that is, anywhere in the United States—for only three cents.[106] This filled the mails with dispatch bills, detailed orders, money drafts, and all sorts of other "commercial paper." If the express companies handled the transactions, they added a small charge to the delivery fee.

Thus, when one of Martin's customers received a shipment of instruments, he or she most commonly paid with a bill of exchange issued upon receipt of the goods. Martin's ledger indicates that his clients favored this last method, sending him "sight drafts," that is, handwritten documents that permitted Martin to receive or "draw on sight" those amounts whenever he presented the documents at the banks on which they were "drawn" (where the customers maintained credit), usually in a specified number of days (most commonly from ten to thirty, sixty, or ninety) at 7 or 8 percent interest. This presumably allowed customers time to sell the goods or otherwise find ways to make sure that their deposits covered the amounts for which the drafts were written. By the 1850s most commercial transactions were completed in this way. Further, because the banks on which customers "drew" notes were often at considerable distances from the creditor, a vigorous trade arose for "discounting" such notes—that is, for allowing them to be traded or sold among different parties and redeemed at other financial institutions at a discount, or at less than face value, often before they were due. The difference between the two amounts constituted the profit on the transaction when a party finally redeemed the note at full value.[107]

Martin's transactions with George Dutch of Marietta, Ohio, indicate how in practice one conducted such business. Dutch ordered a guitar for J. R. Crawford, to be sent to Pittsburgh care of D. J. Morgan. Martin could draw on Crawford "at sight payable at the Bank of Marietta." Dutch added, "Mr. Crawford belongs to the bank and is perfectly good pay."[108] Or, to take another example, when in the spring of 1854 T. C. Loud of Holly Springs, Mississippi, wanted Martin guitars, he explained that hitherto he had gotten them in New York, Philadelphia, and Cincinnati. Now he wanted to order directly from Martin, "to obtain a much lower discount from your manufactory." For terms he wanted "Sixty days" (that is, his note would be redeemable at full value at the end of that period), and if this was acceptable, Martin then could "draw" on him "through the Northern Bank of this place." Loud also offered references, among others, J. E. Gould of Philadelphia and Bruno and Cargill at no. 47 Maiden Lane, New York.[109] This was the kind of note, drawn at smaller banks at a distance from East Coast financial centers, that Martin might wish to discount.

Other customers asked Martin outright how they should pay him. When A. W. Penniman received his order in Columbus, Ohio, for example, he told Martin to send his "bill, and draw on me at your pleasure, or, I will remit you the money as you shall otherwise direct." Still other clients gave Martin the option to redeem their notes at the very banks on which they were drawn. J. P. Reed & Company of Boston, for example, evidently had established credit with the Easton Bank (in Easton, Pennsylvania, only fifteen miles from Nazareth), where Martin might bring notes from this firm. On April 27, 1853, he did just that and redeemed a draft from Reed for $163.55.[110]

Some larger firms such as Peters, Webb in Louisville operated a bit differently. They wrote actual checks on New York institutions with which they had standing accounts. Such payments were particularly convenient because Martin visited that city so frequently. Hence, on November 10, 1852, they paid $149.25 with a check on the Phoenix Bank in New York and on March 18, 1853, with another, for $218.75 at New York's Bank of America. Jonathan Miller of Pittsburgh paid similarly, issuing Martin a check early in 1853 for $112.10 on the American Exchange Bank in New York. Jonathan West of Nashville wrote checks on either New York or Philadelphia banks for his payments.[111]

When a customer issued a sight draft, Martin often relied on financial agents in different cities to redeem them for him. Janon had served this function for him, and in the early 1850s William Hackett frequently performed this service in Philadelphia. The notation "Drawn by Wm Hackett at Ten Days Sight" or "Drawn at Twenty Days Sight by order of William Hackett" is common in Martin's records of accounts paid through that city. For such work Martin also engaged Louis Hartmann and C. F. Hartmann, this last a cousin of Frederick Martin who worked in the guitar firm; William Raddé in New York City, the German bookseller long known to Martin; and "Rev. H. J. Ruetenick." Martin thus relied on a complex web of individuals and institutions through which he received payments at almost any time, not on set days of the month or at the ends of a business quarter or year.

Given such an elaborate system, it should come as no surprise that either Martin or his debtors occasionally incurred some inconvenience. In the summer of 1851, for example, Martin found it unacceptable that one of his largest customers, Peters, Webb in Louisville, had issued its note for ninety days, a much longer period than customary for the company, and he told it so. The company had had some heavy payments coming due, Peters explained, for he and Webb had just bought out a partner's share of the business. For that reason, the company had taken "the liberty to ask as a favor the extension" of the note and would appreciate it if Martin could let the note stand until maturity. Peters, Webb assured him that hereafter he could draw at ten days' sight for all his invoices.[112] In a postscript the firm reminded Martin that "their intention [had] always been to act toward [him] in perfect good faith." If it had unintentionally acted otherwise, Martin might excuse them.

As the firm's response suggests, given unavoidable financial exigencies, customers did all they could to keep Martin's favor. Around the time that Peters, Webb apologized to Martin, for example, West of Nashville sent him a check "on Philadelphia" for $180.00, $1.40 over the amount of his bill. The "exchange being 1½%," the additional amount was to cover interest, for the delay in not remitting more promptly. Business had been exceedingly dull, West explained.[113] A year later he was still having trouble paying on time. Sending Martin another check on a Philadelphia bank, he explained that he would have remitted sooner, but the music business was so slow that he found it difficult to meet his engagements.[114] Even a large firm such as J. E. Gould of Philadelphia sometimes had problems with timely payment. In the winter of 1854 it had been handed Martin's draft on it and had accepted it, but wished to pay at a later date. The firm had not yet received returns from Memphis, it reported, owing to severe storms in the Mississippi River valley. It had many thousands of dollars to pay this month, and many of those owing money had not met their obligations.[115]

Occasionally, the problem was on Martin's end. In the autumn of 1853, for example, Peters & Sons of Cincinnati wrote Martin that it had received his recent letter and paid his draft "at 3 days sight before due." But when the firm examined its accounts more carefully, it discovered that Martin had overdrawn on it, not realizing that he had sent a no. 2 guitar rather than a no. 2½ as the company had requested. Peters & Sons thus asked for a credit of $3.30 on its next order.[116] When customers noticed such minor discrepancies, they usually handled them just as Peters & Sons did, with a polite request for credit toward their next obligation.

GUITAR MAKING, 1839-1855

Sometime in 1849, W. C. Peters, head of a Baltimore music house with satellites in Cincinnati and Louisville, decided to publish a monthly paper devoted to music. He already had had some experience issuing sheet music and in January 1850 launched *The Baltimore Olio and American Musical Gazette*, "A Monthly Parlor Companion for the Ladies, devoted chiefly to music, the arts, and musical intelligence generally" (fig. 3-9). Each issue would contain at least six pages of music, arranged for the pianoforte, guitar, flute, and violin. Its first issue's advertising carried notices from many firms with whom Martin did business, including Nunns, Clark & Company and Lee & Walker. Martin himself had sold guitars to Peters. Now, in addition to taking a subscription to the new paper to support his customer's venture, he too placed an advertisement, one of the few times that he ever did so, usually relying on his agents to tout his guitars in their own notices. He informed "the Musical public generally, that the great favor bestowed on him has induced him to enlarge his Factory, in order to supply the increasing demand for his instruments."[117]

Unfortunately, the extant records are largely silent on the nature of this expansion of his facilities, but we gain some notion of the scale of Martin's operation from his return for the United States census for the year ending June 1, 1850. Martin listed himself as a "Guitar Manufacturer" with a $5,000 capital investment in "real and personal estate in the business." Under the quantities, kinds, and values of raw materials used, he noted a $100 investment in rosewood, $100 in "ivory, &c.," $200 in "German silver," and two hundred "patent screws," valued at $600. Under "motive power, machinery, structure, or resource," he listed one steam-powered saw. Martin also reported that he employed six male hands whom he paid a total of $150 per month. He listed his annual production at 250 guitars, valued at $4,000.[118]

The most important component of the expansion he advertised in Peters's paper was what he noted in the census return under "motive power," a steam engine to run equipment for sawing and shaping lumber. Martin's notice, as well as the census return, indicates that he had installed this machine in the late 1840s. By the fall of 1850 he evidently had replaced it with another, from Philip Deringer of Reading, Pennsylvania, who wrote Martin to say that he would bring the "mashean" by wagon when Martin was ready to install it. He also reminded the guitar maker that "the Lay [lathe] must be put up with

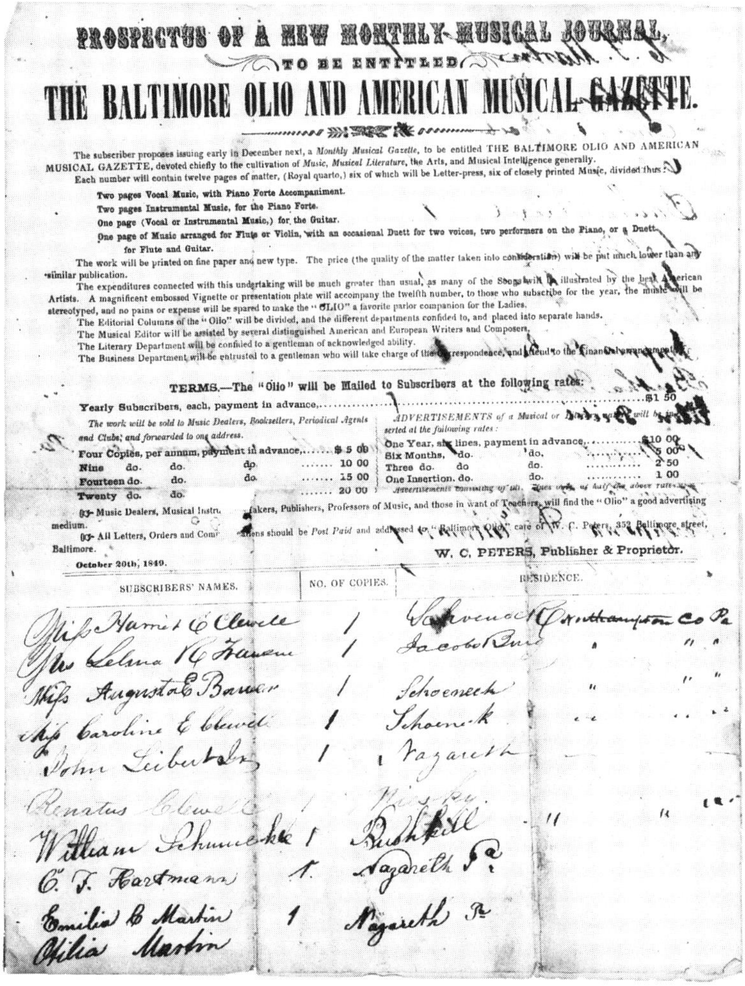
PROSPECTUS OF A NEW MONTHLY MUSICAL JOURNAL,
TO BE ENTITLED
THE BALTIMORE OLIO AND AMERICAN MUSICAL GAZETTE.

The subscriber proposes issuing early in December next, a *Monthly Musical Gazette*, to be entitled THE BALTIMORE OLIO AND AMERICAN MUSICAL GAZETTE, devoted chiefly to the cultivation of *Music, Musical Literature*, the Arts, and Musical Intelligence generally.

Each number will contain twelve pages of matter, (Royal quarto,) six of which will be Letter-press, six of closely printed Music, divided thus:

Two pages Vocal Music, with Piano Forte Accompaniment.
Two pages Instrumental Music, for the Piano Forte.
One page (Vocal or Instrumental Music,) for the Guitar.
One page of Music arranged for Flute or Violin, with an occasional Duett for two voices, two performers on the Piano, or a Duett for Flute and Guitar.

The work will be printed on fine paper and new type. The price (the quality of the matter taken into consideration) will be put much lower than any similar publication.

The expenditures connected with this undertaking will be much greater than usual, as many of the Songs will be illustrated by the best American Artists. A magnificent embossed Vignette or presentation plate will accompany the twelfth number, to those who subscribe for the year, the music will be stereotyped, and no pains or expense will be spared to make the "OLIO" a favorite parlor companion for the Ladies.

The Editorial Columns of the "Olio" will be divided, and the different departments confided to, and placed into separate hands.

The Musical Editor will be assisted by several distinguished American and European Writers and Composers.

The Literary Department will be confided to a gentleman of acknowledged ability.

The Business Department will be entrusted to a gentleman who will take charge of the correspondence, and attend to the financial arrangements.

TERMS.—The "Olio" will be Mailed to Subscribers at the following rates:

Yearly Subscribers, each, payment in advance, ... $1 50

The work will be sold to Music Dealers, Booksellers, Periodical Agents and Clubs; and forwarded to one address.

Four Copies, per annum, payment in advance,				$ 5 00
Nine	do.	do.	do.	10 00
Fourteen	do.	do.	do.	15 00
Twenty	do.	do.		20 00

ADVERTISEMENTS of a Musical or [illegible] *will be inserted at the following rates:*

One Year, six lines, payment in advance,			$10 00
Six Months,	do.	do.	5 00
Three	do.	do.	2 50
One Insertion,	do.	do.	1 00

Advertisements consisting of [illegible] *half the above rates.*

☞ Music Dealers, Musical Instrument Makers, Publishers, Professors of Music, and those in want of Teachers, will find the "Olio" a good advertising medium.

☞ All Letters, Orders and Communications should be *Post Paid* and addressed to "Baltimore Olio," care of W. C. Peters, 352 Baltimore street, Baltimore.

W. C. PETERS, Publisher & Proprietor.

October 20th, 1849.

SUBSCRIBERS' NAMES.	NO. OF COPIES.	RESIDENCE.

Figure 3-9.
Prospectus for The Baltimore Olio and American Musical Gazette, *a "new monthly musical journal," 1850. In an early issue of this periodical, to which Martin subscribed, he announced that he had recently enlarged and had added steam power to his factory owing to the demand for his guitars. (Courtesy of C. F. Martin & Company Archives)*

the mashean." Further, "if you would have your Circle saw ready & have it put up at the same time," he continued, "you will not be sorry for it." Deringer "garrunteed" his machine's dependability. It was well worth its money, he added, and Martin and "Fritz" (Frederick) could use it "for more purposes than for Sawing[,] as it will be three Horse power besides the Ingen [engine]." Deringer worried, though, about who would help him lift the equipment off the wagon, given its considerable weight.[119]

Martin did indeed put the engine to good use, for by the next spring it needed major repair. Deringer was to send along "the piston & two pipes + cock" that Martin needed, but for now, he advised Martin, he should try to make the "old piston do as the New patterns are to[o] large." "Don't put in the springs," he cautioned Martin, "but Pack it with Hemp." Deringer gave further directions for the temporary repair of the machine, and Martin seems to have resolved any further difficulties.[120]

His installation of such equipment should not come as a surprise, for, like so many other craftsworkers in that period, he could boost his production through the time- and labor-saving potential of steam-powered (or water-powered) machinery. With such equipment, for example, he could prepare veneers and sounding boards with a saw run from belts connected to the engine shaft, and rough-cut and shape the necks and blocks of his instruments. He did not relinquish his lifelong commitment to fine workmanship, for he continued to finish the guitars by hand. But to compete in the expanding national marketplace he had to bring more guitars to his customers, and more quickly.

At least since Martin's days with Coupa, his customers had pushed him to fill orders more expeditiously, and this need remained a constant refrain through the 1850s, even after he mechanized his operation. His growing reputation as a maker of quality instruments accounted for the demand. Peters in Cincinnati put the matter succinctly. Martin's guitars were "all the rage and West [another firm in that city] and we have almost made up our mind to keep none else," he reported. D. A. Truax of Dunton & Thurston echoed his remark (fig. 3-10). "Sometime ago I sent you an order," he wrote. The firm needed the guitars soon, for it had calls for them frequently. Jonathan Mellon in Pittsburgh felt the same way and constantly prodded his supplier. Mellon's customers were waiting very anxiously for the instruments they had ordered, he wrote in 1852. Other clients, too, were impatient. "Please advise when you can forward the Guitars ordered," Miller & Beacham wrote from Baltimore. "The *three weeks* has elapsed, and no news of them." Horace Waters, a major New York customer, was the most exasperated of all. "Now is the time to sell," he wrote in the summer of 1853. "Please hurry up the Guitars—most out of all kinds, especially the cheap ones."[121]

In addition to clamoring for more stock, Martin's clients also urged him to send catalogues or standard price lists of his guitars. This, as well as the increased demand, forced Martin to standardize his instruments more than he ever had. As we have seen, when he began to make guitars in New York, he had produced them in great variety, with many built to customers' specifications. But as he sought ways to manufacture his goods more efficiently, he began to restrict himself to a certain number of sizes and styles of decoration. During these years Martin freed himself fully from the kinds of patterns he had learned in Europe and developed a line of instruments that marked his emergence as a unique American maker.

In the early 1850s Martin had named some of these guitar models after players, the "De Goni" the most common example. Coupa regularly referred to that model, as did Rohé & Leavitt when in 1852 the company ordered the "'largest model' which you call 'Do Gonis' or something like that—costing about $18 or $20 in case."[122] Martin regarded it as one of his less expensive, plainer instruments, yet one that had a good sale. As late as 1854 some customers still used the term. In the spring of that year, for example, W. C. Peters of Cincinnati complained that he had not been able to sell a fancy guitar

Figure 3-10. *Letterhead of Dunton & Thurston, a music house in Cincinnati that was one of Martin's regular customers in the early 1850s. (Courtesy of C. F. Martin & Company Archives)*

that Martin had sent earlier that year. "Those generally that want so fine an instrument," he related, "are judges and complain that the tone is not so good as your No. 1[,] De Goni, Pattern."[123]

Through the early 1850s, however, Martin's customers also referred to the guitars in other ways. Some ordered instruments by price. In 1852 Lee & Walker took "1 guitar at $27, 2 guitars at $20, and 1 guitar at $17." Others described instruments by size, as when Peters, Webb & Company took "1 large size $26, 2 second size $24 or $23, 4 small size $15–$21." Most important, as early as 1840, shortly after Martin's move to Nazareth, Coupa already had begun to refer to Martin's guitars by number, though clearly Martin did not yet use these designations with all his clients. In February of that year, Coupa ordered a rosewood instrument that he called a "Model 3," and the next month he ordered a "No. 2" as well as "3"s (plates 3-1–3-7).[124]

Lacking records between 1840 and 1849, we do not know if Martin used these numbers regularly throughout that decade. An elaborate daybook, however, begun in January 1852 and going on into 1858 verifies his institution of a numbering system early in the 1850s, with numbers 3, 2½, 2, 1, and the largest size, 0, added in 1854 (plate 3-8). Further, by 1852 many of his customers also regularly referred to his instruments by these numbers. Jonathan Mellon of Pittsburgh, for example, ordered "No. 2[,] Two small de Goni guitar, no. 2½[,] Two Rosewood, and no. 3[,] Two Rosewood." In the late winter of 1853 Drucke, the music teacher in Philadelphia, asked Martin for the prices of "no. 1 and no. 2" guitars. Ilsley in Albany placed an order that August for "one size 2 rosewood, ivory edge, Ger[man] silver frets, $30," two "size 2½ with lines, Brass pat[ent] heads, $24," and three "size 3 plain, Brass pat. Heads, $17." Through the mid-1850s these were the most common numbers. Horace Waters even suggested that Martin "put a number on the Guitar just under your name + on the outside of the Box." "We deal so much in nos.," he explained, "that it comes handy to us." Waters added that he had "difficulty in finding the cost—please no. them in some way."[125]

For this period there are few indications of where Martin purchased his native wood to make his instruments, though presumably he bought maple, holly, spruce, and whitewood locally. He also continued to import rosewood, mahogany, and ebony through companies in New York. Hawes & Willoughby, at 370–372 Washington Street, for example, told Martin that they could get him an order of rosewood in ten to twelve days, or perhaps earlier, "if the saw plates were in order" for cutting this particular wood.[126] He also bought rosewood, a staple for his guitar bodies, and other species from J. F. Copcutt at 348 Washington Street and from Ogden & Company, at 392 on that same street.[127] As he had in the 1830s, Martin relied on John M. Phyfe at 48 Canal Street to supply other exotic materials, including ebony and elephant ivory. At one point, when Martin had ordered "one small Tooth ivory," Phyfe wrote back apologetically to say that he had none smaller than twenty pounds, at a cost of $1.80 per pound.[128] Another time Martin bought a tusk weighing twenty-nine and a half pounds from P. I. Farnham & Company in the city for over forty dollars.[129] In this decade he also he began to use fancy wood binding and marquetry, instead of ivory, around the sound holes and edges of his instruments. He acquired this material from different sources, including Schatz, now in Boston, who in 1850 glued to the edge of a letter many small samples of patterned wood for Martin's perusal (plate 3-9). Schatz had obtained a stock of this material, as well as different gauges of wire for strings, from Germany.[130]

As the census records for 1850 indicate, Martin's largest regular expense for materials was for tuning machines. These he continued to acquire from Europe, primarily from France, through Fiot in Philadelphia. In February 1852, for example, Fiot wrote that he had received from Mssrs. Hufron & Duhan a small box containing 125 pairs "Mechaniques for guitars" which he had ordered for Martin on his account. The cost, he continued, would probably amount to $182.00 but could not be established before ascertaining the rate of the exchange in Paris. The following January, when he apprised Martin that he was selling his business to J. E. Gould & Company, he also mentioned that a large box of goods ordered from France finally was on its way across the Atlantic. Among other things, it included fifty sets of "Guitar Screws" for Martin, at an estimated cost of over ninety dollars. Six weeks later the firm forwarded these items to Bethlehem by stage and noted that Hufron & Duhan had apologized for having detained the order so long. They had had orders they had to fill in all parts of the world.[131]

As Martin's adoption of standard numbers for sizes suggests, the guitars that he now built had less overall variety than they had in the 1830s, when many orders were customized, but they also mark his emancipation from the style of instruments that he had learned to make at Stauffer's side. His detailed daybook for the 1850s, for example, does not record any instruments made with Stauffer-style peg heads and Vienna machines. Two-sided screws, in different metals, or the older violin-style pegs were now the norm. Also, more and more often his instruments had smaller upper bouts rather than the nearly equal-size upper and lower bouts commonly found on his instruments from the 1830s. And Martin's sound hole decoration now assumed the understated but elegant form that permanently marked his and his successors' work (plates 3-10, 3-11, 3-12). He now more often used concentric rings of light and dark wood, and sometimes ivory, with mother-of-pearl reserved for only his most expensive instruments and even then in unostentatious patterns (plates 3-13, 3-14). He also commonly used what is known as a Spanish-shaped heel rather than the ice cream cone shape typical of his earlier instruments. Other details on some instruments from this period—the occasional use of fan rather than ladder bracing, for example—further suggest that he had Spanish instruments in mind.[132]

Also, more and more of his guitars began to feature cross-bracing, in which some of the braces crossed in an X between the sound hole and the bridge, rather than fan bracing (plates 3-15, 3-16). This design provided much more strength and stability to the tops of the instruments, something increasingly important as the sizes of the instruments continued to increase during the nineteenth century. It is impossible to say just who first utilized this structural design, for by the 1850s one could find it in the instruments of several makers, all German and all known to each other—namely, Martin, Schmidt & Maul, and Stumcke. From the 1850s on, Martin made X-bracing a distinguishing feature of his instruments, so much so that it was primarily through his work that this aspect of construction eventually became the norm for American guitar makers.[133]

Between 1852 and 1856 Martin turned out about one thousand guitars—225 in 1852, 303 in 1853, 270 in 1854, and 211 in 1855, an average of about 250 per year. In his daybook of instruments made during these years (where the total numbers of guitars are slightly more than what the ledger records for the same period because in the ledger he did not always enter single instrument purchases or smaller orders), he used the following categories to describe the guitars: size; of what woods the neck and body were made; ornament, sound hole, edges (extent of purfling around these parts of the instruments); head (tuners); extra ornament (an ivory bridge, for example); whether the customer ordered a case; and price. The majority of his guitars had rosewood, and necks were described as either cedar (that is, natural wood) or painted black. Ornamentation was usually termed line, double line, de Goni, or Spanish. Sound hole ornamentation was described as plain, pearl, chain, de Goni, and Otilia (a designation named after Martin's daughter and sometimes used, as in the phrase "Otilia lines," to describe ornament as well). Edges were black, ivory, or ivory to the nut (that is, a "bound" fingerboard). The headstock could have ivory or ebony pegs, or brass or German silver side screws.

By late 1856, Martin also began to use a standardized system to indicate the degree of ornamentation on his instruments. On October 23, for example, he first used the shorthand designation, adding a second number, that he subsequently employed throughout his career. Specifically, in an order for C. A. Zoebisch & Sons, Martin described the guitars as 2/20, 2½/17, and 3/17, and skipped any mention of sound hole, ornament, edges, and the like. Interestingly, these numbers corresponded to the wholesale prices at which Martin sold the models to Zoebisch—a 2/20 sold for $20.00. For the next nine months he used these style numbers only in his sales to Zoebisch and continued to note other sales in full detail. It was not until July 19, 1857, that another order, to Miller & Beacham, was similarly described, with the style number again keyed to the price.[134] In the late summer of 1858 Martin began to use the designations regularly with a range of his customers.

With regard to sizes, in this four-year period the 2½ was most popular, with 264 made (see Appendix D). He also made 143 no. 1s, 205 no. 2s, and 214 no. 3s in this same four-year period. The records also indicate that he made two size 0, which he introduced in the spring of 1854. He shipped one of these to Peters & Sons on April 25 and the other to Reed on May 11. He also produced a terz guitar, for the New York market, in 1855. The prices for his instruments ranged from a low of $17.00 to $26.00 for plain 2½s and 3s, to more expensive instruments, usually appointed with pearl, in the $30.00 to $37.00 range (plates 3-17–3-22).

Each year between 1852 and 1856, then, with the assistance of a handful of laborers, Martin turned out two to three hundred instruments of several sizes and varied ornamentation. He had a vigorous business and scores of wholesale customers who eagerly sought to stock his guitars. By the mid-1850s, however, he also had to address a new challenge, a threat to his commercial independence from the all important New York wholesalers. These large music houses, which did hundreds of thousands of dollars of business a year in all aspects of the music trade (including the publication of sheet music), began to vie for Martin's business. But they did not simply want wholesale prices and the privilege of a good supply of Martin's instruments. Rather, they sought exclusive rights to sell his guitars throughout the trade, so that a dealer in Cleveland or a customer in Memphis would have to go through them to obtain an instrument.

To complicate matters, for the first time other guitar makers, particularly James Ashborn and William B. Tilton, seriously challenged Martin's supremacy in the trade. By the mid-1850s, for example, Ashborn had already negotiated special arrangements with certain New York music houses and was turning out hundreds more instruments than Martin. And during the same years, Tilton's "improved" guitars became increasingly popular. To maintain his position as America's premier guitar maker, Martin, for the first time, had to attend to the competition.

Plate 3-1.

Front view of C. F. Martin guitar, size no. 3, ca. 1840s. This small-bodied instrument has a fairly long scale (24¼ inches). Because of this, the bridge is positioned farther back toward the end block than on most Martin instruments from the same period. (Courtesy of Frank Ford)

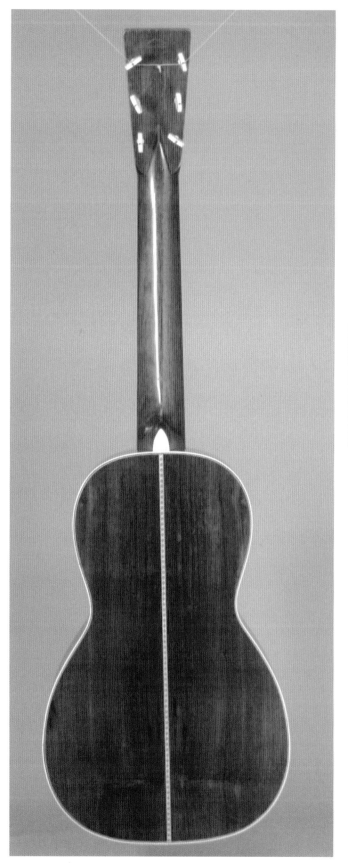

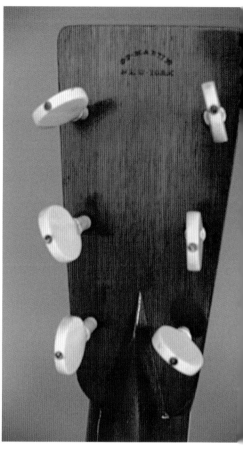

left
Plate 3-2. *Rear view of guitar in plate 3-1.*
(Courtesy of Frank Ford)

top
Plate 3-3. *Close-up of peg head*
of guitar in plate 3-1, stamped
"C F Martin / New York." Note
the simple friction tuners, the least
expensive kind that Martin offered.
(Courtesy of Frank Ford)

Plate 3-4. *Close-up of heel of the guitar in plate 3-1. Note the "Spanish-style" heel and the side center decoration. On this instrument, the sides are book-matched across this center strip, top and bottom, but the side grain does not match from the treble side to the bass side of the guitar. (Courtesy of Frank Ford)*

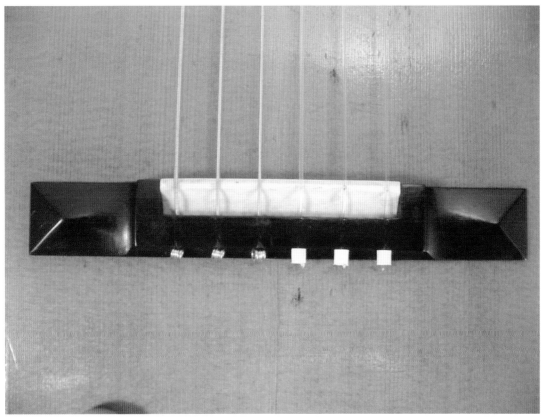

Plate 3-5. *Close-up of bridge on guitar in plate 3-1. This is an early tie block bridge, typical of Spanish construction. (Courtesy of Frank Ford)*

Plate 3-6. *Close-up of the bottom of the guitar in plate 3-1. Notice the decorative striping down the back, in the center of the sides, and down the end. (Courtesy of Frank Ford)*

Plate 3-7. *Close-up of the interior, heel section, of the guitar in plate 3-1. Notice the mahogany plate at the foot of the neck block, and the side reinforcement braces that terminate in yokes to receive the ends of the top and back braces. (Courtesy of Frank Ford)*

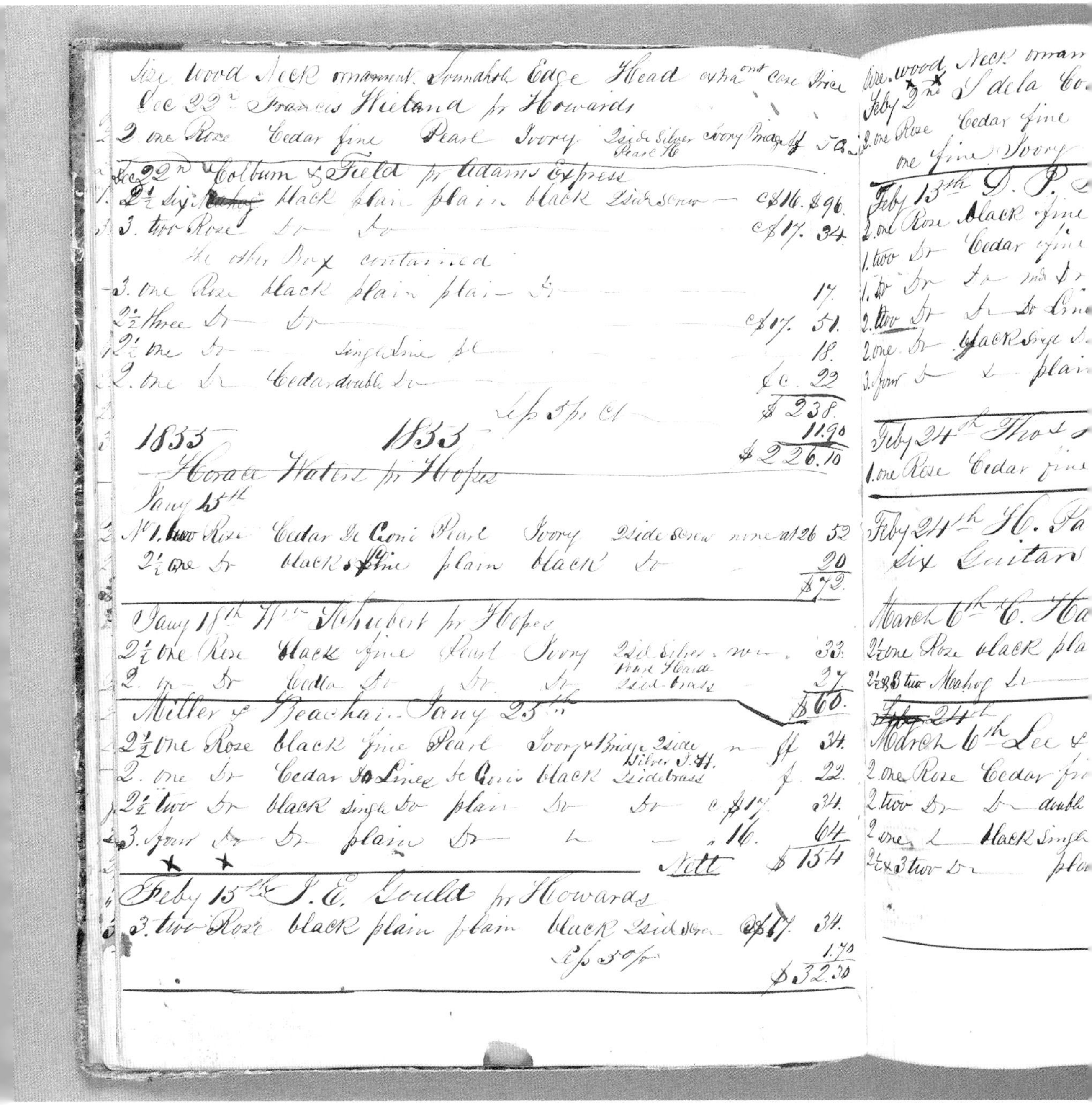

Size wood Neck ornament Soundhole Edge Head extra ornt Case Price
Dec 22d Francis Weiland pr Howards
2. one Rose Cedar fine Pearl Ivory 2side Silver Pearl H Ivory Bridge ff 50
~~Dec 22d Colburn & Field pr Adams Express~~
2½ six Mahog black plain plain black 2side screw c$16. $96.
3. two Rose do do c$17. 34.
The other Box contained
3. one Rose black plain plain do 17.
2½ three do do c$17. 51.
2½ one do single line do 18.
2. one do Cedar double do 22
$ 238.
Less 5 pr Ct 11.90
$ 226.10
1853 1853
~~Horace Waters pr Hopes~~
Jany 15th
No 1. two Rose Cedar do Coni Pearl Ivory 2side screw nine at 26 52
2½ one do black fine plain black do 20
$72.
Jany 18th Wm Schubert pr Hopes
2½ one Rose black fine Pearl Ivory 2side Silver Pearl Head 33.
2. do do Cedar do do do 2side brass 27.
$60.
Miller & Beacham Jany 25th
2½ one Rose black fine Pearl Ivory & Bridge 2side Silver S.H. ff 34.
2. one do Cedar do Lines do Coni black 2side brass f 22.
2½ two do black single do plain do do c$17. 34.
3. four do do plain do do 16. 64
Nett $154
Feby 15th J. E. Gould pr Howards
3. two Rose black plain plain black 2side screw c$17. 34.
Less 5% 1.70
$32.30

Plate 3-8. *Page from Martin's daybook of guitars made in the mid-1850s. The categories across the top of the page provide detailed descriptions of his instruments for these years. (C. F. Martin & Company Archives)*

Plate 3-9.

*Letter from
Heinrich Schatz
to Martin, Boston,
April 29, 1850. On
the back of this letter
Schatz glued samples
of marquetry that he
could provide Martin
for decoration on
his instruments.
(C. F. Martin &
Company Archives)*

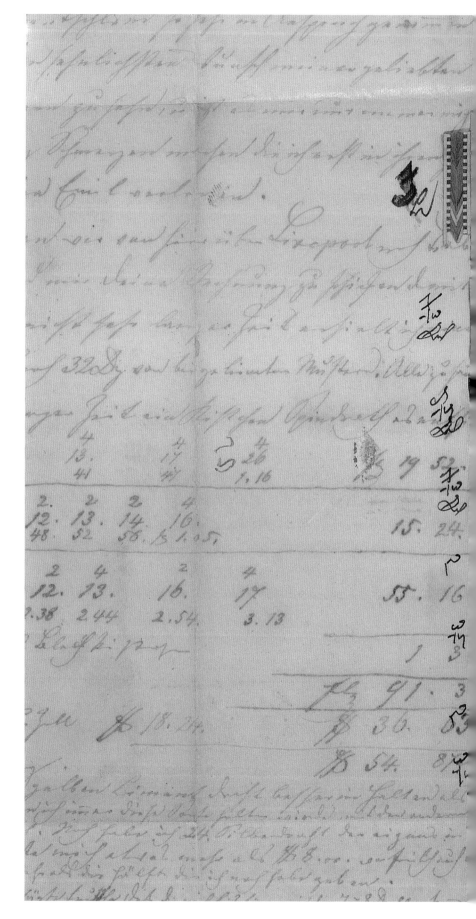

Plate 3-10.
Front view of C. F. Martin guitar, 3-24, ca. 1840s. This instrument has a transitional pin bridge, with its back scooped, as found on earlier tie bridges. (Courtesy of Frank Ford)

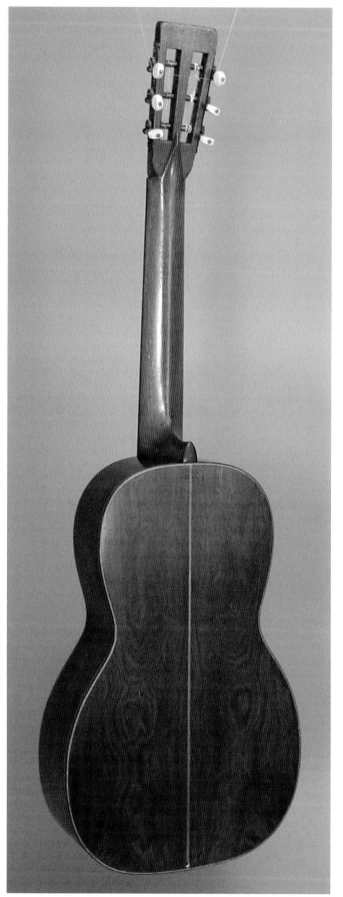

left
Plate 3-11. *Rear view of the guitar in plate 3-10. (Courtesy of Frank Ford)*

top
Plate 3-12. *Close-up of center stripe on bottom of the guitar in plate 3-10, typical of what became known as style 24. (Courtesy of Frank Ford)*

Plate 3-13.
Front view of C. F. Martin guitar, size 4, ca. 1850s. This instrument has rosewood sides and back (laminated); marquetry on back and side edges and through the center of its sides; pearl trim around the top; and an abalone rosette. It is ladder braced. (Courtesy of Elderly Instruments, Lansing, Michigan)

Plate 3-14. *Close-up of top of the guitar in plate 3-13. Note in particular the beautiful abalone sound hole and top trim, found on Martin's highest-style guitars, and the ivory tie bridge. (Courtesy of Elderly Instruments, Lansing, Michigan)*

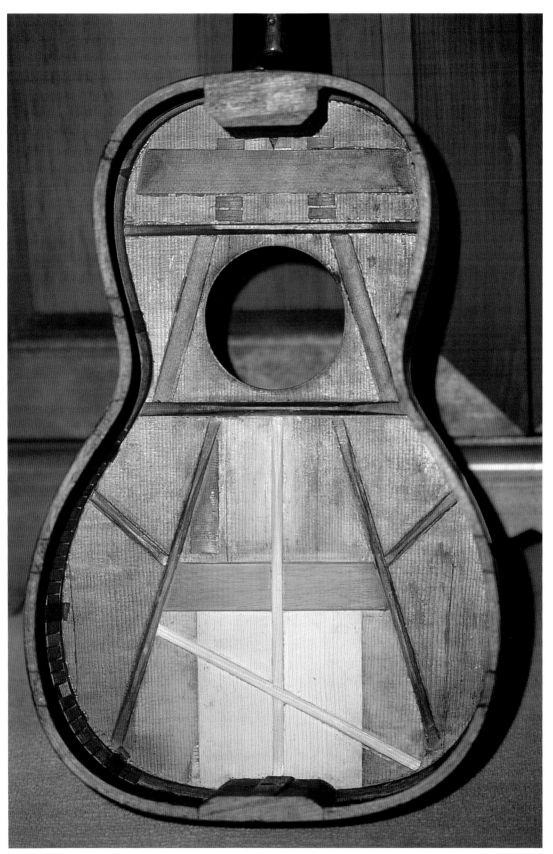

Plate 3-15. *Fan bracing typical of the mid– to late nineteenth century, used on Martin's lower-numbered styles. (Courtesy of David LaPlante)*

Plate 3-16. *X-bracing typical of the mid– to late nineteenth century, used on Martin's styles 21 and above. (Courtesy of David LaPlante)*

Plate 3-17.

Front view of C. F. Martin guitar, 2½-20, ca. 1840. Rosewood sides and back, with back laminated over spruce. The instrument is X-braced. Guitars of this sort show Martin leaving behind the Viennese models and establishing his own conception of the instrument's design. (Courtesy of America's Shrine to Music Museum)

Plate 3-18.

Rear view of the
guitar in plate 3-17.
(Courtesy of America's
Shrine to Music
Museum)

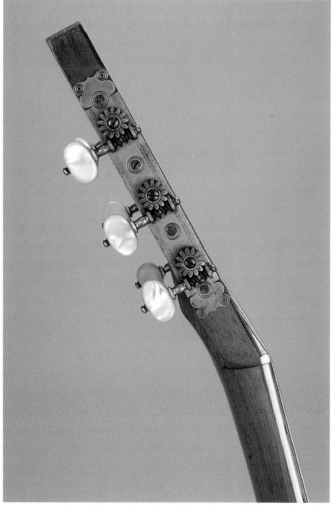

top
Plate 3-19. *Close-up of the top of the guitar in plate 3-17. The guitar features abalone trim around edge of the top and sound hole, and ivory trim around the top and back of the body. (Courtesy of America's Shrine to Music Museum)*

left
Plate 3-20. *Close-up of the peg head of the guitar in plate 3-17. (Courtesy of America's Shrine to Music Museum)*

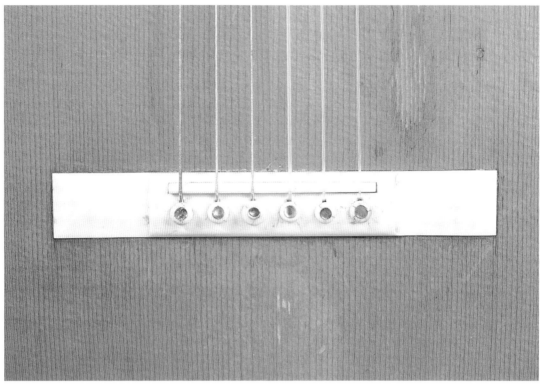

Plate 3-21. *Close-up of the ivory pin bridge on the guitar in plate 3-17. Note the abalone-trimmed pins. (Courtesy of America's Shrine to Music Museum)*

Plate 3-22. *Close-up of the ivory trim and button on the bottom of the guitar in plate 3-17. (Courtesy of America's Shrine to Music Museum)*

Ashborn, Tilton, and the Battle for New York, 1852–1861

MUSIC HOUSES AND THE PROMISE OF SECURITY

In the late spring of 1853, Mayer & Collins of Albany was waiting for a de-layed order of guitars. "We have been obligated," the company wrote Martin, "to furnish in their place New York made guitars." A few months later Hor-ace Waters, a major customer for Martin's instruments, echoed its northern neighbors. "I have written so often for Guitars," Mr. Waters himself told Martin, "that I am almost ashamed to write again." "Perhaps you do not wish me to sell more than I have on hand," he continued, but "unless I can have a better supply I shall have to get some other maker[']s guitars." "I advertise your Guitars, and if I do not have them I might as well give them up."[1]

It is no coincidence that in 1853 both these music firms should have warned Martin about having to buy guitars from other makers. As Martin ex-panded his base of clients west to the Mississippi River, two other guitar manufacturers, James Ashborn of Wolcottville, Connecticut, and William B. Tilton of New York, challenged him in the New York City market and, through it, nationally. By this time a handful of major music houses—specif-ically, Firth, Pond & Company, William Hall & Son, Berry & Gordon, and Horace Waters—had consolidated the city's music trade. These firms con-trolled the lucrative sheet music–publishing industry and sought the same monopoly on the retail instrument trade.[2]

One of Waters's advertisements summarizes its business philosophy. "To Dealers in every variety of business generally through the City" the company announced that its governing rule was "Large Sales and Small Profits," rather than "Small Sales and Large Profits." This enabled it "to fill all orders they may receive from their friends, or business correspondents residing at a distance from the city, for Music Merchandise, upon such terms as will prove to their own, as well as to the advantage of those ordering."[3] Just as large ex-press companies had emerged to facilitate the shipment of goods through the

View of the interior of the Publishers Great Piano & Music Establishments

Figure 4-1. *Lithograph, "View of the Interior of the Publisher's Great Piano and Music Establishment," showing the main sales room for sheet music in Horace Waters's emporium in New York City. In the 1850s Waters attempted to get Martin to make exclusive arrangements for the marketing of his guitars. Such stores sold every conceivable variety of musical instrument as well as hundreds of selections of sheet music. Cover of Thomas Baker's* The Sparkling Polka, *published by Waters in 1859. (Courtesy of American Antiquarian Society)*

country's rail system, music houses such as Horace Waters sought to have all instruments and sheet music go through them (fig. 4-1). Often starting satellite firms or silent partners in other major cities, by the early 1850s they were well on their way to cornering the market in precisely this way.

To manufacturers such as Martin, the advantage of such a system was a single, large outlet for their goods. An instrument maker who signed with a firm like William Hall & Son no longer had to devote himself to tedious and time-consuming correspondence of the sort Martin conducted virtually on a daily basis, or personally visiting representatives in the major markets ("jobbing," as it was termed). The supplier also avoided the aggravation that occupied Martin as he sorted out, say, his rental of a depot in New York, competition for agency in a distant city, or transportation problems to Memphis or Cleveland. Instead, a New York house promised quick, dependable payment at set rates for as many instruments as a maker cared to send. One gained in security what he lost in independence and flexibility.

In the spring of 1856 Firth, Pond & Company spelled out the benefits of signing with one of these houses. The company boasted that it could sell more of Martin's instruments than any house in the trade. "We have the finest store and the best warerooms for sound in the city." Further, Firth, Pond was willing to make "permanent arrangements with de Janon or some other good guitarist" to keep Martin's guitars in good order, if that is what he wanted. At the bottom line, it was to his advantage to have his guitars "in the hands of good Agents in the city, those who have the confidence of the public" (plate 4-1). Indeed, this house thought so highly of Martin's guitars that it was prepared to make virtually any arrangements he wanted, either to receive instruments on consignment or, preferably, to buy them outright for cash, if the discount was right. If Martin chose the latter course, Firth, Pond had no objections to taking large quantities of his guitars and attending to the wholesale trade, saving him "the risk of doing the jobbing business."[4]

Until recently, Firth, Pond & Company had had such an arrangement with James Ashborn, who sold thousands of guitars to just two houses, William Hall & Son being the other house (fig. 4-2). These two firms had come into existence in 1847, when John Firth and William Hall, who had been partners since the 1820s as Firth & Hall, finally parted ways. Now they were rivals who contested the allegiance of New York's amateur and professional musicians and music lovers in general.[5] By the mid-1850s the clamor for guitars had become so loud that Firth, Pond & Company decided to try to recruit Martin into its fold.

If Martin accepted an offer like that from Firth, Pond & Company, his guitars would penetrate all segments of the national market without any effort or expense on his part. Customers, too, would gain from this special arrangement. "Our guitars," Hall & Son explained in one of its advertisements, may be had "of all the Principal Music Dealers in the United States" at the same prices for which they sold in New York, in addition to shipping.[6] But, like virtually all James Ashborn's instruments sold to Firth, Pond & Company (and to Hall & Son), Martin's guitars would prominently display on their center strip not his own name but that of the New York company who jobbed them—hence, Mayer & Collins's locution "New York made guitars." Presumably, this meant that the music house fielded any complaints from customers. The guitar maker was just that: an individual who manufactured goods for another firm and sold under its name.

Eventually, Martin chose a different tack in navigating these complex economic currents. But Ashborn's career, as a guitar maker in the 1850s who pro-

Figure 4-2. *Lithograph, music emporium of William Hall & Son at 239 Broadway, ca. 1850.*
One of the largest music houses in the city, in the 1850s William Hall & Son, like its competitors,
tried to convince independent musical instrument makers to sign exclusive contracts. William
Hall & Son also did a large business in pianos, which it had manufactured at different factories
in the city. Cover of George M. Warren, Broadway Waltzes *(1849). (Courtesy of American*
Antiquarian Society)

duced more instruments than Martin and offered his wares exclusively through two of these large New York firms, throws important light on the difficult choices Martin faced. Detailed records for the 1850s from Ashborn's factory permit a comparison of the country's two most important antebellum guitar makers. In particular, we can contrast Martin's continued emphasis on meticulous hand craftsmanship and economic independence with another maker's eager embrace of industrialization and willing surrender of his rights to his instruments.[7]

ASHBORN IN WOLCOTTVILLE

Ashborn's guitar works were located in Torrington in northwestern Connecticut, thirty miles northwest of Hartford. By the early nineteenth century Torrington was known for its extensive hardwood forests, which contributed to the success of Ashborn's guitar works as well as to the burgeoning wagon-making activity so prevalent in the area. The area also featured plentiful mill sites, situated as it was on the Naugatuck River. By the 1820s Torrington had grown in importance as factories built specifically for the manufacture of woolen and cotton yarn and cloth joined its grist- and sawmills and its artisans' workshops for the production of tool handles, carriages, and other wooden goods.[8] Wolcottville, a village within this larger community, grew up along one of the mill sites on the Naugatuck.

By themselves Torrington's forests and waterpower do not suggest an overriding reason why James Ashborn chose to manufacture guitars there, for the town shared these resources with many communities in the area. His reason may have been personal, for like other immigrants (including C. F. Martin, in New York and Pennsylvania) he might have enjoyed being with others from his home country. Born in England around 1816, in Torrington Ashborn joined a group of thirty-eight of his former countrymen recruited in the late 1830s for a projected brass works that later became the largest manufacturing enterprise in the area. As his patents demonstrate, he had skill as a designer and draftsman, and the investors in the brass factory may have enticed him to Wolcottville to work on their project.

Ashborn had arrived there by the mid-1840s via New York, for the United States Census of 1850 lists him with four children, aged six to sixteen, all born in that state. We know nothing of his first wife, but in 1847 he married Lucinda Smith of Torrington and, in 1859, Maria L. Cook, by whom he had one more child. In 1850 when he was thirty-four, he called himself a "mechanic" (that is, a skilled artisan), and noted two thousand dollars in real estate, an amount that had grown to seven thousand dollars by the next census, at which time he also listed two thousand dollars in his personal estate.[9] Although Torrington's historian says that Ashborn had closed his guitar factory during the Civil War, other evidence suggests that he was still in business as late as 1869. He lived in Wolcottville until his death on December 7, 1876.

Among his belongings at probate were many guitar-making tools and supplies, miscellaneous parts for guitars and banjos (which he also manufactured), a dozen curly maple guitars "not quite finished," and, ironically, one secondhand Martin guitar valued at $5.00 (see Appendix E).[10]

Like many other artisans in that entrepreneurial age, Ashborn sought financial backing from local sources to realize his ambitions, in his case, to build a guitar works to capitalize on the nation's growing interest in music. Whatever his previous training, whether as draftsman or woodworker, somewhere along the way he had become interested in guitars. By embracing the mechanization and division of labor that defined the early industrial revolution, he believed that he could produce these instruments as well as anyone and at a profit. He convinced his fellow townsman Austin H. Hungerford, whose family already was well established in large-scale manufacturing in the area, to become his business partner. In the 1850 census Hungerford listed himself as a "manufacturer," and for several more years he and Ashborn conducted a successful business. Sometime between 1856, when the extant guitar factory records end, and 1860 Hungerford evidently left both the business and the area. In the next federal census (1860) Ashborn assumed the title of "guitar manufacturer."[11]

With Hungerford's capital and connections to the larger commercial world, Ashborn manufactured thousands of guitars and shipped them to New York City via the recently completed Naugatuck Railroad, which by 1850 had transformed the economic landscape of the Naugatuck River valley.[12] With access to a railhead in Wolcottville, Ashborn gained a direct and quick route to New York City and by 1851 (if not earlier) was selling large numbers of guitars there. If the numbering system he used to mark his instruments is reliable, by 1851, when the extant records commence, he had already sent close to two thousand guitars to these firms. His guitar works, employing up to ten workers at any one time, had become not only part of Torrington's booming economy but also the nation's largest supplier of parlor guitars, eclipsing Martin's output by hundreds of instruments per year.

THE WOLCOTTVILLE GUITAR FACTORY

At first Ashborn, like Martin, made his instruments in a modest workshop. Sometime in the late 1840s he purchased a building in which a craftsman had made hay rakes and fork and hoe handles and altered it for his purposes. It would have resembled any small early-nineteenth-century woodworking shop. The large open work area was dominated by a variety of saws and simple lathes run off leather belts and wooden shafts. This belting, however, was run not from a steam engine, as in Martin's shop, but from a waterwheel turned by the Naugatuck River, whose course had been dammed for that purpose. While Martin had to call on Philip Deringer to repair his machine's pistons, Ashborn's main worry was the water level in the Naugatuck or keeping his large wooden wheel and its gearing in repair. Hence, we find such entries in his expense account as that for August 1851 in which he recorded the payment of $10.00 for "repairing [the mill] Wheel" or that in July 1854, when he noted "Repairs to Dam, etc."[13]

For several years the old rake factory served Ashborn's purposes. Like Martin, though, who in 1850 had expanded his works and added steam power to meet an increased demand for his guitars, by the fall of 1852 Ashborn had built a new and larger factory (figs. 4-3, 4-4).[14] Within a few months the size of his shipments of both guitars and strings (which he also made on-site) noticeably increased, without, however, a comparable rise in his expenditure for labor. On average before the new construction, for example, he shipped two to three dozen guitars per month. But in the year following the completion of the new factory in December 1852, he produced as many as one hundred instruments per month, with aggregates in the seventies quite common. Obviously, the innovations in production that the new building made possible allowed him to turn out guitars much more expeditiously.[15]

Figure 4-3. Photograph, late nineteenth century, of the "Fine Woodworking Department" in Stewart and Bauer's musical instrument manufactory, Philadelphia. Although Stewart and Bauer's operation was larger than Martin's, this image gives us a sense of the machinery one found in a small steam-powered factory. This and the following image appeared in S. S. Stewart's Banjo, Guitar, and Mandolin Journal 16, 3 (1899).

Figure 4-4. *Photograph, late nineteenth century, of the "Guitar Finishing Department" in Stewart and Bauer's Philadelphia factory.*

Ashborn's records, as well as his last will and testament, tell us a good deal about the equipment inside the factory. His saws were his most important tools, as well as the most frequently mentioned and expensive.[16] In August 1851, for example, from J. Atkins & Company Ashborn bought a twenty-two-inch veneer saw for the considerable sum of $17.00, and two months later from the same source he secured a twelve-inch circular saw for $3.00 and six scrapers (edge tools used for smoothing wood before final finishing). He also had twelve planes, two "guitar string machines" for winding strings, two machines for cutting screws, and a steam box used for bending the sides of the guitars to the proper shape.

Such equipment brought Ashborn other income from both local and distant sources. On several occasions, for example, he allowed the Alvord Carriage Manufactory, by the 1850s one of Wolcottville's largest employers, to use his saws to prepare wood for its own works. And Ashborn's proximity to the rail line allowed him to perform work for the New York music houses with which he already had established extensive business arrangements.[17] In particular, he often sawed lumber for William Hall & Son's extensive piano factory in New York City. In February 1852, for example, he charged the company nineteen dollars for sawing "long blocks" and another forty-six dollars for "21 days sawing piano work and lumber." Hall & Son had sent some of this lumber from the city, but Ashborn also bought some of it locally, from the same lumbermen who sold him wood for his guitar work, and forwarded it to New York after he had cut it to size. Even the by-product of such contract work had value. On several occasions Ashborn used hogsheads of sawdust as credit toward purchases at the Wolcottville Brass Company, which presumably used the material in their metal casting or as packing material for the shipment of finished goods.

Ashborn stocked other supplies typically used by antebellum guitar makers (or woodworkers, for that matter): many hand tools, hide glue, turpentine, varnish, and other spirits. He also needed a variety of wood. Local suppliers brought him spruce—fifty dollars for fifteen hundred feet seems to have been the common rate for this species. From local traders he also bought maple for use in guitar necks and, in the later 1850s and 1860s, for the bodies of some of his instruments, including banjo rims. Ashborn also frequently prepared maple as part of the piano work he performed for Hall & Son. In 1852 Winthrop Cook, a local lumberman, brought him 141 feet of maple (for $17.63), along with other hardwoods: 300 feet of cherry (for $9.00) and 157 feet of apple (for $9.42).

The New York music houses, themselves deeply invested in piano factories in and around the city, needed exotic woods for such instruments and thus sold Ashborn what he needed for his guitars from their own stock. These supplies constituted one of his major expenses, as they did Martin's.[18] Because tropical woods were hard to obtain outside the city, Ashborn even acted as a broker and sold smaller pieces to local craftsmen. On several occasions, for example, Arvid Dayton, who since 1840 had manufactured pipe and then reed organs in a factory near Ashborn's, bought small pieces of ebony, and Clark Downs, a "trader," took a block of rosewood the same day he brought Ashborn thirty-six hundred feet of hemlock.[19] In February 1855 Ebenezer Welton, a button maker, bought an entire rosewood log for twenty-two dollars, a purchase that presumably went a long way in his craft.

The Connecticut guitar maker differed from his Nazareth counterpart in one significant way: he had his own metal tuning machines, elegant and quite distinctive, made locally. The records show that Ashborn often bought rolled brass from the Wolcottville Brass Company, owned by his partner's father, and employed others to machine it to his specifications. Ashborn paid one of his employees, thirty-year-old Emery Morris (who called himself a "mechanic"), extra money to produce parts for the tuning machines. In July 1851, for example, Morris received thirteen dollars for eleven days' labor and an additional eighteen dollars for seventy-two "sett screws and wheels," a type of entry repeated every few months until April 1852. At that point Ashborn increased both Morris's salary, from $1.25 to $1.50 a day, and the number of days per month that he worked, which suggests that from that point on he performed this work regularly. Although Ashborn did not ship all his guitars with these tuners—he also had patented special wooden ones, as I will discuss—he did not incur Martin's large expenses for the importation of European tuning machines.

ASHBORN GUITARS

With these materials Ashborn and his workers manufactured a large number of instruments. Until July 1854 he meticulously listed by serial number all guitars sent to Firth, Pond & Company and William Hall & Son. A typical entry reads "12 No 3 Guitars and Cases / Nos 2938 to 2949." Even though he inexplicably stopped noting the serial numbers after that date, he continued to enumerate the guitars carefully. Between April 1851 and December 1855 the factory produced 3,152 instruments, an average of 54 per month, with as many as 119 shipped in June 1854 and many fewer in the winter months, perhaps because the Naugatuck River iced over and reduced the amount of water power available. Ashborn most often shipped instruments in increments of twelve, and the most common amounts per shipment were four and five dozen.

He simplified manufacture by making his guitars all the same size and shape, with a body 17¼ inches long and the lower bout 11 inches across, making an instrument comparable in size to a Martin size 3. Ashborn thus set his price scale by the degree of ornamentation on each instrument. He made six different grades, identified by a numeral stamped inside the guitar on its center strip, which also carried the serial number and the name of the New York firm that had purchased the instrument.[20] During the period covered by the extant records, he shipped 916 no. 1s, 1,016 no. 2s, 576 no. 3s, and 406 no. 4s. He built nos. 5 and 6 in very small numbers and occasionally made what he called an "Extra," four of which he made with "Ivory Bands" in December 1851 and sold to Hall & Son for $42.75 each (fig. 4-5; plates 4-2–4-8).

Ashborn expedited the manufacture of these instruments to meet the demands of the New York market. Whatever the guitars' grades, their basic construction was remarkably consistent, as befitted factory production. The top was spruce, braced with a three-stave fan set into a peaked cross brace, a design fairly common to contemporary Spanish guitars. He never used the X-bracing characteristic of Martin's and other German makers' instruments from the 1850s on. Ashborn's guitars had sides of spruce or maple. If the former, he usually veneered them (as did many contemporary makers) with rosewood or mahogany, from two pieces of closely matched grain. His guitar necks were assembled from three pieces of hardwood (often maple) and sometimes veneered with rosewood or mahogany, an uncommon appointment on antebellum guitars.

A few more details of construction are available from advertisements placed by William Hall & Son for Ashborn's instruments. In 1856, for exam-

Figure 4-5. *This advertisement for Charles C. Converse's* New Method for the Guitar *(1855) shows a young woman playing an Ashborn no. 6 guitar, his highest-grade model. The model is distinguishable by the elaborate wooden inlay around the body and sound hole. See plates 4-2 and 4-8. From* New York Musical World *(1856). (Courtesy of American Antiquarian Society)*

ple, the firm observed that Ashborn had improved his manner of fretting the instrument: "The frets are secured in a groove so that they cannot come out, and they are so shaped that the most perfect glide can be made without the least injury or inconvenience to the fingers." Hall & Son also noted that on the high-grade no. 3 instrument the maker used an "oval back, centrifugal bars, [and] fine finished oval blocking," describing Ashborn's refinements to the interior construction of his instruments.[21]

Ashborn's manner of attaching the neck to the body offers a striking illustration of how he adapted traditional design to more rapid factory production. He performed this important task with the use of a dovetailed joint and the addition of a short collar glued to the back, a particularly expeditious manner of assembly. In contrast, the Spanish heel more commonly seen on antebellum guitars was attached by slotting the sides of the body into the neck, which then continues a short way into the body, a method that requires more tedious adjustment and thus allows for more variation among instruments.[22] Finally, Ashborn spliced the peg head to the top of the neck with a distinctive "diamond" joint that permitted a large gluing surface and thus a strong bond.

No doubt because his new factory helped him increase production without incurring significantly greater labor costs, Ashborn kept the prices of his guitars constant between 1851 and 1856, selling the instruments to both of his New York buyers for the same amounts. He charged $8.50 for a no. 1, $9.75 for a no. 2, $11.50 for a no. 3, $14.25 for a no. 4, $17.50 for a no. 5, and $25.00 for a no. 6. It is worth noting that in his June 1855 account with William Hall & Son, Ashborn listed two new items: eight dozen "Maple Guitars & Cases," at $7.50 each, unlined instruments that became the least expensive of the company's productions, and a dozen "No. 3 Guitars & Cases New Style" at $13.00, more expensive than the standard no. 3s. As these figures make plain, Ashborn sold his guitars for much less than Martin, whose *lowest-priced* guitars in this period ranged from $17.00 to $20.00.

ASHBORN'S PATENTS

As these details of Ashborn's guitar construction suggest, his training as a "mechanic" inclined him to innovative solutions to what he regarded as problems with the instrument's design. In the early 1850s, for example, he turned his attention to the guitar's tuning mechanism—specifically, the wooden friction tuner—and developed two different variations of it that he thought significant enough to patent. He installed these on some of his guitars, but he also sold them separately.[23] Rather than purchasing the geared tuners that Martin imported from Europe, Ashborn experimented with modified, more efficient versions of wooden violin-style tuners that allowed the same precise tuning that the patent heads did. Because he could turn these wooden pegs on his own lathes, they were considerably less expensive than metal geared machines, which, as we have seen, he also had built to his own specifications, probably later in the 1850s.[24]

On April 16, 1850, Ashborn obtained U.S. patent no. 7,279 for a "Guitar-Head and Capo Tasto," that is, a peg head tuning mechanism and a capo for changing the pitch of the strings (fig. 4-6). His tuner is like a windlass, a peg-and-spindle mechanism to enable one to tune more easily and precisely than with the violin peg-style tuner or the metal patent heads. Ashborn found the latter undesirable not only because of their considerable cost but also their weight, which adversely affected the vibration of the instrument. To solve the problem he made a larger-size spindle to attach to the head of the guitar but not to protrude on the backside, connected by catgut to a regular-shafted violin tuner passing all the way through the peg head, slightly behind the spindle for that string. When the violin tuner was turned, the resulting action was like that of a windlass: easier, more accurate adjustment without the cost or the weight of the brass tuning machines. This was indeed a solution worthy of someone who termed himself a "mechanic."

Ashborn's second patent, for a "Tuning-Peg for Guitars," is even more ingenious. Like his first innovation, it is made wholly of wood in a shape that he easily could produce on his lathe. This patent is for what might be termed a "multiratio" tuning peg. Citing the same defects in tuning mechanisms

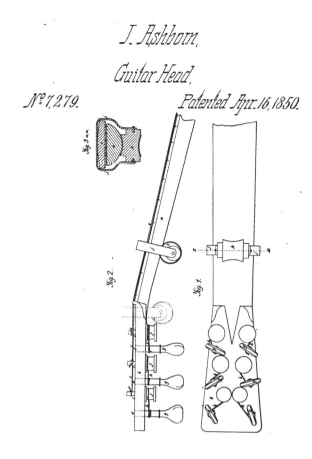

J. Ashborn,

Guitar Head,

Nº 7,279.   Patented Apr. 16, 1850.

Figure 4-6. *Patent drawing for James Ashborn's "Guitar Head," 1850. Ashborn constantly tried to improve his guitars and banjos, in this case by making lighter and more effective tuning mechanisms made of wood. This particular patent is for a peg and spindle mechanism that operated like a small windlass to allow fine tuning.*

that he had noted in his 1850 patent description, in U.S. patent no. 9,268, issued September 21, 1852, Ashborn developed a new model. He described a tuner with "that part of the wooden peg which is fitted to and turns in the handle of the instrument, and which may be called the journal, of much greater diameter than the barrel or part on which the string is coiled." This gave "such leverage to the surface of which makes friction and which resists the tension of the string as effectually to hold the string without the necessity of wedging or driving the peg too hard." The result was a larger hole in the peg head into which the journal was fitted, but the ease with which such pegs could be made and the efficiency and accuracy gained in tuning were significant.[25]

The other half of his patent of 1850 also displays Ashborn's penchant for elegant innovation. With his tuning peg he offered as well a version of what was called a "capo de astra," an accessory to hold down the strings at a certain fret to change the pitch of all strings played above that point.[26] Ashborn's refinement of the capo was simple and its principle is still used. Though this item did not bring him a lot of income, he marketed it at a good profit. In October 1851, for example, he sent Hall & Son four hundred of them at twenty-five cents each. This was a sizable markup over the $22.50 that Ashborn paid Morris, who by the mid-1850s also made Ashborn's specially designed (though not patented) metal tuners, to produce them. Two years later Hall & Son took a thousand at the same price. More important, this capo, like the wooden tuning pegs, speaks of this mechanic's willingness to challenge conventional wisdom about the ways items could best be designed and produced.

ASHBORN'S FACTORY SYSTEM

Ashborn differed significantly from Martin not only in his willingness to adapt traditional craftsmanship to the market economy, specifically through his modification of the construction of his guitars in a mechanized workshop, but also in his open embrace of the division of labor that marked new modes of industrial production. Departing from the usual practice, with its origin in the European guild system, in which a master worked by hand on instruments from start to finish and trained apprentices in the same steps until they made masterpieces, Ashborn used water-powered machinery and a small number of specialized employees whom he supervised in particular tasks. In this way he could produce standardized instruments more cheaply.

His division of labor was crucial, for the reassignment to individual workers of the discrete tasks in manufacture, rather than the wholesale mechanization of such tasks, marked industrialization's early stages. I have already discussed Emery Morris, who machined parts for Ashborn's distinctive brass tuners when he began to use that style. Equally important is Isaac Thornton's work as a "polisher," as he termed himself in the census of 1850.[27] An Englishman about the same age as Ashborn, like his employer (and perhaps with him) he arrived in Torrington from New York. Ashborn paid him well for "polishing" or "polishing and bridging" the guitars, his rate of pay set by the style of instrument on which he worked. In June 1851, for example, he received $10.08 for polishing a dozen no. 1 guitars, $10.80 for a dozen no. 2s, and $12.00 for work on no. 4s, rates that remained standard through the period. If Thornton bridged the guitars as well (that is, properly set the height of the bridges and saddles and glued the bridges into place), he received almost a dollar more per dozen instruments.

By 1852, though, Ashborn had stopped noting such pay for individual jobs and simply listed the number of days these men worked. As noted above, Morris received a raise in April 1852 to $1.50 per day, the highest rate Ashborn paid. Such changes in the way Ashborn kept the labor account were directly related to his move toward a factory system in which specialized work that hitherto was performed in addition to one's regular duties now became one's main task.

Variation in pay among his employees further differentiates the work performed in his factory. At the top of the scale were four employees who remained with Ashborn through the period covered by the extant account book: Morris, Charles Lamb (in 1850 a forty-two-year-old "mechanic"), Cornelius Rinders, and Burris Manville. In May 1852 thirty-five-year-old John

Huke, who had recently arrived from Prussia with his family, also joined the workforce at the top rate. In the census of 1860, Lamb, Thornton, and Huke all listed themselves as "guitar makers," a description that presumably reflected their considerable responsibilities in the factory, while Manville, who left the firm in the late 1850s, had become a wagon maker. Elisha Loomis, a "mechanic" who worked for Ashborn for only eight months but at the high rate, subsequently became a gunsmith.[28]

Chester Smith, who in 1850 at the age of thirty had declared himself a "mechanic" but a decade later was another of Ashborn's "guitar makers," led a second tier of employees whose wages were between $1.00 and $1.30 per day. A bachelor who boarded with a family in Torrington, Smith had as peers Ernest Young, who made $1.30 a day, and Timothy Hart, who began at $1.10 but soon worked himself to the higher rate. By July 1852, George Sherman, another "mechanic" with Ashborn throughout the period, moved up the pay scale from $1.05 to $1.33, clearly a member of this second group of skilled employees.

Workers with wages below one dollar a day, the rate of unskilled laborers in that decade, occupied the factory's lowest tier and may have made guitar cases (as Martin's lowest-paid employees did), or they may have wound the strings that Ashborn manufactured in the shop and which constituted an important part of his income, even meriting lengthy mention in one of Hall & Son's advertisements.[29] Among this group there was not much loyalty to the enterprise. Some, like Dennis Kelley and Andrew Booter, worked only a couple of months at the rate of one dollar. Thomas Woodrow and Martin Judd stayed fewer than six months at $.50 per day. Alexander Inwood worked for about a year at $.65 a day. When he departed, Mrs. Brown, who also worked for $.50 per day, was the only steady employee left from this lower-paid group, who, in part because of their transience or their lack of specialized skills, never moved up the wage scale as, say, Hart or Sherman had.

At its largest, Ashborn's workforce numbered about ten but more regularly consisted of eight employees, two more than Martin had during the 1850s.[30] They evidently worked twelve-hour days, on the average. The core of the labor force—Chester Smith, Lamb, Rinders, Sherman, Judd, and Manville— put in between twenty and twenty-five days per month, though in some months that dropped to fifteen to seventeen days. Interestingly, such short months do not seem to bear any relation to seasonal agricultural work, as might have been the case earlier in the century. The longest workdays in the factory were in the spring and summer and the shortest in the colder season. This reverses our expectations about laborers who might work for the guitar factory in the winter while tending their farms in the warmer months. It suggests that the factory operated less efficiently in colder months when the river froze and when extremes in temperature and humidity might affect the use of glue.

ASHBORN'S NEW YORK CONNECTION

Ashborn and Hungerford's financial arrangements with William Hall & Son and Firth, Pond & Company were complicated, but the scale of production in the Wolcottville factory resulted from the support of and sales to these music houses. In contracting to sell his guitars through these firms, Ashborn not only avoided having to job his own guitars to dealers around the country but also allied himself to two of the giants of the American music trade. In 1855, for example, a New York trade paper reported Firth, Pond & Company's annual income at $150,000: $70,000 from sheet music, $50,000 from pianos, and $30,000 from other musical merchandise.[31] Against such numbers the income from Ashborn's or Martin's guitar factories looks small, but such operations as theirs fueled the growth of large music companies by providing merchandise that was not being made in enough quantity, or could not be made as cheaply, in the city. The New York merchants' willingness to market as many guitars as Ashborn or Martin could produce verified such entrepreneurs' hunches that Americans were eager to purchase well-made, indigenous instruments.

Ashborn may have learned to what lengths the New York music houses would go to control their supplies of goods when John Firth and William Hall, as partners in Firth & Hall, had purchased Asa Hopkins's Litchfield, Connecticut, flute manufactory, not far from Torrington.[32] Hopkins had been in business since 1834, but after being bought out he made flutes exclusively for Firth & Hall, whose instruments thereafter carried their names, not his. Such large firms always looked for ways to expand their empires. Early in 1855, however, for some reason Ashborn ended his relationship with Firth, Pond & Company, which might account for that firm's overture to Martin a few months later. Thus, it may have been at this time that Ashborn broached (if he already had not) the possibility of an arrangement similar to that of Hopkins and gave his business fully to William Hall & Son, essentially masking his role as maker of these guitars.[33]

This would explain, for example, Hall & Son's proprietary tone in their full-page advertisement in the *New York Musical World* in 1856.[34] Under the heading "Hall's Guitars," the firm claimed that, because of "greater perfection in our machinery and consequent facility for making Guitars," it not only had "added to the strength of the Instrument, but increased the volume of tone and made it sweeter and more sonorous." Hall & Son, of course, had no guitar manufactory and was talking about Ashborn's as though it were the firm's.[35]

The changes that Hall & Son announced in the numbering system of its guitars point to the same conclusion. The company told the public that it was doing away with the old-style no. 1 and replacing it with "an elegant Rosewood Instrument, superior in appearance as well as in tone to the old No. 2." The new no. 2 was the equal of the old no. 4, and the new no. 3 like the former no. 5. Moreover, Hall & Son would sell any "extra styles" according to the amount of work on them. Prices for the three new numbers were $18.00, $25.00, and $35.00, respectively. These were the same guitars that I noted above as Ashborn's "new" models, first shipped that very year. He sold the first two of these new grades for $7.50 and $13.50 each, and Hall & Son's prices for these instruments indicate the considerable markup—about double—from Ashborn's wholesale prices. A few years later Hall & Son again revamped the numbering system, announcing yet another new arrangement. The firm sold a no. 0 maple guitar, in a bag, for $7.50; a no. 1 "curl" maple guitar, in bag, for $10.00; a no. 1 "elegant rosewood," with patent heads, in a case, for $18.00; a no. 2, like the no. 1 but with rosewood neck, for $22.50; a no. 3, with oval back, centrifugal bars, and fine finished oval blocking, for $29.50; and a no. 6, essentially a no. 3 but highly decorated, for $50.00.[36]

More evidence of Hall & Son's relationship with Ashborn came in the company's description of the new "Patent Heads" on these guitars. These tuning devices, the company claimed in the same advertisement, were better made, of less weight, and were less liable to get out of order than other tuners. Such heads could be attached to any guitars for five dollars and required no more power to turn than other tuners. These may have been the wooden tuning pegs with which Ashborn had experimented in the early 1850s. But Hall & Son's notice that they could be attached to any guitar suggests that they more likely were the elegant brass machines made for Ashborn in Wolcottville in the mid-1850s and later, with his name stamped on them. Hall & Son's advertisement of a new capo d'astra—the same patented by Ashborn in 1850—right beneath the notice of these tuning machines seals the case. The company obviously had reached some understanding with Ashborn, perhaps having bought the rights to his patents.[37] Whatever the arrangement, Ashborn was on special terms with this giant in the New York musical world, the logical conclusion of a relationship that had developed since at least the early 1850s.

Ashborn's accounts with Hall & Son, and as well with Firth, Pond & Company, the other New York firm with which he did business, indicate the complexity of such financial arrangements. Each month he meticulously recorded all transactions with them. Typically, he listed as debits the amounts of the different grades of guitars he shipped. He noted (at least for several years) the instruments' serial numbers, as well as the quantity of strings, in dozens, and other items provided or work his employees performed. Under this category were numbers of patent tuners, capos, or bridges, for example, or the "piano work" Ashborn carried out or, occasionally, the repair of some instrument such as a violin, accordion, or guitar that one of the companies had forwarded. Ashborn also indicated the days on which the factory shipped the items or performed the work.[38]

The companies in turn credited Ashborn in one of two ways. First, they issued bank drafts payable in 10, 20, 30, 60, 90, and occasionally up to 120 days. Or they credited him through goods, usually materials he needed for his business but could not obtain locally: such exotic woods as rosewood, mahogany, and ebony, for example, or the silver wire and silk needed for the string manufacture he also carried out in the factory. Occasionally, the companies supplied other items: reams of paper, for example, or, in July 1852, three refrigerators, or most surprising of all, in April 1854, oysters, for which Ashborn and Hungerford split the cost, almost thirty-five dollars.

When Hall & Son or Firth, Pond & Company wrote their bank drafts to Ashborn, they often issued a series of them on one day, payable at different times over the next few months. They did so only once or twice in a given month, even if the guitar works shipped items in several different batches, presumably as Ashborn completed the instruments. Most commonly, Hungerford, who kept the business records, handled both the accounting and the drafts.[39] But although Hungerford was Ashborn's financial angel and accountant, he seems to have allowed Ashborn to attend to most of the direct business with the New York companies, for the records show him frequently reimbursed for travel to the city, and Hungerford, only a few times.

Over the five years for which we have records for Ashborn, he did approximately 75 percent of his business, worth forty thousand dollars, with Hall & Son, and the remainder, about seven thousand dollars, with Firth, Pond & Company. In February 1855, probably at the request of Hall & Son, the accounts were audited, for, in another hand at the bottom of the page, it reads: "We ex[amined] accounts of W. H. & Son and A. N. Hungerford April 20 to Feby 1st 1855 & find bal[ance] in favor of Wm H & Son 2113.09." Other evidence of such external audits appears on the very last page of the ledger. In yet another hand, in pencil, is written "Cr[edit] by 2578.26 bal[ance] as ex[penses]." These audits, and the degree of Ashborn and Hungerford's indebtedness to Hall & Son, may have pertained to whatever final arrangement the parties reached about Ashborn's guitars and patents.

Finally, in addition to drawing cash from the factory's bank account, on three occasions Ashborn and Hungerford each took a substantial amount listed as a dividend, indicating that they shared profits from the enterprise. In April 1852, for example, each took $1,294.62; the following April, $1,324.74; and in November 1853, $1,869.67, at which time Hungerford also gave his partner a note for $245.69 from the general account. These amounts indicate that, whatever the precise condition of Ashborn and Hungerford's accounts with the New York music houses, their enterprise provided a substantial return.

Without doubt, Hungerford kept other account books for this company. For example, standard numbers that are prefixed to each account throughout the journal indicate that he transferred the information into a more formal ledger in which each party was debited and credited by corresponding number. Furthermore, we know that Ashborn also made banjos for the same two

New York firms, as well as for William Pond & Company, successor to Firth, Pond & Company. But in the extant record book kept by Hungerford, there is no mention of this instrument.[40] The information on Ashborn's guitar factory, however, provides much insight into the ways a rural artisan, by securing local capital and entrepreneurial expertise and by locating a large and dependable market, adapted his craft from workshop to factory, the better to produce goods for New York retailers. At precisely the same time, the large city firms offered C. F. Martin the same opportunity. If he so wished, a skilled craftsman such as Martin, who hitherto had jobbed his own goods around the country, now had the incentive to expand his operation in new ways and move his wares exclusively through the nation's largest mercantile center.

WILLIAM B. TILTON'S PATENTS

William B. Tilton, who manufactured violins and guitars in the city from 1853 through 1867, as well as banjos in the 1860s, was another major player in New York's guitar wars of the 1850s. Like Ashborn, he experimented with instrument design and held patents for violin, guitar, and banjo improvements and was thus aptly described as "an ingenious American mechanician."[41] But, unlike Ashborn, who continued to manufacture guitars with his patents, even if he sold exclusively to one or two large houses, Tilton fairly quickly sold his rights to large wholesalers — first in New York, later in Boston — who then had guitars with the Tilton patent built for them. Like Ashborn, too, he represents the culture of innovation — or, put another way, of endless tinkering — that, with the spread of industrialization, affected even the most traditional handcrafts.

On September 2, 1851, Tilton, a New Hampshire native then living in Carrollton, Alabama, registered his first patent (U.S. patent no. 8,338), for the "construction of violins, &c." (fig. 4-7), an improvement that garnered considerable attention in the United States and abroad.[42] With it he tried to improve the volume and quality of the tones of stringed instruments that were "acted on by the finger or the bow," a definition that included, as he intended, the guitar. Tilton explained that the end blocks glued to such instruments — he had in mind the violin family — were so large as to impair the vibration of the instrument's sounding board. Traditionally, such blocks had been constructed to add strength to the sounding board, under great tension from the strings. Tilton proposed to insert a longitudinal bar between the neck and tail blocks and taper the blocks to meet this bar, leaving them wide only where they met the instrument's body. Doing so would relieve "the sounding board altogether from the duty of sustaining the longitudinal force of tension of the strings," he explained and thus allow the craftsman to reduce the sounding board's thickness for better tonal quality. Tilton's bar essentially functioned like the dowel of a banjo, traversing the instrument from head to tail and thus offering it support, an improvement that had some cur-

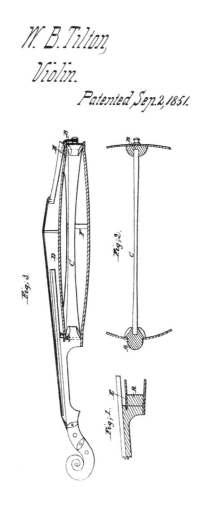

W. B. Tilton,
Violin.
N.º 8338.
Patented Sep. 2, 1851.

Figure 4-7. *Patent drawing for William B. Tilton's improvement for bracing violins, guitars, and other stringed instruments, 1851. Tilton proposed building the instruments with a dowel right through the body of the instrument, as in the construction of a banjo, to strengthen the top of the design. This proved a popular feature and even led to the conversion of extant instruments.*

rency. As late as 1867, for example, one of Martin's clients told him that he thought such Tilton instruments with the neck fully through the body still proved the strongest.[43]

Three years later, now living in New York amid the music houses' active competition to procure more and better guitars for the American market, Tilton registered another improvement, one that applied and extended his previous patent specifically to guitars (fig. 4-8). His object in U.S. patent no. 10,380 (January 3, 1854) was to stretch the strings to the foot of the guitar— that is, beyond the bridge—"so as to give greater vibration to the sounding board, and consequent clearness of tone to the instrument." Tilton essentially had attached the strings to a tailpiece like those found on contemporary banjos or on violins, for that matter. As he put it, he attached the strings at the foot of the guitar and carried them "through perforations in permanent pins, at the usual place of fastening," and then over a bridge directly in front of these pins. This rendered the strings incapable of lateral movement over the bridge, Tilton explained in his patent description, and provided an additional length of string between the pins and the bottom of the guitar. In this im-

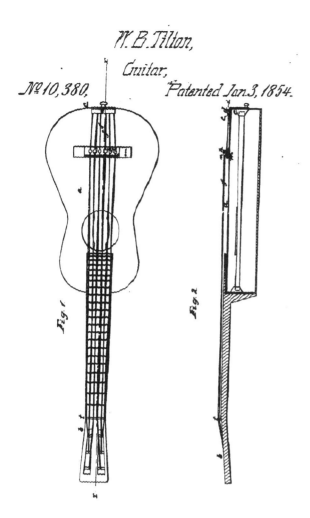

W. B. Tilton,
Guitar,
№ 10,380.
Patented Jan. 3, 1854.

Fig. 1

Fig. 2

Figure 4-8. *Patent drawing for William B. Tilton's improvement for the guitar bridge, 1854. Here Tilton proposed using a tailpiece attached, like a violin's, to the bottom of the instrument, and to have the strings go through holes in the bridge pins, presumably to alleviate excess pressure on the top of the instrument. This improvement, coupled with that of 1851, made his guitars very popular.*

provement, he added, the bridge became a fulcrum for increasing the tension of the strings, by the downward action of the pins, with "the advantage gained in tone by the additional string between the pins and the foot" of the instrument (plates 4-9–4-13).[44]

The main point was the increased string length. In this construction, one did not have to brace the guitar as heavily behind the bridge, something that had a tendency to injure the tone of the instrument. Other craftsmen, Tilton observed, had attached the strings at the bottom of guitars, but without his proposed improvement at the bridge, the strings on such instruments were too loose and produced only a "discordant twanging." His patent, he concluded, gave "the requisite tension to the usual length of string, upon which every note is made." Further, the extra string length and the elimination of heavy bracing beneath the bridge area permitted "a vibration which gives a fullness and richness of tone not obtained on any instrument of this character." To make the instrument still lighter, he reminded people, one could also build into the guitar his earlier innovation, the dowel, although this was not absolutely necessary for the application of the present improvement.

These new patents were well-received (fig. 4-9). In 1854, for example, a writer in *Musical World and New York Musical Times* who had played one of Tilton's guitars touted his improvement as "an important one to the Art of music."[45] A year earlier, at the annual fair of the American Institute, the major New York City mechanics' exhibition, Tilton and Company, 65 Chatham Street, had been awarded a silver medal for improvements on the guitar and violin. Two years later, Tilton received another medal from the institute, again for both instruments, and the awards committee noted the Tilton guitar as the best in the show.[46] Tilton showed his instruments elsewhere too. The writer for the *Musical World* observed that the guitar maker "would have obtained another [award] from the Musical Jury of the World's Fair [the Crystal Palace Exhibition] . . . had his improvement been submitted in time to come into competition."[47]

The judges who examined the guitars submitted to the American Institute in 1855 also were convinced that if Tilton's improvements were added to Hall & Son's guitars, such composite instruments would be superior to all other makes.[48] Indeed, as one writer editorialized, one of the chief advantages of Tilton's improvement was that such a change of structure could be easily effected without any detriment to the instrument whatever. Many customers evidently sough this modification, for the *Musical World* noted that Tilton and Company could hardly "attend to all the old instruments which are sent in to be remoddelled [*sic*]." The reporter for *Musical World* opined that he himself had so much faith in Tilton's improvement that he was going to have a "$100 guitar, used in his family, altered conformably thereto." The following week, in his regular advertisement, Tilton himself noted that "the fact that we are improving those [guitars] of Martin's and Schmidt & Maul's make, so justly celebrated as they are," was convincing proof of the success of his innovation.[49]

Appended to James Ballard's *History of the Guitar* are scores of pages of testimonials from people who had seen guitars so modified in such cities as Albany, New York, and Philadelphia. Even Martin's longtime customer William Schubert touted the "improvement," for example, and another of his Philadelphia clients, J. E. Gould, sent at least two lots of instruments, including Martin guitars, to Tilton to be refitted with his improvements. Boardman & Gray of Albany similarly sent Tilton instruments, including Schmidt & Maul guitars, for "improvement." Indeed, at least one Martin guitar modified with some of Tilton's improvements is extant, but no one has yet seen an Ashborn—that is, a "Hall & Son"—guitar so altered.[50]

The main attraction of Tilton's improvements was that they evidently transformed inexpensive, mediocre-sounding violins and guitars into instruments with much improved tonal qualities. Indeed, as Tilton put it, "for a very moderate sum . . . every professional Performer and Every amateur" could "*possess a good Instrument at a reasonable price.*"[51] Thus, by the mid-

Figure 4-9. *Cabinet card, ca. 1880, by R. Miller, North Baltimore, Ohio. Both women have Tilton guitars. The one on the left has a medallion, visible in the sound hole of the guitar, mounted on the instrument's internal dowel. The other has a Tilton tailpiece. (Collection of the author)*

1850s Tilton's two patents had made his guitars and violins so popular that he secured the backing of a wealthy New York businessman, James E. Smith, and erected, at considerable expense, a large factory for the manufacture of violins and guitars that employed a considerable workforce. Tilton even hired a traveling business agent, the "energetic and trustworthy Mr. Augustus Morand, a member of the New York Board of Education," to drum up business among new retailers.[52] Tilton and Smith, and perhaps Morand, constituted Tilton and Company. To puff his guitars even more, Tilton engaged James Ballard, the New York music teacher, to write *A History of the Guitar*, in which he argued that Tilton's recent improvements marked the apogee of the instrument's design. Tilton appended scores of pages of testimonials in a separate advertisement for his instruments.[53]

Before Tilton turned his attention to the banjo, an increasingly popular instrument, he offered the public one more improvement for the guitar.[54] Once again he modified an instrument's construction so that the sounding board vibrated more freely and thus produced a more brilliant tone. In U.S. patent no. 14,378 (March 4, 1856) he proposed a modification in the guitar's bridge to strengthen the instrument and yet make it lighter because, again, not as much bracing was required.

In ordinary guitar construction, Tilton explained, the bridge was quite large because it had to "sustain the strain of the strings and give space to fasten the pegs into." But this reduced the guitar's vibration, something he had tried to address in a different way in his previous patent. Now he proposed paring down the bridge to a minimum size "simply for the purpose of pressure" and connecting it to a metal tailpiece that did not touch the soundboard but lay just above it. This much resembled a violin tailpiece, he noted, but its front end was permanently fixed to the bridge and attached to the bottom of the instrument, providing strength. Because the strings connected to this tailpiece like violin strings, there was no need for bridge pins. Tilton's patentable feature here consisted in "the combination of the bridge and rim of a guitar or other stringed instrument by a tail piece firmly attached to both substantially and in the manner and for the purposes set forth" (fig. 4-10). In this way much of the strain was taken from the bridge, whose size was greatly reduced with the result of better tone.

This innovation proved particularly worthwhile and lucrative. A year after Tilton registered his patent, for example, Horace Waters wrote Martin to see if he would consider making a guitar with just such a bridge.[55] And by about 1860 the New York firm of Ferdinand Zogbaum and Rufus Fairchild had bought the rights to Tilton's patents and was manufacturing guitars prominently stamped with both their label and another indicating the use of Tilton's patent of 1856 on the instrument (plates 4-14, 4-15, 4-16).[56] More important, in the late 1860s John C. Haynes, whom Oliver Ditson of Boston had made head of the musical instrument division of his business, also secured rights to the 1856 patent and manufactured guitars with it.[57] Haynes announced both the patent and its awards prominently on the metal disks and tailpieces of these instruments (fig. 4-11). By then, the Ditson firm, based in Boston, was challenging the supremacy of the New York firms and later in the century, through partnerships in New York, Philadelphia, and Chicago, emerged as a new giant in music publishing. Ditson had full confidence in Haynes's judgment of musical instruments and presumably had given him the go-ahead to secure Tilton's patent.

Tilton thus became the third important player in the New York guitar wars of the 1850s, and his instruments remained a significant presence in the market for the next twenty years (fig. 4-12). In the mid-1860s, for example, one of Martin's clients in Connecticut had a good supply of Tiltons on hand but also wanted to carry some of Martin's models.[58] And in 1868, on a copy of a price list enclosed with one of his receipts, Bruno listed several models of Tilton guitars as well as Martin's complete line of instruments (fig. 4-13). Like Ashborn's unpatented modifications in guitar construction, Tilton's patents offer important examples of the technological experimentation carried out in the 1850s as industrialization began to affect even the most traditional crafts.

Figure 4-10. *Carte-de-visite, ca. 1870. This early promotional photograph for Tilton's guitar shows his 1856 patent, with the tailpiece affixed to the bridge. Here in the sound hole one also sees the silver medallion affixed to the dowel. Elaborately engraved, these medallions carried both Tilton's patent information and the name of the maker to whom Tilton sold or licensed the "improvements." On guitars that Tilton himself made, only his name appears, with a serial number. Compare this with the guitars in fig. 4-9. (Courtesy James F. Bollman)*

In this decade and the next, one sees such technological experimentation everywhere among banjo makers.[59] Even violin makers, among the most conservative artisans, were not above seduction by the lure of such "improvements." In the early 1850s, for example, William Sidney Mount, renowned as an artist but also a musician, patented his own design for a violin. In his description he stressed the commercial advantages of his instrument, for its

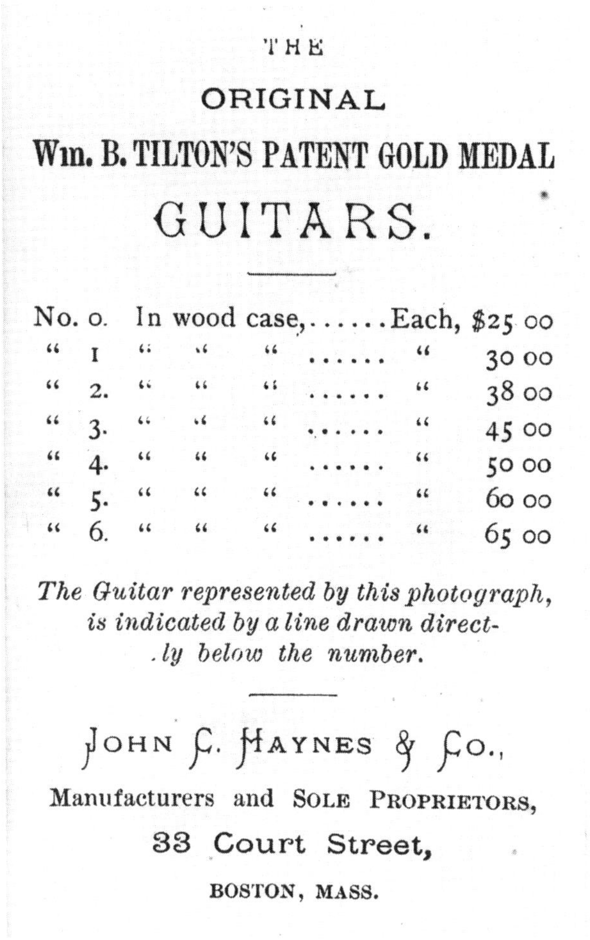

Figure 4-11. *Advertisement (reverse of the carte-de-visite illustrated in fig. 4-10), ca. 1870, for John C. Haynes & Company, Boston, which bought the rights to Tilton's guitar improvements and thereafter prominently advertised Tilton's awards for the designs that he had patented. (Courtesy of James F. Bollman)*

THE

ORIGINAL

Wm. B. TILTON'S PATENT GOLD MEDAL

GUITARS.

No. 0.	In wood case,			......	Each,	$25 00
"	1	"	"	"	......	"	30 00
"	2.	"	"	"	......	"	38 00
"	3.	"	"	"	......	"	45 00
"	4.	"	"	"	......	"	50 00
"	5.	"	"	"	......	"	60 00
"	6.	"	"	"	......	"	65 00

The Guitar represented by this photograph, is indicated by a line drawn direct-
.ly below the number.

JOHN C. HAYNES & CO.,

Manufacturers and SOLE PROPRIETORS,

33 Court Street,

BOSTON, MASS.

manufacture required only twenty-eight or thirty parts, which could be mass-produced, not the fifty-six handmade parts that went into a fully hand-crafted instrument.[60] Martin, however, obviously believed that his guitars represented the apogee of the instrument's form, like, say, a Stradivarius violin. Thus, with the exception of X-bracing, he rejected all such experimentation and opted instead to continue the tradition of artisanry that had always characterized his labors. He never had any trouble finding people to whom to wholesale his instruments, nor customers to buy them. And he continued to offer them on his own terms.

C. A. ZOEBISCH & SONS

By the late 1850s, though, Martin had begun to see the justness of Firth, Pond & Company's suggestion that he avoid the risks—and the loss of time—that came with the jobbing business. But he did not throw in his lot with any of the major New York City music houses. Instead, he shifted more and more of his business to C. A. Zoebisch & Sons, a city firm with family roots in Neukirchen, thus continuing the pattern set since his emigration of patronage of other German immigrants. But this relationship, which grew through

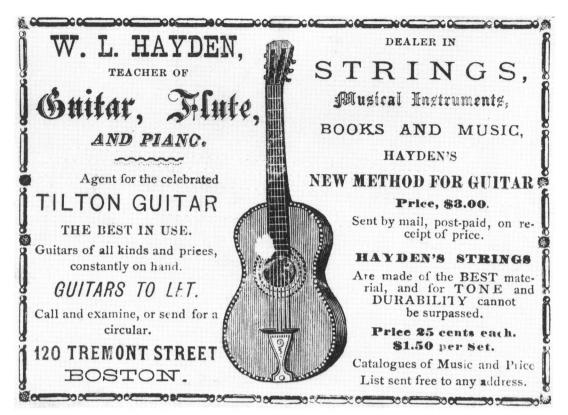

Figure 4-12. *Advertising card for W. L. Hayden, music teacher in Boston, ca. 1875. The illustration is of the same sort of guitar shown in fig. 4-10, with the 1856 patent. Tilton's models remained popular through the 1880s. (Courtesy of James F. Bollman)*

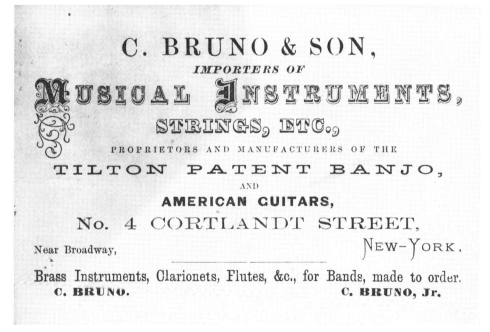

Figure 4-13. *Trade card, ca. late 1870, for C. Bruno & Son, a large New York musical instrument firm that over the years did much business with Martin. Here, however, during a period when he had fallen out with Martin, he prominently announces that he carried Tilton's banjos and guitars.*

the 1860s until C. A. Zoebisch & Sons was Martin's largest (though not his sole) distributor, was not always smooth and took several years to solidify. In the early 1860s, Martin finally gave a majority of his business to Zoebisch & Sons, with the understanding that he would maintain control over the name on his instruments. Unlike Ashborn, who accepted the fact that Hall & Son shamelessly advertised his instruments as "Hall's Guitars," Martin never allowed Zoebisch to claim that it manufactured the guitars that he sold. Rather, the firm had to be content to advertise his facilities as the chief "Depot for C. F. Martin's Celebrated Guitars," and the instruments carried the stamp "C. F. Martin / New-York," from the guitar maker's deference to the city that remained the center of the nation's music trade.[61]

The Zoebisch family had come from Neukirchen and very likely had made brass instruments there. In 1842 Charles A. Zoebisch Jr. (1824–1911) immigrated to the United States and settled near Martin in Cherry Hill, Pennsylvania. His father and the rest of the family, including Charles's brothers Gustav and Herman, arrived five years later and established themselves as musical instrument dealers in the Lancaster area. While in Pennsylvania the family imported musical goods for the Moravian community and also began to manufacture their own brass instruments, which received an award at the American Institute fair in New York City in 1847. By 1847 the family had relocated to that city, with business addresses in that year at 411½ Broadway, then on Mott Street through 1853, and on William Street through the mid-1860s. The patriarch's name disappears from the city directories during the early 1860s, when Charles Jr. took over leadership of the company.[62]

Martin's first recorded business with Zoebisch came in 1849 when, newly established in New York City, Zoebisch ordered several guitars for his store.[63] But given Coupa's and Janon's relationships with Martin through early 1852, Martin believed he already had good representation in the city. After he terminated his arrangement with Janon, Martin turned to J. M. Jaques as his major wholesaler, sending him twenty instruments between September 1852 and mid-February 1853. When Jaques subsequently was bought by Horace Waters as part of that firm's bid to rise to the top of New York's musical world, Waters got the bulk of the guitars Martin shipped to New York, a total of eighty-five through mid-1855. Waters had bought instruments from Martin since at least 1851, adding only two dollars to each guitar purchased from him.[64]

In June 1855, Zoebisch & Sons placed its first order in the new bidding wars and by that fall had taken twenty-seven instruments, all paid for in cash. And during the winter and early spring of 1856, Martin had purchased substantial numbers of tuning machines from the firm, one bill amounting to over two hundred dollars. But the extant correspondence records *no* communication between Martin and Zoebisch from late summer 1856 until 1860, when Martin began to send the firm very large orders. The last of the missives from Zoebisch to Martin, July 29, 1856, had been quite cordial, with Zoebisch himself telling Martin that he had just sent fifteen gallons of wine by express and to look for the shipment the next day in Easton. Martin was to let the wine sit for six to eight days, he added. Then, silence.

Zoebisch's ostensibly unscrupulous business ethics, as reported by other of Martin's customers, caused this interruption in their budding relationship. William M. Peters, one of the sons in a family that by that time owned music emporiums in several of the nation's largest cities, tipped off Martin to Zoebisch's duplicity (fig. 4-14).[65] In the autumn of 1856 Peters had decided to open a store in New York City, territory on which he had not yet marched, and had spoken of his plans to William Schubert, the Philadelphia teacher and longtime Martin customer who had just relocated to the metropolis. In the course of their conversation, the musician had complained about Zoebisch & Sons's wish to retail Martin's guitars in New York. Further, he had provided instances of the firm's having sold them to individual customers at very low rates and reported that he had frequently heard the same from other sources. When Schubert had asked Zoebisch why he undersold the retailers, he replied that he "could not sell them at the Broadway places [that is, in the large music emporiums such as Hall & Son and Firth, Pond & Company], because they controlled the market in that area of the city and was satisfied with the smaller profit."

But Zoebisch & Sons was supposed to be Martin's *wholesale* agent, not a retailer, and therein lay the ethical problem. "The conduct of Mr. Zoebisch surprises me," Peters wrote, "for you remember how tenatious [*sic*] he was of his right as a wholesale agent." Thus, Peters continued indignantly, Zoebisch & Sons should be the last firm to lessen the guitars' value. If Peters and other retail dealers had to get guitars from him, Zoebisch was duty bound not to retail a single guitar in New York, or if he did, he should charge a higher price rather than a lower. Peters knew that Firth, Pond & Company, William Hall & Son, or anyone else to whom Zoebisch & Sons sold Martin's guitars would agree, for by the firm's actions it, too, was injured, for such conduct "would soon prevent safe men from taking the right interest in their sale."

Peters then went to the heart of the matter. Zoebisch & Sons's activities had given him pause about doing business on Broadway, Peters admitted, because he believed the firm sought to monopolize the entire trade, wholesale and retail, in Martin's guitars. Peters lamented that the whole cause of his not getting guitars directly from Martin was not so much Zoebisch & Sons's wanting the small profit it could make from Peters in such transactions. Rather, Zoebisch & Sons did not wish to be deprived of the retail sales it also coveted. And any reduction in the retail prices of Martin's guitars "by a large house like Zoebisch & Sons would be felt throughout the whole United States."

Peters, of course, wanted a piece of the action, specifically in New York. He hoped to induce Martin to let him have a certain number of guitars a year, for which he promised to pay cash. Eventually, he hoped that Martin would make him the sole agent for retail and wholesale in New York City and thus confine Zoebisch & Sons strictly to wholesale in other cities where Martin as yet had no agents. Realizing the presumption of his plan, Peters also admitted that he would settle for the New York retail trade. If Martin agreed to such an arrangement, Peters observed, Zoebisch might pretend to be very angry but eventually would have to accept the change, for "he would not give up for a good deal a half even of what benefit he has in your agency." Peters then urged Martin to keep a promise about at least giving him the agency of the guitars previously earmarked for Horace Waters, with which Martin evidently had terminated business. "I hope soon," Peters said, "to show you I can work to your Interest as well as any of them [the large music companies] if not better as far as New York City is concerned." He ended with a request that, for the immediate future, Martin let the matter rest because Peters did not wish "any difficulty with Mr. Zoebisch." Moreover, he insisted, the information he had provided about the latter's activities were in confidence. "I would not have you use it coming from me," he concluded.

This self-serving missive goes far toward explaining the cooled relation-

First Floor and Salerooms of

JOHN F. STRATTON & CO., 49 Maiden Lane,
NEW YORK.

Figure 4-14. *Back cover of* Catalogue of Holiday Goods Issued by John F. Stratton and Co. *(1882). This interior view of Stratton's large music emporium gives a good idea of the size and scale of the large city firms that vied for Martin's wares in the booming postwar economy. (Courtesy of James F. Bollman)*

ship between Martin and Zoebisch & Sons in the late 1850s. What seemed, in the fall of 1855, like the beginning of a new and important relationship did not materialize for several more years. But neither did Martin grant Peters the agency he wanted. Instead, as Martin's correspondence indicates, after this flurry of courtship by New York entrepreneurs who sought varying kinds of exclusive rights over his instruments, Martin again jobbed his own instruments through the elaborate network of dealers he had cultivated over the previous decade. He sought to hold off the competition by doing what he always had done best: making guitars and marketing them himself.

ASHBORN VERSUS MARTIN

A comparison of Martin's business with Ashborn's and Tilton's in the 1850s raises one more question. Why precisely was Ashborn willing to sell his guitars to William Hall & Son and Firth, Pond & Company so that his own part in their production was subordinated, a course of action that Tilton followed with different firms? It may have had to do with these makers' late entry into the nation's superheated musical instrument market. By the late 1840s, for example, when Ashborn moved to Connecticut to seek Hungerford's backing for a guitar factory, Martin was already well established on the New York music scene. In addition to his personal knowledge of many of the key musicians, craftsmen, and dealers, he also had established connections to performers and teachers in New York City, Philadelphia, and other eastern cities. By the mid-1850s his instruments were even more widely known and appreciated throughout most cities east of the Mississippi (fig. 4-15).

On the other hand, Ashborn presumably had no such entrée to New York City's musical world, and Tilton did not emerge in it until the mid-1850s. Instead both men had a hunch that the manufacture of guitars, given the instrument's rising popularity, could make them financially successful. We also know that Ashborn, in particular, believed that the water- or steam-powered factory made possible a more rapid and efficient production of goods, including musical instruments, which hitherto had been handcrafted. With Hungerford's assistance, he captured the attention of two of New York's largest musical instrument purveyors and convinced them that his product would do as well in the market as Martin's or anyone else's, and at a fraction of the price.

The proof was indeed in the pricing. Horace Waters made two dollars on each Martin guitar that he sold. William Hall & Son was able to *double* the prices at which it bought instruments from Ashborn and still undersold Martin. And its terms called for Ashborn to stamp each instrument with Hall & Son's name on the center strip. Given where Ashborn came from, a world in which goods were beginning to be mass-produced, this concession probably seemed a small price for the greater economic benefit the companies' patronage bestowed.

Figure 4-15. *Sixth-plate tintype, ca. 1860s. Through the 1860s, even with the disruption of the Civil War, there was a steady market for parlor guitars of the sort that Martin produced. Here a budding musician holds her instrument in front of the photographer's painted backdrop. (Collection of Daniel A. Gura)*

More than Tilton, Ashborn proved a real and long-term threat to Martin's supremacy in the market. In 1866, for example, the Chicago music firm of Root & Cady advertised Hall & Son maple guitars at from $25.00 to $30.00 and in rosewood at $30.00 to $50.00. Right next to them were Martin guitars, ranging from $45.00 to $100.00.[66] And as late as 1869 Zoebisch still worried

Plate 4-1. *Half-plate ambrotype, ca. 1860. Through the 1850s Martin continued to have agents in New York City who brought his instruments to the attention of musicians and often supplied a depot for his guitars. The well-dressed man in this ambrotype might well have been a professional player who patronized Martin's representatives. (Courtesy of George Eastman House)*

Plate 4-2.

*Front view of guitar
by James Ashborn,
ca. 1864–65. Stamp of
Firth, Son & Company.
The body is rosewood
veneer and the finger-
board ebony. The
decoration marks the
highest style Ashborn
regularly produced
and, while not marked,
is similar to that on
the no. 6 shown in plate
4-8. (Collection of the
author)*

left

Plate 4-3. *Rear view of the guitar in plate 4-2. (Collection of the author)*

top

Plate 4-4. *Close-up of the sound hole of the guitar in plate 4-2. Notice the elaborate and striking "dog tooth" inlay. Ashborn did not decorate his instruments with the kinds of marquetry found on Martin's guitars, nor with pearl or abalone, but rather with what most resembles intarsia (wood inlay). (Collection of the author)*

Plate 4-5. *Close-up of peg head of the guitar in plate 4-2. Ashborn had his elegant brass tuners made by local craftsmen and had his name stamped on them. Note the hexagonal bone buttons. On his lower-grade models they were made of rosewood. (Collection of the author)*

Plate 4-6. *Close-up of bottom of the guitar in plate 4-2, showing the striking inlay around the end button. (Collection of the author)*

Plate 4-7. *Original case for a James Ashborn guitar. Ashborn made his own cases for his instruments. Several of those extant are similarly lined with cloth of equally striking patterns. (Collection of the author)*

Plate 4-8.

*Front view of guitar
by James Ashborn,
style no. 6, ca. 1854.
Stamp of William Hall
& Son. While very
similar to the guitar
shown in plate 4-2, the
inlay pattern on this
instrument is more
rounded than sharp-
toothed. The rosette
around the end pin
also is different and
matches the design
around the top of the
body. (Courtesy of
Tony Creamer)*

Plate 4-9.
Front view of William B. Tilton guitar, no. 275, ca. 1853–54. This instrument, whose silver medallion carries only Tilton's name and the 1851 patent notice, was very likely built by Tilton himself. In addition to the dowel running through the body, it features bridge pins with holes through them for the strings, a feature he patented in 1854. Thus, the guitar probably was built just before he patented this new kind of bridge. It is fan braced. (Courtesy of Bailey Adams)

Plate 4-10. *Back view of Tilton guitar in plate 4-9. The back is made of two pieces of rosewood, but the sides are very unusual. They are rounded and are built up from twenty-one rosewood laminations, and there is no lining. The binding is maple and the fingerboard, stained maple. The heel shape is also unusual. (Courtesy of Bailey Adams)*

Plate 4-11. *Close-up of the bridge on the Tilton guitar in plate 4-9. Notice the unusual bone bridge pins, with holes through them for the strings and capped with beautiful abalone, and the separate, signed tailpiece. Tilton patented both these features in 1854. (Courtesy of Bailey Adams)*

Plate 4-12. *Close-up of the tuning machines on the Tilton guitar in plate 4-9. They are signed "Jerome" and feature ivory buttons in a striking sculptured design. Martin, too, used Jeromes on his higher-end guitars (see plate 5-12). (Courtesy of Bailey Adams)*

Plate 4-13. *Close-up of the silver medallion on the Tilton guitar in plate 4-9. It sits on the patented dowel which goes through the instrument from heel to end and which was its patented feature. Unlike late Tilton "patent" instruments, this one carries only Tilton's name and not that of a manufacturer (see plate 4-16). This strongly suggests that Tilton himself made this instrument. (Courtesy of Bailey Adams)*

Plate 4-14.
Front view of Zogbaum and Fairchild guitar, ca. 1860–68, with William B. Tilton's patent improvements. The silver medallion in the sound hole is mounted on the patented dowel that Tilton built into his instruments, and the strings go through, not over, the bridge (compare with plate 4-11). The tailpiece is not original. In the 1856 patent it is actually connected to the bridge. (Collection of the author)

left

Plate 4-15. *Rear view of the guitar in plate 4-14. The light color in the rosewood is heartwood. (Collection of the author)*

top

Plate 4-16. *Close-up of the engraved silver medallion on the guitar in plate 4-14. It carries Zogbaum and Fairchild's name and indicates as well that the guitar has Tilton's various patented improvements. There is a serial number stamped on the back of the peg head and not on the medallion, as on the guitar in plate 4-9. (Collection of the author)*

Figure 4-16. *Cabinet card, ca. 1875. This elegant woman, playing a large guitar comparable to Martin's size 0, typifies the nation's infatuation with the guitar as a parlor instrument in the post–Civil War period. In these years, Martin's guitars retained their supremacy in the market. (Collection of the author)*

about Ashborn's contracts in the city, now with William A. Pond, who had taken over his father's business in the early 1860s. Zoebisch told Martin that he had convinced Pond to sell Martin's guitars, but Zoebisch could not yet get him to take many of them. Pond still wanted to "feel the market," Zoebisch continued, but he thought it a victory that Pond had even begun to stock Martin's guitars. Pond's father, of course, had long traded with Martin's rival Ashborn, and by making headway with Pond's successor, Zoebisch believed that he could "drive the Ashburn [*sic*] Guitars out of the market."[67]

New York's guitar wars of the 1850s proved at least one thing: the vitality of the American guitar trade and its undeniable success in vanquishing the European competition. As a writer for *Musical World* put it in 1854, though there were some "doubters and cavillers" who did not believe that anything good could come out of Nazareth or New York, the quality of American instruments such as those of Martin, Ashborn, and Tilton put such chattering to rest. And in the same year, in his *Encyclopaedia of Music*, John W. Moore observed that "the demand for this beautiful and graceful instrument has of late so increased that several American houses had commenced the manufacture of them." He had recently seen some of these native instruments, he added, made after the Spanish model. They were of superior tone and finish and, made in the United States, would stand the severest tests of the climate.[68] Moore also observed that the guitar now had come into very general use, so that Martin, Ashborn, and other American makers—Tilton and Schmidt & Maul in New York City, for example, and John Berwind in Philadelphia— had plenty of opportunities to carve up the market share (fig. 4-16).[69]

By this date, if New York did not offer the passe-partout to success in the industry, its competitive music houses and dealers certainly fired the competition to produce more and better instruments for this trade. And while Ashborn's lucrative business with Hall & Son did not survive beyond the 1860s and Tilton's patent found only a small niche, Martin's reputation continued to grow, his instruments everywhere described as "Martin's celebrated guitars."[70] This renown had much to do with the latter's unwillingness to capitulate fully to a manufacturing and marketing system that, in various ways, finally devalued one's products. It remained to be seen whether Martin could continue his independence and financial success into the 1870s, when mass production became de rigueur among most musical instrument manufacturers.

Ensuring the Legacy, 1857–1873

THE PANIC OF 1857

In the autumn of 1857, as Martin continued to job his own guitars, he received an apologetic letter from longtime client Jonathan B. West in Nashville. Martin recently had dunned West for payment on a shipment of guitars, and West explained that he had had ample funds, deposited in the Bank of Nashville, to meet all his debts. But this institution, he continued, had suspended payment so that he could not access his money. "Our Currency is very much deranged," he reported, and "no exchange [is] to be had at any price." West did not do enough business to cover even his store expenses, he told Martin with some embarrassment. Moreover, he did not think that he would be able to make a payment until the next year, when he hoped to receive a dividend on some deposited funds. West promised, however, that Martin would not "loose [sic] anything" by him.[1]

West was describing firsthand the debilitating effects of the panic of 1857, one of the most serious antebellum depressions, and unfortunately, among Martin's customers his story was not unique. The Washington, D.C., firm of Hilbus & Heitz, close enough to Martin for him to entrust the partners with his Crystal Palace guitar to display at local mechanics' fairs, also had failed. In 1858 John Heitz apologetically told Martin that his present income did not enable him to cancel even in part the debt owed Martin by Hilbus & Heitz. Now living in Leesburg, Virginia, Heitz sincerely hoped that his prospects would improve, for nothing would please him more than to liquidate the debt.[2] Martin no doubt knew that when Firth, Pond & Company, Horace Waters, and other large firms tried to convince him to sell his instruments exclusively to them on an immediate cash basis, their sheer size somewhat protected them (and thus him) from the personal and financial embarrassment and hardship such economic downturns engendered.

The nation's first large-scale financial panic had occurred in 1837, just before Martin left New York for Pennsylvania. The following two decades saw the emergence of an extensive market economy characterized by industrialization, new transportation and communication systems, and complex financial networks of credit and exchange. But as the historian Edward Balleisen puts it, "even as impersonal market exchange was fostered by heightened application of division of labor, development of a sophisticated banking system, growth of large, anonymous cities, tied to ever-expanding hinterlands, and transformations in the law of negotiable instruments, intensely personal relationships continued to mediate entrepreneurial schemes and strategies." The new economy was structured "as much around borrowed money and promises of payment as it was around the routes of rivers, canals, and . . . railroads."[3] Thus, we read of the embarrassment and chagrin of such dealers as West, Hilbus & Heitz, and others who paid Martin with promissory notes and counted on selling their goods before these notes came due, only to be blindsided by the economic crisis.

Unfortunately, Martin's accounts for 1857 and 1858 are missing, but extant correspondence indicates that during these years he received regular orders from his long-term customers, particularly W. C. Peters in Cincinnati and Miller & Beacham in Baltimore, and as well from a newer client, C. F. Meyer, in Lexington, Kentucky. Martin's deposits at the Easton (Pennsylvania) Bank speak to the significance of these clients as well as another, Charles Bruno, who reappears in Martin's records in 1858 with the purchase of significant numbers of instruments for the business he had recently opened in New York. But the panic indeed affected Martin, for we miss the large-scale expansion into new markets that had characterized his business five years earlier. After 1856, a new client rarely appears in his records.

Fragmentary accounts indicate the income Martin drew from the business during the 1850s and thus allow one to gauge, at least partially, how the panic affected him. From 1854 through 1856, for example, he paid himself at the rate of $9.00 a week, for a total of $468.00 in wages each year. At the first of the year in 1854 and 1855, he further credited himself from his daybook for about $360.00, presumably profit from the business itself, but this payment fell to $240.00 at the beginning of 1856, which marks the beginning of the economic downturn. The detailed records stop at that date, but the next entry, for January 1, 1859, reads "credit from April 1st 1856 to date, $685.09," indicating an annual amount near the 1856 level. Clearly, the country's economic difficulties affected Martin, as they did so many other business owners throughout the eastern half of the country.

THE CIVIL WAR YEARS

In the late 1850s Frederick Martin relocated from Cherry Hill to Nazareth proper, a move which suggests the family's success in weathering the financial depression (figs. 5-1, 5-2). Since its founding in the 1740s as a closed community administered by the Moravian Church, Nazareth had developed under the strict control of a church council. But persistent financial difficulties through the early nineteenth century persuaded the church fathers gradually to relinquish their oversight. For example, by the 1850s they had begun to allow nonchurch members to rent farmland from the religious community. Finally, in the spring of 1854, the church council decided to sell off some of the church's assets and thus opened Nazareth to new economic activity. Within a few years it became a flourishing, secular business community, its cabinetmakers, carriage and coach makers, and blacksmiths now joined by druggists, harness and saddle makers, tobacconists and jewelers, and even a millinery store owner.[4]

Figure 5-1. *Photograph of Christian Frederick Martin Jr., known as "Frederick" or "Fritz," late 1870s. During this decade C. F. Martin shared more and more of his business responsibilities with his son and in 1867 formed a partnership with him and his cousin, C. F. Hartmann. (Courtesy of C. F. Martin & Company Archives)*

With his father's backing, in August 1857 Frederick took advantage of these new economic opportunities and purchased an entire block on North Main and High Streets for $685.00. Two years later, at a cost of $2,900.00, he built a large residence on the corner of the two streets (fig. 5-3).[5] Behind it, he and his father constructed a large workshop where they continued to make guitars (fig. 5-4).[6] There is nothing to indicate that they installed equipment other than that which they had bought for the Cherry Hill works a few years earlier. This new outbuilding on Frederick's home lot constituted the factory works through Martin Sr.'s lifetime.

Martin himself did not move from Cherry Hill to Nazareth until 1862, but from 1859 on, he (as well as his son) became more involved with the Moravian community in Nazareth. For example, he regularly performed simple repair work for students and teachers at Nazareth Hall and also for members of what, in a small account book of this period, he called the "Nazareth Congregation." His most frequent task was the repair—by which he probably meant the rehairing—of violin bows, at the rate of $.13 each. He also took in drums, providing new heads, at $1.25 each and regularly sold small quantities of strings for violins and cellos.[7] Clearly, he was seen as the town's chief resource for this kind of work.

As the nation tumbled into the chaos of the Civil War, however, Martin's

Figure 5-2. *Photograph, ca. 1870s, of Lucinda Rebecca Leibfried, Frederick Martin's second wife, whom he married in 1862. (Courtesy of C. F. Martin & Company Archives)*

business, like so much of the northern economy not related directly to the war effort, was hit hard. In the census of 1860, for example, for the year ending June 1, 1860, Martin reported strong business. He listed $2,000 capital invested in real and personal estate in his business and had on hand $1,800 in raw materials. He employed four workers whose salaries cost him $144 a month and who helped him manufacture about 300 guitars a year, valued at $6,000.[8] From extant accounts we see that, just before the outbreak of hostilities, Martin's sales remained robust, with 243 instruments manufactured in 1859 at a worth of about $5,200 and close to 300 through 1860, as he reported (see Appendix F).

The next two years, however, saw a large drop in Martin's production and income. In 1861 he produced only eighty-two guitars, worth about $1,600, and eighty-five the following year, at a value of close to $1,900. For some inexplicable reason, sales rebounded at the midpoint of the war, for in 1863 he produced 204 guitars, worth over $4,800. This trend continued through the first half of 1864 (when this set of records ends), with 165 instruments manufactured, at a value of close to $3,400.

As one might expect, Martin's customer base shrank considerably during the first years of the war. In 1859 and 1860, for example, he had had about

Figure 5-3. *Martin guitar factory on North Street, adjacent to Frederick Martin homestead (behind tree on right). (From* Two Centuries of Nazareth, 1740–1940 *[1940])*

Figure 5-4. *Lithograph of the Martin family residence, a vignette from a bird's-eye-view map of the community made in 1885. The Martins's partner and relative, C. F. Hartmann, built right aside Frederick, and his home looks more like that pictured in fig. 5.3. The guitar manufactory is visible to the left of the picture. (Courtesy of Rare Books and Manuscripts, Boston Public Library)*

twenty different clients, some of whom took large shipments, others but a guitar or two. In 1860 and 1861, however, his years of restricted production, these numbers fell to eight and twelve, respectively. Further, as he pulled out of the war years, Martin either did not regain or did not seek to expand his customer base. Instead, he returned to the pattern developed in the immediate prewar years and sold larger and more frequent shipments to fewer firms. In particular, Martin favored three music houses: C. A. Zoebisch & Sons, Charles Bruno (or between 1860 and 1862, Bruno & Morris) of New York City, and Peters & Sons (or, later, Peters & Brothers) of Cincinnati (fig. 5-5).[9] In the years covered by the extant accounts, 70 to 80 percent of production went to these three firms, the largest shares going to the New York dealers.

Two complementary documents indicate the factory's full rebound by the war's end. In a manuscript "Statement of Shop in 1864," Martin noted $1,975.00 for wages of his employees, $1,800.00 in materials for 200 guitars (at $9.00 each, presumably his cost), and $1,210.00 for 110 more guitars (at $11.00 each). He also listed his receipts for 310 guitars at $6,322.00. After all expenses, Martin's calculated his profit as $831.00. His statement of income for his annual taxes to the United States Internal Revenue for 1865, based in part on this summary, corroborates these figures. Under expenses he listed the rent of his manufactory at $60.00, fuel at $45.00, wages for employees of $2,325.00, and $2,546.73 for taxes and material. He noted $5,001.73 in total deductions and $6,322.00 in receipts, for an income of $1,291.73. This difference in income from that listed on the "Statement of Shop" is probably due to Martin's inclusion, for tax purposes, of his and his son's wages in the expenses.[10]

In these years the reappearance in Martin's records of Charles Bruno, of whom there had been no trace since Martin left for Nazareth almost two decades earlier, comes as a surprise. After a hiatus of a decade or so, Bruno had resurfaced in New York in 1851 as a partner in Bruno & Cargill, manufacturers and importers of instruments, first at 62 Liberty Street and then at 47 Maiden Lane, which displayed at the Crystal Palace Exhibition. This partnership lasted until 1853. A year later Bruno teamed up with Herman W. Wiessenborn in Bruno, Weissenborn & Company, instrument makers at 2 Maiden Lane, an arrangement that lasted until 1857. At that point Bruno reappears in Martin's records and for the next several years ordered large numbers of guitars. Indeed, immediately before and during the Civil War, only C. A. Zoebisch & Sons provided Martin with more income. Moreover, Bruno, like Zoebisch, received Martin's largest discount, 10 percent off regular wholesale (other firms received only 5 percent), for a total of around 30 percent.[11]

Despite the indictment by William M. Peters of Zoebisch & Sons's duplicity in representing Martin's guitars, Martin and Zoebisch were reconciled,

Figure 5-5. *Carte-de-visite, ca. 1861–64, of members of the 99th Regiment, Ohio Volunteer Infantry. This rare image shows soldiers, whose regiment saw much service in Tennessee and Georgia, in the field with their instruments. Interestingly, they carry the full complement of minstrel show instruments—banjo, violin, tambourine, triangle, and bones, as well as a guitar, held by the soldier in the middle. Martin's sales declined a bit in the first years of the war but later rebounded. (Courtesy of James F. Bollman)*

for the firm remained by far Martin's largest buyer during the war years. By the mid-1860s Zoebisch & Sons had eclipsed Bruno as Martin's chief representative in the city (fig. 5-6). In 1859, for example, shortly after Bruno's reappearance on Martin's books, he handled 63 instruments, to Zoebisch & Sons's 84; the following year, 81 to the latter's 123. But once the war began, Zoebisch & Sons won supremacy: Bruno and his new partner Morris only took 7 in 1861, to Zoebisch & Sons's 35. The pattern repeated itself the next year, with Bruno and Morris taking 6 to the latter's 39. In 1863, when Martin's business began to recover, the proportion stayed the same: 22 for Bruno and Morris and 118 for Zoebisch & Sons. For whatever reason—perhaps it was still the German connection—during the 1860s Martin felt confident entrusting more and more of his guitars to this one firm. As we shall see, within a few years he would have more than enough reason completely to halt his dealings with Bruno. With regard to the mid-1860s, however, Martin evidently found his relationship with Zoebisch satisfying and lucrative.

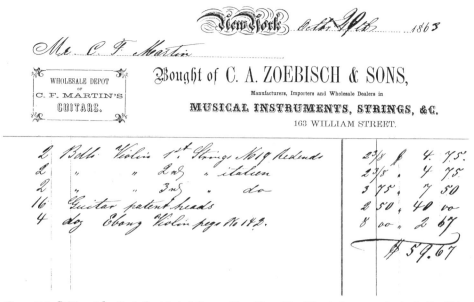

C. F. MARTIN & COMPANY, 1867

The eulogist at Martin's funeral in 1873 recalled that Martin had suffered a stroke twenty years earlier but had made a full recovery. This accords with Stephen Hess's comment, in a letter to C. F. Hartmann in 1855, that he was sorry to hear that Mr. Martin was not enjoying good health.[12] But it also suggests that, by the time Frederick moved to Nazareth and brought the factory with him, his father might have begun to think about passing on more and more control of the business (figs. 5-7, 5-8).[13] By this time, too, the younger Martin had a large family to support.[14] Thus, at the age of seventy, with grandchildren all around him, Martin transferred key parts of his holdings to Frederick. At the end of April 1866, Martin paid off the $1,100 mortgage on the property on North Main Street and also drew out $3,200, the "Money advanced on House & Lot, No. 29 N. Main St." He then gave Frederick the "House & Lots No. 33 & 35 North Main St. as specified in Deed of April 9th," a transaction worth $2,000, as well as $3,000 more (presumably from the money advanced against his own property), "by Gift as general division." By their signatures, father and son indicated their consent to this accounting.[15]

An even more far-reaching financial realignment occurred the next year. In a handwritten document dated July 20, Martin took into the business as full partners both his son and his nephew, Christian Frederick Hartmann. The latter had come to the United States in 1839 and had lived for many years in the Nazareth area, working both as a farmer and in Martin's guitar factory. Clearly, the patriarch believed that he could trust Hartmann to main-

left:

Figure 5-7. *Carte-de-visite by Philip Zorn, 730 Spring Garden Street, Philadelphia, ca. 1867, the only extant photograph of C. F. Martin. (Courtesy of C. F. Martin & Company Archives)*

right:

Figure 5-8. *Carte-de-visite by Philip Zorn, 730 Spring Garden Street, Philadelphia, ca. 1867, of Ottilie Martin, C. F. Martin's wife, taken at the same sitting as the image in fig. 5-7. (Courtesy of C. F. Martin & Company Archives)*

tain and forward the firm's prospects. Henceforth, guitars left Nazareth stamped "C. F. Martin & Co."

The agreement itself was fairly brief. It made the three men equal partners in the newly constituted entity after the two junior members each contributed an amount based on the value of Martin's stock and fixtures, appraised at $2,000, and the shop, valued at $900. An "Inventory of Stock and Fixtures taken on entering in Copartnership," part of a daybook from that period, provides a snapshot of the business at that moment (see Appendix G). In addition to large stocks of rosewood, cedar, ebony, spruce, and basswood, Martin listed a "circular saw," and two "spinning machines" (presumably for winding strings), two "turning lathes," a "rolling machine," and many other supplies, including fifty dollars' worth of "models" (molds to shape the guitars' sides) and fifty dollars' worth of "pearl shells." The shop also was furnished with four work benches and seventy-five dollars' worth of "fixtures and tools."

To finance their investment, Frederick Martin and Hartmann each took out two bonds, for $667 and $300 (that is, about a third of the estimated value), payable with interest to Martin, as their investment in the new firm. Another provision named the elder Martin the partner responsible for business correspondence, financial records, and bank transactions for the new company. The three men were equally to divide profits from the business after expenses. Similarly, they met equally any expenses the business incurred. Finally, they agreed to announce their partnership for the next six months by printed notices inserted in all business correspondence (fig. 5-9). A bill from the Moravian Publication Office in Bethlehem in August of that year records work done for "100 Notices," presumably the announcements specified in the agreement (fig. 5-10).

Although this new business entity did not relieve Martin of many of the duties he had performed for decades (he probably did not want it to), it ensured that, as he grew older, his younger partners could maintain the business at a level of craftsmanship that always had been its hallmark. The partnership also prepared Martin's business for the fiercely competitive marketplace of the Gilded Age.

THE FACTORY IN THE LATE 1860S AND EARLY 1870S

Through the late 1860s and early 1870s Martin produced between 164 and 309 guitars a year (see Appendix H).[16] His largest output came in 1869, when C. A. Zoebisch & Sons, trying to corner the market with Martin's guitars, called on him to ship as many as thirty instruments at a time. After inexplicably low production (188) the following year, Martin rebounded and until his death in 1873 produced close to 250 instruments per year. He continued to do most of his business with Zoebisch & Sons, with Bruno a distant second until 1869, when Martin ceased all dealings with him, which I discuss below. Martin's main Philadelphia customers now were Richard Schmidt and Lee & Walker, though Louis Tripp (later Tripp & Linton) also placed orders regularly.

By this time Martin had developed a line of instruments of standard size and ornamentation. He sold most of the very plain style 17. Some of his customers, however, also continued to request fancier, pearl-decorated styles, and even the very small guitars, nos. 4 and 5. A few even ordered a fairly unusual "ten-string guitar," most likely a harp guitar, of which one is extant (plates 5-1–5-4).[17] Martin and a few employees manufactured all these instruments at the one-story North Main Street factory, virtually unchanged since he had built it in 1859. Two receipts issued to Frederick from the Lebanon Mutual Insurance Company in 1868 (in the company archives) indicate that he valued his home and the factory and its contents at $3,000 and $3,675, but unfortunately we lack the full policies and thus do not know which property was insured at which amount.

Although Martin was now in his seventies and had suffered a stroke, he did

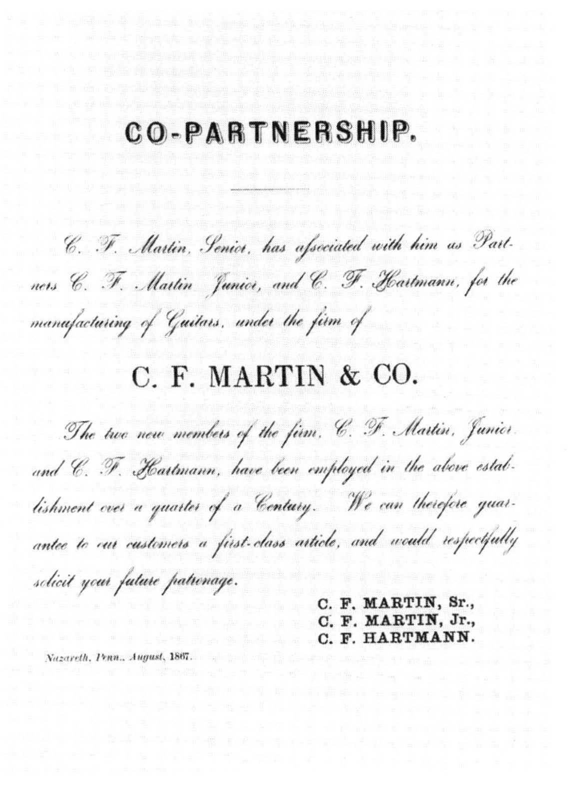

CO-PARTNERSHIP.

C. F. Martin, Senior, has associated with him as Partners C. F. Martin, Junior, and C. F. Hartmann, for the manufacturing of Guitars, under the firm of

C. F. MARTIN & CO.

The two new members of the firm, C. F. Martin, Junior, and C. F. Hartmann, have been employed in the above establishment over a quarter of a Century. We can therefore guarantee to our customers a first-class article, and would respectfully solicit your future patronage.

C. F. MARTIN, Sr.,
C. F. MARTIN, Jr.,
C. F. HARTMANN.

Nazareth, Penn., August, 1867.

Figure 5-9. *Printed sheet, C. F. Martin & Company copartnership agreement, 1867. C. F. Martin, his son Frederick, and C. F. Hartmann agreed, among other things, to insert this notice in all correspondence for six months following the agreement. (Courtesy of C. F. Martin & Company Archives)*

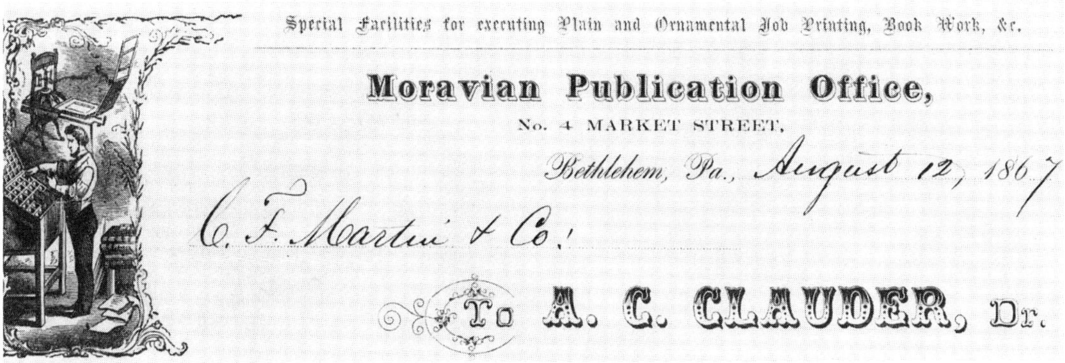

Special Facilities for executing Plain and Ornamental Job Printing, Book Work, &c.

Moravian Publication Office,
No. 4 MARKET STREET,
Bethlehem, Pa., August 12, 1867
C. F. Martin & Co.
To A. C. CLAUDER, Dr.

Figure 5-10. *Billhead of Moravian Publication Office, Bethlehem, Pennsylvania, 1867, on the bill for printing one hundred copartnership notices. (Courtesy of C. F. Martin & Company Archives)*

not withdraw from his craft in the factory. He, Frederick, and C. F. Hartmann still comprised the core of skilled workers in the company. But like James Ashborn, who in his Connecticut guitar factory had hired people at different rates depending on their skills and the demands of their tasks, Martin also began to differentiate among his employees and their labor. For example, he employed Augustus Clewell, from a family of woodworkers in nearby Schoeneck, to make guitar cases at $1.25 each. In 1868 this woodworker produced 178 cases worth $222.50.[18] Christian Blum of nearby Filetown also made cases for the company but, for some reason, only at the rate of $1.12½ per unit. In 1868 he was paid for 176 cases. The total that Clewell and he manufactured that year—over 350—jibes with Martin's own yearly production of guitars, though this estimate has to be adjusted downward slightly because he occasionally sold cases separately, at $32.00 a dozen, to Zoebisch & Sons.

Clewell and Blum worked at the lower end of the wage scale, but Martin also employed a few other men to work on the guitars themselves. In 1868, for example, Reinhold Schuster of Nazareth worked 208 days at $2.00 per day and continued to work into 1869 at that same rate. H. A. Goetz, also of Nazareth, who received $9.00 per week, joined him. In his ledger on January 24, 1868, Martin posted twenty-four weeks of work beside Goetz's name. In the 1860s and early 1870s, Schuster and Goetz appear to have been the only other skilled employees, but Martin occasionally hired other crafts workers. In 1870, for example, for several months Hiram Johnson appears at the rate of $10.00 a week, and in 1867 he paid one Knobloch ten dollars for "carving necks." Martin added other men as orders dictated. Even with these additional individuals joining the two Martins and Hartmann, in these years the factory operated on an intimate scale.[19]

Martin's expenses had not changed greatly since the 1850s. He procured some materials locally, particularly the coal he needed for his steam engine and some of the wood for guitar building.[20] But he continued to obtain many of his other supplies, imported and domestic, through New York. In 1869, for example, he bought a huge cedar log (for guitar necks) from P. M. Dingee, a "commission merchant in foreign and domestic woods," on the East River.[21] Occasionally, Martin had such logs sawn by the dealer himself. In 1873, for example, he bought 980 feet of sawed holly and 160 feet of sawed rosewood from A. Parker & Company at 166 Centre Street in the city (fig. 5-11). Other times he brought his rare woods to some other firms for processing. In 1871, for example, Julius Rayner charged him $12.00 for sawing three rosewood logs. A year later, in a more detailed bill, he charged $54.52 for sawing 462 feet of rosewood, $3.60 for "Slab[b]ing Rosewood 12 cuts," $2.60 for "Trucking" a total of 5,200 pounds of it, and $13.52 more for "*Lumber, labor, nails &c for boxes*," presumably in which to ship it.[22]

Martin needed other exotic, and expensive, materials available only through New York or other port cities. In 1867, for example, he bought an ivory tusk, for inlay and binding work, from Henry Ingalls in New York, at a cost of $172.25. As extraordinary as that price sounds, Martin always paid dearly for this item, with which he decorated his higher-end guitars. In November 1869 he bought another tusk, from Brown & Greene at 165 Water Street, for $228.54.

With the same shipment came, at $1.40, a more mundane but necessary commodity that Martin usually acquired from F. Marx & Company (later Marx & R. A. Wolle), "Manufacturers of Coach, Carriage, and Furniture Varnishes," but which by 1871 he purchased in Nazareth from R. F. Babp & Company. Thomas Hartzell also supplied such goods, in May 1869 providing

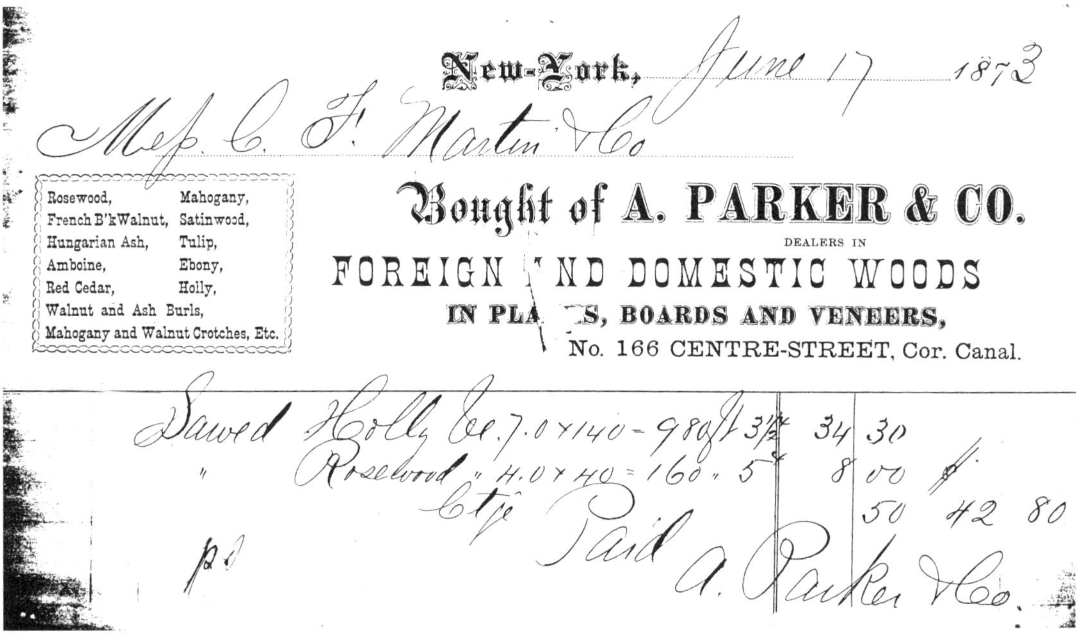

New-York, June 17 1873

Mess. C. F. Martin & Co

Rosewood, Mahogany,
French B'k Walnut, Satinwood,
Hungarian Ash, Tulip,
Amboine, Ebony,
Red Cedar, Holly,
Walnut and Ash Burls,
Mahogany and Walnut Crotches, Etc.

Bought of A. PARKER & CO.

DEALERS IN

FOREIGN AND DOMESTIC WOODS

IN PLANKS, BOARDS AND VENEERS,

No. 166 CENTRE-STREET, Cor. Canal.

Sawed Holly Ve. 7.0 × 140 = 980 ft 3½ 34 30
" Rosewood " 4.0 × 40 = 160 " 5 8 00
Ctg 50 42 80

Paid A. Parker & Co.

Figure 5-11. *Billhead of A. Parker & Company, New York City, 1873, indicating that Martin had holly and rosewood logs sawed for him. (Courtesy of C. F. Martin & Company Archives)*

Martin five gallons of linseed oil and a quantity of brown paint, brushes, and other similar items, for $18.39. Schoonmaker & Close, 5 Chatham Square in New York, a dealer in paints, oils, and paperhangings, also on occasion provided glue (fig. 5-12). If Martin needed hardware for the cases Clewell and Blum made, he acquired it from firms such as Hubinger & Krumm, dealers in hardware and cutlery, at 188 Grand Street, or from W. N. Seymour & Company at 4 Chatham Square. In the inventory Martin made in 1867, Martin listed fifty dollars' worth of "Case Trimmings."[23]

One bill from Seymour (March 18, 1868) carries this notation: "Bill to Zoebisch & Sons / 46 Maiden Lane, N.Y." Frequently, Martin acquired supplies in this manner, through Zoebisch & Sons, which then forwarded shipments to Martin by Hope's Express Company. This was particularly the case with glues, varnishes, and shellacs, essential and quickly utilized materials. In the late 1860s and early 1870s, Zoebisch & Sons also became Martin's main supplier of the geared tuning machines now common on Martin's guitars. These were expensive imported items often in short supply. Zoebisch usually charged $2.00 a set, but one lot that he provided cost $2.75 per unit. In the summer of 1872, for example, Zoebisch wrote Martin that he "went out to see whether we couldn't get any Pat[ent]. Heads we can use, but nobody has any, the dealers out there don't get them to furnish customers here, all sell only cheap make[s]."[24] Martin acquired them whenever and wherever he could, including a shipment of five dozen from Bruno on April 18, 1868, at $2.00 a set, the same price Zoebisch usually asked. Another dependable source was Klemm & Brother of Philadelphia, to which he also often turned for imported strings.

Figure 5-12. *Billhead of S. Schoonmaker, New York City, 1864. This firm provided Martin with glue for the construction of his guitars. (Courtesy of C. F. Martin & Company Archives)*

Silk thread for winding the heavier strings that Martin's workers produced also came from Philadelphia, most commonly from John J. Smith, silk manufacturers, at 15 North Fourth Street and later from the firm of which Smith became president, the Williams Silk Manufacturing Company. Martin also frequently patronized Richard T. Schmidt, who dealt in Italian strings at 610 Arch Street. In February 1870 Martin bought $75.33 worth of this commodity, the entire shipment designated as "Roman" strings. John Sherman, at 52 Beekman Street, agent for the Waterbury Brass Company in Waterbury, Connecticut, supplied silver wire, wrapped around a silk core for the wound heavier strings that Martin manufactured.

MARTIN'S LINE OF GUITARS

By the early 1870s Martin was producing a line of guitars in standard sizes and ornamentation.[25] Most styles were specific to certain body sizes, unless one requested a special order. He identified the sizes by numbers that he had begun to use with some customers in the 1850s, namely, from largest to smallest: 0, 1, 2, 2½, 3. His own printed description reads "No. 3—Small Size. No. 2½ and 2—Ladies' Size. No. 1—Large Size. No. 0—Largest Concert Size" (see Appendix I). In addition, one could special-order the tiny no. 4 or no. 5, which were tuned a third higher than standard guitar tuning.

Martin signaled the degree of ornamentation by a second number, from the style 17, the simplest, through the 42, which was richly decorated with pearl. As one moved up from the 17, the styles were determined first by degrees of wooden marquetry around the sound hole, top, and back and center seams, and then by similar work done in ivory or pearl (see Appendix J and plates 5-5–5-9). Martin's choice of wood for the body still was rosewood, though he occasionally made mahogany-bodied instruments (plates 5-10–5-14). The necks were usually of cedar—hence, his purchase of the large logs from Dingee in New York—and his fingerboards, of ebony or rosewood.

The earliest extant price list for Martin's guitars comes from a manuscript appended to a bill from Bruno and labeled "Price List as ordered to be printed April 28, 1868" (see fig. 5-13).[26] The amounts for some of these sizes and styles on Bruno's printer's copy ranged from $24.00 for a 2½- or 3-17 to $36.00 for a 1-26 that was ivory bound, to $60.00 for a 2-42, with pearl decoration and a "screw neck" of the kind that Martin had produced earlier in his career (see Chapter 2). Interestingly, at the bottom of this sheet Bruno also included a "List of Tiltons," at $30.00, $38.00, and $45.00 for instruments of varying ornamentation with ebony pegs, and $38.00 and $55.00 for those with ivory pegs.

In 1874, a year after Martin's death, Zoebisch began to print his retail price list on the back of his stationery (fig. 5-14).[27] By that time the same Martin models (that is, a 3-17, a 1-26, and a 2-42) were priced at $36.00, $54.00, and $90.00, respectively, with comparable increases for all other models, the same as those listed by Bruno. The amount of these differences—33⅓ percent—suggests that Bruno intended his as wholesale prices. Also, Zoebisch's amounts included both the cases that Martin's workers made and the proper packing of the instrument to prevent damage in transit.

Through this period Martin used both the fan bracing typical of Spanish-school instruments and also X-bracing. As noted above, however, from the 1850s on other makers also used this latter method, and another maker actually patented this construction feature. On December 24, 1867, Joseph E. Bini, of Mount Vernon, New York, took out U.S. patent no. 72,591 for an "Improvement in Bracing the Sounding-Boards of Guitars," assigning it immediately to James E. Jouett and Charles H. Cushman (fig. 5-15). Little is known of Bini, but he was probably related to the "veteran guitarist" who played with Schnepf at a concert in 1844 and was active through the 1850s.[28] And he probably was the same "J. B. Bini" who appears in Martin's ledger for 1837–38 at 302 Hudson Street, charged twenty dollars for sundries, and for whom there is an early receipt, from 1836, to Martin and Bruno for ten dollars.[29]

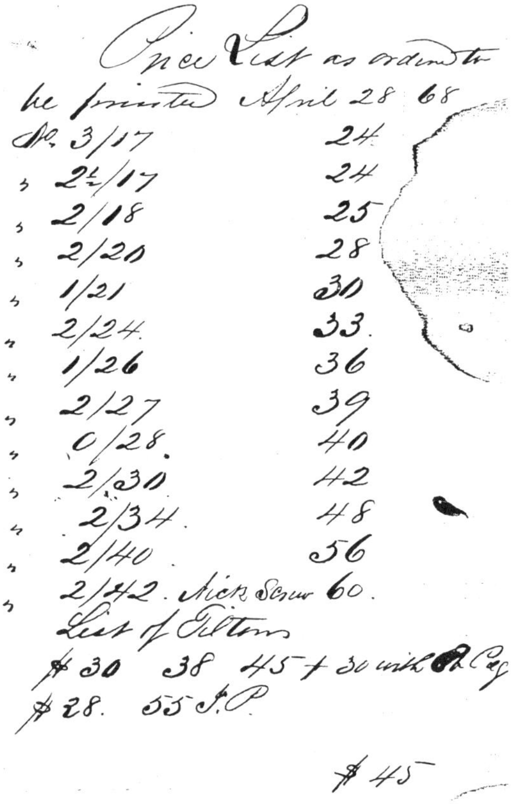

Handwritten manuscript (left):

Price List as ordered to
be printed April 28 68
No 3/17   24
" 2½/17   24
" 2/18   25
" 2/20   28
" 1/21   30
" 2/24   33
" 1/26   36
" 2/27   39
" 0/28   40
" 2/30   42
" 2/34   48
" 2/40   56
" 2/42. Nick Screw 60.
List of Tiltons
30   38   45 + 30 with 2 Peg
28.   55 S.P.

45

Printed price list (right):

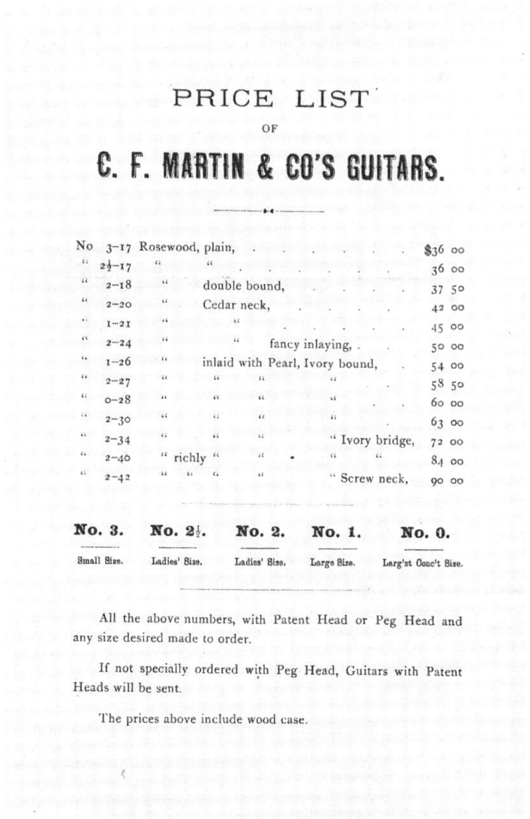

PRICE LIST

OF

C. F. MARTIN & CO'S GUITARS.

No					
No 3–17	Rosewood, plain,				$36 00
" 2½–17	"				36 00
" 2–18	"	double bound,			37 50
" 2–20	"	Cedar neck,			42 00
" 1–21	"	"			45 00
" 2–24	"	"	fancy inlaying, .		50 00
" 1–26	"	inlaid with Pearl, Ivory bound,		.	54 00
" 2–27	"	"	"	"	58 50
" 0–28	"	"	"	"	60 00
" 2–30	"	"	"	"	63 00
" 2–34	"	"	"	" Ivory bridge,	72 00
" 2–40	" richly	"	"	" "	84 00
" 2–42	" "	"	"	" Screw neck,	90 00

No. 3.	No. 2½.	No. 2.	No. 1.	No. 0.
Small Size.	Ladies' Size.	Ladies' Size.	Large Size.	Larg'st Conc't Size.

All the above numbers, with Patent Head or Peg Head and any size desired made to order.

If not specially ordered with Peg Head, Guitars with Patent Heads will be sent.

The prices above include wood case.

left:
Figure 5-13. *Manuscript, printer's copy of a price list for Martin's guitars, prepared by Charles Bruno, 1868. This is the earliest price list known for someone selling Martin's instruments. Bruno had appended it to a bill he sent Martin. Note at the bottom that Bruno also sold Tilton's guitars. (Courtesy of C. F. Martin & Company Archives)*

right:
Figure 5-14. *Price list of Martin's guitars, verso of C. A. Zoebisch & Sons Stationery, 1874. The year after Martin's death, Zoebisch began to print this price list on the back of all his stationery. (Courtesy of C. F. Martin & Company Archives)*

In his patent description, Bini noted that his improvement consisted in substituting for the old method of applying a small number of braces, placed at right angles to the length of the grain of the wood of the sounding board and "unconnected with each other"—what we would call ladder bracing— with a larger number of braces, placed diagonally to the grain and connected to each other. There was also a "main brace to the whole system, upon which it depends, so placed as to greatly increase the power and tone of the treble strings, as compared to the bass strings." Bini distributed and arranged the braces on the treble side in a manner different and distinct from those on the bass side, giving, he thought, "greater musical power" to the instrument.

He also dispensed with the transverse braces usually placed to the rear of the sound hole and instead attached the one long main brace "from the swell

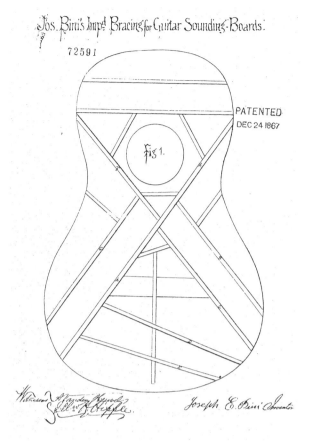

Jos. Bini's Impd Bracing for Guitar Sounding-Boards.

72591

PATENTED
DEC 24 1867

Fig 1.

Witnesses

Joseph E. Bini Inventor

Figure 5-15. *Patent drawing for Joseph Bini's design for bracing the top of a guitar. This pattern of wooden braces is remarkably similar to that used by C. F. Martin and other German makers from the 1850s on.*

[bout] of that part of the sounding board on the treble side to that of the front part on the bass side, of such length, and at such an angle, as it shall pass underneath . . . the treble side of the bridge." By this means, Bini claimed, the vibration of the treble strings was transmitted over a larger part of the sounding board in the same direction as the grain. He placed the other braces for a similar end, to obtain the best possible vibration from different strings. "I produce an arrangement of braces on the one side different from that on the other," he concluded, so that "by the whole system, the general power and tone are increased and improved."

As illustrated in his patent drawing, Bini's pattern essentially replicates what we know as Martin's X-bracing, save for a few more braces, particularly in the lower part of the "X." Interestingly, Bini nowhere mentions the reason usually given for X-bracing's popularity on Martin's instruments—that it strengthened the sounding board enough for one to use steel strings (which require more tension to bring them to pitch). As Bini indicated, it was the improvement in tone and balance, particularly of the treble strings, that compelled him so to brace instruments.

The popularity of Bini's patent is unclear, but Jouett and Cushman evidently transferred it again, for in one of his catalogues from the 1870s, musical instrument wholesaler J. Howard Foote of New York and Chicago prominently featured "the Bini Guitars" as "the best in the world!" Foote claimed to be the "*sole owner* of the patent right for making these *Celebrated Guitars*" and praised the bracing for giving the guitar "greater strength and durability, while the sounding boards, being so much thinner than in the old method, are at the same time more sensitive to sound." The arrangement, he continued, "has the effect to equalize the entire scale, producing every note full and perfect." "The *Bini Guitars* are all made in New-York, under my *personal supervision*, and are *fully warranted* not to crack, or become damaged in any way, with proper care. In *Tone, Power,* and *Durability*, they have *no equal!*"[30]

There is little physical documentation of Bini instruments, for collectors and curators of late-nineteenth-century guitars have previously not examined enough X-braced instruments carefully to determine if Bini's pattern is indeed that which appears in them. Further, if Martin knew of Bini's patent, there is no record of his having been exercised by it. If he did know, he obviously did not think that Bini infringed on his own use of the X-bracing system. Concomitantly, Martin probably was confident that his own method, which utilized a slightly different number and distribution of the braces, did not infringe on Bini's rights. This suggests, again, that by the 1860s several American makers were using this method of construction.

JUSTIN HOLLAND AND OTHER PLAYERS AND PERSONALITIES

As the reputation of Martin's instruments grew, he continued to receive the special orders and requests that had marked his success in the 1850s. Often these clients wanted customized instruments or adjustments to Martin guitars that they already owned. Others wanted particular kinds of sizes or models for their students or protégés. As late as 1868, for example, William Schubert still patronized his longtime friend, ordering a terz as well as a fairly expensive instrument, an 0-28. Janon, too, was still teaching, now in New Haven, Connecticut; in 1869 he also ordered an 0-28. Martin usually honored such requests from old customers—he even continued to give Janon a 20 percent discount—and built special instruments for them. Indeed, such work marked his devotion to handcraftsmanship, an attitude evident as well in his resistance to the overt standardization and simplification of production that characterized James Ashborn's factory.

As I have noted, some customers still requested smaller terz guitars, which Martin built on demand through these years. There were calls for even more unusual instruments. D. Schuyler in Buffalo, a person who had wanted Martin to make him a guitar like "Tilden's [*sic*]," a couple of weeks later requested another instrument, "the handsomest and most perfect, in *tone* and *touch* that you can make." Schuyler's interest was peculiar. He was starting a collection of musical instruments, he explained, "from the *Grand Piano* down to the *smallest* instrument made," and he intended "to have *each one* of them the most *perfect* and *beautiful* of its kind."[31] Schuyler's selection of Martin to make the guitar for this collection speaks to the high regard in which discriminating people held his work. Occasionally, though, such custom orders were more trouble than they were worth. In 1871 Mellor & Hoene, a music house in Pittsburgh, wrote Martin that the lady for whom he had made a fine guitar was unable to take it. The firm returned it because it was entirely too expensive an instrument for its market.[32]

Special requests could be more mundane. In 1867, for example, Anna Polster, a concert player from Baltimore, had problems with a "Grand Guitar" (model o) that she had bought from Martin and sent it back for another. She was particularly eager to replace the instrument because she had several invitations to play guitar music at concerts.[33] She wrote again on October 7 to say that the latest guitar still did not please her as well as her old one. "The first string at the 5th & 6th frets & the second string at the 5th, 6th & 8th frets jingle so much," she explained, that she could not make use of the instrument, "otherwise than as a simple accompaniment." She had considered having someone in Baltimore adjust the new guitar but previously had had a bad experience in such matters. She ended by asking Martin if he could recommend anyone in the city in whom he had confidence to adjust her instrument, but she made it clear that she still would rather have him attend to it. To smooth the waters, she added that she soon would need one or two of his plainest and cheapest instruments for her pupils (fig. 5-16).[34]

Martin sometimes came by such devoted, if particular, clients in interesting ways. Mrs. A. G. Gourlay, a teacher in Philadelphia, previously had acquired her guitars through John Berwind, a respected Philadelphia maker who had decided to go into the piano-manufacturing business. Berwind had been good enough to recommend Martin to her, and in 1872 she inquired about instruments for her students, particularly for a "young lad, a scholar." She wanted an immediate reply because procrastination would lose the sale.[35] Martin likely put up with such presumption because he enjoyed knowing that performers and teachers thought so highly of his guitars.

Another unsolicited letter came from Louisa C. Van Vleck, who wrote Martin from Salem Academy, a Moravian school in Salem, North Carolina, where she taught guitar. After reminding him that she was the daughter of his old friend the Reverend Charles A. Van Vleck, inspector at Nazareth Hall, she asked about the prices of some of his lower-end guitars for her students. She always had had a preference for Martin's guitars, she said, and took pleasure in recommending them. At the close of the Civil War, for example, she had bought a fine, highly embellished instrument from one of Martin's agents. Later, she had tried to sell it to one of her charges but still had it on hand, she explained, because of the scarcity of money in the South. "I fear owing to the war," she wrote, "for the last ten years, there has not been much call for guitars." She enclosed two stamps for him to answer her.[36]

Figure 5-16. *Cabinet card by "The Central," Kansas City, Missouri, ca. 1875. The guitar's popularity soared in the post–Civil War period, and even young children continued to value guitar playing as one of their accomplishments. Instructors continued to write Martin for advice on which of his instruments to purchase. (Collection of the author)*

Martin occasionally was asked to make more unusual instruments or accessories. In 1869 Zoebisch asked him if he knew what a "Lyre" (presumably a lyre guitar) was and "how it is constructed, how many strings, &c." A customer "in a convent out West" wanted one, he explained. "Could you make one and at what price?," he asked.[37] Zoebisch even proffered investment opportunities to his associate. He once told Martin of a good guitar player in the city with an interesting invention, "a kind of stand like a music stand," which he placed in front of him "and screws the Guitar fast [that is, tight to it] when he plays, instead of holding it in his lap." The fellow wanted to sell the rights to it, and Zoebisch asked Martin if he wanted "to take hold of it." Zoebisch also recalled that Coupa had had something like it, which indeed he may have, for the stand sounds much like that developed by the great Italian player Dionisio Aguado in the 1830s.[38] "Please let me know about it, or rather what you think," Zoebisch said, for the man with the idea also was negotiating with Ferdinand Zogbaum, another wholesaler in the city.[39]

Perhaps Zoebisch's most interesting proposition was the opportunity to buy a great violoncello. In 1872, after he had told Martin, for the umpteenth time, to "hurry up the Guitars," Zoebisch confided that he had acquired "Knoop's Cello," that is, the instrument of the internationally acclaimed cellist George Knoop, who had died in 1849.[40] The instrument, the one on which he had played all his concerts, Zoebisch reported, was "yellow looking" and had "an Amati ticket inside." It had to be repaired a bit, for it was "out of glue," but it had good tone. "If you wish to speculate," he told Martin, "make me an offer for it."[41]

Martin evidently passed up the opportunity to represent the storied cello, for he took more pleasure and satisfaction from supplying his own instruments to new masters of the guitar. In this regard, the most important client whom he acquired in the 1860s was the guitarist, composer, and arranger Justin Holland (1819–87), resident during these years in Cleveland, Ohio (fig. 5-17). Holland, an African American, was born in Norfolk County, Virginia. Shortly after Nat Turner's Rebellion rocked the region, he moved to Massachusetts, settling in Chelsea, near Boston, when he was fourteen. From an early age Holland had shown an interest and proficiency in music and now began to study it more formally. Mariano Perez, a Spanish guitarist then playing in Boston, particularly influenced him, and Holland decided that the guitar was his instrument. He thereupon took lessons from Simon Knaebel and then from William Schubert, Martin's longtime client, through whom Holland presumably acquired his taste for Martin's instruments.[42]

In 1841 Holland enrolled in the Oberlin Collegiate Institute, the first institution of higher learning to educate blacks alongside whites. He became so interested in guitar pedagogy, however, that he remained only a year, opting instead to move to Mexico to learn Spanish so that he could study Aguado's guitar method in the original language. Later, he also mastered both French

Figure 5-17. *Engraving of Justin Holland, 1881. Holland, an important African American guitar instructor and arranger who settled in Cleveland, remained one of Martin's most loyal customers through the 1870s. (From James M. Trotter,* Music and Some Highly Musical People *[1881])*

and Italian, to read the tutors of Sor, Carulli, Giuliani, and others. By 1844 he had settled permanently in Cleveland where, its population aware of his proficiency in music, he began a long career as a teacher. He did not very often perform in public but devoted himself to his students and to arranging guitar music. As his first biographer explained, Holland did not aspire "to distinction as an original composer of music," though he had some compositions to his credit. Rather, "of modest pretensions, and rather practical character, he has considered that he could do more for music and the guitar in seeking to make the meritorious compositions of others for other instruments available for guitar practice by skillful arrangements."[43] By 1881, when these words were written, Holland's arrangements already numbered more than three hundred.

He published most of this work through S. Brainard's Sons of Cleveland, the by-now-venerable music house, and some through other publishers, notably J. L. Peters & Company in New York, which convinced him to write his own instruction book. In 1874 this firm issued *Holland's Comprehensive Method for the Guitar*, and two years later Brainard engaged him to do another, more condensed tutor, which it published in 1876 as *Holland's Modern Method for the Guitar* (figs. 5-18, 5-19). Highly acclaimed in their time, these books established Holland as one of the country's preeminent guitar instructors.

Beginning in 1861, when he purchased a 2½-24 from Martin, Holland remained a devoted customer who frequently corresponded with Martin and, after his death, with his son.[44] In 1865 he sent a brief note to Nazareth, observing that he had written several weeks ago to learn the prices of "one two, or three good, plain guitars with ivory pegs," instruments "not to be of the largest size."[45] In 1868 he bought two instruments and received the 20 percent discount that Martin accorded his good customers.

But Holland, like other instructors, could aggravate Martin, intentionally or not, with his demands. In 1869 he wrote a lengthy letter to Frederick Martin to custom-order a guitar for a very fastidious young woman, a letter that reveals how picky clients could be in demanding special work from Martin. Holland was very specific about what his tutee sought: an instrument of excellent tone, with a body of "the *blackest* rosewood," ivory pegs, and the decoration corresponding to a 2-27 but as near in size to a 1-21 as Martin could

HOLLAND'S
MODERN METHOD
——FOR THE——
GUITAR;

BEING AN IMPROVEMENT ON ALL OTHER METHODS FOR
THIS INSTRUMENT IN

PROGRESSIVE ARRANGEMENT, ADAPTATION & SIMPLICITY,

AND CONTAINING THE BEST SELECTIONS FROM

CARCASSI, CARULLI, SOR, MERTZ, GIULIANI, AGUADO,
AND OTHER
CELEBRATED COMPOSERS.
——THE WHOLE EDITED AND COMPILED BY——

JUSTIN HOLLAND.

PUBLISHED BY

The S. BRAINARD'S SONS CO., CHICAGO.

Figure 5-18. *Title page of Holland's important tutor* Modern Method for the Guitar *(1876). Note his familiarity with the methods of all the earlier European virtuosos. Throughout his career Holland sang the praises of Martin's instruments. He was well known to the family and even sent some manuscript music to Frederick's daughter when she was learning the guitar.*

make it for a lady's use. She preferred no pearl trimming, he continued, for she "says it looks 'Dutchy.'" If it had to have pearl, Holland explained, "select a good one with the pearl ring as narrow as may be, and with the inlaying around the rim next to the ivory band, very narrow." The price for this special guitar was not to exceed sixty dollars.[46]

This special order started a brouhaha, for Martin did not want Holland as a middleman. Instead, he directed the teacher to have the lady order the guitar through S. Brainard & Sons, now his agent in that city. Holland was hurt by Martin's reply, but because he wanted her to have a Martin guitar, he sacrificed his own feelings in this matter and offered to take her to Brainard's to help her describe and order the instrument. But the young lady's father, a "square man" and one of the city's oldest and most prominent citizens, was indignant at the idea of being forced to deal with Brainard's firm.

First, Holland explained, the fellow objected to Martin's working with just this one company, for in a city of over seventy thousand inhabitants with five large music stores, he thought that the public "would be better served & at fairer rates, [and] the instruments become better known & far more sold by free trade & competition than to allow one to monopolize who takes little pains to bring them to the notice of all." Further, for whatever reason, the father's personal animus toward S. Brainard & Sons was severe: "He said," Holland reported, "that he would not have an instrument through them at any price."

MANNER OF HOLDING THE GUITAR.

Figure 5-19. *Frontispiece to Holland's* Modern Method for the Guitar *(1876).*
Note that although Holland was African American, the player is white.

Holland finally calmed this parent enough to make him understand the superiority of Martin's work and thus the desirability of acquiring one of his instruments in whatever way he could. The two thereupon came upon a novel, if duplicitous, solution. The client would bypass Brainard by having Martin send the guitar to one of their relatives in New York rather than directly to Cleveland. The party promised to forward payment as soon as Martin set a price, and if the instrument were spoken of at all, "it will be, as having been obtained in New York." Holland then appended another description of the instrument—a variation of a 2-27—and gave Martin the address to which it was to be sent, to N. H. Hilliard at the St. Nicholas Hotel, New York City.

Martin evidently complied, for on April 1 he recorded a 1-27 that he sold to Holland for $58.50, before the 20 percent discount that he regularly allowed him. Holland knew that he had compromised Martin but shared his client's disgust at S. Brainard & Sons' lethargy in the promotion of Martin's instruments. For one thing, he knew that with the stock he had from Martin and that he had bought up from other parties in the city, he could "make a larger trade" in Martin's guitars "than has been done in the stores here this winter."[47] In other words, for Holland, as for so many others who had grown to love Martin's instruments, it came down to his asking for the guitars' agency in Cleveland.

Despite this unpleasant episode, Martin remained on good terms with Holland and continued to sell him guitars. He remained a steady customer through the early 1880s, even though, given Zoebisch & Sons's growing control over Martin's stock and who carried it, he never gained the exclusive agency he desired. But the Martins understood his significance to American music and appreciated his considerable talent. The same year of the haggling over S. Brainard & Sons, for example, Frederick acknowledged Holland's reputation as a composer/arranger by requesting several pieces of music for his teenage daughter Emma. Holland's example and music moved many others as well. In 1870, W. R. Hoeg wrote Martin from Cincinnati to order a 1-21 guitar. He wanted the strings rather low, he said, so it would be easy to perform on, "like the one you sent Justin Holland, for his own use."[48] For his part, Holland continued to champion Martin's instruments. In 1884 he was pleased to report to Frederick that the members of the Cleveland guitar club, which he had founded, all played Martin guitars.[49] Martin's association with Victorian America's premier arranger for the guitar surely brought many other such benefits.

MARTIN, ZOEBISCH, AND THE VAGARIES OF THE MARKET

The new stamp that announced "C. F. Martin & Co." still included "New-York" as the guitars' place of origin. In part, this was testament to the city's continuing centrality to the American music trade but also signaled Martin's long-standing and now increasing reliance on C. A. Zoebisch & Sons as his main wholesaler. Extant correspondence from 1864, for example, shows that the firm ordered virtually all the guitars Martin made, over 285. By the next year Martin had returned to his pattern of sending a few smaller orders to Philadelphia and to Cincinnati. But from this point on, he clearly relied on Zoebisch & Sons to job his guitars in New York and through that city to other markets all over the United States.

The reason for Zoebisch's success, and thus for Martin's continued respect for him, was quite simply his single-mindedness, epitomized in his comment that he "should like to go in the Country a week but [couldn't] get away," for he had to have his eyes "open & move about to make things go."[50] Zoebisch's correspondence with Martin from the late 1860s until the latter's death in 1873 offers rare glimpses of just how he did so in the cutthroat economic climate of the Gilded Age. Fewer and fewer large companies sought to monopolize more and more of the market, in this case for guitars, and Zoebisch wanted to emerge a winner. Complicating matters, between 1867 and 1869 the country's overall financial condition remained weak, causing a serious recession that affected wholesalers such as Zoebisch who had invested in the expansion of their facilities and stock. Thus, when the two friends' correspondence resumed in 1867 (extant letters from 1865 and 1866 are few), Zoebisch frequently reported on national market conditions, as he understood them. In particular, he complained about the scarcity of both customers and capital, the main reason for his subsequent attempts to manipulate the market in favor of Martin's instruments.

"Money is very scarce," Zoebisch lamented late in 1867. "Can't collect of the best houses, I never saw the like." "Drawing checks is the order of the day," he continued, "and nothing coming in, pretty hard work, which takes a good Check Book to hold out." Nor was this situation restricted to the city, for trade was "very dull and every body complains, here as well as all over the country." As if this were not enough, Zoebisch thought that the worst was yet to come. He was owed from thirty-eight to forty thousand dollars, he explained two weeks later. "I will collect all I can right after Newyear because I am afraid in Spring we will have a scare."[51]

These straitened conditions had gripped the national economy for some time and continued to do so through the early 1870s. Earlier, in 1867, Bruno had told Martin that between November 1866 and March 1867 he had retailed only one guitar. Referring to one of the nation's previous depressions, when he had worked with Martin, he added, "It beats 1837." In a refrain that Zoebisch echoed, Bruno noted that southern customers were purchasing very little, and what was worse, they could not pay for what they had bought the previous fall, for their notes came back "protested" (that is, returned because of insufficient funds). This was the case with "western papers" (notes), too, he reported. Within the last week, Bruno told Martin, he should have received sixteen hundred dollars from drafts due but had been able to collect only two hundred dollars, accompanied by letters begging him to wait for the balance.[52]

Zoebisch, constantly on the lookout to strengthen his presence in the national market, explained that the West was "hard up again" because "grain fetches only about half price, and then in some sections it was very poor." Western merchants could not collect, he went on, and consequently could not pay.[53] Nor was it any better in the South, where sales were not up to expectations. E. A. Coldridge, one of Martin's Alabama clients, explained why: "Owing to the particular failure of the Cotton Crop in this section, and the very low price of the same," nothing more could be done in the way of selling Martin's instruments. "The Cotton Crop is the one which Southern people can only count on for Resources," he explained, "and when that fails they are broke."[54]

In Zoebisch's eyes, all this was linked to the falling price of gold. "Gold is the cause," he suggested in 1869, as the economy stayed stagnant. "It is about [$]123 [per ounce]." "We are now, as the gold goes down," he continued, "feeling that people are taking care and holding on to greenbacks." A week later, things had not improved, for gold was down again, to $119¾. "Until Gold takes a decided stand," he lamented, "business can't get better, because it upsets every thing & creates distrust in [the] values of things."[55] Some firms slashed the prices of goods to cover expenses. In New York, Zoebisch reported, "many houses go down and eat themselves up owing to heavy Rents and expenses, [and] goods are sold at cost and under only to raise money." While he himself had not yet taken this tack, he had had to mark down many guitars (including, presumably, Martin's) in the hope that some cash would be forthcoming. The question on Zoebisch's mind, as well as on those of many others, was how to maintain the prices of goods, given such an unstable currency and depressed market. If collecting debts was almost out of the question, as he reported, "and customers buy only in a small way from week to week what they can sell," how might he and Martin ensure good market prices for the latter's guitars?[56] Zoebisch wanted a long-term solution, and in several letters to Martin in 1871 outlined a plan so that once and for all he, with Martin on his coattails, could rise above the vagaries of the economy.

ZOEBISCH'S MACHINATIONS

On May 19, 1870, Zoebisch elaborated his grand plan to push his competitors' instruments from the market. He wrote Martin, cryptically, that he would "see what can be done and try to force it as much as possible," that is, to make people think that there was a great demand for Martin's instruments, so much so that orders could not be filled. "Of course in doing this," he continued, "[we] must be carefull and watch the chance, so not to appear too anxious, else it would do harm if people found out and the demand is not equal to the supply."[57] Reading between the lines, Zoebisch here suggested that he would make it appear as though he had only a limited number of Martin guitars in stock. Concomitantly, he would not appear too eager to sell the instruments that he had on hand. Then, as word circulated that Martin's guitars, so well regarded, were difficult to acquire, Zoebisch & Sons could begin to sell its stock. Other makers' brands, for which there was not as much demand, would then fall in value.

Zoebisch revealed another part of his plan: he would make Martin's guitars so financially attractive to other major music houses that they would want to carry *only* his instruments, obtained, of course, solely through C. A. Zoebisch & Sons. Zoebisch had begun to implement this strategy as early as 1868, when he had tried to persuade William Pond & Company to take Martin's guitars on sale so that he and Martin could "drive the Ashburn Guitar out of the market."[58] Now Zoebisch worked on Bruno. On one occasion, for example, this dealer, whom Martin no longer directly supplied, had been in Zoebisch's store, and Zoebisch promised him a little "extra discount as well as [the] same as [that given] some other large city houses." Zoebisch wrote Martin that he thought "that they [Bruno] will take hold of it too"—that Bruno would begin to carry Martin's guitars exclusively (acquiring them, of course, through Zoebisch). Bruno also had told him that his firm now "ran [carried] their own Guitars." Zoebisch assured Martin, though, that as far as he knew, Bruno was simply bluffing, for Bruno had no guitars to "run." "It will take a little time," he assured Martin, "but [I] think they [Bruno] will all fall in line as it is in their interest to do so."[59]

Zoebisch understood that it would take time to manipulate the public perception of the market in the way that he wanted and over the next months urged Martin to supply him with the guitars he needed to perform such squeeze plays. The most important thing was for him to get guitars from Martin as cheaply as possible, to make it attractive to the other houses to carry them. "Could you," he asked Martin in March 1871, "if I take a lot of Guitars, say 3 cases of 10 each—30 Guitars in all, give me the 5% extra [discount], the pay to be deducted from the $500 loan[?]" If Martin agreed to this, Zoebisch continued, he could get rid of his indebtedness, and Zoebisch could force business the way he wanted to, a course of action from which Martin, too, would share the benefit. "I shall leave no stone unturned to go on against all competition," Zoebisch added. "Mind, I don't want to screw you down," he reassured Martin. "I look to your interest as well as mine."[60]

Occasionally, the two mixed up their signals about pricing and orders, cause for mutual embarrassment, but particularly for Zoebisch. At one point, for example, he was surprised that Martin could not send a quantity of old stock he had indicated as on hand. If Zoebisch had known this, he would have held back some guitars from market and sold them later, as the demand rose. "I put them in" (that is, he advertised as having the old stock that he thought

Martin would send), adding that all this was *"confidential."*[61] Zoebisch also knew that if Martin provided him with so many instruments, he had fewer to sell to other clients, who then would have to buy them through Zoebisch & Sons. The big payoff would come down the road, when Martin, through Zoebisch, controlled the national market. Eventually, the system began to work as Zoebisch desired. "I have drummed up people in every corner," he told Martin in 1872, "and we must now do all to supply every order that comes in." "I must have stock," he continued, "and be able to supply Guitars when wanted at once, else sales and too much time is [*sic*] lost and I am continually in hot water and don't know where to turn." He then asked Martin to send no fewer than one hundred instruments.[62]

Zoebisch's gambit depended on his control of both the supply and prices of Martin's instruments. Things became complicated, however, when Martin (who was under no contractual obligation to move such numbers of instruments through Zoebisch & Sons) continued to make special arrangements with other of his long-standing customers. On one occasion, for example, Zoebisch inquired if Martin had sold any of his old stock at a higher discount than $33\frac{1}{3}$ percent. "I pulling one way, and you another won't do," he reminded his friend, for "between us we will spoil the thing."[63] He meant that if one of them sold some guitars at lower rates and other customers heard about such preferential pricing, rivalries among competitors that, under regular market conditions, were sublimated could surface, turning ugly and personal.

This is precisely what happened in 1871. Word got around of such favoritism—either on Martin's or Zoebisch's part—enough so to threaten Zoebisch's grand strategy. The precipitating complaints came from two parties, John C. Haynes & Company of Boston and Klemm & Brother in Philadelphia, both new but already important players in the world of music wholesaling. The first hint of trouble came when Zoebisch heard from a customer who supposedly had had an offer of Martin's guitars at more than 40 percent off. He asked Zoebisch whether he could do as well. Zoebisch wanted to be sure that Martin had not arranged this sort of deal with other customers without his knowing it, for he had understood Fritz Martin to say that the firm did not sell at a higher discount than $33\frac{1}{3}$ percent to anybody.[64] A week later Zoebisch reiterated the question, explaining to Martin that he was not inclined to believe the charge because the still unnamed party who had asked him about this matter was "greedy and sneaky and does anything to get an article cheaper than any body else can buy it in order to undersell." But Zoebisch wished to be absolutely sure that Martin had not made any special arrangements of which he was unaware. After Martin assured him that he had not, Zoebisch took it upon himself to "put him [the other party] aright."[65]

By May, Martin knew who this "greedy and sneaky" person was, for Zoebisch had forwarded the letter in which the party had made the charge. The aggrieved was none other than John C. Haynes & Company of Boston, a firm

This engraving represents the famous factory of John C. Haynes & Co. Boston, Mass., the musical instrument department of the great Ditson houses where the celebrated **Bay State Guitars, Mandolins, Banjos and Zithers, and the Haynes Excelsior and Wm. B. Tilton Gold Medal Guitars** and other musical goods are manufactured.

A visit to this busy place will repay all people who are interested in the musical art, and who care to know how these wonderfully perfect goods are made.

Figure 5-20. *Illustration of John C. Haynes & Company's large factory in Boston, ca. 1889. By the 1870s Haynes, a spin-off of Oliver Ditson's musical empire, tried to obtain the same discount for Martin's instruments as enjoyed by Zoebisch & Sons. (Courtesy of James F. Bollman)*

which had recently bought the rights to the Tilton patent and which constituted the wholesale instruments division of Oliver Ditson's musical empire (fig. 5-20). Haynes told Zoebisch that he did not want the guitars "at any price different from 33% & 10%[,] as we can get them for that." "If you cannot sell for that," Haynes continued high-handedly, "we shall return those

Plate 5-1. *Front view of C. F. Martin harp guitar, size 1, ca. 1850. This is the only known harp guitar made by C. F. Martin, although his records indicate occasional requests for "ten-string" guitars. The squared upper shoulders of the body are unusual, but compare them with the guitar in plate 2-20. Also note the lyre-shaped peg head, made from two Vienna-style curls. This instrument was found in Mississippi, where Martin had several clients. (Courtesy of Frank Ford)*

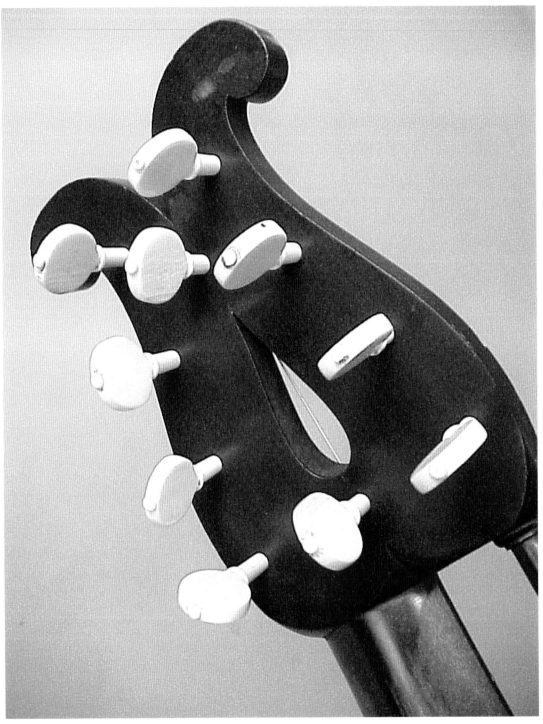

Plate 5-2. *Close-up of the lyre-shaped peg head on the guitar in plate 5-1. All ten of the ivory pegs are original and show the elegance of Martin's friction tuners. (Courtesy of Frank Ford)*

Plate 5-3. *Close-up of the sound hole and body of the guitar in plate 5-1, showing herringbone marquetry. (Courtesy of Frank Ford)*

Plate 5-4. *Close-up of heel of the guitar in plate 5-1. The neck is one-piece black maple, very unusual on a Martin instrument. (Courtesy of Frank Ford)*

Plate 5-5. *Close-up of Martin style 20 rosette and binding. (Courtesy of David LaPlante)*

Plate 5-6. *Close-up of Martin style 20 back stripe. (Courtesy of David LaPlante)*

Plate 5-7. *Close-up of Martin style 17 back stripe. (Courtesy of David LaPlante)*

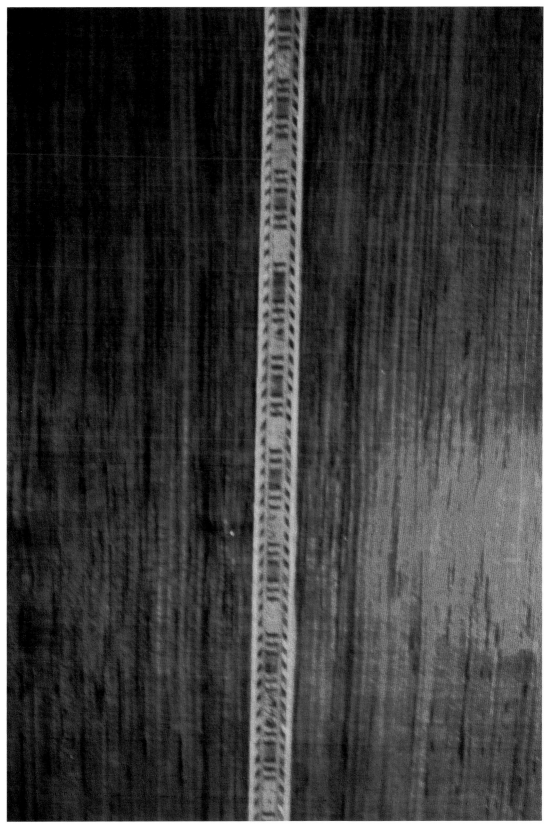

Plate 5-8. *Close-up of back stripe on early Martin style 28 guitars. (Courtesy of David LaPlante)*

Plate 5-9. *Close-up of rosette and binding on early Martin style 40, 42, and (later) 45 guitars. (Courtesy of David LaPlante)*

Plate 5-10.

Front view of Martin guitar, 2$^1/_2$-24, pre-1867. During the 1850s and 1860s, Martin's guitars attained their quintessential sizes and styles. This is a fine example of one of his midrange instruments. (Collection of the author)

left
Plate 5-11. *Rear view of the guitar in plate 5-10. (Collection of the author)*

top
Plate 5-12. *Close-up of tuning machines on the guitar in plate 5-10. The tuners are stamped "Jerome" and presumably were imported from Europe. Note the elegantly sculpted buttons. (Collection of the author)*

Plate 5-13. *Close-up of the sound hole of the guitar in plate 5-10. (Collection of the author)*

Plate 5-14. *Close-up of the marquetry around the bottom seam and end button on the guitar in plate 5-10. (Collection of the author)*

you have sent us: do not send the others." As an afterthought at the top of the letter he asked, "Could you do better than 33% on Martin Guitars?" for he had been offered a better discount.[66] Puzzled as he was by the origin of the offer, Zoebisch still would not play this game, for Haynes already had emerged as a major player in the musical instrument market and did not need any further advantage.

About the same time, someone told Martin that *Zoebisch* was making such special offers, specifically to Klemm & Brother of Philadelphia, a firm with which Martin had done business since at least 1867 when he had sent them a circular announcing the new partnership of Martin & Company.[67] When Martin asked Zoebisch about this new rumor, he quickly protested that he had never made such an offer. "In fact I don't know anything about offering them Guitars at all, if they have written about prices they certainly got an answer that ⅓ off is the price." He had never sold the firm any of Martin's guitars, he added emphatically, and did not recall that Klemm & Brother even wrote for prices. Confessing that in the past he occasionally had made such special arrangements, Zoebisch reminded Martin that whenever he had done so, he had told the guitar maker about it and had "never taken advantage or [had] recourse to underhand work." Zoebisch did admit being surprised that, in the attempt to get guitars at a better rate, the firm was willing to stoop to such prevarication. Moreover, he added haughtily, "Klemm can't sell any way many Guitars."[68]

Given Zoebisch's other machinations in the face of the depressed market and his evidently duplicitous behavior in acting as both wholesaler and retailer in the late 1850s, it is entirely possible that when he needed cash he sold Martin's guitars more inexpensively. He may have done this with Klemm, who then sought to turn it to his advantage with Martin himself. Whether true or not, such rumors about preferential discounts undeniably affected the market, as other firms sought comparable arrangements. About the same time, for example, Lee & Walker, another Philadelphia firm, asked Martin if he could do better for it in the way of a discount and let it have the sole agency of his instruments. "If you can," the partners continued, "we will pay you every month for all we may order, and advertise the Instruments, not only in this city, but through the whole Country, for which we possess unusual facilities."[69] But Zoebisch was a step ahead of them, for he, too, was advertising nationally. Two years earlier he had had new circulars printed, which he sent all over the country "to raise the wind" about Martin's guitars.[70]

Despite Zoebisch's intense efforts to control the market for Martin's stock, even minor players in the music business continued to aggravate matters. For example, Zoebisch once asked Martin if he had recently sent any guitars directly to Hoeg, the Cincinnati guitar teacher, for local stores had complained that somehow he undersold them (fig. 5-21). Then, when Hoeg had needed more instruments for his students and the stores offered him a discount of

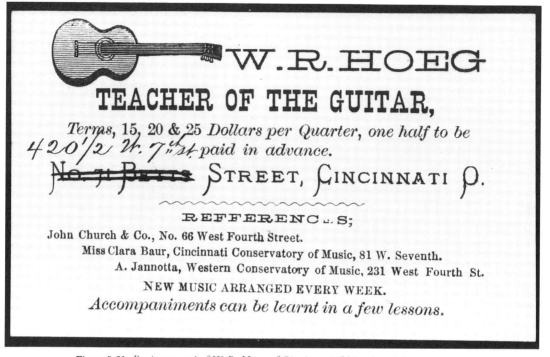

Figure 5-21. *Business card of W. R. Hoeg of Cincinnati, Ohio. A well-known guitar teacher, in 1867 Hoeg tried to undersell some of the local music houses with which Martin had long had special arrangements. (Courtesy of C. F. Martin & Company Archives)*

only 20 percent, he wrote to Zoebisch to see if the New York wholesaler could do better. "I referred him to the Stores there to make his arrangements," Zoebisch reported. "He teaches only & has no store & hurts them."[71] Even E. A. Coldridge, in Demopolis, Alabama, thought that he could help Martin. He asked for nothing less than "the General Agency for the United States for the sale of your Guitars in any of the cities." He had no doubt of his qualifications. Under more favorable circumstances (his region was suffering economically because of the failure of the cotton crop), he could sell his townspeople almost anything, he explained, "from a wooden nutmeg to an Eliphant."[72] The battle for supremacy in the national guitar market thus centered on control of Martin's inventory, for his instruments set the standard for players of any seriousness and discrimination. With everyone wanting a cut of the action, C. A. Zoebisch & Sons had its hands full.

BRUNO'S TREACHERY

Before making his presumptuous offer, Coldridge had written to pay Martin the forty-five dollars he owed for a ten-stringed guitar that Martin had made for him. Coldridge reported that he was offered so much money for the last instrument Martin had made for him that he was almost inclined to sell the new one. "I think and know," he continued, that "Martin Guitars are the best made and feel so shur of it that I could nearly Preach it."[73] In his praise

Coldridge echoed what by then was a national sentiment, for most dealers believed, as S. Brainard's Sons of Cleveland did, that "Martin Guitars are the finest in the world."[74] Indeed, by the late 1860s, Martin's guitars had become so highly regarded and in demand that they spawned a market in counterfeits peddled by unscrupulous dealers. As early as 1854, as discussed in Chapter 3, some unknown party was selling spurious Martin guitars in Memphis. This practice persisted into the 1860s, and most surprising, the individual primarily responsible for the deception was none other than Charles Bruno, associated with Martin in one way or another for the past forty years.

Zoebisch accidentally had uncovered this forgery during his attempt to manipulate the supply and prices of Martin's guitars. From his brother Bernhardt in Neukirchen in the spring of 1869, Zoebisch learned that Bruno was having "Ivory Pegs Guitars" made in that town. He now awaited further word from Bernhardt, who had "sneeked some away" so that he could study them more closely. Zoebisch also assured Martin that he would "watch and have a hand in every thing they [Bruno] attempt and have no doubt we can manage them." "He can't do no harm," Zoebisch concluded, for, using the Martin instruments that he had stockpiled, he would sell at cost the same "Style of Guitars they want to run" and thus "spoil the whole thing for them."[75]

A little over a week later Zoebisch had more to say about this business. Evidently earlier that year Bruno had sent around a circular in which he announced that his son Charles Jr. was going to Europe to "get up Goods suitable to this [America's] market." His father had "made a noise when his son went away," that is, he had bragged to his fellow dealers about the boy's prospects. Thus, Zoebisch found it humorous that the young Bruno had returned after only five weeks, presumably because he did not have much success in procuring suitable goods for the American market. But Zoebisch had other news, too, for after Bernhardt had examined the guitars, he thought that his brother should see them and had shipped several to New York, where Zoebisch eagerly awaited them. Zoebisch was particularly curious because Bruno had been telling people that he now had "a Guitar which beats yours [Martin's] & any other Guitar in the market & still will be more perfected."[76] Presumably, that is what the young Bruno had acquired in his abortive attempt to "get up goods" for the American market.

Zoebisch finally received the instruments in early June and was astonished to find that they were direct copies of Martin's own. They seemed to be well made, he reported, and he concluded that they must have had Martin's guitars, "taken out [i.e., over] by Bruno," for patterns. Further, from what he could tell of the workmanship, he surmised that no one could have made them "but Durschmidt or Heberlein who worked at Schatz's," that is, two men who had worked for Martin's longtime friend Heinrich Schatz in Boston at least until 1845 and then presumably had emigrated. The instruments in question were patterned after several of Martin's well-known and popular styles, including the 2½-17, 2-24, 2-27, and the 0-28, and were made with either simple pegs or patent heads.

Zoebisch told Martin not to fret over Bruno's perfidy, though, for there was no danger that the guitars would harm the American market. In the first place, he assured him, the Europeans could not finish such guitars in large enough quantities to affect the American market. Second, the difference in price was not enough for dealers to buy them and run the risk of "splitting, &c.," evidently a reference to the fact, frequently recounted, that European instruments did not fare well in the American climate.[77] As a postscript, Zoebisch remarked on Bruno's cleverness in leaving nothing to chance. The guitars came in cases just like those made for Martin by Augustus Clewell, the worker whom Martin employed for that purpose.[78]

Zoebisch never said if these instruments actually carried a forged Martin stamp. But the immediate effect of Bruno's bald action was Martin's severance of all business with him. Through the 1860s, for example, Bruno, with his European connections, had regularly supplied Martin with patent heads. Now Martin began to acquire them exclusively through Zoebisch or Klemm & Brother in Philadelphia. Furthermore, Bruno's attempts to secure more Martin guitars in this unscrupulous way played directly into Zoebisch's hands, for with his connection to Martin ended, the only way that Bruno could get Martin guitars was through Zoebisch himself. By the 1870s, Bruno had been reduced, as his business card indicated, to being the chief depot for Tilton's "American Guitars," not for C. F. Martin's, as Zoebisch proudly proclaimed in his advertisements (figs. 5-22, 5-23).

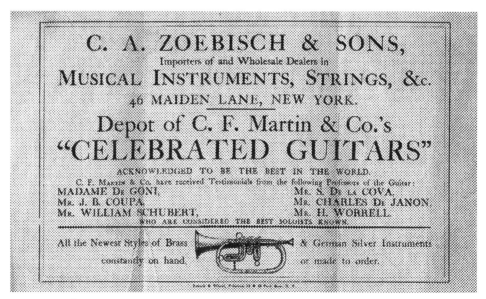

Figure 5-22. *By the 1870s, as this advertisement indicates, Zoebisch & Sons in New York City touted itself as the chief depot for Martin's "Celebrated Guitars, acknowledged to be the best in the world." (Courtesy of C. F. Martin & Company Archives)*

LYON & HEALY AND THE BATTLE FOR NEW MARKETS

The problem of spurious guitars resurfaced in 1871 when Martin and Zoebisch met their largest challenge for the market share of instruments. This time the problem was not Bruno or even New York. It had to do with a new competitor in the music wholesaling business, in the growing metropolis of Chicago. By 1864 Oliver Ditson, the Boston-based music house that had set up Haynes as a wholesaler and manufacturer, was extending its tentacles to other cities. Ditson had considered San Francisco and St. Louis as well as Chicago and finally decided on the last, no doubt because of its rapid growth and its centrality to the new American economy. Ditson sent two of its employees, forty-four-year-old George Washington Lyon and twenty-four-year-old Patrick Joseph Healy, to start a branch of the business in the great midwestern city. The decision was a good one: in its first year the firm did one hundred thousand dollars' worth of business.[79]

Lyon & Healy had bought guitars from Martin since the early 1870s.[80] Like other firms, it sought to acquire as many of his instruments as it could and by

DESCRIPTIVE PRICE LIST.

————•·•————

C. BRUNO & SON,

ESTABLISHED 1834,

IMPORTERS AND WHOLESALE DEALERS IN

Musical Instruments,

STRINGS, Etc.,

NO. 4 CORTLANDT STREET,

P. O. BOX 4963.   *NEW YORK.*

1874.

Entered according to Act of Congress, in the year 1874, by
C. BRUNO & SON,
in the Office of the Librarian of Congress, at Washington, D. C.

NEW YORK:
PRESS OF WYNKOOP & HALLENBECK, 113 FULTON STREET.

Figure 5-23. *Title page of Charles Bruno's* Descriptive Price List *(1874). In this catalogue Bruno, having lost out to Zoebisch as Martin's chief distributor, advertised Tilton's guitars. (Courtesy of James F. Bollman)*

that December was regularly ordering ten to twenty instruments at a time. Zoebisch quickly became aware of this new competitor and, given the incestuous connections among Ditson, Haynes, and Lyon & Healy, finally deduced who was behind the rumors of his and Martin's supposed collusion for preferential treatment of some customers. Simply put, it was not merely Haynes who was interested in larger discounts but Lyon & Healy as well. "I presume the trouble comes from the blowers, Lyon & Healy," he told Martin. "Haynes & Co. in Boston are the party and they, through Ditson, are all connected in one way or another." A month later Zoebisch revisited the subject, telling Martin that Lyon and Healy seemed to have taken it in their heads to work against him. "Certain it is," he continued, "that if they enjoy the discounts you gave them so far, it will hurt the Guitar trade out West because other dealers will not be satisfied to see L[yon] & H[ealy] have an advantage, and it won't take long before this thing is out all over." Even if Martin extended preferential discounts to them, Zoebisch explained, "I shall first get the blame[,] people thinking I am doing it," he protested. Besides, he concluded, "as in the case of the J. C. Haynes & Co., people doubt my word and get distrustful."[81]

Lyon & Healy's orders clearly were beginning to impact the market. Further, the firm was making noise to Martin about even better discounts, Zoebisch explained, because it could not "get enough imitation Guitars from people here [that is, from Bruno] who get them made in Neukirchen, nor can [it] get along with only a few of *Evans* [another wholesaler?], because Zogbaum, Bruno, Sontag all want those Neuk[irchen] Guitars."[82] The consequence, Zoebisch continued, was that no one ever had enough of the spurious Martin guitars "to bother with, to make it pay." Lyon & Healy thus had turned to Martin to see what could be done, for formerly it had stocked only Martin's instruments and had had them on hand. As long as there were copy instruments readily available in the market, Lyon & Healy did not want to take more than a few from Martin himself, for they cost too much. Zoebisch expected Lyon & Healy to raise the issue with Martin and urged his friend to support him "in regard to [the] discount" to them, so that he would know how to act in selling to them.[83]

Soon thereafter Martin queried Lyon & Healy about the prices at which the company sold his guitars. Using precisely the ploy that Zoebisch thought it might, the firm repeated Haynes's charge: it had not sold guitars at any lower rate than Zoebisch had, so had it not a right to sell as low to others? "We certainly desire to keep up prices, but we do not see why Mr. Zoebisch should sell lower than we do."[84] Martin followed up with an inquiry for more information about Zoebisch's supposed arrangements, and Lyon & Healy again wrote at length: the firm had evidence that Zoebisch & Sons had sold at extra discount to three different houses and surmised that he had done the same on many other occasions. Then switching to the offensive, to make Martin offer it the same supposed discounts, "We do a larger wholesale business and have all the facilities for doing such a trade, and as a consequence we are prepared to compete with any NY or Boston houses." Signaling the rapacity with which the firm was willing to attack the competition, Lyon & Healy added: "We don't like to know that we can be undersold by any of them."

The firm also reminded Martin that it had introduced his instruments into new channels throughout the Midwest and thus would doubtless need the guitars in even larger quantities thereafter. This was indeed significant, for as powerful as Zoebisch was, Lyon & Healy was poised to open and to monopolize vast new markets in the interior of the country. In essence, the firm offered Martin the same opportunity, in the new markets, that such firms as William Hall & Son and Firth, Pond & Company had offered in New York fifteen years earlier. It hoped that Martin would come around to their view and shape his arrangements to supply them promptly, closing by noting that the firm itself had entirely discontinued the manufacture of guitars.[85]

Such negotiations continued through the early fall of 1871 but were halted by the cataclysmic fire that destroyed the city's downtown business area, including Lyon & Healy's huge salesrooms and warehouse (fig. 5-24). By chance, Zoebisch had been traveling to different cities where he and Martin had business—namely, to St. Louis, Louisville, and Cincinnati—and had arrived in Chicago shortly after the event. In a letter to Martin thereafter, he left a vivid account of the disaster. Lyon & Healy, then located at 150 S. Clark Street, had lost everything, he reported, including the valuable stereotype plates from which it printed sheet music. The equally important house of Root & Cady had also been wiped out, as well as E. Bauer & Company, another music dealer. The company (unnamed) with which Zoebisch did business had been fortunate enough to save its account books and stereotype plates because these items had been kept in a separate vault, but losses still amounted to $140,000.

But as terrible as these losses were to the music trade, the general devastation shocked Zoebisch even more. The city looked frightful, he told Martin, and nobody could form any idea unless he had seen it. Imagine New York, he continued, "burned down from North to East River[,] then from & including Wall St. up to Union Square, and you have the burnt district of Chicago," the most important part of the city. Zoebisch had gone over the whole ground in a buggy with a friend. While he declared it "awful!," he was already "filling orders to enable our friends to take their stand again at once and supply their customers," he told Martin, "and so do most New York houses in every branch."[86]

Chicago survived this tragedy, and by the next summer Lyon & Healy, fully insured, had reestablished itself in a large building on the corner of State and Monroe Streets. Anticipating its reopening, in May the firm had placed an order with Martin for eight guitars, but the next month it asked

Figure 5-24. *Printed notice of Lyon & Healy, Chicago, 1874. The dramatic vignettes on an announcement that Lyon & Healy had reopened at new quarters after the great Chicago fire of 1871 had destroyed its previous operations give a sense of that terrible conflagration. Within a few years this firm emerged as a major force in the world of musical instrument sales and production. (Courtesy of C. F. Martin & Company Archives)*

why he had not filled it in accordance with the arrangement he supposedly had made with Lyon.[87] After consulting with Zoebisch, Martin balked again. This prompted Lyon & Healy to remind him of Haynes's discount from Zoebisch. The firm also included evidence of its charge: a letter from one of Haynes's clerks in which he admitted that, while he could not place his hands upon the bill from Zoebisch & Sons that gave Lyon & Healy a 40 percent discount, he could distinctly say that Haynes & Company had had them for that figure.[88] Here the matter stopped, without any concessions on Martin's part. In the next few years the Chicago house continued to order guitars from him but did not raise any more fuss about the rate at which it received them. Instead, it began to make plans to manufacture its own instruments.

Whatever his culpability in these shenanigans, Zoebisch, who understood the strategic importance of Chicago, was not willing to let that market fall entirely to Lyon & Healy. In the autumn of 1872 he again went out west, on short notice, because of "trouble in Chicago, things look blue." He had been considering the purchase of one of the city's music firms but after the trip decided not to pursue the option immediately. A couple of weeks later he still deliberated the right course of action and sent an agent to examine the prospect. The cost would be considerable, for to acquire the firm he would need to invest fifty thousand dollars cash and twenty to twenty-five thousand dollars more to stock it and run it properly. The creditors were so eager to have him purchase the whole business outright, though, that they were willing to sell it to him at fifty cents on the dollar. "Business is business," he wrote philosophically, and "always involves more or less risk." Ever alert to being beaten to the punch, he added, "Keep these remarks confidential."[89] Two weeks later, however, he told Martin that he finally had declined the

Figure 5-25. *Cover of* The Washburn American Guitar, *Chicago, ca. 1880s, in which Lyon & Healy advertised an entire line of instruments to challenge Martin's. (Courtesy of James F. Bollman)*

offer. Rather, in his usually ruthless way, he considered starting his own house there and then buying the other firm's imported goods if he could get them at a bargain. Ever the businessman, Zoebisch observed as a matter of fact that his coup de grace would be his wooing one or two of the firm's best men to his own concern.[90]

As Zoebisch's activities indicate, in these years the music wholesaling business more and more involved travel to clients distant from New York, something that he did not personally enjoy. Thus, early in 1873, he hired a man "for travelling purposes," someone who knew his business and had been doing this kind of work for five years. Other houses had such representatives to tout their clients' wares, he noted, and he did not want "to be behind the age!" It was "asking a man's life to every day be out on the rail Roads," he observed, and he would rather pay someone else to do it.[91]

Zoebisch's new agent was to begin work on February 1, none too soon because trouble over pricing still bedeviled the Chicago houses. A Western customer had told him "he has Guitars offered less than ⅓ off," Zoebisch related to Martin a week after announcing that his new man was on the job. "I think to protect the business for the future," he continued, "it would be best to stop this Chicago affair," for it made people "undecided & only makes trouble." It is unclear what he meant by the phrase "Chicago affair," but it may have had to do with the continued haggling with Lyon & Healy over discounts or his own attempts to start a proxy there. Once his agent began to serve such new markets, things would improve, Zoebisch wrote, with Martin's guitars continually offered to the best houses and thus kept prominently in the trade.[92]

WASHBURN GUITARS.

Standard Size.

No. 102.

Figure 5-26. *Illustration of guitar from* The Washburn American Guitar, *ca. 1880s. Though not as well made as Martin's instruments, Washburn guitars were made more quickly and economically and sold in large numbers. (Courtesy of James F. Bollman)*

THE LARGEST MUSICAL INSTRUMENT FACTORY IN THE WORLD.

LYON & HEALY FACTORIES, UNION PARK, CHICAGO.

Figure 5-27. *Lithograph, Lyon & Healy Factory, Chicago, ca. 1898, frontispiece to* Catalogue of Musical Merchandise Imported and Manufactured by Lyon & Healy *(1898). By the last decades of the nineteenth century, Lyon & Healy had become the country's largest manufacturer of stringed instruments, dwarfing C. F. Martin & Company and other competitors. (Courtesy of James F. Bollman)*

Zoebisch thus prepared to play, as he never had before, in the national arena, a market that now centered as much on Chicago as New York, and Martin knew that he had to go along with him. But while for the moment they had fought Lyon & Healy to a draw, the ambitious firm would be heard from again. In the late 1870s, for example, it took the radical step of issuing elaborately illustrated catalogues of all its goods, complete with detailed descriptions of each instrument and model (figs. 5-25, 5-26). This obviated the need for the kind of traveling salesmen in whom Zoebisch placed his faith. Moreover, by the 1880s Lyon & Healy was bypassing the kinds of troubles it had had with Martin and, presumably, other suppliers and had begun to manufacture its own line of instruments under the "Washburn" label.[93]

In immense steam-powered factories at 211–15 South Canal Street, it produced thousands of instruments of all kinds and thus posed a challenge of an entirely new magnitude to C. F. Martin & Company, as well as to other musical instrument manufacturers (fig. 5-27). It typified what one historian has identified, in a company's emphasis on cutting costs and increasing production, as indicative of a shift from "batch" to "bulk" production, which often led to a decline in overall quality.[94] In batch production, goods (Martin's guitars, say) were made in small lots of various sizes, often on the basis of aggregated advance orders. In bulk production of the kind in which Lyon & Healy was engaged, the manufacturer made much larger numbers of goods based on what it perceived as the potential size of the market for them.

The ubiquity of such low-priced instruments—they were turned out in other large cities as well, by firms such as Haynes's and, increasingly, Bruno's—provided C. F. Martin & Company with the opportunity to distinguish what it considered its finer, "legitimate" instruments from the massproduced, and thus inferior, goods now sold (in Lyon & Healy's case) with the "George Washburn" label. Frederick Martin and his son, Frank, had to confront this challenge directly and eventually did so with great success. But this was a battle fought primarily in the 1880s.

Epilogue:
Final Years

On June 29, 1871, N. Marache, a New York guitar teacher at 34 Wall Street, inquired about a guitar for which he had placed a special order. He already was a bit annoyed, for Martin had made him order it through Zoebisch & Sons. Marache had done so, but the instrument had not arrived by the date promised. Zoebisch informed Marache that he probably could not get it for another fortnight and explained why. As Marache redacted the message to Martin, "it was owing to your sickness that the work on Guitars had to be suspended." "Sickness is of course excusable and cannot be avoided," he continued, but he impressed on Martin how much he needed the instrument. Two weeks later the customer still clamored for his order. He calls every day, Zoebisch wrote, adding at the end of the letter, "Marache is sitting here now again."[1]

Martin had been in declining health since 1871. His eulogist recalled that that year he had suffered a relapse from his stroke of twenty years earlier, and this time the effects were more permanent, with weakened memory and damaged mental powers.[2] This explains Justin Holland's having written to Frederick Martin rather than to his father. It also suggests that, after the summer of 1871, Frederick had assumed many of Martin's duties, particularly the correspondence with Zoebisch, a task that took on even more importance now that Martin could not communicate with his old client base, some of whom had been with him since the 1840s. The third partner, Hartmann, had never been involved in marketing instruments and presumably devoted his energy to production.

Martin's wife, Ottilie, had died on December 24, 1872, after several months of painful illness, and thereupon Martin moved into his son's home, next door to his own. Despite his diminished mental powers, he remained in sound physical health and continued to go to the shop, voluntarily, but only for short periods, to carry out tasks to which he had been habituated for fifty

Figure E-1. *Half-plate tintype, ca. 1870. In the 1870s and 1880s the guitar was found in all strata of society. In this unusual outdoor, rural image, the musicians have three banjos, a fiddle, a flute, and a guitar. Here we have the makings of what, by the 1920s, would be called a "country string band." (Collection of the author)*

years. Two weeks before he died he attended church services, as he always had, but needed to be taken home before they commenced. He began to fail physically and died peacefully on February 16, 1873. His eulogist from the Moravian church in nearby Bethlehem testified both to Martin's deep faith and to his humility. "In his time of greatest powers," he reminded the mourners, "he cast his light before others without putting on special airs to call attention to himself."[3]

Frederick Martin and C. F. Hartmann took over the company at a time of another national economic downturn. The year following Martin's death was particularly bleak financially. As usual, Zoebisch had his pulse on the economy. In the early autumn he reported, "We had awful times here, but hope the worst is over now." Stocks had fallen 30 percent to 50 percent, and the

Figure E-2. *Albumen photograph, ca. 1890. By the 1890s, many colleges and municipalities claimed banjo, mandolin, and guitar clubs. These accomplished young women, probably from one of the early women's colleges, have no fewer than four guitars to accompany their banjos and mandolin. Unlike the banjo, which earlier in the century had been very much associated with men, the guitar had always fit well into the hands of genteel women. (Courtesy of James F. Bollman)*

banks had been at the point of closing, he continued, "and of course if New York gives out all the rest of the Country is nowhere." A few weeks later, he could see little improvement. Things in the city were a bit better, but "outside of New York it is yet bad." "Nobody can pay notes," he continued, and banks were not yet paying checks at sight. "It takes a great check book to get along nowadays," he opined. The news the following week was no better: "Our banks have to keep the whole Country agoing," Zoebisch wrote, and "can't get any cash from any quarter." He was grateful that he had no debts and thus could wait until his customers "came up to time."[4]

But the guitar remained a popular instrument among all sorts of players, and Frederick Martin and Hartmann kept production fairly steady during these tough times (figs. E-1, E-2, E-3). In 1873, for example, they produced 245 instruments, and 226 the following year. But the next five years showed a progressive reduction (see Appendix H), with only 97 guitars leaving the shop in 1878. Not until 1882 would the company return to more normal production, with 192 guitars.

Figure E-3. *Albumen photograph, ca. 1890. From the early nineteenth century on, the guitar had always been associated with recreation and the family as well as with performance.*

Here a group of picnickers in their best Victorian costume enjoy some guitar and banjo music in a pastoral setting. (Courtesy of James F. Bollman)

Martin and Hartmann also continued to market their instruments primarily through Zoebisch, who in the years immediately following the elder Martin's death handled from 80 percent to 90 percent of them. While the company continued to sell to such individuals as Holland and to smaller firms like Charles Loag of Lancaster, Pennsylvania, all other merchandise circulated through New York. The only other large musical house to which C. F. Martin & Company sold regularly was Klemm & Brother of Philadelphia, which in return continued to supply Martin with strings and tuners.

By the mid-1880s Hartmann had left the partnership, though he continued to work for the firm through the early 1890s. In 1887 Frederick oversaw a major expansion of facilities, adding more space and purchasing steam-powered band saws and other equipment. He died November 15, 1888, and his wife and his son, Frank Henry Martin, inherited the firm. In the early 1890s Frank Martin ended the company's decades-long involvement with Zoebisch and returned to what his grandfather had done so well in the early 1850s: he marketed his guitars on his own, head to head with Lyon & Healy, which, with its own factories, was now churning out thousands of instruments a year for a national market. These guitars are not considered the equal of Martin's, for their mass production resulted in overall lower quality.

Frank Martin and his descendants rose to such challenges over and over again in the firm's 170-year history. But in large measure the firm's supremacy was possible only because of the example, in business as well as in craftsmanship, set by C. F. Martin himself. No one spoke better to his devotion to and success in his craft than his ever-bothersome but utterly loyal customer Marache. After hearing of Martin's death, he wrote to console Frederick. "Allow me to sympathize with you & family in the great loss you have sustained in the death of your good father & mother," he wrote. In Frederick's father, whose memory Marache revered, "the world has lost, not only a good man, but an ingenious and truly great artist in his line, for who has not heard of the world-renowned 'Martin Guitar'?"[5] Remarkably, one would answer his obviously rhetorical question the same way today as in 1873.

APPENDIXES

A. Martin Record Books, 1834–1873

The extant financial records of C. F. Martin and C. F. Martin & Company are of various sorts. I here list in chronological order all substantial items. As was the custom in the nineteenth century, businesspeople kept various kinds of records. In *daybooks* Martin recorded each transaction at the time it was made. At the end of each month he consolidated and transferred such records into *journals*, where he credited accounts for sums paid for goods and debited both goods and moneys received. Periodically, he also entered such information in *ledgers*, in which he organized the journal accounts, often alphabetically, by customer.

1. Daybook, 1834–1837. 5 pp. of accounts at front (June 7, 1834–Jan. 3, 1836), then beginning at p. 142, 25 pp. Ledger for years 1834–35. All in German.
2. Journal, 1836–1837. Journal entries through p. 140 (January 1, 1836–June 6, 1837). At p. 143, 10-page list of "Orders Received" (May 10, 1838–February 12, 1839). At p. 236, 30 pp. "Inventory," in German, of instruments and parts.
3. Inventory, 1837–1838. 32 pp. of instruments sold in New York City. At p. 34 there is another "Inventory," 19 pp. of the sale of his stock to Ludecus & Wolter, May 29, 1839. From back of this book, pages upside down, Martin kept a daybook for 1852–1858, consisting of 78 pp., January 22, 1852–December 23, 1858, listing in detail all the guitars that he made, with size, style of decoration, and other details (see no. 9).
4. Ledger, 1837–1840. 92 pp. + 12 pp. index at the end.
5. Journal, 1837–1838. 94 pp. (April 1, 1837–November 29, 1838). At p. 40 a note in German states that the accounts following are those of Martin & Bruno (May 1, 1838–November 1, 1838). These records are in Bruno's hand.
6. Inventory of Sale to Ludecus & Wolter, 1839 (see no. 3).
7. Ledger, 1849–1858. Begins with alphabetical index. Then 3 pp. of C. F. Martin's accounts, from December 1849 through 1859; then 1 p. of C. F. Martin Jr.'s accounts. Then accounts with various people, from the 1850s until 1889.
8. Accounts of C. F. Martin Jr., 1850–1852. Preliminary sheet, "C. F. Martin Jr. dr to C. F. Martin, Sr. New York 1850." 11 pp. Then 8 pp. of accounts with other individuals.
9. Daybook of Guitars Made, 1852–1858 (see no. 3).
10. Miscellaneous Accounts, C. F. Martin Jr., 1851. 10 pp. (May 27, 1851–October 30, 1851).
11. Accounts with Easton, Pennsylvania, Bank, 1851–1860. 53 pp. (May 1, 1851–May 17, 1860).
12. Ledger, 1852–1857. 73 pp.+ 2 pp. at end and inside rear cover of accounts with Nazareth Hall, 1857.
13. Daybook, 1859–64. 101 pp. + 8 pp. miscellaneous accounts, 1850–51.
14. Journal, 1859–1867. On cover, "1859 C. F. Martin d[ebtor] in acc[oun]t with

C. F. Martin, Jr." 89 pp. (March 28, 1859–July 24, 1867; second to last p., 1871, statement of worth of his "third of shop and business").

15. Accounts with Easton, Pennsylvania, Bank, 1860–1866. 32 pp. (May 19, 1860–November 28, 1866).

16. Daybook, 1867–1874. 106 pp. (August 3, 1867–June 17, 1874). Inside flyleaf, "Guitars Sold."

17. Daybook, 1867–68, 1874–84. Begins with a four-page "Inventory of Stock and Fixtures taken on entering in Copartnership July 20, 1867." This is followed by eleven pages of "materials bought since July 31 [1867], through December 21, 1868. One-hundred-four-page list of guitars sold, by date, follows.

18. Ledger, 1867–1871. 8 pp. accounts from 1869, then 2 pp. from 1867. Later, more from 1867 and then 50 pp. through 1871.

19. Daybook, 1869–1871. On cover, "Day Book of C. F. Martin's Co. Jan[uar]y 1869." 128 pp. (January 1, 1869–January 17, 1871).

20. Ledger, 1873–1885. Ledger for 210 pp. At p. 301, 10 pp. of "Business Expenses" for 1879–1882, by year. At pp. 317–26, daybook for guitars made (January 17, 1873–April 6, 1885). At p. 327, Martin's expenses. At p. 330, "Extraordinary Expenses." Then pp. 331–44, "Expenses for Business" (1873–1878).

B. Martin Accounts

Martin's accounts are listed in the order in which they appear in the ledger for 1837–40, with addresses supplied from the ledger entries and occupations, if known, added.

Charles Bruno, New York (musical instruments)
Mr. [Frederick] Schnepf, 41 Greenwich Lane, New York
    ("professor" of the guitar)
Mr. George Coe, New Haven, Conn. (musical instruments)
Mr. T. Lucchesi, "Westpoint" ("music leader")
William Schubert, Boston
Mr. Boucher, 38 John Street, New York
Mrs. Stone, 59 Grand Street, New York
Mr. Hoffman, New York
Mr. Prier, 226 Greenwich Street, New York
John Coupa, 198 (and, later, 385) "Broad-way," New York (music teacher)
Mr. Jacob Hartmann, 28 Cherry Street, New York (brass instruments)
Mr. Bacher, 25 Ferry Street, New York
Mr. Witthaus, North Fulton Street, New York
Mr. Rieber Jr., 85 Essex Street, New York
Peter Retter, No. 48 West Street, New York
P. H. Taylor, Richmond, Va. (musical instruments)
John F. Nunns, Philadelphia (musical instruments)
Joseph F. Atwill, 201 Broadway, New York (musical instruments)
O. Scheitz, "West-Point" (musical instruments)
Mr. Godonne, 412½ Broadway, New York
F. L. Hewitt, 239 Broadway, New York

F. M. Austrup, New Haven, Conn. (musical instruments)
Edward Baak, No. 28 Cherry Street, New York ("flutemaker")
Charles H. Keith, 61 Court Street, Boston (musical instruments)
H. Andrae, Quebec, "U[pper] C[anada]" (musical instruments)
Mr. Eckle, New York; Mr. Benss, "U.S. Musician at Westpoint"
Dr. Kiefer, 77 Franklin Street, New York
Charles G. Christmann, 404 Pearl Street, New York (musical instruments)
Mssrs. Brauns & Focke, Baltimore (musical instruments)
Henry G. Guetter, Bethlehem, Pa. (musical instrument maker)
Mr. [Edward] Fehrman, 76 Walker Street, New York (musical instruments)
Charles Stumcke, Nazareth, Penn. (musical instrument maker)
Frederick William Rasche, 212 Fulton Street, New York (employee)
"Miss Collins, at Mrs. Smith," No. 35 Fifth Avenue, New York
Andreas Berger, No. 59 Crosby St., New York
Mr. Ludwig Albert Hallstein, Bridgeport, Conn. ("cabinetmaker," case maker)
Mr. Kohlsaat, No. 77 Murray Street, New York
Mr. Hoyer, 303 Broadway, New York
Mr. Legget, No. 42 Dominick Street, New York
Mrs. Bertrand, No. 107 Norfolk Street, New York
August Rönnberg, Richmond, Va.
Mr. Henry Schatz, Millgrove, Pa. (musical instrument maker)
Mr. C. L. Heizman, Reading, Pa.
Mr. [Richard] Schroeder, 177 Elizabeth Street, New York ("flutemaker")
James B. Mills, No. 27 Morton Street, New York
Mrs. Mary Okill, No. 685 Clinton Place, New York
    (boardinghouse and schoolkeeper)
John F. Burnton, No. 189½ Hudson Street, New York
Jacob Ackerman, "corner of Christopher & West streets," New York
Wolter & Helfrich, Louisville, Ky. (musical instruments)
Charles A. Bruckmeyer, New York
H. Goodwin, Hartford, Conn.
Mssrs. F. W. Randolph & Co., Richmond, Va.
Charles Ahlborn, New York
Edward Ludecus, New York (musical instruments)
Charles Berg, Petersburg, Va.
H. Wiese; Franz Alvary, West Point
Prof. Druck (music teacher)
Professor Cammener (music teacher)
William Rönnberg, 92 Fulton Street, New York
J. B. Bini, 302 Hudson Street, New York (guitar maker and instructor)

C. Martin's Ledger Book

Listings of customers in Martin's ledger book, 1852–57, appear in order of entry, with date of first and last account, and numbers of guitars purchased. Totals at end in parentheses represent count from Daybook of Guitars Made, 1852–58.

	1852	1853	1854	1855	1856	1857
Charles F. Meyer (Lexington, Ky.)	4		3	2		
G. P. Reed & Company (Boston)	12	15	4	6		
Peters, Webb & Company (Louisville, Ky.)	20	14	20			
Peters & Sons (Cincinnati)	16	32	23	30	15	
Jonathan H. Miller (Pittsburgh)	15	18	8			
H. Parson (New Orleans)	6	12	6			
Jonathan B. West (Nashville, Tenn.)	6	8				
P. H. Taylor (Richmond, Va.)	4	4	10			
E. P. Nash & Company (Petersburg, Va.)	8	17	9	3	4	
Lee & Walker (Philadelphia)	12	10	10	8	16	3
A. Fiot and Gould & Company (Philadelphia)	11	34	14	32		
F. D. Benteen & Company and Miller & Beacham (Baltimore)	12	16	16	8		
Balmer & Weber (St. Louis, Mo.)	12	12	18	6	6	
Charles de Janon (New York City)	14			1		
Rohé & Leavitt (New York City)	7					
Colburn & Field (Cincinnati)	12	24	26	6		
E. Pique (Philadelphia)	3	3				
Joseph Mickey		2				
Francis Funck		4				
Philip Deringer			1			
Mr. Addeton			1			
Charles Demming (Philadelphia)	3					
F. I. Ilsley and Mayer & Collier (Albany, N.Y.)	9	6	5			
M. Schmitz (Philadelphia)	4					
J. Brainard (Cleveland, Ohio)	6	16	8	6		
J. M. Jaques & Horace Waters (New York)	16	26	34	14		
John Harvie (Port Gibson, Miss.)	4	4				
William Schubert (Philadelphia)	2	5	9			
A. D. Truax (Cincinnati)		10	8			
Hilbus & Hitz (Washington, D.C.)		4	7			
A. W. Penniman (Columbus, Ohio)		6	4			
James Miller (Wheeling, Va.)			4	4		
Mould & Greene (Chicago)			6	6		
J. H. Macmichael (Natchez, Miss.)			6			
E. A. Benson (Memphis, Tenn.)			6			
Fauld, Stone & Morse (Louisville)			10	12		
C. Hall & Co. (Norfolk, Va.)				6		
C. A. Zoebisch & Sons (New York City)				29		
A. G. Crane & Company (Indianapolis)				4		
Charles F. Geist (Boston)	4					
Total	222	302	276	183	41	3
	(225)	(303)	(270)	(211)		

D. Total Guitars Made, 1852–1855 (with Numbers of Each Size)

	1	2	2½	3	Other	Total
1852	27	54	71	73		225
1853	49	53	101	100		303
1854	37	48	86	97	size o (2)	270
1855	30	50	96	34	terz (1)	211
Total	143	205	354	304	3	1009

Source: Figures from Daybook of Guitars Made, 1852–55.

E. Guitar-Making Tools and Supplies in Rooms and Shop, James Ashborn's Last Will and Testament, Probated December 27, 1876

North Room

1 Lathe with Foot Power attachment	$25.00
1 Guitar String Machine perfect	25.00
1 Guitar String Machine not perfect	10.00
1 Iron Saw Frame & Counter Shaft	10.00
1 Hand Power & Balance Wheel & [?]	6.00
1 Small Saw Frame	1.00
1 Work Bench with tail & Head screw	10.00
Tools in Drawer & Rack	5.00
10 Hand Screws	2.00
1 Tool Chest & Contents	30.00
1 Box with Marking Stamps	.50
3 Screw Wrenches	2.50
2 Cases of Drawers & Contents	10.00
1 Second Hand Melodeon Piano Rosewood Style	25.00
1 Martin's Guitar Second hand	5.00
12 Curly Maple Guitars not quite finished	75.00
1 Stove & Pipe	1.00
1 Old Violin (small)	5.00
1 Violin J. Ashborn's Make	10.00
1 Double Violin Case	2.50
1 Villoume [*sic*] Bow	2.00
1 Imitation Villoume [*sic*] Bow	1.00
10 Circular Saws (small)	8.00
1 Lot of Guitar Tools not mentioned in above	10.00

Back Room Hall

1 Bass Viol	5.00
2 Veneer Saws	4.00
1 Thickness Saw	1.00
3 Saws	3.00
1 Saw Set	.25
2 Machines for Cutting Screws	2.00

12 planes	5.00
2 Guitar Cases	4.00
2 Violins & Double Case	25.00
1 Cremona Violin and Double case not finished	12.50

South East Bedroom upstairs, including unfinished
Guitar Cases, Mettalic [*sic*] Heads and
    Parts of Guitars, Banjos, Tools, &c.   62.50

Workhouse

2 Work Benches	10.00
1 Vise & Bench	3.00

Shop

1 Lot Hoop Iron	4.00
1 Pair Tinners Shears	2.00
About 75 Hand Screws	15.00
Guitar Tools & Stock up Stairs in Shop	10.00
Guitar Tools & Stock down Stairs in Shop	10.00
Lumber for Guitars in Barn	5.00
1 Lot of Dies & Punches for Guitar Work	5.00
1 Press for joyning [*sic*] Rims	2.00
1 Steam Box	3.00
Lumber & Tools in Wagon house	3.00

Source: Original in Connecticut State Archives, Hartford.

F. Production of Guitars, 1859–1864 (Largest Customers Noted)

1859	243	(Bruno: 63; Zoebisch: 84; Peters & Sons: 31)
1860	291	(Bruno, or Bruno & Morris: 81; Zoebisch: 123)
1861	82	(Bruno & Morris: 7; Zoebisch: 35; Peters & Bros.: 20)
1862	85	(Bruno & Morris: 6; Zoebisch: 39; Peters & Bros.: 11)
1863	204	(Bruno: 22; Zoebisch: 118; Peters & Bros.: 25)
1864	165[*]	(Bruno: 32; Zoebsich: 82; Peters & Bros.: 24)

Source: Figures derived from Daybrook, 1859–64.

[*]Records through July 1 only

G. Inventory of Stock Fixtures Taken on Entering Copartnership, July 20, 1867

Rosewood	$125.00
Ivory	172.00
Cedar	190.00
Ebony	140.00
Spruce	75.00
Basswood & cases	100.00
Mahogany & other remnants of woods	50.00
Glue	25.00
[Indecipherable]	75.00
Hickory wood in shed	8.00
German silver wire	20.00
Gut string & Silver wire	30.00
Counter Desk & Wardrobe	12.00
Stoves	6.00
Circ[u]l[a]r Saw & 2 Spinning machines	125.00
2 Turning Laths [sic]	35.00
2 Grind Stones	8.00
4 Work Benches	80.00
20 Models	50.00
Fret Saw & Machine	15.00
Fixtures & Tools	75.00
Case Trimmings	50.00
Paper	5.00
Rolling Machine	15.00
Pearl Shel[l]s	50.00
Cotton Flannel 120 yds.	30.00
Bridge Pins & Guitar trimming	32.00
Guitar Machines	400.00
Shop	900.00
	2,900.00

Source: Daybook, 1867–68, 1874–84.

H. Production of Guitars, 1867–1883

1867	164	1873	245	1879	113
1868	199	1874	226	1880	128
1869	309	1875	212	1881	159
1870	188	1876	104	1882	192
1871	238	1877	118	1883	268
1872	232	1878	97		

Source: Figures derived from Daybook, 1869–74, and Ledger, 1873–84.

I. Sizes of Martin's Standard Models, 1870s (in Inches)

	Total Length	Body Length	Width of Upper Bout	Width of Lower Bout	Scale Length
Size 5	33	16	8¼	11¼	21.4 or 22
Size 4	33	16	8¹⁵⁄₁₆	11½	22
Size 3	36	17⅜	8⅛	11¼	23⅞
Size 2½	36½	17⅞	8¼	11⅝	24.5
Size 2	37	18¼	8½	12	24.5
Size 1	37¾	18⅞	9¼	12¾	24.9
Size 0	37¾	19⅛	9½	13½	24.9

Source: From Walter Carter, *The Martin Book* (San Francisco: GPI Books, 1995), 76–77.

J. Descriptions of Styles, ca. 1870s

Style 17 Introduced 1856. Two or four rosewood sound hole rings, with checkered purfling or green and white rope pattern in center of rings. Five-ply top binding with Rosewood outer layer, unbound back. White back stripe. Brass tuner plates, ivory buttons.

Style 18 Introduced 1857. Much like style 17. No top edge purfling. Rope pattern colored wood sound hole ring. Brass tuner plates, ivory buttons.

Style 20 Introduced 1850s. Herringbone sound hole ring or red, white, and green wood. Five-ply top binding and three-ply back with rosewood outer layer. Herringbone back stripe of red, white, and green wood.

Style 21 Introduced 1860s. Much like style 20. Colored wood herringbone sound hole ring between four rosewood rings (between two groups of five rings after 1869). Colored wood pattern herringbone back stripe. Diamond-patterned figures on end piece, engraved tuner plates, ivory buttons.

Styles 22, 23 Introduced 1850s. Herringbone sound hole ring between two groups of five rings. Four-ply top binding with ivory outer layer, ivory-bound back.

Style 24 Introduced 1850s. Sound hole ring of green and white wood in Z pattern (line of long diagonals between two short diagonal lines) between two groups of five rings. Rosewood top binding, top purfling of green and brown wood in diagonal pattern (some with additional checkered pattern lines). Thin line of side binding with rosewood outer layer. Back stripe of red, green, brown, and white wood in long arrow pattern. Engraved brass tuner plates, ivory tuner buttons. Diamond-patterned figures on end piece.

Style 26 Introduced 1850s. Sound hole ring in 5-9-5 grouping. Ivory-bound top, black and white rope pattern top purfling, one- or three-ply back binding with ivory outer layer. Zigzag back stripe.

Style 27 Introduced 1857. Sound hole ring of four groups of five rings with pearl ring in center. Ivory-bound top purfling of green and brown wood in long diagonal pattern, three-ply back binding with ivory outer layer. Zigzag back stripe. Ivory-bound fingerboard and peg head.

Style 28 Introduced 1860s. Pearl sound hole ring through 1870, later with black and white rings in 5-9-5 ring grouping (two ivory rings in center). Herringbone top purfling, ivory-bound top, three-ply back binding with ivory outer layer. Zipper pattern (horizontal pieces between two diagonal lines) back stripe.

Style 30 Introduced 1860s. Sound hole rings of four groups of five rings with pearl ring in center. Herringbone top purfling around top border; ivory binding on top, back, and fingerboard.

Style 34 Introduced 1870s. Pearl sound hole ring, top purfling of red, green, and white herringbone. Ivory-bound top, three-ply back binding with ivory outer layer, ivory bound fingerboard.

Style 40 Introduced 1860s. Pearl top borders but not around fingerboard. Pearl trim around top edge, ivory-bound figure. Zipper-patterned back stripe (line of horizontal inlays between two diagonal lines). Ivory bridge. German silver tuners, pearl buttons.

Style 42 Introduced 1870s. Pearl sound hole ring. Pearl trim around top edge, pearl trim on top around fingerboard, ivory-bound fingerboard. Zipper-patterned back stripe (line of horizontal inlays between two diagonal lines). Listed in 1870 with "screw neck." Ivory bridge. German silver tuners, pearl buttons.

Source: Walter Carter, *The Martin Book* (San Francisco: GPI Books, 1995), 83.

GLOSSARY

Action: Height of strings above the fingerboard; determines playability of the guitar.

Bass side: The side of the guitar on which the three lower strings are found.

Binding: Decorative strips (usually wooden or mother-of-pearl) around the edges of the guitar.

Bout: Outward curves of the guitar above and below the guitar's waist.

Braces: Wooden struts glued to the inside of the sounding board and back of the guitar to provide added strength.

Bridge: Part of the guitar glued onto the soundboard to which the strings are attached.

Bridge pin: Secures string to the bridge.

Buttons: Wooden or bone attachments to the ends of patent pegs by which the pegs are turned.

End pin: Bone or wooden pin set in the bottom of the guitar for holding one end of a shoulder strap (the other end is usually tied around the peg head).

Fan bracing: Braces for the soundboard in the shape of a fan.

Fingerboard: Part of the neck, usually made of ebony, rosewood, or some other resilient wood, on which the notes are fingered. Usually fretted.

Frets: Small raised strips of metal inlaid into the neck to mark finger positions for notes.

Friction pegs: Tuners kept in place by friction of pegs in holes in the peg head. Also called *violin-style tuners*.

Heel: Where the neck meets the body of the guitar. Usually thicker than the rest of the neck.

Ladder bracing: Braces for the soundboard set parallel to each other, like the steps of a ladder.

Lining: Thin wooden strips joining top and back of the guitar to the ribs that strengthen the instrument.

Marquetry: Decorative wooden patterns inlaid on the top, sides, or back of the guitar.

Neck: Long, thin part of the guitar, including the heel and peg head, on which the notes are fingered.

Neck block: Part of the neck that is attached to the inside of the guitar.

Nut: Piece of wood or bone at the top of the fingerboard, near the peg head, over which the strings pass in notches. These determine the spacing of the strings.

Patent pegs: Metal, geared tuning pegs. Sometimes called *machine heads, patent heads*, or *tuning machines*.

Peg head: Top of the neck, where the tuners are found. Also called the *headstock*.

Pin bridge: Type of bridge on which the strings are secured by bridge pins.

Purfling: Another term for binding.

Ribs: Sides of the guitar.

Rosette: Decorative inlay around the sound hole.

Saddle: Part of the bridge over which the strings pass. Usually made of bone.

Scale: Length of the strings from the nut to the bridge. Double the distance from the nut to the twelfth-fret position.

Soundboard: Top of the guitar, usually made of spruce.

Sound hole: Hole in the soundboard of the guitar that allows sound projection.

Tie bridge: Type of bridge on which the strings are knotted to secure them.

Treble side: The side of the guitar on which the three higher-pitched strings are found.

Tuners: Wooden or metal parts in the peg head by which the strings are tightened. Also known as *tuning pegs*.

Violin-style tuners: See *friction pegs*.

Waist: The middle of the guitar, between the two bouts.

X-bracing: Braces for the soundboard set in the shape of an *X*.

NOTES

All references to the C. F. Martin & Company Archives, Nazareth, Pennsylvania, will be abbreviated CFM.

PREFACE

1. The only music industry for which there are any remotely comparable sources is piano making. There is good documentation of Steinway & Sons, renowned piano makers, but its records for the antebellum period are nowhere near as rich as Martin's. See Richard K. Lieberman, *Steinway & Sons* (New Haven, Conn.: Yale University Press, 1995). See also Gary J. Kornblith, "The Craftsman as Industrialist: Jonas Chickering and the Transformation of American Piano Manufacturing," *Business History Review* 59 (1985): 349–69. For brass instruments, see Robert E. Eliason, "The Meachams, Musical Instrument Makers of Hartford and Albany," *Journal of the American Musical Instrument Society* 5–6 (1980): 54–73, and "Charles G. Christman, Musical Instrument Maker in Nineteenth-Century New York," ibid., 27 (2001): 84–119; and, in general, Laurence Libin, *American Musical Instruments in the Metropolitan Museum of Art* (New York: W. W. Norton, 1985).

CHAPTER ONE

1. Herman Melville, *Pierre; or, The Ambiguities* (Evanston, Ill.: Northwestern University Press, 1971); all quotations concerning Isabel and her guitar are from pages 125–27 and 149–53.

2. Herman Melville to Sophia Hawthorne, January 8, 1852, in *The Letters of Herman Melville*, ed. Merrell R. Davis and William H. Gilman (New Haven, Conn.: Yale University Press, 1960), 146.

3. As early as the 1830s, for example, sheet music compositions recorded the kinds of preternatural effects supposedly wrought by the guitar. One writer of popular song thus apostrophized the instrument: "Many a feeling fraught / With wildest ecstasy / Many a gloomy thought, / Is strangely link'd with thee; / Feelings, though sweet, too deep / Too wild for souls all blest— / Dark thoughts that will not sleep, / Nor let the bosom rest. / Adieu, my sweet Guitar! / My day of song is o'er, / And to the midnight star / I'll wake my chords no more." W. M. Robinson, *The Guitar: A Serenade* ([Philadelphia]: Fiot, Meignen & Co., [ca. 1830s]). See fig. 1-2.

4. Information about the early development of the guitar is available in Stanley Sadie, ed., *New Grove Dictionary of Musical Instruments*, 3 vols. (London: Macmillan, 1984), 2:87–109. But see also Graham Wade, *The Traditions of the Classical Guitar* (London: John Calder, 1980), 3–23; Harvey Turnbull, *The Guitar, from the Renaissance to the Present Day* (New York: Charles Scribner's Sons, 1974), 5–62; Alexander Bellow, *The Illustrated History of the Guitar* (Rockville Centre, N.Y.: Franco Colombo Publications, 1970), 53–147; Frederic V. Grunfeld, *The Art and Times of the Guitar: An Illustrated History of Guitars and Guitarists* (New York: Macmillan, 1969), 61–162; and Peter Päffgen, *Die Gitarre: Grundzüge ihrer Entwicklung* (Mainz: Schott, 1988).

5. Turnbull, *Guitar*, 66.

6. A. P. Sharpe, *The Story of the Spanish Guitar*, 4th ed. (London: Clifford Essex, 1954), 15–18; Stewart Button, *The Guitar in England, 1800–1924* (New York: Garland Publishing, 1989), 210–41.

7. Sharpe, *Spanish Guitar*, 18–22. On Lacote see also Constant Pierre, *Les facteurs d'instruments de musique[,] les luthiers[,] et la facture instrumentale* (Paris: Ed. Sagot, 1893), 275.

8. Wade, *Traditions*, 100–101.

9. On Sor see particularly Brian Jeffrey, *Fernando Sor: Composer and Guitarist* (London: TECLA Editions, 1977), but also Philip J. Bone, *The Guitar and Mandolin: Biographies of Celebrated Players and Composers*, 2d ed. (London: Schott & Company, 1954), 335–43; Wade, *Traditions*, 114; and Turnbull, *Guitar*, 82–85.

10. From an article in the British periodical *Giulianiad* in 1833, quoted in Jeffrey, *Sor*, 38.

11. Quoted in Jeffrey, *Sor*, 71–72.

12. Sor speaks to this collaboration in the introduction to his *Method for the Spanish Guitar*, trans. A. Merrick (London: R. Cocks and Company, [1830]), 9.

13. See Thomas F. Heck, *Mauro Giuliani: Virtuoso Guitarist and Composer* (Columbus, Ohio: Editions Orphée, 1995); Bone, *Guitar and Mandolin*, 137–45; Turnbull, *Guitar*, 85–100; and Wade, *Traditions*, 103–25.

14. The piece was written in 1830 and published in *Giulianiad* later; see Wade, *Traditions*, 116, also 118–19.

15. Bone, *Guitar and Mandolin*, 2–5; Wade, *Traditions*, 119–21.

16. Bone, *Guitar and Mandolin*, 70–75.

17. Wade, *Traditions*, 124–25; Bone, *Guitar and Mandolin*, 67–70.

18. Wade, *Traditions*, 109.

19. Cited in ibid., 127.

20. Grunfeld, *Art and Times*, 202.

21. *Giulianiad* 1 (1833): 2.

22. Cited in James Ballard, *The Elements of Guitar-Playing* (New York: Geib and Walker, 1838), 4.

23. Cited in Grunfeld, *Life and Times*, 174.

24. C[harles] de Marescot, *La Guitaromanie, Op. 46.* (Paris: chez L'Auteur, [c. 1830]). The book is exceedingly rare; the only copy known in the United States is in the collection of the author.

25. Nicholas Tawa, *High-Minded and Low-Down: Music in the Lives of Americans, 1800–1861* (Boston: Northeastern University Press, 2000), 246.

26. For a wonderful evocation of the complexity of New York City's musical life in these years, see Vera Brodsky Lawrence, *Strong on Music: The New York Music Scene in the Days of George Templeton Strong, 1836–1875*, 3 vols. (Chicago: University of Chicago Press, 1988–99). See also Ronald L. Davis, *A History of Music in American Life*, 3 vols. (Malabar, Fla.: Robert Krieger Publishing, 1982), 1:95–121.

27. "On the Evidences of Musical Taste," *American Musical Journal* 1, 1 (1834): 17.

28. Richard Crawford, *America's Musical Life: A History* (New York: W. W. Norton, 2001), 221.

29. See, for example, Russell Sanjek, *American Popular Music and Its Business: The First Four Hundred Years*, 3 vols. (New York: Oxford University Press, 1988), 2:1–125; Dale Cockrell, "Nineteenth-Century Popular Music," in *Cambridge History of American Music*, ed. David Nichols (New York: Cambridge University Press, 1998), 158–85; Gerald Boardman, *The American Musical Theater* (New York: Oxford University

Press, 1978); Robert C. Toll, *Blacking Up: The Minstrel Show in Nineteenth-Century America* (New York: Oxford University Press, 1974); Nicholas Tawa, *Sweet Songs for Gentle Americans: The Parlor Song in America, 1790–1860* (Bowling Green: Bowling Green State University Press, 1980), and *A Music for the Millions: Antebellum Democratic Attitudes and the Birth of American Popular Music* (New York: Pendragon Press, 1985); W. Porter Ware and Thaddeus C. Lockard Jr., *P. T. Barnum Presents Jenny Lind: The American Tour of the Swedish Nightingale* (Baton Rouge: Louisiana State University Press, 1980).

30. Lawrence, *Strong on Music*, 1:94, and Tawa, *High-Minded and Low-Down*, 71; see also Crawford, *America's Musical Life*, 240–71.

31. Lydia Maria Child, *Letters from New-York* (New York: Charles S. Francis and Co., 1843), 180.

32. Tawa, *High-Minded and Low-Down*, 71.

33. Henry D. Thoreau, *Familiar Letters* (Boston: Houghton Mifflin, 1895), 367.

34. Lawrence, *Strong on Music*, 1:94–95. Crawford, *America's Musical Life*, 230, describes how America's unique social conditions contributed to a musical culture much less closed than that in Europe, where there was a sharper distinction between elite and popular forms. The difference was the economy, for in America "the popular sphere and commercial interests . . . enjoyed more clout."

35. *New York Sunday Morning News*, cited in Ballard, *Elements of Guitar-Playing*, "Critical Remarks"; John W. Moore, *Complete Encyclopaedia of Music: Elementary, Technical, Historical, Biographical, Vocal, and Instrumental* (Boston: John P. Jewett, 1854), 353; and *Musical World and New York Musical Times*, July 1, 1854, 108.

36. But see Crawford, *America's Musical Life*, 233–40, who notes the continuing prevalence of pianos, whose prices decreased somewhat in the 1840s and 1850s with the mass production of the instrument's constituent parts.

37. Tawa, *High-Minded and Low-Down*, 101.

38. *Circular and Catalogue of the Albany Female Academy* (Albany: C. Van Benthuysen & Co., 1843); *[Boston] Musical Quarterly*, August 17, 1846, 116. Even as far west as Illinois, musical instruction was in demand. An advertisement in a fledgling musical review in 1857 asked for "a lady capable of teaching the piano and German." The "Female Seminary" in northern Illinois also noted that it sought someone "practical and thorough, rather than showy," and if the individual were able "to teach the guitar and painting, all the better." *Chicago Musical Review* 2, 8 (1857), 120.

39. *New-York Mirror*, cited in Ballard, *Elements of Guitar-Playing*, "Critical Remarks."

40. *Letters of William Gilmore Simms*, ed. Mary C. Oliphant et al., 6 vols. (Columbia: University of South Carolina Press, 1952), 1:90; John Pendleton Kennedy, *Memories of the Life of William Wirt*, rev. ed., 2 vols. (Philadelphia: Lippincott, 1860), 1:128; and Mrs. N. P. Lasalle, *Annie Grayson; Or, Life in Washington* (New York: Bunce, 1853), 70.

41. In his survey of the instrumentation in early minstrel shows, Robert B. Winans finds that, particularly before the 1850s, the guitar was rarely present on the minstrel stage. See "Early Minstrel Show Music, 1843–1852," in *Musical Theatre in America*, ed. Glenn Loney (Westport, Conn.: Greenwood Press, 1984), 71–97.

42. *New-York Mirror*, cited in Ballard, *Elements of Guitar-Playing*, "Critical Remarks."

43. William Ransom Hogan and Edwin Adams Davis, eds., *William Johnson's Natchez: The Ante-bellum Diary of a Free Negro* (1951; reprint, Baton Rouge: Louisiana State University Press, 1979), 350.

44. David Ritter, *A Key to the Study and Practice of the Accordeon*, 5th ed. (Philadelphia: Smith and Peck, 1841), 3, 5.

45. Louisa C. Tuthill, *The Young Lady's Home* (Boston: William J. Reynolds and Co., 1847), 72.

46. Ballard, *Elements of Guitar-Playing*, 3, "Critical Remarks."

47. *New Instructions for the Spanish Guitar, Containing a Variety of Songs and Pieces by a Professor* (Philadelphia: G. Willig, [ca. 1816]), 2). The American Antiquarian Society's copy of this rare book was dated by the music historian and bibliographer Richard Wolfe. Another early tutor available in the United States was *New Instructions for the Guitar, to which is added A Collection of Popular Aires, by M. Carcassi, with French and English Text* (Philadelphia: Klemm and Brother, [ca. 1820]), essentially a republication of Carcassi. As its title suggests, John Siegling's *Complete Instructor for the Spanish and English Guitar, Harp, Lute, and Lyre* (Charlestown, S.C.: J. Siegling, 1828), is a potpourri devoted to a variety of stringed instruments, including the English guitar, a ten-course instrument struck with a plectrum that derives from the cittern. As early as 1819, Edward Riley, proprietor of a music store and publisher of engraved sheet music, advertised that, in addition to lessons on the pianoforte, flageolet, flute, and violin, he offered them on the "guitarr." See Edward Riley, *Riley's Flute Melodies*, vol. 2 (New York: Edward Riley, [1819]), 100.

48. Otto Torp, *New and Improved Method for the Spanish Guitar* (New York: Torp & Unger, 1834). See also Torp, *Instruction Book for the Spanish Guitar, selected from the Works of F. Carulli, F. Molini & M. Giuliani, Professors to the Conservatory of Paris* (New York: E. Riley, 1829).

49. Letter from W. Penson to D. Walker, and *Family Magazine*, both in Ballard, *Elements of Guitar-Playing*, "Critical Remarks." In 1861 Ballard was still listed in New York City as a "Teacher" of "Guitar and Singing"; see *American Musical Directory* (1861; reprint, New York: Da Capo, 1980), 117. Ballard also wrote *A History of the Guitar, from the Earliest Antiquity to the Present Time* (New York: William B. Tilton & Company, 1855), a work published by a guitar maker in which Ballard touted Tilton's patented "improvement" for stringed instruments (see Chap. 4 in this volume).

50. Ballard, *Elements of Guitar-Playing*, "Critical Remarks."

51. Ibid.

52. Ibid., 1–2.

53. Ibid., 3.

54. *Sunday Morning News*, cited in ibid., "Critical Remarks."

55. Ballard, *Elements of Guitar-Playing*, 44.

56. [Elias Howe], *Howe's Instructor for the Guitar* (Boston: E. Howe, 1846); this title was reissued by Oliver Ditson in 1851.

57. Richard Culver, *The Guitar Instructor: An Easy Method Containing the Elementary Principles of Music with Examples & Lessons Requisite to Facilitate the Progress of the Pupil* (Boston: Oliver Ditson, 1846), 3–4.

58. Charles C. Converse, *New Method for the Guitar, Containing Elementary Instructions in Music, Designed for Those Who Study without a Master* (New York: William Hall & Son, 1855). In an advertisement Converse placed in 1854 he announced that he now had made New York City his residence and proposed "to give Instruction on the Guitar, Singing and Pianoforte." He could be contacted, he added, at Firth, Pond & Company (*Musical World*, November 4, 1854, 121). On Frank Converse see Philip F. Gura and James F. Bollman, *America's Instrument: The Banjo in the Nineteenth Century* (Chapel Hill: University of North Carolina Press, 1999), 84–85. Other

instruction books from this period include N. P. B. Curtiss, *Progressive and Complete Method for the Spanish Guitar* (Boston: Oliver Ditson, [ca. 1850]), and Louis Bail, *Guitar Without a Master* (Boston: Oliver Ditson, 1851).

59. Ballard, *Elements of Guitar-Playing*, 3.

60. U.S. Patent registered October 6, 1831. Patents issued prior to July 1836 were not assigned a patent number at the time they were granted. Numbers were assigned retrospectively after that date and are designated with the prefix "x." Hence, Scherr's patent now is no. x6788. Emilius Nicolai Scherr was a Danish immigrant who made pianofortes and organs in Philadelphia. See Laurence Libin, *American Musical Instruments in the Metropolitan Museum of Art* (New York: W. W. Norton, 1985), 130–32. Several of his harp guitars are extant. In one edition of his tutor, Torp took the occasion to tout Scherr's invention and included as one of his illustrations a lithograph of two players with Scherr's guitars (fig. 1-21). See Torp, *New and Improved Method for the Spanish Guitar* (New York: Torp and Viereck, 1834), facing p. 5. Ballard was the one who noted the reasons that Scherr's patent did not gain much popularity; see his *History of the Guitar*, 21.

61. *Longworth's American Almanac, New-York Register, and City Directory* (New York: Thomas Longworth, 1837), leaf 1v. The "latest Pattern" may refer to three tuners on each side of a rectangular peg head, rather than the six-on-a-side tuners associated with German, particularly Viennese, makers. See Chapter 2 for a discussion of such tuning machines.

62. Moore, *Complete Encyclopaedia*, 353.

63. Journal, 1837–38, January 26, 1838, CFM.

CHAPTER TWO

1. Basic biographical information on Martin is available in Mike Longworth, *Martin Guitars: A History*, 3d ed. (Nazareth, Pa: Longworth, 1988); Walter Carter, *The Martin Book* (San Francisco: GPI Books, 1995); Jim Washburn and Richard Johnston, *Martin Guitars: An Illustrated Celebration of America's Premier Guitarmaker* (Emmaus, Pa.: Rodale Press, 1997); and Lloyd Farrar, "Under the Crown and Eagle," *Newsletter of the American Musical Instrument Society*, October 1983, 3–4. See also Bernhard Zoebisch, *Vogtländer Geigenbau: Biographien und Erklärungen bis 1950* (Horb am Neckar: Verein der Freunde und Förderer des Musikinstrumenten-Museums e. V. Markneukirchen, 2000), for biographical information about the Martin family and other musical instrument makers in Saxony.

2. On Stauffer see Harvey Turnbull, *The Guitar, from the Renaissance to the Present Day* (New York: Charles Scribner's Sons, 1974), 70; A. P. Sharpe, *The Story of the Spanish Guitar*, 4th ed. (London: Clifford Essex, 1954), 19–20; and Helmut Ottner, *Der Wiener Instrumentenbau, 1815–1833* (Tutzing: Hans Schneider, 1977), 144–45.

3. On Panormo see Turnbull, *Guitar*, 68–70; Alexander Bellow, *The Illustrated History of the Guitar* (Rockville Centre, N.Y.: Franco Colombo Publications, 1970), 173, 177–79; Stewart Button, *The Guitar in England, 1800–1924* (New York: Garland Publishing, 1989), 210–41, 311–15; and Sharpe, *Spanish Guitar*, 15–16.

4. Turnbull, *Guitar*, 70.

5. Three other children, Emily Clara (September 2, 1835), Hermann Henry (May 10, 1839), and Nathalie Eleanora Susanna (October 7, 1842) followed, all born in the United States.

6. On instrument making in this region see *Musikinstrumenten-Museum Markneukirchen* (Munich: Deutscher Kunstverlag, 2000).

7. Quotations here and in the following two paragraphs come from Sharpe, *Spanish Guitar*, 20–21, and Berthold Gotz, "Geschichte der Saiteninstrumentmacherinnung," in *Anlasslich der Gemeinschaften Gedenkfeier du Saiteninstrumentmacher . . . und der Saitenmacherinnung zu Markneukirchen* (Markneukirchen, 1927), 41–44. I thank Richard Rust for help in translating from the latter.

8. On the impact of the "market revolution" see especially Charles Sellers, *The Market Revolution: Jacksonian America, 1815–1846* (New York: Oxford University Press, 1991).

9. In an article on the Martin Company, Lloyd Farrar mentions a manuscript in German in which Martin described his Atlantic voyage, but I could not find the item in the Martin archives. See "Under the Crown and Eagle," *Newsletter of the American Musical Instrument Society*, October 1983, 3.

10. Manifest of the ship *Columbia*, "Passenger Lists of Vessels Arriving at New York, 1820–1897," microfilm reel 21, item 820, National Archives, Washington, D.C. This group of nine, the first names listed on the manifest, is set off with a large bracket. Martin was listed as thirty-seven years old; his wife, twenty-eight; his son, Christian Frederick, eight; and daughter, Otilia, one-and-a-half. Including the Martins, there were 191 passengers aboard the ship. John W. Hartman, Johann Georg Martin's brother-in-law, also was the father of C. F. Hartmann, who later worked for Martin and, in 1867, went into partnership with him and his son Frederick (see Chapter 5).

11. See manifest of ship *Columbia*. Robert Ernst, *Immigrant Life in New York City, 1825–1863* (1949; reprint, Port Washington, N.Y.: Ira J. Friedman, 1965), 12–14, offers details of the immigrant experience when the Martins embarked.

12. Ernst, *Immigrant Life*, 37–40. On the importance of cartmen to the city's economy, see Graham Russell Hodges, *New York City Cartmen, 1667–1850* (New York: New York University Press, 1986), esp. 129–50.

13. See Tyler Anbinder, *Five Points: The Nineteenth-Century City Neighborhood that Invented Tap Dance, Stole Elections, and Became the World's Most Monstrous Slum* (New York: Free Press, 2001).

14. The best study of housing in New York City in this period is Elizabeth Blackmar, *Manhattan for Rent, 1785–1850* (Ithaca, N.Y.: Cornell University Press, 1989), esp. 109–48. See also Ernst, *Immigrant Life*, 42–43. On the German community in New York during the antebellum period, see Stanley Nadel, *Little Germany: Ethnicity, Religion, and Class in New York City, 1845–80* (Urbana: University of Illinois Press, 1990), esp. chap. 2.

15. Klaus Wust, *Guardian on the Hudson: The German Society of the City of New York* (New York: German Society of the City of New York, [1984]), 22–28. See Journal, 1836–37, February 1, 1837, and Journal, 1837–38, May 1, 1837, CFM, for rent payment. See also ibid., May 4, 1838. An entry for August 2, 1837, in ibid., indicates that his tax bill on the property was $21.69. Blackmar, *Manhattan for Rent*, 240, notes that another rental on Hudson Street went for $87.50 per quarter.

16. Nancy Groce, *Musical Instrument Makers of New York: A Directory of Eighteenth- and Nineteenth-Century Craftsmen*, Annotated Reference Works in Music no. 4 (Stuyvesant, N.Y.: Pendragon Press, 1991), xi. See also Blackmar, *Manhattan for Rent*, chaps. 4 and 5, and Richard B. Stott, *Workers in the Metropolis: Class, Ethnicity, and Youth in Antebellum New York City* (Ithaca, N.Y.: Cornell University Press, 1990), 124–25.

17. Daybook, 1834–37, CFM. This book has a bookseller's tag that reads "J. T. Burton, Bookseller + Stationer. 189½ Hudson-St.," a short distance from Martin's shop.

18. See Russell Sanjek, *American Popular Music and Its Business: The First Four Hundred Years*, 3 vols. (New York: Oxford University Press, 1988), 2:57–92.

19. On Eisenbrandt see Laurence Libin, *American Musical Instruments in the Metropolitan Museum of Art* (New York: W. W. Norton, 1985), 74–75, and "The Eisenbrandt Family Pedigree," in *Studia Organologica: Festschrift für John Henry van der Meer zu seinem fünfundsechzigsten Geburstag*, ed. Friedman Hellwig (Tutzing: Schneider, 1987), 335–42. On Boucher see Philip F. Gura and James F. Bollman, *America's Instrument: The Banjo in the Nineteenth Century* (Chapel Hill: University of North Carolina Press, 1999), 55–65.

20. Daybook, 1834–37, Store Receipts, May–July 1834; ledger entry, ibid., for Fehrman, and for Rönneberg, June 16, 1834; and Groce, *Musical Instrument Makers*, 134. Fehrman published at least one piece of music that he arranged for guitar, namely, Henry Russell's *My Heart's in the Highlands* (New York: James L. Hewitt & Company, [ca. 1830s]), itself derived from Robert Burns.

21. Daybook, 1834–37, ledger entry for Jacob Hartmann, presumably related to August.

22. Journal, 1836–37, April 8 and May 26, 1836.

23. See William Waterhouse, *The New Langwill Index: A Dictionary of Musical Wind-Instrument Makers and Inventors* (London: Tony Bingham, 1993), 261.

24. Although Martin continued to do some business with Hartmann, his last large order, totaling $385.11, came in the summer of 1838, and Martin sent him a last bill of exchange, for "$400 Rheinish or $170," later that autumn. Journal, 1837–38, August 5 and October 29, 1838.

25. On tariffs see Leander Bishop, *History of American Manufactures from 1608–1860*, 3d ed., 3 vols. (Philadelphia: Edward Young, 1868), 2:342–43, chap. 5.

26. Journal, 1836–37, August 26 and September 23, 1836, and January 24, 1837.

27. On January 28, 1836, for example, Martin noted the following expenses: "for duty of one box no. 15 and other expenditures," $39.64; "Land and Sea freight for the same," $14.86; "for duty of a box, no. 14, received on the 11 January," $29.80; "Land Sea freight of the same," $13.08. For Meyer see Journal, 1836–37, January 28 and September 23, 1836, and May 29, 1837, and Journal, 1837–38, July 18 (for goods that arrived on the *Isabella*) and August 8, 1837 (shipment on the *Constitution*). For Schmidt & Son see ibid., October 1, 1838, payment "for freight of goods from Hamburg."

28. Journal, 1836–37, April 14, 1837, for example, and see Journal, 1837–38, August 17, 1838, for this account: "Paid a cartman for carrying a Piano from Mr. Opal's, 196 Hudson Street, to the store 212 Fulton Street (including 3 helpers), $1.75." See also Hodges, *New York City Cartmen*, chap. 10.

29. Journal, 1836–37, November 4, 19, December 2, 1836.

30. On Gütter see Stewart Carter, "The Gütter Family: Wind Instrument Makers and Dealers to the Moravian Brethren in America," *Journal of the American Musical Instrument Society* 27 (2001): 48–83.

31. Journal, 1836–37, June 28, 1836. See also May 17, August 25, September 23, 27, 1836, and March 18 and 29, 1837. The violoncello cost Martin $15.00.

32. Ibid., April 18, 28, June 9, October 6, 1836, and January 9, 10, March 3, 1837.

33. Journal, 1837–38, May 9 and 18, 1838. On Stumcke see Christine Merrick Ayars, *Contributions to the Art of Music in America by the Music Industries of Boston* (New York: W. H. Wilson, 1937), 227–28. By 1853 he had relocated to San Francisco. The *New York Musical World*, May 2, 1857, 282, reported that since that year "Mr. Charles Stumcke, an old gentleman of Bremen, who learned his trade 35 years ago in Verona,

Italy, [was] now manufacturing musical instruments [in San Francisco], but particularly Guitars." One instrument label from the period reads "CHARLES STUMCKE / Manufacturer of all Kinds of / GUITARS / No. 8 Winter Street (upstairs) / Boston / N. B. All kinds of stringed instruments repaired at the shortest notice." See <www.vintage-instruments.com> (December 2001). On Schatz in Boston, see Ayars, *Contributions*, 277, 306.

34. Robert E. Eliason, "Charles G. Christman, Musical Instrument Maker in Nineteenth-Century New York," *Journal of the American Musical Instrument Society* 27 (2001): 84–119, and Groce, *Musical Instrument Makers*, 30–31.

35. Journal, 1836–37, April 13, November 7, 10, 1836; Journal, 1837–38, June 19, 1838. The brass instrument cost $20.00.

36. For Schroeder see Journal, 1836–37, April 11, 12, 25, 1836, February 21, 1837, and Groce, *Musical Instrument Makers*, 139. For Baack, Journal, 1837–38, January 27, 1838, and Groce, *Musical Instrument Makers*, 5.

37. In one transaction, Martin paid Geib & Walker $30.00 for twenty bundles of "E" strings, $12.00 for six bundles of "A" strings, and $7.50 for three bundles of "D" strings (Journal, 1837–38, March 26, June 27, and September 9, 1838). See Journal, 1836–37, April 5 and August 9, 1836, for the account with Geib & Walker.

38. Journal, 1836–37, March 4 and 10, 1836, February 2 and May 12, 1836, and May 12, 1837.

39. In his journal for such daily transactions, Martin recorded the patron's name if the amount of the sale was sizable but rarely did so if the transaction was under a few dollars. He also identified the customer if he or she had a regular account with him, in which case the transaction appears in the "Account" column rather than under "Cash" and later would be entered in Martin's ledger book as well.

40. Journal, 1836–37, February 2, June 2, December 12, 1836.

41. For the violoncello see Daybook, 1834–37, November 1, 1836. For the cello bow, see ibid., April 9, 1836.

42. Journal, 1836–37, March 17, 1837, and November 19, 1836.

43. Journal, 1837–38, November 11, 1838. On another occasion, "Mr. Bennet, No. 688 Greenwich Street, got a G trompete with 4 Crooks[,] to try it" and left a "copper bugle and $2.00 for security." See Daybook, 1834–37, June 20, 1836, C. F. Martin & Company Archives. Martin's largest order for brass came at the suggestion of a "Dr. Sens" of New York. On his recommendation, "Captain Thomas Swords, the United States Quartermaster at Fort Leavenworth," bought three copper bugles at $15.00 each, a tenor trombone for $18.00, a bass trombone for $20.00, a copper basshorn for $36.00, a French horn "with all crooks" for $26.00, and a trumpet with three valves and four crooks for $30.00. A week later "Mssrs. Schuyler and Swords" (the latter probably the client's relative), 142 Broadway, paid Martin in full for the instruments, as well as for some extra mouthpieces, "bought by order of Captain Swords," to a total of $194.00. See Journal, 1837–38, November 11, 1838.

44. Journal, 1837–38, March 13, 1838. The horns cost $50.00 total.

45. Ibid., April 3, 1837.

46. Journal, 1836–37, January 1, 1836.

47. Ibid., November 23, 1836, May 13, 1837, March 22, 1836, May 10, 1836, and September 22, 1836.

48. Journal, 1837–38, July 10, 1838. See also October 17, 1838, for the sale of Carcassi's exercises.

49. Ibid., July 19, 1838, for the sale of a Giuliani tutor.

50. Journal, 1836–37, June 11, 1836.

51. On one occasion, Martin recorded that Mr. Wiesner, "a black man," brought in his violin for a seventy-five-cent repair, and in his records Martin noted that he had worked on this client's instrument before, in 1835. See Journal, 1837–38, September 6, 1838. For rehairing the cello bows, see Daybook, 1834–37, July 6, 1836.

52. He returned one guitar, received on May 14 from "Miss Collins, at Ms. Smith's. No. 3 5th Avenue," for a $1.25 repair, a week later. On May 31 someone brought in one of Martin's own guitars, to have the bridge raised; he did the work at no charge and returned it on June 10. See Journal, 1836–37, "Orders Received," which continue into 1838.

53. Daybook, 1834–37, April 9, 1836, for Schroeder's work.

54. On Paulus, see Groce, *Musical Instrument Makers*, 5. He may have been related to Martin through Martin's mother, Eva Regina Paulus Martin.

55. Journal, 1837–38, May 13, 1838.

56. Given the many business connections among German immigrants and their compatriots across the Atlantic, it seems likely that this Jacob Hartman may have been related to August Hartmann, the Markneukirchen exporter. Daybook, 1834–37, June 27, 1836, and November 10, 1836.

57. Journal, 1837–38, November 19, 1837.

58. An order for $128.43¾ followed in November, another for $84.32 in December, and a third for $70.75 later that month. See Daybook, 1834–37, November 6, December 2, 17, 1835.

59. Ibid., ledger entry for Charles H. Keith and S. G. Miller.

60. See Journal, 1837–38, September 31, 1837, for example.

61. In April 1836, for example, he sent a shipment worth eighty dollars to Coe and another valued at sixty-nine dollars to Nunns, Clark & Company. See Daybook, 1834–37, April 1, 1836.

62. In 1833 Samuel Bromberg and Company was listed as a music store at 329 Broadway. See *Longworth's American Almanac, New-York Register, and City Directory* (New York: Thomas Longworth, 1833), 144.

63. The latest entry in 1839 is in the account for Schnepf, on March 4, providing some sense of when Martin closed out his business in the city. However, there is one notation for 1840 (on the page that also records the account of "Professor Druck") that settles an account with Ludecus & Wolter, which a year earlier had bought Martin's entire stock.

64. On one occasion, for example, Martin sent Taylor a large order ($261.91) whose details are worth noting. He included, among other items, a dozen "violins No. 3 [designation of a grade] with bows" at $8.50; six violins "double inlaid" with bows at $19.00; two violins "with pearl ornaments," two bows, and two cases, at $13.50 each set; a violin "with backprints" (perhaps a marquetry design on the back?), case, and bow for $10.50; two copper bugles at $8.25 each; a rosewood guitar for $63.00; two "Post trumpets" at $1.75 each; and three hunting horns at $1.00 each. See Journal, 1837–38, September 6, 1837.

65. Journal, 1836–37, January 22, 1836; see also May 26, 1836.

66. Ibid., November 7, 1836, and Journal, 1837–38, January 27 and May 18, 1838.

67. Journal, 1836–37, May 5, 1836, "Sent to Mrs. Hasbrook (O'Kill's Boarding School) a Guitar with Patent screws, ordered by Mr. Fehrman. $25," and May 28,

"Sent to Mrs. O'Kill a Guitar with patent screws and a case. $24." This was Mary Okill, listed as running a boardinghouse (and, evidently, a school) at 8–10 Clinton Place. See *Doggett's New York City Directory for 1844–1845* (New York: Doggett, 1844), 264.

68. Journal, 1836–37, February 12, 1836, for piano rental, and November 21, 1836, for flute. Other examples are in ibid., January 15, February 6, June 27, July 1836, and Journal, 1837–38, July 17 and 27, 1838. See Ledger, 1837–40, Boucher's account, CFM, for cello.

69. Martin's Daybook, 1834–37, is the source of the data and speculation in this paragraph.

70. Berger previously had done "painting" for Martin; see Journal, 1837–38, July 15, 1837. On the importance of such signage to New York's commerce, see David M. Henkin, *City Reading: Written Words and Public Spaces in Antebellum New York* (New York: Columbia University Press, 1998), chap. 3.

71. Journal, 1837–38, May 14, June 16, and August 11, 1838.

72. Journal, 1836–37, October 13, 1836.

73. On one occasion Martin bought 89 feet of pine for only $2.22 and 159 feet of holly veneer for $9.54 (Journal, 1836–37, November 28, 1836). Another large order, for unspecified veneers, from Peck & Ridner, was $14.82 (Journal, 1837–38, June 28, 1838).

74. Journal, 1836–37, February 14 and April 28, 1837, and November 28, 1836.

75. In 1845 Heinrich Eduard Baack's advertisement in one of the city directories had him carrying "Kammer's Patent Heads for Guitars," the only hint we have of what European firm supplied these in the 1840s. See *Sheldon & Co.'s Business and Advertising Directory* (New York: John F. Trow, 1843), 129.

76. Journal, 1837–38, June 8, 1838.

77. On February 14, 1837, for example, Martin paid Phyfe twenty-four dollars for "six sets" of ivory. The year before he recorded the purchase of "2 sets ivory Piano keys, extra fine, at $4 each" (Journal, 1836–37, November 11, 1836). As we shall see, in the 1850s Martin still patronized Phyfe, who sold him actual ivory tusks by the pound. In a business directory for this decade, Phyfe is listed as a "Dealer in Ivory and Hard Woods" and sold, besides ivory and the many objects he made from it, "Sea Horse and Whale Teeth," boxwood, ebony, "cocoa [cocus] and granadilla," "satin, partridge, palm," and "lignumvitae." See *Wilson's Business Directory for New York City for 1852–1853* (New York: John F. Trow, 1852), opposite p. 177.

78. Daybook, 1834–37, December 2, 1835.

79. Insurance policy with North River Insurance Company, May 21, 1838, CFM.

80. Daybook, 1834–37, "*Ausgaben für Holtz*, &c.," for the lithographer's work, and Daybook, 1836–37, March 21, 1837, for the engraving and printing. "Harris" is probably James Harris, an engraver at 58 Nassau Street (see *Longworth's American Almanac, New-York Register, and City Directory* (New York: Thomas Longworth, 1837), 295. This same transaction is recorded in the Journal, 1837–38, April 1, 1837. See also Henkin, *City Reading*, 72–74, on the importance of trade cards for advertising in the city.

81. Thomas Heck notes that "at the time of the first flowering of the classic guitar in Vienna (1800–1820)," instrument makers "produced a great many sizes and shapes of guitar, depending on the needs of the customer." See his *Birth of the Classic Guitar and Its Cultivation in Vienna, Reflected in the Career and Compositions of Mauro Giuliani*, 2 vols. (Ph.D. diss., Yale University, 1971), 1:56–57. For examples of Martin guitars from the 1830s, see Washburn and Johnston, *Martin Guitars*, 18–23, 27–40, and Carter, *Martin Book*, 10–11, 14–15, 18–19.

82. Journal, 1837–38, May 19, 1838. Brazilwood is a very heavy, red wood, growing in the tropics.

83. Journal, 1836–37, September 16, 1836, and July 15, 1837. For examples of such guitars see Washburn and Johnston, *Martin Guitars*, 19, 28. Journal, 1837–38, January 26, 1838, for Ballard.

84. On such veneering seen among the European makers, see Jose L. Romanillos, *Antonio de Torres, Guitar Maker—His Life and Work*, rev. ed. (Westport, Conn.: Bold Strummer, 1997), 80.

85. Washburn and Johnston, *Martin Guitars*, 28–31, 38–39; Carter, *Martin Book*, 10–11, 14–15, 18–19.

86. See, for example, Journal, 1837–38, April 23, 1838. On Torres's innovation, see Romanillos, *Antonio de Torres*; Sharpe, *Spanish Guitar*; and Graham Wade, *Traditions of the Classical Guitar* (London: John Calder, 1980), 133–42.

87. Journal, 1837–38, August 25, 1837. See also in "Orders" appended to Journal, 1836–37, listings for September 10 and 26, 1838, both for "Spanish" guitars. The "Spanish" bridge refers to the kind through which the strings are tied off, rather than being held through a bridge plate by pins.

88. Journal, 1836–37, June 20, October 12, December 5, 1836.

89. Zebrawood is a fairly tight-grained wood with pronounced light and dark stripes. It comes from such West African countries as Nigeria and Cameroon.

90. Journal, 1836–37, September 17, 1836, and January 5, 1837, and "Orders Received," October 26, 1838.

91. See "Orders Received," in Journal, 1836–37, under dates noted in text.

92. Journal, 1837–38, April 21, 1838.

93. "Orders Received," in Journal, 1836–37, September 10 and 26, November 1 and 17, 1838. Ibid., August 22, 1836. This was probably the wife of Ogden E. Edwards, owner of a leather store at 18 Ferry Street, with his home at 28 Varick. See *Longworth's American Almanac, New-York Register, and City Directory* (New York: Thomas Longworth, 1839), 268.

94. Journal, 1836–37, "Orders Received." Another source records forty-eight guitars sold between August 1837 and January 1838 and indicates types of woods and other appointments. This may well be the list of guitars Martin actually produced. Inventory, 1837–38, folios 15–16, CFM.

95. Daybook, 1834–37.

96. On Schatz, see Groce, *Musical Instrument Makers*, 104.

97. See ibid., 107, 137. In 1835 Maul was listed as a cabinetmaker at 184 Canal Street.

98. Journal, 1837–38, June 6, July 12, August 14, 1838.

99. Ibid., October 12, 1838, and September 20, 1838, for Kretchmann; April 21, 1838, for string turning. Ledger, 1837–40, "Rasche." During this period the three lower strings for the guitar were made of silver wire wrapped on a fiber core, and the other three were of catgut, usually imported.

100. Journal, 1836–37, October 6, 1836, Martin notes that he forwarded goods to Schatz by this transportation company.

101. Ibid., June 9, 1836.

102. *Longworth's American Almanac* (1837), 123. The next year Bruno was listed under "musical instruments" at 212 Fulton Street. See *Longworth's American Almanac, New-York Register, and City Directory* (New York: Longworth, 1838), 124.

103. See Groce, *Musical Instrument Makers*, 23.

104. Journal, 1837–38, May 3 and 21, 1838.

105. Complicating matters, there is a two-months' overlap (April 1–June 9, 1837) between the journal for 1836–37 and that for 1837–38, with both seemingly in the same hand but not with all the same transactions. This suggests that the later book, that which eventually became the book for Martin & Bruno, may have begun as the record book for the Bruno/Martin store on Fulton Street. Evidence for this comes from the entry of April 6, 1837, for strings being brought to Fulton Street, which comes from the earlier record book.

106. Journal, 1837–38, May 1, 1837, for the rental payment.

107. See Vera Brodsky Lawrence, *Strong on Music: The New York Music Scene in the Days of George Templeton Strong, 1836–1875*, 3 vols. (Chicago: University of Chicago Press, 1988–99), 1:142, 170, 223, 596n for some of Coupa's public appearances. Like other popular instructors, he also arranged music; see J. B. Coupa, *Theme and Variations for the Guitar* (Baltimore: W. C. Peters, 1843), "entered . . . by F. Nunns in the southern district of New York." Coupa also published an early instruction book with a Boston imprint, which suggests that when he came from Spain he first lived in that city. See J. B. Coupa, *Instruction Book for the Guitar, extracted from the best French and Italian Authors* (Boston: Coupa, 1826). In 1870 this text was still available; see *Complete Catalogue of Sheet Music and Musical Works, Published by the Board of Music Trade of the United States of America, 1870* (New York: Board of Music Trade, 1871), 568. Ledger, 1837–40, under "Coupa" for his settlement of bill.

108. Groce, *Musical Instrument Makers*, 104–5.

109. Washburn and Johnston, *Martin Guitars*, 33–37. Journal, 1837–38, July 16 and September 1, 1838, records postage for letters from Nazareth, one entry noting "Postage for a letter from Nazareth, to Mr. C. F. M.," and the other, "Postage for a letter to [from?] Mr. Martin, (Nazareth) to Mrs. Martin."

110. Ledger, 1837–40, "Ludecus" and "Ludecus and Wolter." In 1839 Ludecus was listed under "musical instruments" at 212 Fulton Street, and Wolter under "music" at the same address; the firm of Ludecus & Wolter was listed at 320 Broadway as "importers and dealers in musical instruments, repairers of instruments," and, not surprisingly, "agents for Martin's and Schatz's warranted Guitars." See *Longworth's American Almanac* (1839), 417, 719. In the early 1840s Ludecus was listed as an importer and Wolter as a musician. See *Doggett's New York City Directory for 1844–1845*, 216, 385.

111. On the causes of the panic of 1837 see Peter Temin, *The Jacksonian Economy* (New York: Norton, [1969]), chap. 4; on its effects on New York labor see Sean Wilentz, *Chants Democratic: New York City and the Rise of the American Working Class, 1788–1850* (New York: Oxford University Press, 1984), 299–359. Martin's records do not indicate that he was significantly affected by the financial depression of the late 1830s. Oral history within the Martin family suggests that the reason for the move was personal: the family wished to be in the kind of rural landscape they had left behind in Neukirchen.

CHAPTER THREE

1. Jim Washburn and Richard Johnston, *Martin Guitars: An Illustrated History of America's Premier Guitarmaker* (Emmaus, Pa: Rodale Press, 1997), 33–37.

2. See, for example, [Various Contributors], *Two Centuries of Nazareth, 1740–1940* (Nazareth: Nazareth, Pennsylvania, Bicentennial, 1940), 1–12, and John Hill Martin, *Historical Sketch of Bethlehem in Pennsylvania, with Some Account of the Moravian Church* (Philadelphia: For Orrin Rogers by John L. Pile, 1872), 5–11.

3. A eulogy at Martin's funeral in 1873 places him in the Schoeneck congregation until 1862 (transcription in CFM). See also [Various Contributors], *Two Centuries of Nazareth*, 34–36.

4. [Various Contributors], *Two Centuries of Nazareth*, 158.

5. Richard Crawford, *America's Musical Life: A History* (New York: W. W. Norton, 2001), 52–55.

6. Eliza Southgate Browne, *A Girl's Life Eighty Years Ago* (New York: Scribners, 1887), 173–74.

7. In a detailed search of the C. F. Martin & Company Archives, I could find no documentation for these years, nor has any previous historian of the company mentioned such records.

8. Through June of that year, Drucke continued to buy strings and guitars from Martin. Martin also had a debit of $25.00 on February 1 to "Messrs. Ludecus & Wolters Account." On the credit side Drucke paid $25.00 cash on June 12, claimed an $8.60 commission on a $48.00 guitar sold to Mrs. Okill at her New York boardinghouse, and claimed another commission on December 24, for $1.00, for bringing Martin a guitar for repair. Although no address for Drucke is given in the ledger, he was paid a commission for a guitar sold to Mrs. Okill, to whom Martin sold other instruments. This indicates that Drucke was in the city at this time.

9. Significantly, on the credit side there is no entry after May 1839, which suggests that Coupa's bill was carried over into another, now missing ledger.

10. Coupa to Martin, New York, January 14, 1849; all letters are from CFM, unless otherwise noted.

11. Ibid., April 2, 1849. See also Coupa to Martin, April 3, 1849.

12. Coupa to Martin, New York, April 25, 1849, and see a letter with no year but dated April 5 in which Coupa mentions the measles. When his child's illness passed and the family finally got resettled, he told Martin, he intended to take his family "in the country to get some rest." Like many others who lived in the city and could afford the luxury, Coupa also had a house outside New York to which his family retreated during the hot summer months, in this case, a thirty-six-acre farm he had "7 miles from Newark/West Bloomfield." But by June things were only worse. His daughter remained "very low" with severe complications from her initial illness. "We have no hopes," Coupa lamented, writing now from Canterbury, New York, for "the disease[,] which had the origins in the heart, has gone to the brain—she is delirious, [and] when she has the fever, it is frightful." They were "resigned and prepared" for her death. In this missive Coupa also mentioned that he had this land for sale, presumably because he wanted a different country retreat. Coupa to Martin, Canterbury, New York, June 29, 1849.

13. Coupa to Martin, New York, undated (1849). Jonathan Mellon to Martin, Pittsburgh, June 30, 1848, an order for seven guitars; Thayer and Collins to Martin, Albany, New York, July 24, 1849, in which the firm writes that it has received the three guitars recently shipped and needs two more.

14. Coupa to Martin, New York, September 8, 1849.

15. Coupa to Martin, New York, October 15, 1849. On de Goni see Vera Brodsky Lawrence, *Strong on Music: The New York Music Scene in the Days of George Templeton Strong, 1836–1875*, 3 vols. (Chicago: University of Chicago Press, 1988–99), 1:96, 107, 223, 353. De Goni's husband also was a guitarist, but in 1845 she married George Knoop, a renowned cellist, after Sr. de Goni discretely left the scene. See also James Ballard, *A History of the Guitar, from the Earliest Antiquity to the Present Time* (New

York: William B. Tilton & Company, 1855), 21–22. Ferranti (1802–78) was influenced by Paganani and was famous among his contemporaries for his ability to sustain notes and chords longer than other players. He toured the United States in 1845. His instrument was described as similar to the design of an instrument made for the Italian guitarist Luigi Legnani by Stauffer. It also had an extra sounding board beneath the guitar's top and was copied in the United States primarily by Schmidt & Maul. See Ballard, *History of the Guitar*, 22, and Philip J. Bone, *The Guitar and Mandolin: Biographies of Celebrated Players and Composers*, 2d ed. (London: Schott & Company, 1954), 113–17.

16. Coupa to Martin, New York, October 15, 1849.

17. Malthaner, another German immigrant, was a piano maker who had moved from New York City to Bethlehem in 1837. See Joseph Levering, *A History of Bethlehem, Pennsylvania, 1741–1892* (Bethlehem, Pa.: Times Publishing Company, 1903), 717, and Nancy Groce, *Musical Instrument Makers of New York: A Directory of Eighteenth- and Nineteenth-Century Craftsmen*, Annotated Reference Works in Music no. 4 (Stuyvesant, N.Y.: Pendragon Press, 1991), 103.

18. Coupa to Martin, New York, November 24 and December 17, 1849.

19. Ibid., February 3 and February 4, 1850.

20. Susan Coupa to Martin, New York, March 12, 1852.

21. Bill from William Raddé to Martin, New York, December 6, 1856, CFM. Raddé (1800–1884) was born in Berlin and had come to Philadelphia in 1832 to work with his friend Johann Georg Wesselhöft, an importer and publisher of German books and of works on homeopathy. Wesselhöft set up Raddé as his agent in New York City beginning March 1, 1834. See Robert E. Cazden, *A Social History of the German Book Trade in America to the Civil War* (Columbia, S.C.: Camden House, 1984), 102–4, 109 n. 30. On Raddé's letterhead he is described as "Importer, Bookseller, Publisher and Foreign Agent, No. 300 Broadway / Also, dealer in Homeopathic medicine, and homeopathic books and journals in the English, French, and German languages."

22. Susan Coupa to Martin, New York, March 12 and 23, 1852.

23. Coupa to Martin, New York, August 28, 1849. In this same letter Coupa says that he may come in to town "to see if any of [his] friends are returning, but [was] afraid it is too hot yet for them to return."

24. See, for example, Coupa to Martin, New York, December 17, 1849. An 1851 directory has Maul living at 388 Broadway, the same address as the guitar-making firm of Schmidt & Maul. See *Doggett's New York City Street Directory, for 1851* (New York: John Doggett, Jr., 1851), 72, and Groce, *Musical Instrument Makers*, 107, 137.

25. A fragmentary ledger of business accounts shows that in 1850 and 1851 Martin was in the city for considerable periods of time. On February 1, 1851, for example, he took a $276.96 credit from the business "while in New York from September 1 to date," evidently for guitars made and sold in that period. On the opposite page, for January 1851, he debited his business $147.00 for "five Months work in the shop before I left for New York," and on February 1, 1851, for $300.00 more, for "Eight Months Labor in New York." Ledger, 1849–58, CFM. Through the 1850s Martin continued to travel to New York regularly. In a May 23, 1856, letter to him, Charles Lohman wrote that he and his wife had hoped to see Martin "as we were under the impression that you came to the city every five weeks."

26. The "Index of Conveyances Recorded in the Office of the Register" (1862), held by the New-York Historical Society, on January 24, 1851, records that Christian F. Martin was grantor (probably of this property) to Jasper Grosvenor in an instrument dated

May 22, 1850 (reference to "lib. 552, p.445," a volume presumably at the City Registers Office). But a directory for 1851–52 still lists Martin "upstairs" at 385 Broadway, perhaps now in a space he rented (*New York City Directory, for 1851–1852* [New York: Doggett & Rode, 1851], 362). *Doggett's New York City Street Directory, for 1851*, 72, also lists the following at 385 Broadway: J. M. & J. D. Jaques ("music"), Harriet Wilson ("millinery"), and R. A. Kidder ("dressmaker").

27. A small book of accounts between Frederick and his father dated "New York 1850" records expenses from July of that year. Frederick primarily bought fancy goods — "1 pair gloves," "pocketbook," "straw basket," "Box containing Christmas Presents — Cartage from Boat," for example — but also listed such expenses as "Freight on 11 barrels and art — $4.95" and "Passage for Home — $2.50" that indicate his attention to the family business. He also took time to enjoy the city, for there are several entries recording admission to "Niblo's Garden," a chief venue for all sorts of popular music and theatrical entertainment. Another fragmentary account book for 1851 with some letterhead tucked in at the end indicates that C. F. Martin, "Manufacturer of Guitars and Guitar Strings," now had a depot at "585 Broadway" (a typographical error for "385," the address all other records during these years indicate). These accounts show Frederick traveling with his brother, Hermann, from Nazareth ($4.50 in expenses) and housekeeping in the city. Frederick recorded, for example, expenses (a few dollars at a time) for "kitchen use," clothes, and foodstuffs; rent of $85.33 paid on August 1 (presumably for a quarter's stay); and even $12.60, "Water Rent (Croton)," for a water supply from the newly opened Croton aqueduct. Accounts of C. F. Martin Jr., 1850–52, CFM.

28. Policy no. 80973 with United States Fire Insurance Company, 69 Wall Street, policy expiration date June 28, 1851, CFM.

29. The next summer he also sold strings and did repair work — he had bought a workbench for $9.00 — for a total income of $41.34.

30. Bone, *Guitar and Mandolin*, 182–83, lists a Charles de Janon (1839–1911), a native of Cartagena, Colombia, who as a child had come with his family to New York. From his teens he was known as an outstanding performer and, like other stage personalities, soon began to teach. This Janon was "ranked among [the guitar's] most accomplished performers" whose "versatile and musicianly arrangements for guitar" were "familiar to all performers in America" and were "among the best and most popular publications for the guitar in America." Among his publications are *Theme and Variations for the Guitar* (Boston: Oliver Ditson, 1851), *Variations Brillantes on the Favorite Air, Katy Darling* (New York: Horace Waters, 1858), and *Cluster of Musical Gems: A Collection of Choice Melodies Arranged as Solos for the Guitar* (n.p., 1885). It is unlikely, however, that Martin gave his agency to a twelve-year-old, and our Charles de Janon more likely was an older relation, perhaps an uncle. In *Wilson's Business Directory for New York City for 1852–1853* (New York: John F. Trow, 1852), 218, Charles de Jannon [*sic*] is still listed at 385 Broadway, as a "Musical Instrument Maker," which he was not. On Leopold de Janon see Lawrence, *Strong on Music*, 1:142.

31. "Articles of Agreement," C. F. Martin Sr. and Charles de Janon, January 1851, CFM. Also, Susan Coupa had asked Martin to make her a guitar to take with her when she left the country, but unfortunately he did not have time to do so. Intent on securing one of his instruments before she left, she asked if she could select one "from amongst those Mr. De Janon has at 385 Broadway." See Susan Coupa to Martin, New York, March 12 and 23, 1852.

32. As early as 1835 people in the music trade shared this property. In that year the

piano maker Albert G. Smith gave 385 Broadway as his address, and the music store of Jollie & Millet was also listed there. See *Longworth's American Almanac, New-York Register, and City Directory* (New York: Thomas Longworth, 1835).

33. See Elizabeth Blackmar, *Manhattan for Rent, 1785–1850* (Ithaca, N.Y.: Cornell University Press, 1989), chap. 7. On the ubiquity of boarders in New York in this period see Kenneth A. Scherzer, *The Unbounded Community: Neighborhood and Social Structure in New York City, 1830–1875* (Durham, N.C.: Duke University Press, 1992), 97–110, and Elizabeth C. Cromley, *Alone Altogether: A History of New York's Early Apartments* (Ithaca, N.Y.: Cornell University Press, 1990).

34. Wilson is listed in an 1851 city directory under "millinery"; see note 26, above.

35. Charles de Janon to Martin, New York, February 21, March 3, 1851.

36. Ibid., March 20, 1851. Martin's city property continued to be a burden, for soon there was more trouble with a renter. Mrs. Wilson was out of the scene, but a Mr. Beckman was having difficulty making payments. He had told Janon that he would have the money "in the Course of the Week," and Janon gave him a bit of slack. "I think he is an honest man," Janon wrote. But two weeks later Janon still had not resolved matters, and Martin had to send him one hundred dollars to cover the rent. Beckman paid back some of this, but in January 1852, Janon again asked Martin to cover the rent for a while. Janon to Martin, New York, October 25 and November 7, 1851, January 13, 1852. In a letter of December 8, 1851, Janon told Martin that Beckman had paid thirty-five dollars on the one hundred owed and had assured him of fifty dollars more that afternoon.

37. Janon to Martin, New York, June 19, November 7, 15, 1851.

38. Ibid., February 21, June 13, 1851.

39. Ibid., December 8, 1851.

40. By November things finally were looking up a bit, if Martin would fill the orders. Janon wrote that he had sold four guitars that week and wanted four or five more. Ibid., October 25, November 7, 1851.

41. Janon to C. F. Martin Jr., New York, January 21, 1852. We also hear again of Martin's friend William Raddé, who earlier had settled Martin's bill with Susan Coupa and eventually assumed some of Janon's financial duties. Janon wrote Martin that he would call on Raddé "and also upon others that you have commitianed [*sic*] me to." Raddé resurfaces in his next letter, February 1, as having collected "the first bill that you [Martin] gave him," but he had not yet remitted the amount because he had no orders from Martin to do so. Janon to Martin, New York, February 1, 1852.

42. In a letter dated April 28, 1852, Frederick wrote Janon that, on his way home from New York, Martin realized that he had forgotten to "charge" Janon's account for money still owed him from different transactions, including a $50.00 bill from the guitar makers Schmidt & Maul, $16.00 for strings Janon had bought, $34.50 to the Adams & Company Express for shipment of "[de la] Cova's G[uitar]," and the $32.52 that Martin had paid for the rent of another recalcitrant tenant and which Janon supposedly was to have collected.

43. In a letter of August 2, 1852, to one of the Martins, William Fleiss of Great Jones Street wanted to use the Martin's dog for breeding. "When you come to New York again," he wrote, "will you bring your slut with you[.] I have one of the finest Newfoundland dogs, and should like to have a couple of pups from him. The above address is where you went to hear Mr. Tropel[?] play on his instrument."

44. The ledger from the 1850s shows that through September 14, 1852, Janon received several more guitars to sell but then none until 1855, when he took one. It is unclear for what he was still indebted to Martin in 1856.

45. Janon to Martin, New York, May 13, 1856.

46. See Stephen Foster, "Old Uncle Ned" (Philadelphia: E. R. Johnston & Company, 1849), and "Oh! Susanna" (Philadelphia: E. R. Johnston & Company, 1849), and Henry Russell, "We Have Been Friends Together" (Philadelphia: A Fiot, 1849), all arranged by Pique; "Anvil Polka" (Philadelphia: A Fiot, [ca. 1850]), which he composed. For the order see Edward Pique to Martin, Philadelphia, February 20, 1852. See also September 17, 1850, May 28 and June 6, 1851, and January 30, 1852, with a peg sketched.

47. William M. Peters to Martin, New York, December 6, 1856.

48. *Philadelphia Public Ledger*, February 28, 1848, p. 1, col. 3. Schubert also arranged music; see *Garibaldi's Quickstep, arranged for the Guitar by Wm. Schubert* (n.p. [Philadelphia?], n.d. [1840]).

49. Fiot also published music. See, for example, "My Switzer Home" (Philadelphia: A. Fiot, [184?]), where he is listed as "Publisher and Importer of Music and Musical Instruments" at 196 Chestnut Street.

50. J. E. Gould & Company to Martin, Philadelphia, January 25, 1853.

51. Thayer and Collins to Martin, Albany, N.Y., July 24 and September 13, 1849. The following spring this firm decided to concentrate on piano sales and spun off its musical instrument business to F. I. Ilsley, who became Martin's regular customer. See Thayer and Collins to Martin, Albany, N.Y., April 27, 1850.

52. George Hilbus to Martin, Washington, D.C., July 18, 1851. Perhaps related to Jacob Hilbus (1787–1858), an organ builder from Westphalia, Germany, who in 1808 came to the Washington, D.C., area. See Orpha Ochse, *A History of the Organ in the United States* (Bloomington: Indiana University Press, 1975), 180.

53. A. W. Penniman to Martin, Columbus, Ohio, April 19, 1853.

54. Truax and Baldwin to Martin, Cincinnati, July 29, 1856.

55. A. Brainard to Martin, New York, May 3, 1852, and Cleveland, February 4, 1853.

56. Churchill & Company to Martin, Memphis, Tenn., July 18, 1854.

57. E. H. Benson to Martin, Memphis, Tenn., November 17 and September 22, 1854. See also Churchill & Son to Martin, New York, August 29, 1854.

58. James Mellon to Martin, Wheeling, Va., October 7 and December 8, 1853.

59. Edward Hopkins to Martin, Troy, N.Y., December 8, 1853.

60. Horace Waters to Martin, New York, April 18, 1851.

61. M. Chambers to Martin, New York, January 3, 1853.

62. Among Sulzner's compositions were "The Slave's Return" (New York: William Hall & Son, 1851), part of a series called Sulzner's Southern Melodies, and "The Soldier's Dream" (Mobile, Ala.: J. H. Snow, 1852). Perhaps he wanted one of Martin's models with a neck that was adjusted with a key? F. Sulzner to Martin, Huntsville, Ala., October 30, 1853.

63. John Harvie to Martin, Port Gibson, Miss., February 22 and June 5, 1852.

64. Ibid., June 10 and 11, 1852; Francis Funck to Martin, Port Gibson, Miss., June 14, 1852.

65. D. Drucke to Martin, Philadelphia, February 4, 1853.

66. Anson Tucker to Martin, Lafayette, Ind., April [?], 1853.

67. H. Worrall to Martin, Cincinnati, August 21, 1856.

68. S. de la Cova to Martin, Panama (City), Panama, March 16, 1853, and New York, November 29 and December 1, 1853.

69. De la Cova to Martin, Havana, Cuba, January 29, 1854.

70. De la Cova to Martin, Panama (City), Panama, October 2, 1855. He also hoped

that his "sounding or harmonic seat or stool," evidently earlier described to Martin, "would come soon" and again enclosed a drawing of the item, as he had by the last "Express." This stool apparently was a hollow seat that de la Cova thought would augment the guitar's sound.

71. De la Cova to Martin, New York, November 25, 1853.

72. See Robert C. Post, "Reflections on American Science and Technology at the New York Crystal Palace Exhibition of 1853," *Journal of American Studies* 17 (1983): 337–56, and Edwin G. Burrows and Mike Wallace, *Gotham: A History of New York City to 1898* (New York: Oxford University Press, 1999), 669–72.

73. See *Report of the Jury on Musical Instruments at the Crystal Palace, New York, 1853* (New York: Baker, Godwin & Co., 1853), 12, and *Official Catalogue of the New York Exhibition of the Industry of All Nations* (New York: George P. Putnam & Co., 1853), 96.

74. George Hilbus to Martin, New York, [?] 31, 1853.

75. W. C. Peters to Martin, Cincinnati, October 12, November 8 and 24, 1852.

76. Ossian E. Dodge to Martin, "Museum Sanctum," Boston, September 21, 1853. Some facts about Dodge's life — he was born October 22, 1852, for example — are available in Flodoardo Scott's *Biographical, Historical, and Incidental Sketches of Ossian E. Dodge* (New York: Flodoardo Scott, [ca. 1851]), in Scott's Dime Library, no. 10. This pamphlet includes a phrenological sketch of Dodge by "his old friends, O. S. and L. N. Fowler." Dodge's periodical is a trove of short stories and sketches, occasionally by authors of some note, written specifically for the paper. In the autumn of 1852, for example, Dodge even announced a contest, with a three-hundred-dollar prize for the best "original tale about 'American life.'" Caroline Lee Hentz won the prize, for "Neglecting a Fee: The Young Physician and His Fortunes." See *Literary Museum*, November 20, 1852.

77. John Townsend Trowbridge, *My Own Story, with Recollections of Noted Persons* (Boston: Houghton, Mifflin and Co., 1903), 164.

78. See *Concert: A Branch of the Hutchinson Family, associated with the Misses Caroline and Ellen Rogers, and Ossian E. Dodge . . . at the Melodeon . . . January 17, 1849.* The Hutchinson twins, Joshua and Caleb, were the Hutchinsons who participated. Dodge was described as "Comic and Barytone [*sic*]." Dodge to Martin, Nantucket, November 5, 1853.

79. Trowbridge, *My Own Story*, 164.

80. Ossian Dodge, *Ossian's Serenade as Sung by Ossian Dodge* (Boston: Oliver Ditson, 1850).

81. Trowbridge, *My Own Story*, 165–66; [Flodoardo Scott], *Sketches of Ossian E. Dodge*, iv.

82. Dodge to Martin, Boston, September 21, 1853.

83. Dodge to Martin, November 5, 1853. By late December Martin had sent Dodge a beautiful rosewood guitar, but it was not to his liking. He wrote Martin "on the wing" to an engagement in Portland, Maine, that, as splendid as the new instrument looked, its tone did not equal that of Schatz's guitar. Dodge evidently had owned yet another Martin instrument, probably the one listed in Martin's daybook — with pearl sound hole and ivory edges, pegs, and bridge at a cost of $30.00 — as sold to him in December 1853 (Daybook of Guitars Made, 1852–58, December 1, 1853, CFM). Although he had recently sold it, he had retained "the privilege to use it if I wish till the first of July next" and presumably would do so for his upcoming performance. He wanted Martin to make him *yet another* instrument, on Martin's own schedule. If that one did

not please him, he would rest satisfied with the one that he had recently received. Dodge to Martin, "On the Wing," December 22, 1853.

84. Dodge to Martin, Brandon, Vt., March 9, 1854.

85. Dodge to Martin, Cleveland, June 1, 1857.

86. Dodge to Martin, Cleveland, July 30, 1857. Dodge ended this brash letter with a bit of coercion. In a previous missive he had evidently asked the price of a guitar but had not actually ordered it. Martin had misunderstood his intention and sent it to Cleveland. Dodge promptly had returned it but, not wanting Martin to "suffer from sending it" (that is, by paying for the shipping), had paid all charges on it, for a total of $53.75. So, given the price of the guitar, he actually had paid more than it was worth and essentially owned it! But Dodge knew that he could not sell the instrument for the $50.00 he had invested in it and thus placed the matter "exclusively upon your [Martin's] honor," that is, he wanted some reimbursement.

87. Daybook of Guitars Made, 1852–58. Hilbus & Heitz to Martin, Washington, D.C., November 15 and 20, 1854; *Record of the First Exhibition of the Metropolitan Mechanics' Institute* (Washington, D.C.: H. Polkinhorn, 1853), 12. Martin also showed his instruments at the fairs of the Franklin Institute in Philadelphia. His listing in an 1851 New York City directory, for example, notes that he "received twice the highest premium at the Franklin Institute, Philadelphia" (*New York City Directory, for 1851–1852*, 362).

88. For a magnificent treatment of the expansion of the nation's transportation system during this period, see D. W. Meinig, *The Shaping of America: A Geographical Perspective on 500 Years of History*, 4 vols. to date (New Haven: Yale University Press, 1986–), vol. 2 (*Continental America*), pt. 2. On express companies see A. L. Stimson, *History of the Express Companies; and the Origin of American Railroads, Together with Some Reminiscences of the Latter Days of the Mail Coach and Baggage Wagon Business in the United States* (New York: For the Author, 1859); Alvin F. Harlow, *Old Waybills: The Romance of the Express Companies* (1934; reprint, New York: Arno Press, 1967); and Horace Greeley et al., *The Great Industries of the United States* (Hartford: Burr & Hyde, 1872), 713–21.

89. Alfred D. Chandler Jr., *The Visible Hand: The Managerial Revolution in American Business* (Cambridge: Harvard University Press, 1977), 126–28. The Adams Express Company was such a fixture in the public's imagination that it was made the butt of jokes on the minstrel stage. In 1855, for example, Sanford's Minstrels offered this joke to its audience: "For what purpose was Eve created? For Adams' Express Company." See Harlow, *Old Waybills*, 69, and Greeley et al., *Great Industries*, 714–15.

90. *Sheldon & Co.'s Business and Advertising Directory* (New York: J. F. Trow, 1845), leaf 2r.

91. Chandler, *Visible Hand*, 83–86, on railroad expansion, and 126–28, on express agents. See also Harlow, *Old Waybills*, 25–70, and, on the railroads in general, Albert Fishlow, *American Railroads and the Transformation of the Antebellum Economy* (Cambridge: Harvard University Press, 1965).

92. J. E. Gould to Martin, Philadelphia, June 17, 1853.

93. In 1853, Gould & Company bought A. Fiot's business and became Martin's largest outlet in Philadelphia. See Fiot to Martin, Philadelphia, January 12, 1850.

94. On the Adams Express Company, one of the oldest and largest, see Harlow, *Old Waybills*, 25–32, 48, 61–70.

95. Lee & Walker to Martin, Philadelphia, May 27 and 28, 1852.

96. George Dutch to Martin, Marietta, Ohio, September 19, 1850.

97. E. P. Nash to Martin, Petersburg, Va., March 5, 1856, and June 27, 1857.

98. Nunn, Clark to Martin, Philadelphia, January 20, 1853.

99. John Harvie to Martin, Port Gibson, Miss., February 22 and June 5, 1852.

100. James Demarest to Martin, New York, May 13, 1853, and John Harvie to Martin, Port Gibson, Miss., June 8, 1853.

101. T. C. Loud to Martin, Holly Springs, Miss., May 15, 1854. Loud probably was related to the Loud family in Philadelphia, prominent piano makers. See Laurence Libin, *American Musical Instruments in the Metropolitan Museum of Art* (New York: W. W. Norton, 1985), 177–79.

102. James Mellon to Martin, Pittsburgh, Pa., December 31, 1853.

103. J. H. Macmichael to Martin, Natchez, Miss., October 10, 1854. Unfortunately, Macmichael died shortly after this order, and his wife wrote Martin for advice on how to liquidate the guitars her spouse had received. See Mrs. J. H. Macmichael to Martin, Natchez, November 3, 1854.

104. During this period, historians note "a general shift away from long-term credit toward doing business for cash, or on account with monthly billing." See Glenn Porter and Harold Livesay, *Merchants and Manufacturers: Studies in the Changing Structure of Nineteenth-Century Marketing* (Baltimore: Johns Hopkins University Press, 1971), 125–26.

105. Edward J. Balleisen, *Navigating Failure: Bankruptcy and Commercial Society in Antebellum America* (Chapel Hill: University of North Carolina Press, 2001), 27.

106. Allan Pred, *Urban Growth and City-Systems in the United States, 1840–1860* (Cambridge: Harvard University Press, 1980), 147–48.

107. On banking in general during this period, see Howard Bowderhorn, *A History of Banking in Antebellum America: Financial Markets and Economic Development in an Era of Nation-Building* (New York: Cambridge University Press, 2000).

108. George Dutch to Martin, Marietta, Ohio, September 19, 1850.

109. T. C. Loud to Martin, Holly Springs, Miss., May 15, 1854.

110. A. W. Penniman to Martin, Columbus, Ohio, May 16, 1853. Ledger, 1852–54, "J. P. Reed," CFM.

111. Ledger, 1852–54, "Peters, Webb," "Jonathan Miller," and "Jonathan West."

112. Peters, Webb to Martin, Louisville, Ky., August 16, 1851.

113. West to Martin, Nashville, Tenn., August 29, 1851.

114. Ibid., December 4, 1852.

115. Gould to Martin, Philadelphia, January 24, 1854.

116. W. C. Peters & Sons, to Martin, Cincinnati, October 28, 1853.

117. *Baltimore Olio and American Musical Gazette*, January 1850, 1.

118. U.S. Census, 1850, Manuscript Returns, Northampton County, Pennsylvania, National Archives, Washington, D.C.

119. Deringer was not yet happy with some "brass castings" on it, however, and told Martin that he would attend to them before he came. Philip Deringer to Martin, Reading, Pa., September 22, 1850.

120. Ibid., May 14, 1851, and March 21, 1852, when Deringer wrote that he wished to purchase a guitar.

121. C. Peters to Martin, Cincinnati, April 18, 1855; D. A. Truax to Martin, Cincinnati, April 16, 1853; Jonathan Mellon to Martin, Pittsburgh, June 18, 1852; Miller & Beacham to Martin, Baltimore, August 1, 1853; Horace Waters to Martin, New York, September 6, 1853.

122. Rohé & Leavitt to Martin, New York, April 9, 1852.

123. W. C. Peters to Martin, Cincinnati, May 1, 1854.

124. Lee & Walker to Martin, Philadelphia, April 27, 1852, and Peters, Webb, Louisville, Ky., January 31, 1851; Ledger, 1837–40, entries for Coupa at February 3 and March 26, 1840.

125. Jonathan Mellon to Martin, Pittsburgh, April 20, 1852; D. H. Druck to Martin, Philadelphia, February 4, 1853; Ilsley to Martin, Albany, August 2, 1852; R. G. Greene to Martin, Chicago, May 24, 1852; and Horace Waters to Martin, New York, May 1, 1853. Presumably these were not serial numbers because they were to be on the case as well. See also Waters to Martin, March 9, 1853, for an order by number.

126. Hawes & Willoughby to Martin, New York, November 2, 1858.

127. Bills from J. F. Copcutt, New York, and Ogden & Company, New York, both dated December 29, 1849, CFM.

128. John M. Phyfe to Martin, New York, September 9, 1858. A letter of August 22, 1857, has Martin ordering ebony from him.

129. Bill from P. I. Farnham & Company, December 29, 1849.

130. Schatz to Martin, Boston, April 29, 1850.

131. A. Fiot to Martin, Philadelphia, February 24, 1852, and January 12 and February 28, 1853.

132. Washburn and Johnston, *Martin Guitars*, 34–42.

133. Ibid., 38–40. Musical instrument dealer Fred Oster of Vintage Instruments (Philadelphia) thus describes a guitar by Stumcke: "Boston, Two-piece rosewood back veneer over spruce, rosewood ribs, two-piece wide-grained spruce top, cone heel, slotted head, nickel tuners with ivory rollers and elaborate buttons, pearl soundhole inlays, cross-braced + 4 fans." See ‹*www.vintage-instruments.com*› (December 2001).

134. Daybook of Guitars Made, 1852–58, July 9, 1857.

CHAPTER FOUR

1. Mayer & Collins to Martin, Albany, N.Y., June 4, 1853, and Horace Waters to Martin, New York, September 23, 1853; all letters from CFM, unless otherwise noted.

2. See Russell Sanjek, *American Popular Music and Its Business: The First Four Hundred Years*, vol. 2 (New York: Oxford University Press, 1988), 65–71.

3. *Brooklyn Director and Yearly Advertiser, for 1847–48* (Brooklyn, N.Y.: Lees & Foulkes, 1847), advertisement.

4. Firth, Pond & Company to Martin, New York, June 18, 1856.

5. Sanjek, *American Popular Music*, 2:59, 65, 71–72. In *Musical World and New York Musical Times*, January 1, 1853, 45, Firth, Pond & Company advertised "Guitars of Our Own Manufacture, of Superior Tone and Finish, in Lined Case, for $15 to $50." These undoubtedly were Ashborn's instruments, for the company had no guitar factory of its own.

6. *New York Musical World*, March 8, 1854, 120.

7. The main source for this chapter is Ashborn's accounts journal for the period April 1851 to January 1856, in the author's possession. It outlines supply, improvement, and building accounts; expenses for labor; numbers and types of guitars manufactured; and Ashborn's financial arrangements with the New York music trade. On Ashborn as a banjo maker, see Philip F. Gura and James F. Bollman, *America's Instrument: The Banjo in the Nineteenth Century* (Chapel Hill: University of North Carolina Press, 1999), 66–73.

8. Historical information about Torrington comes primarily from Samuel Orcutt, *Torrington, Connecticut, from Its First Settlement in 1737, with Biographies and Genealogies* (Albany, N.Y.: Munsell, 1878).

9. On the ship's manifest documenting his arrival in New York City, Martin was listed as a "mechanic," though he was a member of the cabinetmakers' guild. The customs officers obviously used a few shorthand terms to cover many different occupations, and one wonders if Ashborn, too, used this designation on the census because he had been so labeled on his immigration.

10. This information is gleaned from Orcutt, *Torrington*; from the manuscript "United States Census (Population) of 1850" and of 1860; and from "Estate of Jas. Ashborn/His Last Will & Testament," "Approved and accepted and allowed in open Court Dec. 27, 1876," recorded in vol. 4, pp. 465–66, Litchfield County, Connecticut, Connecticut State Archives, Hartford. My data and arguments about Ashborn are presented in more detail in "Manufacturing Guitars for the American Parlor: James Ashborn's Wolcottville, Connecticut, Factory, 1851–1856," *Proceedings of the American Antiquarian Society* 104, part 1 (Spring 1994): 117–56.

11. U.S. Census, 1850, Manuscript Returns, Litchfield County, Connecticut and U.S. Census of 1860, Litchfield County, Connecticut, in National Archives, Washington, D.C. On Hungerford see Orcutt, *Torrington*, 512–13.

12. The Naugatuck Railroad was completed in 1849 and ran from the manufacturing town of Winsted (north of Torrington) through Waterbury to Bridgeport, where it connected with the New York and New Haven Railroad. See Sidney Withington, *The First Twenty Years of Railroads in Connecticut*, Connecticut Tercentenary Pamphlet (New Haven: Connecticut Tercentenary Committee, 1935).

13. In May 1852, for example, Charles Bradley paid Ashborn twenty-five cents for the use of his lathe. On waterpower in this period see Charles Howells, "Colonial Watermills in the Wooden Age," in *America's Wooden Age: Aspects of Its Early Technology*, ed. Brooke Hindle (Tarrytown, N.Y.: Sleepy Hollow Restorations, 1975), 120–59.

14. In his new "Building" account, Ashborn noted considerable expenditures for the building's construction: three thousand bricks ($1,800.00), lumber ($66.10), foundry castings ($328.85), shafting ($73.32), and belting ($5.75). In addition to paying Russell Goodnow and his carpentry crew, Ashborn also recorded expenses for a "machinist," an "Irishman," and the chief builder, Willys Curtiss, who received $281.53.

15. The new factory, however, did not seem to have affected the production of strings as much. The factory shipped this item regularly between April 1852 and June 1853, and then more sporadically, often a few months going by before another shipment. During that period of steady production, Ashborn shipped as few as 48 dozen (in September 1852) and as many as 252 dozen (in February 1853, shortly after the factory was completed). It seems more likely that Ashborn used the new space for speedier manufacture of the instruments and perhaps sought the new building because, once he undertook string making, his space had become cramped.

16. In July 1851 he also bought files for $3.00 and once paid $.50 to someone for "filing [a] saw." In 1854, perhaps to outfit further the new factory building for increased production, he purchased a "saw arbor" for $14.00, a "saw frame" for another $12.00, and subsequently noted the acquisition of a crosscut saw and several more circular saws for $15.00. See "Estate of Jas. Ashborn/His Last Will & Testament."

17. Gary J. Kornblith, "The Craftsman as Industrialist: Jonas Chickering and the Transformation of American Piano Manufacturing," *Business History Review* 59 (Autumn 1985), notes that in an attempt to economize by division of labor, the piano man-

ufacturer Jonas Chickering utilized workers in several locations around Boston to prepare components of his instruments (360–62). See also Sean Wilentz, *Chants Democratic: New York City and the Rise of the American Working Class, 1788–1850* (New York: Oxford University Press, 1984), who observes that New York, "with its immense labor pool, its credit facilities, its access to prefinished materials from Britain and New England, and its transportation lines, was a superb site for producing finished consumer goods, for local consumption or shipment elsewhere." The out-of-shop contracting that characterized such work, he concludes, created a kind of "bastard artisan system" in which the old distinctions among craftspeople on the basis of skill was undermined as manufacture was subdivided into various tasks, as at Ashborn's factory (111–13).

18. At the same time that Ashborn bought a sizable amount of basswood from Hall & Son in July 1851, for example, he took two rosewood logs for $30.00 and a thirteen-inch mahogany plank for $8.16. A year later he acquired ninety feet of mahogany for $14.40 and in April 1854 a log of rosewood for $40.50. Ebony was equally dear. He paid $22.19 for an unspecified amount in December 1853 and $65.00 for another shipment in 1854.

19. On Dayton's activities see Orcutt, *Torrington*, 84–85, 428–32. He built his first pipe organ in 1840, and in 1846 his first reed organ, one of the earliest of its kind in America. In 1855 he developed a different sort of board for the organ's reeds that, Torrington's historian writes, "proved to be the greatest improvement in reed organs, that has been effected." Orcutt continues, "This invention consisted in arranging the reed board so as to have two and a half sets of reeds (or more) to operate with one set of valves, having dampers placed over each half set to be raised by stops, so that either set or half set, can be played alone or at the same time" (432).

20. "1 Box with marking stamps" was listed in Ashborn's will. Although the ornamentation varies somewhat within each grade of guitar that has been seen, his no. 1 had a minimum of decorative binding around the top perimeter and the sound hole. In addition, unlike on the higher-grade models, the fingerboard sometimes was made of a local hardwood rather than of rosewood or ebony. The no. 2 has its maple sides and spruce back veneered with rosewood, more decorative binding around the top, and three-line purfling around the bottom edge. The fingerboard was ebony, and the peg head veneered on the front with the same wood and with rosewood on the back. No no. 3 has been recorded, but the no. 4 also has rosewood veneer over sides and back, ebony binding and white side purfling around its body, three-line purfling around its neck, neck and peg head veneered with rosewood, ebony fingerboard, and many-lined rosette rings. The no. 5 is similarly appointed but with a nine-ply binding around the top, five-ply around the back, and five-ply around the edges of the sides as well. The no. 6s that have surfaced have elaborate wooden decoration around the sound hole and top, as well as around the strap button on the bottom of the instrument. One no. 6 also has simple pearl dots as fret markers, the only use of pearl noted on Ashborn's instruments. His decoration on his no. 6 instruments is made from cut pieces of wood and more resembles intarsia, an inlay, than marquetry, made of veneers of differently colored wood glued together and then cut through to make the pattern. Martin always used marquetry. See plate 4-4 and F. Hamilton Jackson, *Intarsia and Marquetry* (London: Sands & Company, 1903), 1–2.

21. *New York Musical World*, January 5 and March 8, 1856.

22. For this insight and for my general description of the construction of Ashborn guitars, I am indebted to Juris Poruks of Montreal, Quebec, a collector of Ashborn guitars (letter to the author, March 23, 1994).

23. They appear in the records as "Pat[ent] Heads wood parts" or "pat[ent] peg heads & wood parts," shipped in batches of six or a dozen at the price of two dollars per set, to be resold to other guitar manufacturers in the city or elsewhere.

24. The elegant geared tuners had Ashborn's name stamped on them but had no patentable features. In the following discussion of Ashborn's patent innovations I am indebted to Edmund Britt of Wakefield, Massachusetts, who has generously shared his knowledge with me.

25. It is difficult to gauge the success or popularity of Ashborn's patent innovations because most of his extant guitars carry the more traditional brass tuning machines, which leads one to believe that most of his instruments left the factory so equipped.

26. During this period a capo usually consisted of a metal or wooden bar faced with buckskin and attached around the guitar neck to hold down the strings at a certain fret. Tension was provided by a gut string wrapped once around the neck and tightened with a short fiddle-style peg fitted to a hole in the top of the bar. In his 1850 patent, however, Ashborn noted that hitherto the use of a capo was "attended with great difficulty" because the tension on the strings might easily be lessened or released if the gut slipped. He modified this design so that the capo could be more easily adjusted by "an eccentric roller, the periphery of which is turned down in the middle to correspond with the underside of the handle." When the roller was properly positioned, "the capo tasto or pressure plate is drawn down tight on the strings." When it was turned halfway around, however, "then the plate is not drawn onto the strings and the whole apparatus can be pushed back onto the head" (U.S. Patent no. 7,279).

27. U.S. Census, 1850, Manuscript Returns, Litchfield County, Connecticut, in National Archives, Washington, D.C.

28. Ibid., and U.S. Census, 1860, Manuscript Returns, Litchfield County, Connecticut, in National Archives, Washington, D.C.

29. Hall & Son noted that its "covered" strings (that is, those with wound silver wire on them) were made from "the best American floss, which has a much stronger fiber than any other." The firm also noted that Ashborn had "a new plan for manufacturing them . . . [that] gives them a greater strength than any other string. . . . The three catgut strings" (the unwound strings) were "the very best Italian." *Musical World and New York Musical Times*, July 1, 1854, 108.

30. As was the case in other such mill villages, some of Ashborn's workers took part of their wages in goods, which he and Hungerford provided either through their local connections or those in the city. Chester Smith and Thornton occasionally took barrels of flour, at $5.75 per barrel. Once Smith took a no. 1 guitar at $8.00, the same amount for which Ashborn sold the model to the city. Other arrangements also were made between employer and employee. Hart, for example, rented a house from Ashborn, paying $5.50 for fifty days. And occasionally a worker was remunerated for some task not related to his guitar work. In July 1851, for example, at the height of the haying season, Martin Judd received $2.00 extra, for haying.

31. *New York Musical Review* (1855), quoted in Sanjek, *American Popular Music*, 72.

32. On Hopkins's flute works see Nancy Groce, *Musical Instrument Makers of New York: A Directory of Eighteenth- and Nineteenth-Century Urban Craftsmen*, Annotated Reference Works in Music no. 4 (Stuyvesant, N.Y.: Pendragon Press, 1991), 52.

33. In February 1855, Firth, Pond returned eight guitars to Ashborn, the only time any firm had done so, and thereafter the extant record does not record any further sales to the company. Hungerford left the Wolcottville area sometime in 1857 or 1858.

This, too, may have been related to Ashborn's business arrangement with Hall & Son. In the early 1860s, however, Ashborn sold to Firth, Son & Company (1864–65), one of the successors to Firth, Pond & Company. The guitar in plate 4-2 carries its stamp. Only one Ashborn guitar has been seen with a stamp other than those of the large New York companies, namely, "J Sage & Sons / 209 Main St. / Buffalo / American Guitar." There is no model number but it conforms to a no. 2.

34. *New York Musical World*, March 8, 1856, 120.

35. In 1861 the *American Musical Directory* still had an advertisement for "Hall & Son's Celebrated Guitars, warranted to stand the climate; superior in tone to any foreign instrument" (1861; reprint, New York: Da Capo Press, 1980), advertisements following text.

36. *Musical World*, October 22, 1859, 12.

37. Every guitar I have seen that was stamped Hall & Son was made in Ashborn's factory, an observation verified by other informants as well. One occasionally finds guitars with "Ashborn" stamped on the heel block, and as I have noted, some of the patent metal tuners carry his name as well. The same is true for Firth, Pond & Company's instruments, though Ashborn's larger account was with Hall & Son.

38. In any given month he often sent goods to the firms in several different shipments.

39. A frequent notation in his account book shows the company paying him fifty cents for "Going to the Bank." On banking in Connecticut in this period see Francis Parsons, *A History of Banking in Connecticut*, Connecticut Tercentenary Pamphlet no. 42 (New Haven: Connecticut Tercentenary Commission, 1935), and Joseph G. Woodward, "Commerce and Banking in Connecticut," in *The New England States*, ed. W. T. Davis, 4 vols. (Boston: Hurd, 1897), 2:617–82.

40. This fact suggests that Ashborn may have begun to manufacture banjos after Hungerford left. This theory is undercut, however, by the patent Ashborn filed in 1852 for a "guitar key" which shows four of the tuning pegs in what unmistakably is a banjo, not a guitar, head stock, of the same trapezoidal shape as his extant banjos.

41. "On Stringed Instruments," *Musical World and New York Musical Times*, June 10, 1854, 63. Reprinted as "A Resonant Testimonial," *American Musical Instrument Society Newsletter*, Summer 2002, 11–12.

42. In the discussion of Tilton's improvements appended to James Ballard's *History of the Guitar, from the Earliest Antiquity to the Present Time* (New York: William B. Tilton & Co., 1855), there are reports and testimonials about this improvement in papers and journals from Alabama (where Tilton resided in 1851) to New York, and even to London and other European cities. See pp. 68–105.

43. D. Schuyler to Martin, Buffalo, N.Y., December 14, 1867.

44. One other guitar maker, William H. Towers of Philadelphia, similarly rethought the bridge and interior design of the instrument. On May 16, 1851, he registered a patent (no. 10,934) that described hollow bridge pins pushed into the soundboard itself, and through which the strings passed, obviating the need for a bridge per se. Moreover, two of these pins extended to the bottom of the guitar and functioned like the sound post in a violin.

45. "On Stringed Instruments," 63. Through this period Tilton paid for a weekly advertisement in this periodical, the only guitar maker to do so with such regularity, which may account for the fulsome editorial notice he received in this issue. See also Ballard, *History of the Guitar*, 68–105.

46. Groce, *Musical Instrument Makers*, 157.

47. "On Stringed Instruments," 63. In his advertising supplement to Ballard's *History of the Guitar*, Tilton printed a testimonial from the judges of the Crystal Palace Exhibition to the effect that, had his instruments been submitted earlier, they would have "without hesitation" granted him the highest medal (66–67). Napoleon W. Gould, guitar player for Christy's Minstrels, exhibited another interesting guitar at the Crystal Palace Exhibition. It had an adjustable nut so that he could lower the pitch of the instrument a halftone and play it in a flat key without changing his fingering. Gould, however, later added his name to the testimonials for Tilton's improvements. See Ballard, *History of the Guitar*, 22, 83–84.

48. Groce, *Musical Instrument Makers*, 157.

49. *Musical World and Times*, June 17, 1854, 60.

50. "On Stringed Instruments," 63; Ballard, *History of the Guitar*, 82–83, 88–89. In Philadelphia much was made of a Martin guitar for Franklin Peale, "a distinguished Amateur of the Guitar" and an official at the United States Mint, who had his instrument modified by Tilton. See Ballard, *History of the Guitar*, 77–82. For a picture of one Martin guitar so refitted, see Jim Washburn and Richard Johnston, *Martin Guitars: An Illustrated Celebration of America's Premier Guitarmaker* (Emmaus, Pa.: Rodale Press, 1997), 31. One guitar that Zoebisch sent to Martin for repair had been so modified. "Be sure all the 'Tilton affaire' is removed," Zoebisch instructed Martin, adding that the client wanted the "Tilton arrangement & Pegs returned with the Guitar." C. A. Zoebisch & Sons to Martin, New York, February 20, 1870.

51. Ballard, *History of the Guitar*, 96.

52. "On Stringed Instruments," 63.

53. Ballard's whole title is instructive: *A History of the Guitar, from the Earliest Antiquity to the Present Time, including a Sketch of the Different Experiments That Have Successively Been Made in Its Construction, and a Full Explanation of the Character and Merits of Tilton & Co.'s Patent Improvement of Which Can Be Attached to the Instruments of Any Other Maker.* Indeed, the cover title of this 105-page book reads "Tilton's Patent Improvement." Note the similarity of this advertising ploy to that of S. S. Stewart in his *The Banjo!: A Dissertation* (Philadelphia: S. S. Stewart, 1886), in which the Philadelphia banjo maker reviews the history of this instrument, to arrive at the conclusion that his own banjo marks the height of the instrument's design. See Gura and Bollman, *America's Instrument*, 164–65.

54. Tilton registered his banjo patent (no. 54,264) on April 24, 1866. It consisted of a novel way of tensioning the head of the instrument. See Gura and Bollman, *America's Instrument*, 92–94.

55. Horace Waters to Martin, New York, October 24, 1857.

56. Tilton continued his advertisements in the *Musical World* at least through 1859. On Zogbaum and Fairchild see Groce, *Musical Instrument Makers*, 176–77.

57. On Haynes see Sanjek, *American Popular Music*, 109; William Arms Fisher, *Notes on Music in Old Boston* (Boston: Oliver Ditson, 1918), 40, 73–74, 77; and Michael I. Holmes, "John C. Haynes Company," *Mugwumps* 4, 2 (1975): 16–18.

58. C. M. Loomis to Martin, New Haven, Conn., June 8, 1866.

59. See, for example, Gura and Bollman, *America's Instrument*, esp. chap. 3.

60. Mount's patent was entered June 1, 1852. See Alfred Frankenstein, *William Sidney Mount* (New York: Abrams, 1975), 79–94; Peter G. Bulkeley, "'The Place to Make an Artist Work': Micah Hawkins and William Sidney Mount in New York City," in *Catching the Tune: Music and William Sidney Mount*, ed. Janice Gray Armstrong (Stony Brook, N.Y.: Museums at Stony Brook, 1984), 22; and Laurence Libin, "In-

strument Innovation and William Sidney Mount's 'Cradle of Harmony,'" in ibid., 56–66.

61. The *American Musical Directory* has an unnumbered advertising page for Zoebisch that identifies the firm as the "Exclusive Wholesale Depot of C. F. Martin's Celebrated Guitars" (rear advertisement).

62. In 1847 C. A. Zoebisch exhibited a case of musical instruments at the American Institute fair. See *Catalogue Containing a Correct List of All the Articles Exhibited at the Nineteenth Annual Fair of the American Institute in the City of New York* (New York, 1847), entry no. 942. See also Groce, *Musical Instrument Makers*, 176; Lloyd Farrar, "Under the Crown and Eagle," *Newsletter of the American Musical Instrument Society*, February 1994, 2–3; and Washburn and Johnston, *Martin Guitars*, 44–48. William Waterhouse (*The New Langwill Index: A Dictionary of Musical Wind-Instrument Makers and Inventors* [London: Tony Bingham, 1993], 19) has C. A. Zoebisch as a maker of brass instruments in Neukirchen. Presumably, this is the same man who subsequently emigrated.

63. C. A. Zoebisch to C. F. Martin, New York, October 4 and December 22, 1849. Also, in 1849 John Coupa wrote Martin that he had "sent word to Zoebisch to call" and that he would pay him the thirty dollars Martin wanted. See Coupa to Martin, New York, October 17, 1849.

64. When Waters first assumed Jaques's orders, he took instruments on consignment but thereafter, trying to curry favor with Martin, usually paid immediately by cash or check. Horace Waters to Martin, New York, April 18, 1851, for the two-dollar increase in price.

65. William M. Peters to Martin, New York, December 6, 1856.

66. *Root & Cady's Illustrated Catalogue and Price List* (Chicago: Root & Cady, 1866), 63.

67. C. A. Zoebisch to Martin, New York, February 13, 1869.

68. *Musical World and Times*, June 10, 1854, 63; John W. Moore, *Encyclopaedia of Music: Elementary, Technical, Historical, Biographical, Vocal, and Instrumental* (Boston: John P. Jewett, 1854), 353.

69. Berwind exhibited at the Franklin Institute exhibition in 1856; see *Catalogue of the Twenty-Fifth Exhibition of American Manufactures Held in the City of Philadelphia* (Philadelphia: William S. Young, 1856), 74.

70. See, for example, *Musical Times* (Boston), February 25, 1860, 13, where both Charles Bruno and C. A. Zoebisch & Sons used this phrase to describe Martin's wares. In *Musical World and Times*, February 18, 1854, 83, Horace Waters advertised "Martin's Unrivalled Guitar."

CHAPTER FIVE

1. Jonathan B. West to Martin, Nashville, Tenn., October 23, 1857; all letters from CFM, unless otherwise noted.

2. John Heitz to Martin, Leesburg, Va., December 13, 1858.

3. Edward J. Balleisen, *Navigating Failure: Bankruptcy and Commercial Society in Antebellum America* (Chapel Hill: University of North Carolina Press, 2001), 17, 27.

4. [Various Contributors], *Two Centuries of Nazareth, 1740–1940* (Nazareth: Nazareth, Pennsylvania, Bicentennial, 1940), 120–24, 195–96.

5. Ledger, 1849–59, accounts with C. F. Martin Jr., CFM.

6. [Various Contributors], *Two Centuries of Nazareth*, 193–94.

7. A eulogy at Martin's funeral in 1873 places him in the Schoeneck congregation

until 1862. Transcription in CFM. Ledger, 1852–57, CFM, accounts with Nazareth Hall, 1857, appended.

8. U.S. Census for 1860, Northampton County, Manuscript Returns, "Manufactures," National Archives, Washington, D.C.

9. By this time, Cincinnati had its own guitar maker, F. Holtvoight. In 1860 his guitars won a "small silver medal" at the exhibition of the Ohio Mechanics' Institute in that city. The instruments were described as "highly credible to the maker." See *Report of the Eighteenth Exhibition of the Ohio Mechanics' Institute* (Cincinnati: Ohio Mechanics' Institute, 1860), 88.

10. "Statement of Shop in 1864," and United States Internal Revenue, statement of income, both in CFM. Other accounts for this period, for example, show that they drew nine dollars or ten dollars a week for their own labor at the factory. See Daybook, 1859–64, and Journal, 1859–67, CFM.

11. In 1854 Bruno, Weissenborn & Company advertised that it was an agent for "Schmidt & Maul's Celebrated Guitars" (*Musical Times*, November 24, 1854, 160). By 1858, though, Bruno was announcing himself as selling Martin's instruments (*Musical World*, August 28, 1858, 554). Between 1860 and 1863 Bruno once again was in partnership, this time with Richard M. Morris. He then worked on his own until the late 1860s, when his son Charles Jr. joined him as Bruno & Son. Martin did business with them until 1869. Nancy Groce, *Musical Instrument Makers of New York: A Directory of Eighteenth- and Nineteenth-Century Urban Craftsmen*, Annotated Reference Works in Music no. 4 (Stuyvesant, N.Y.: Pendragon Press, 1991), 23–24.

12. Stephen Hess to C. F. Hartmann, [Pennsylvania], March 26, 1855.

13. This is readily apparent in Daybook, 1859–64, about 1860.

14. In 1849 Frederick had married Ann Marie Allerman of Cherry Hill, with whom he had three children: Clara Emilie (b. 1850); Otto Franklin (b. 1852), and Emma Natalie (b. 1854). Ann Marie died in 1861, and the following year the young Martin married Lucinda Rebecca Leibfried. They eventually had five children: Agnes Ottilie (b. 1862); Laura Lucinda (b. 1864); Frank Henry (b. 1866), who eventually took over the family business; Anna Caroline (b. 1868); and Mary Harriet (b. 1871).

15. C. F. Martin Accounts with C. F. Martin Jr. in Journal, 1859–67. In another entry, however, added to the account book five years later (but in space available on the very next page, that is, for 1866, of the accounts), Martin clarified this transaction, for he had made a credit error of $2,914.16. "Being about to make a settlement we find that I [C. F. Martin Sr.] had charged myself with the House & Lot, No. 29 Main Street," the entry reads. Rather, he had intended "Said House & Lot" to be "embodied in the Gift of $3000," it continued. Martin, his wife Ottilie, and his employee (and relative) C. F. Hartmann had then signed "in evidence of the above Explanation." This left Frederick with that amount of credit on his father's books.

16. Information in this chapter is based on Martin's Ledger, 1867–71; Daybook of C. F. Martin & Company, 1869–71; Daybook of "Guitars Sold," 1869–74; and Ledger, 1873–84. All from CFM.

17. Guitars sold to Olaf Ericson, January 4, 1860, at thirty-five dollars each; see Daybook, 1859–64.

18. Other members of the Clewell family did occasional woodworking for the Martins. In 1872, for example, Henry Clewell billed Martin for "sawing out Table legs" and making some "chair bows," and Martin also had accounts with Augustus Clewell. Daybook, 1867–74, CFM.

19. Daybook, 1867–74.

20. For coal, Martin patronized either Jefferson & Schweitzer in nearby Hecktown, a "dealer in Lehigh and Wilkesbarre Coal," or William H. Frankefield at "Brodhead Station," on the Lehigh and Lackawanna rail line. A. Heberlein provided seventy-two feet of spruce, for the sounding boards of his instruments, at $4.32. In the fall of 1869 John Kinds, another local businessman, sold him a large quantity of "bass board," perhaps for cases, for $51.50. Information in this and the next four paragraphs is taken from the collection of bills in the C. F. Martin & Company Archives, under the dates listed.

21. Other shipments from Dingee over the next few years were of three "large Rosewood" logs at $37.92; three more, weighing a total of 1,406 pounds, at $112.48; and, in 1872, six more logs (5,200 pounds) at $234.00.

22. In another set of transactions in the spring of 1873, Martin bought three more cedar logs from what now was P. M. Dingee & Son, for $126.02. Four days later he had it trucked to the Rayner & Brother mill at 11 and 13 Cannon Street, where that company sawed it into planks ("4 cuts") and shipped it to Nazareth. Occasionally, Martin secured such wood through Philadelphia. Prestien & Berwind, for example, who made pianos, sent Martin one hundred feet of rosewood veneers, as well as fifty ebony fingerboards.

23. On January 6, 1868, for example, he purchased handles, clasps, locks, finishing nails, and screws, to a total of $42.17, from Hubinger & Krumm. See Daybook, 1867–68, 1874–84, CFM.

24. C. A. Zoebisch to Martin, New York, July 24, 1872. The more expensive tuners to which Zoebisch referred may have been the elegant ones stamped "Jerome" that are found on some of Martin's instruments from this period. See plate 5-12.

25. He still manufactured custom orders on demand. As Zoebisch put it in the circular that graced the back of all his stationery, "all the above numbers, with Patent Head or Peg Head, and any size desired made to order."

26. "Price List as ordered to be printed, April 28, 1868," in CFM.

27. C. A. Zoebisch to Martin, New York, March 11, 1874. "As you see, had price list printed on back of letters, so to keep continually before customers & everybody we write to."

28. Vera Brodsky Lawrence, *Strong on Music: The New York Music Scene in the Days of George Templeton Strong, 1836–1875*, 3 vols. (Chicago: University of Chicago Press, 1988–99), 1:274, 414, 490, 2:500.

29. A guitar made by Bini in New York, dated 1852, has been recorded. See the Vintage Instruments Web site, ‹*www.vintage-instruments.com*› (January 7, 2002). "Guitar, BINI, JOSEPH, New York, 1852, two piece Brazilian rosewood back, matching ribs, one-piece spruce top, 2 piece cedar neck, ebony fingerboard, missing bridge & pegs, lob 316mm, scale 16-½"; Pequeno [small] guitar?" This instrument is fan-braced and smaller than a terz guitar.

30. *J. Howard Foote's Descriptive Catalogue of Musical Instruments, Strings, &c.* (New York, [ca. 1870s]), 23. Foote was at the address 31 Maiden Lane, New York, listed on this catalogue from 1862 to 1882. See Groce, *Musical Instrument Makers*, 54.

31. D. Schuyler to Martin, Buffalo, N.Y., December 26, 1867.

32. Mellor & Hoene to Martin, Pittsburgh, May 12, 1871.

33. Anna Polster to Martin, Baltimore, September 16, 1867.

34. She had brought a terz guitar to a local repairman for similar adjustment but had had it returned looking so bad that now she wanted to sell it. Ibid., October 7, 1867.

35. Mrs. A. G. Gourlay to Martin, Philadelphia, May 3, 1872. Berwind had personally written to Martin on April 29, 1872, regarding his decision to go into the piano-making business with Prestien.

36. Louisa C. Van Vleck to Martin, Salem, N.C., February 6, 1871.

37. C. A. Zoebisch & Sons to Martin, New York, May 1, 1869.

38. On Aguado see Philip J. Bone, *The Guitar and Mandolin: Biographies of Celebrated Players and Composers*, 2d ed. (London: Schott & Company, 1954), 2–5, and Graham Wade, *The Traditions of the Classical Guitar* (London: John Calder, 1980), 119–21.

39. C. A. Zoebisch & Sons to Martin, New York, February 13, 1869.

40. Zoebisch said that he had bought it "off a friend of his." Knoop had toured with, and later married, the guitarist Dolores de Goni (the same performer after whom Martin had named one of his earlier models). Lawrence, *Strong on Music*, 1:118–19, 137–39, 223, 353, 616 n.

41. C. A. Zoebisch & Sons to Martin, New York, May 31, 1872.

42. For Holland's biography see James M. Trotter, *Music and Some Highly Musical People [with] Sketches of the Lives of Remarkable Musicians of the Colored Race* (Boston: Lee & Shepard, 1881), 114–30. Knaebel was well known as an arranger, particularly for "Ned" Kendall's brass band, of which Schubert was also a member.

43. Ibid., 120.

44. November 25, 1861, in Daybook, 1859–64.

45. Justin Holland to Martin, Cleveland, December 20, 1865.

46. Ibid., March 6, 1869.

47. Ibid., March 18, 1869.

48. W. R. Hoeg to Martin, Cincinnati, September 23, 1870.

49. Jim Washburn and Richard Johnston, *Martin Guitars: An Illustrated Celebration of America's Premier Guitarmaker* (Emmaus, Pa.: Rodale Press, 1997), 75.

50. C. A. Zoebisch & Sons to Martin, New York, September 1, 1869.

51. Ibid., December 9 and 23, 1867.

52. Charles Bruno to Martin, New York, March 21, 1867.

53. C. A. Zoebisch & Sons to Martin, New York, December 13, 1867.

54. E. A. Coldridge to Martin, Demopolis, Ala., October 8, 1867.

55. C. A. Zoebisch & Sons to Martin, New York, December 13, 1869.

56. Ibid., December 3, 21, and April 10, 1869.

57. Ibid., May 19, 1870.

58. Ibid., February 13, 1868.

59. Ibid., May 30, 1870.

60. Ibid., March 31, 1871.

61. Ibid., April 24, 1871.

62. Ibid., July 16, 1872.

63. Ibid., April 5, 1871.

64. Ibid., March 30, 1871.

65. Ibid., April 5 and 12, 1871.

66. Ibid., May 30, 1871, forwarding letter from John C. Haynes & Company to Zoebisch & Sons, Boston, April 19, 1871. Zoebisch had asked for the missive's return, but for some reason Martin kept it.

67. Klemm & Brother to Martin, Philadelphia, September 11, 1867.

68. C. A. Zoebisch & Sons to Martin, New York, April 12, 1871.

69. Lee & Walker to Martin, Philadelphia, April 19, 1871.

70. C. A. Zoebisch & Sons to Martin, New York, December 13, 1869.

71. Ibid., September 11, 1867.

72. E. A. Coldridge to Martin, Demopolis, Ala., October 8, 1867.

73. Ibid., October 8, 1867.

74. *Western Musical World*, October 1867, 157, where Brainard's Sons also announced that it had "a large stock of French and American Guitars" for sale, as well as the "celebrated *Martin Guitars*."

75. C. A. Zoebisch & Sons to Martin, New York, April 10, 1869.

76. Ibid., April 19, 1869.

77. In one of William Hall & Son's advertisements for Ashborn's guitars, for example, the firm quoted from the report of the American Institute to the effect that the guitars "were constructed in such a manner as to withstand the changes of any climate." *New York Musical World*, January 5, 1856, 12.

78. C. A. Zoebisch & Sons to Martin, New York, June 11, 1869.

79. John Teagle, *Washburn: Over One Hundred Years of Fine Stringed Instruments* (New York: Musical Sales, 1996), 18–20.

80. Lyon & Healy to Martin, Chicago, January 11, February 16, March 30, and April 5, 1870.

81. C. A. Zoebisch & Sons to Martin, New York, April 24 and May 30, 1871.

82. On Ferdinand Zogbaum, another wholesaler, see Groce, *Musical Instrument Makers*, 176–77; on Herman Sonntag, in the same business, ibid., 146.

83. C. A. Zoebisch & Sons to Martin, New York, May 30, 1871.

84. Lyon & Healy to Martin, Chicago, June 7, 1871.

85. Ibid., June 12, 1871.

86. C. A. Zoebisch & Sons to Martin, New York, October 23, 1871. Zoebisch had not been able to see either Lyon or Healy, he told his friend. The former had been in the East at the time of the conflagration, for Zoebisch had actually seen him just before his own trip, in his own store in New York, where the Chicago businessman had purchased some guitars for stock. And Zoebisch had missed Healy because he evidently lived on the west side of Chicago, "too far away to get to him handy," Zoebisch wrote.

87. Evidently, Healy had been present at some meeting in New York that Martin had attended but had not made himself known to him. The latter had written to find out why. "We supposed," the letter continued, "that there was some influence at work against us," and if such were the case Martin might have said something at the interview that he would not have had he known Healy was there. Lyon felt assured that, "as the matter now [stood]," the firm would be treated fairly, by which he meant that they expected the largest discount possible, the same supposedly offered preferred clients. Lyon & Healy to Martin, Chicago, May 3 and June 20, 1872.

88. John C. Haynes & Company to Martin, Boston, July 29, 1872, and Lyon & Healy to Martin, Chicago, July 31, 1872.

89. C. A. Zoebisch & Sons to Martin, New York, November 6 and November 21, 1872.

90. Ibid., October 24 and November 21, 1872.

91. Ibid., January 9, 1873.

92. Ibid., January 17, 1873.

93. Teagle, *Washburn*, 18–20.

94. Philip Scranton, *Endless Novelty: Specialty Production and American Industrialization, 1865–1925* (Princeton: Princeton University Press, 1997), 10–12.

EPILOGUE

1. N. Marache to Martin, New York, June 29 and July 12, 1871; all letters from CFM.

2. Transcription from eulogy at Central Moravian Church, Bethlehem, Pennsylvania, CFM.

3. Ibid.

4. C. A. Zoebisch & Sons to C. F. Martin Jr., New York, September 30, October 17 and 27, 1873.

5. N. Marache to C. F. Martin Jr., New York, October 28, 1873.

INDEX

Page numbers in *italics* refer to illustrations.

—parts: tuning machines, 117–18, 122, 125, 226 (n. 25), pl. 4-5; bouts, 118; bracing, 118; top, 118; neck, 118, 119, 125, 225 (n. 20); body, 118, 225 (n. 20), pl. 4-2, pl. 4-8; joints, 119; Spanish heel, 119; back, 119, 125, 225 (n. 20); frets, 119, 225 (n. 20); peg head, 119, 225 (n. 20), pl. 4-5; bridge, 122; blocking, 125; patent head, 125; edges, 225 (n. 20); fingerboard, 225 (n. 20), pl. 4-2; sides, 225 (n. 20); sound hole, pl. 4-4; bottom, pl. 4-6; end pin, pl. 4-8

Atwill, Joseph, 53, 54, 55, 60, 62

B. K. Mould & Robert G. Greene, 98
Baack, Heinrich Eduard, 46, 52, 55, 212 (n. 75)
Bail, Louis, 207 (n. 58)
Baker, Thomas, *110*
Ballads, xi
Ballard, James, 24–29, *26*, 30, 33, 59, 130, 206 (n. 49), 207 (n. 60), 228 (nn. 47, 53), pl. 2-28; and Tilton, 132, 206 (n. 49)
Balleisen, Edward, 144
Balmer & Weber, 78, 84, 97–98
Baltimore, Md., 19, 41, 54, 61, 94, 95, 98, 101, 103, 144, 161
Baltimore & Ohio Railroad, 95, 97
The Baltimore Olio and American Musical Gazette, 101
Bands, military, 54, pl. 2-8
Banjo, 12, 16, *22*, 41, 114, 127, 128, 132, *149*, *187*, *188*, 227 (n. 40), 228 (n. 53); and minstrelsy, 19; method for, 29; rims, 117; dowel, 127; improvements to, 133; associated with men, *186*; clubs, *186*
Bank of America, 99

Bank of Marietta, 99
Bank of Nashville, 143
Banks, xiv, 186
Barnum, P. T., 13, 91, 93
Bass, double, 44, 47, 52, 63, 64, 69
Bassoon, 44, 69, 74; cost of, 47; reeds, 69
Basswood, 151
Benson, E. H., 84; counterfeiting of Martin guitars by, 84
Berlioz, Hector, xi, 8; *Symphony Fantastique*, 8
Berry & Gordon, 109
Berwind, John, 142, 161, 229 (n. 69), 232 (n. 35)
Bethlehem, Pa., 44, 45, 64, 68, 74, 105, 152, 186, 216 (n. 17)
Bini, Joseph E., 157–59, *159*, 160, 231 (n. 29)
Birch, 59
Blum, Christian, 153, 154, 155
Boak, Dick, xvi-xvii
Boardman & Gray, 130
Boccherini, Luigi, 8
Bodhran, pl. 2-4
Bone: for guitar ornamentation, 57, pl. 2-31, pl. 4-5, pl. 4-11
Bones, *48*, *49*, *149*
Booter, Andrew, 123
Boston, Mass., 12, 40, 46, 53, 57, 64, 66, 67, 71, 87, 93, 96, 99, 105, 132–33, *134*, *135*, 163, 171, *172*, 175, 179, 209 (n. 33), 225 (n. 17), pl. 3-9; "Music Hall," 91
Boucher, William, 41, 55
Boxwood, 47, 55, 212 (n. 77)
Bradley, Charles, 224 (n. 13)
Brainard, Alonso, 83, 94, 97
Brainard's Sons, 233 (n. 74). *See also* S. Brainard & Sons
Bransford Female Institute, 87
Brass, 104, 107, 156
Brass works, 113
Brauns & Focke, 61
Brazilwood, 59, 213 (n. 82)
Bremen, 35, 38, 209 (n. 33)
Bridge, Spanish. *See* Guitar parts: bridge

Bridgeport, Conn., 46, 53, 224 (n. 12)
Broadway Waltzes, 112
Bromberg and Company, 54
Brower, Ogden, & Company, 57
Brown, Mrs., 123
Brown & Greene, 154
Bruno, Charles, xiii, 64–67, 87, 148, 149, 152, 155, 157, *158*, 168, 170, 178, 183, 213 (n. 102), 230 (n. 11), pl. 2-11; as Martin's bookkeeper, 65–66; carries Tilton and Martin guitars, 133; opens business in New York, 144; guitars by, 170; advertising by, 175; sale of counterfeit Martin guitars by, 175–77; and Tilton guitars, 176; price list by, *177*; and Tilton guitars, *177*
Bruno, Charles, Jr., 175, 230 (n. 11)
Bruno, Weissenborn & Company, 148. *See also* Bruno, Charles
Bruno & Cargill, 99, 148. *See also* Bruno, Charles
Bruno & Morris, 148, 149. *See also* Bruno, Charles
Bryant Park, 89
Bugle, 46, 69, 210 (n. 43), 211 (n. 64); keyed, 44, pl. 2-5; cost of, 47, 50
Burns, Robert, 209 (n. 20)
Bushkill Township, Penn., 73

C. A. Zoebisch & Sons, xiv-xv, xviii, 84, 107, 134, 136–39, 148, 149, 154, 155, 167, 168, 170, 171, *172*; roots in Neukirchen, 134; duplicity of, 148; billhead of, *150*; attempt to corner market by, 152, 175; supplies tuning machines to Martin, 155; prices charged by, *158*; seeks exclusive agency for Martin guitars, 167; jobs Martin guitars in New York, 168;

Greene, Robert G. *See* B. K. Mould & Robert G. Greene

Grosvenor, Jasper, 216 (n. 26)

Guilds, xv, 37, 41, 71, 122; cabinetmakers, xii, 35–38; violinmakers, 36–38

Guitar, 12, *13*, *45*, 46, 53, *88*, *149*, 215 (n. 15); sizes, xiii; ornamentation, xiii, pl. 2-1, pl. 2-2, pl. 2-3; as romantic icon, 1, 17; literary images of, 1–2, 7, 9, 17, 19; fascination with, 2, *3*; popularity of, 2, 5, 6, 8–9, 17, 19, 24, 28, 30, 36, *162*, 186; early evolution of, 2–5, 7; origins of, 3–5; Spanish, 4, 5, 7, 17, 19, 24, *25*, 26, 31, 33, *33*, 37, 50, 60, 61, 76, 106, 118, 142, 157, 213 (n. 87), pl. 2-16, pl. 2-30, pl. 2-31, pl. 3-5; terz, 7, 42, *43*, 55, 59, 75, 89, 231 (nn. 29, 34); accessibility of, 9, *11*, 17, 24; associated with parlor, 13, 19; as sign of prosperity, *16*, 27, 29, pl. 1-6, pl. 1-8, pl. 2-34; cost of, 17, 31, 33, *33*, 176; and women, 17–19, *20–21*, 24, 80, 86, *140*, *141*, *186*, pl. 1-1, pl. 1-6, pl. 1-8, pl. 2-34, pl. 2-37; and American music culture, 17–19, 22–24; instruction in, 18, 19, 22, 206 (nn. 47, 58), pl. 1-7; as positive moral influence, 19, 22, *22*, *23*; power of, 19, pl. 1-1; cross-racial appeal of, 19, pl. 1-7; ease in learning to play, 22–23, *23*, 24; as accompaniment for vocals, 24, 28, 30; as instrument for concert performance, 28; music for, 29, 101, 209 (n. 20), pl. 1-2; poor quality of, in United States, 30; harp, 31, *31*, *32*, 207 (n. 60), pl. 5-1, pl. 5-2, pl. 5-3, pl. 5-4; German, 33, 62, 178, pl. 2-2; French, 33, pl. 2-22; improvements to,

35–36, 157–60, *159*, 227 (n. 44); and guild disputes, 36–37, 38; similarity to other stringed instruments, 37; European, 44, 60, 62, pl. 1-8, pl. 2-28, pl. 2-34, pl. 2-37; placed on commission, 46; repair of, 50–52, 125; ornamentation of, 57, 59, 64, 223 (n. 133); shield, *70*; demand for, 111, pl. 2-2; parlor, 114, *140*; tone of, 129, 130; vibration of, 132; size, *141*, 212 (n. 81); general use of, 142; American trade in, 142, 174; and children, 162, pl. 1-2; lyre, 163; pedagogy, 163; arrangements for, 164, 167; Washburn American, *181*, *182*, 183; clubs, *186*; associated with family, *187–88*; and minstrel stage, 205 (n. 41); English, 206 (n. 47); Vienna, 212 (n. 81), pl. 2-2, pl. 2-3

—parts, 44, 114; sounding board, 2, 4, 5, 7, 35, 60, 64, 77, 103, *159*, 160, 215 (n. 15); sound hole, 2, 4, 59, 64, *131*, *133*, 158, 220 (n. 70), pl. 2-1, pl. 4-14; bracing, xiii, 2, 4, 59–60, 118, 157–60, *159*, 231 (n. 29), pl. 2-28, pl. 2-29, pl. 2-30; strings, 4, 7, 36, 42, 44, 45, *45*, 46–47, 51, 52, 53, 54, 55, 63, 66, 67, 69, 76, 80, 87, 89, 105, 120, 121, 125, 128, 129, *129*, 132, 145, 155, 156, 158, *159*, 213 (nn. 87, 99), 226 (n. 29), pl. 4-14; bridge pins, 4, 46, 51, 57, 132, 227 (n. 44); bridge, 4, 54, 59, 60, 69, 77, 89, 125, 128–29, *129*, 132, 213 (n. 87), 227 (n. 44), pl. 2-1, pl. 4-14; fingerboard, 5, 35, 36, 50–51, 57, 59, 69, 231 (n. 22), pl. 2-1; sides, 7; head, 33, 59, 80, 223 (n. 133), 226 (n. 23), pl. 2-3, pl. 4-16; patent screws,

33, 60, 101, 211 (n. 67), 212 (n. 75); neck, 35, 59, 60, 61, 69, 76, 77, 117, pl. 2-1; pegs, 45–46, 47, 57, 61, 69, 77, 81, 120, 157; tuning machines, 47, 54, 57, 59, 60, 61, 63, 80, 105, 106, 117–18, 120, 122, 125, 155, 207 (n. 61), 223 (n. 133), 226 (nn. 23, 24), pl. 2-1, pl. 2-3; tailpiece, 47, 128, *129*, *131*, 132, pl. 4-14; heel, 59, 60; kerfed linings, 60; frets, 61, 89; dowel, 129, *131*, *133*; exotic, 212 (n. 77); cone heel, 223 (n. 133); bouts, pl. 1-8

See also Ashborn, James: guitars; Martin guitars; Tilton, William B.: guitars

The Guitar, A Serenade (Meignen), *4*

Guitar cases, 54, 55, 56, 60, 66, 67, 120, pl. 4-7

Guitar Instructor (Culver), 29

Guitar makers, 63, 90, 107, 123, 139, 157, 206 (n. 49), 207 (n. 60), 212 (n. 81), 215 (n. 15), 226 (n. 23), 227 (nn. 44, 45), 230 (n. 9); lack of, in United States, 30–31; American, 30–31, 33–34; German, 33, 60, 106; English, 35; French, 35; tools used by, 56; supplies for, 56–57; European, 59, 60, 63, 176, 118, *159*, pl. 2-1; Spanish, 60, pl. 2-16, pl. 2-30; as anonymous manufacturers, 111; competition among, 127, 133, 169–70; technological innovation by, 133; Vienna school of, pl. 2-1

Guitarmania, xi, 9, 34, 35, pl. 1-2, pl. 1-3, pl. 1-4

Guitar methods. *See* Guitar tutors

Guitar mold, pl. 2-13

La Guitaromanie (Marescot), 204 (n. 24), pl. 1-2, pl. 1-3, pl. 1-4

pl. 2-8, pl. 2-21, pl. 2-36; and Zoebisch, xii, xiv, xv, 134, 136–39, 140, 142, 148, 149, *150*, 152, 157, 163–83 passim, *172*, *176*, 229 (n. 61), 232 (n. 40, 66); as entrepreneur, xii, xv; immigration to United States, xii, xv, 37–40, 62, 72, 208 (nn. 9, 10), pl. 1-2, pl. 2-25; and economic circumstances, xii, xv, 82, 214 (n. 111); reputation of, xii, 37, 71, 82, 86, 103, 142, 160, 190, pl. 2-37; repair work by, xii, 40, 46–47, 50–52, 54, 60, 62, 66, 69, *75*, 76–77, 87, 89, 145, 211 (nn. 51, 52), 217 (n. 29), 228 (n. 50), pl. 2-7; death of, xii, 152, *158*, 164, 186, 190; as chief craftsman of C. F. Martin & Company, xii, 153; and "market revolution," xiii; and Bruno, xiii, 64–68, 133, *135*, 144, 148, 149, 152, 157, 168–69, 214 (n. 105), 230 (n. 11), pl. 2-11; leaves for Pennsylvania, xiii, 65, 67, 68, 69, *70*, 71–72, *75*, 87, 113, 144, 148, 214 (n. 111), pl. 2-35; personal connection with clients, xiii, 81, 82; and success in market, xiv; and streamlining of labor, xiv, xv; and Tilton, xiv, 107–8; and competition from other makers, xiv, 107–8, 109, 113–42 passim, 152, 177; and Ashborn, xiv, 107–8, 113, 139–42; independence of, xiv, 113, 142; rejects mass production, xv; ties to Europe, xv; and guild system, xv, 37; and Lyon & Healy, xv, 177–81, 183, 233 (n. 87); personal life of, xvi; biography of, xvi, 35–36; purchases by, xviii, 55–57, 136, pl. 2-12; clients of, *20–21*, 40–42, *40*, *45*, 47,

50–52, 60–61, 68–69, 71, 76–90 passim, 94, 96–98, 101, 103, *104*, 128, 130, 133, 134, 137, 143, 146, 148, 152, 156, 160, 163, 164, 167, 171, 210 (nn. 39, 43), 211 (nn. 61, 62, 64, 67), 215 (n. 8), 219 (nn. 51, 62, 70), 222 (n. 103), 233 (n. 87), pl. 1-6, pl. 2-4, pl. 2-7, pl. 2-8, pl. 2-27, pl. 2-35, pl. 2-37, pl. 4-1, pl. 5-1; and Ballard, *26*, *33*, 59, pl. 2-28; early guitarmaking by, 33, 34, 40, 45, 55–68, 103, 217 (n. 27); and design, 33–34, pl. 3-17; contribution of, to American guitar culture, 34; business partners of, 34, 62–68; and musicians, 34, 85–89, *88*, 163; in Vienna, 35–36; apprenticed to Stauffer, 35–36, 56, 60, 64, 106, pl. 2-1, pl. 2-25; apprenticed to Kühle, 36; marriage of, 36; returns to Neukirchen, 36; at 196 Hudson Street, 39–41, 208 (nn. 15, 17), pl. 2-21, pl. 2-25; as distributor, 40; business records of, 42, *43*; costs of, 42, 44, 45, 105, 148, 154, 155, 209 (n. 27), 28, 217 (n. 29); suppliers for, 42, 44, 46, 52, 80, 154–55, 157, 212 (nn. 75, 77), 231 (nn. 20, 22, 23), pl. 2-17; and Merz, 42, 71; American goods sold by, 44; early stock of, 44–46, *45*; and Schatz, 45–46, 62, 63–64, *65*, 68, 71, 77–78, 105, 175, 213 (n. 100), pl. 2-4, pl. 2-14, pl. 2-24, pl. 2-27, pl. 3-9; and barter and trade, 46; and used instrument trade, 46; prices of goods stocked by, 46–47, 50; as retailer, 46–47, 62, 63, 66, 79, 80, 87, 137, 173, 210 (n. 43), pl. 2-8; and violin sales, 47, pl. 2-4; cello

sales, *48–49*; and Baack, 52; and Paulus, 52; and Schroeder, 52; and use of subcontractors, 52, 54, 63; and Christman, 52, 54–55, 71; and Hartman, 52, 55, 71; as wholesaler, 52–55, 61, 79, 81–85, 94, 96, 103, 107, 137, 173; use of English by, 53; account books of, 53, 54, 55, 56, 58, 62, 65–66, 67, 74, 104, 106, 144, 149, 203 (n. 1, Preface), 210 (n. 39), 214 (nn. 105, 111), 217 (n. 27), pl. 2-10, pl. 2-11, pl. 3-8; early profits from guitarmaking, 54; and other instrument makers, 54; sale on commission by, 54, 55, 60; extension of credit by, 54–55; and Atwill, 54–55, 60, 62; rentals by, 55; and Schnepf, 55; and Coupa, 55, 60, 65, 67–68, 74–78, 103, 136, 229 (n. 63), pl. 2-35; and Fehrman, 55, 61; discounts offered by, 55, 82–83, 94, 111, 148, 160, 164, 167, 170, 171, *172*, 173–74, 178, 179–80, 181, 233 (n. 87); wood purchases by, 55–57, 105, 154, *155*, 212 (n. 73); expanding business of, 56, 94, 96, 109, 127, pl. 2-37; and expenses of establishing guitarmaking shop, 56–58, *58*, pl. 2-21; and insurance, 57, 76, 78, 152; valuation of business by, 57, 152; and advertising, 58, 101; loaning of instruments by, 61; wages paid by, 62, 63, 123, 144, 148, 153, 154; agents of, 62, 67, 68, 72–85 passim, *87*, 94, 100, 101, 110, 111, 136, 138–39, 149, 161, 165, 167, 173, 174, 214 (n. 110), 217 (n. 30), 221 (n. 93), pl. 2-35, pl. 4-1; employees of, 62–64, 78, 107, 123, 146, 152, 153–54,

157, pl. 2-11; manufactures his own strings, 63; and Maul, 63, 78; identified as violin maker, 64, pl. 2-4, pl. 2-21; at 212 Fulton Street, 66, 87, 214 (n. 105); begins use of inventory numbers, 67; at 385 Broadway, 67, 79–80, 216 (n. 26), 217 (nn. 27, 32); sale of inventory to Ludecus & Wolter, 69, *70*, 71, 74, 211 (n. 63), pl. 2-36; ethnic and cultural networks of, 71; and sales on commission, 71; and Schmidt, 71; and Stumcke, 71; establishes home at Cherry Hill, Pa., 73, 136; gap in records for, 74; guitarmaking as secondary business for, 77; ongoing visits to New York, 78, 99; and Janon, 78–81, 136, 160, 218 (nn. 36, 40, 41, 42, 44); as landlord, 80, 218 (nn. 36, 42); and westward expansion of business, 83–84, 97–98; business terms offered by, 84, 143; commissions paid by, 85; and expanding market, 85; and music instructors, 85–87, *87*, 89, 104, *162*; and de la Cova, 87, 89; replacement parts sold by, 87, 89; and Crystal Palace Exhibition, 90–91, 92–94; and Dodge, 91, *92*, 93–94, 220 (nn. 76, 83); and shipping, *95*, 96, 97, 209 (n. 27), 211 (n. 61), 213 (n. 100); and New York market, 96, 97–98, 103, 109–11, 127, 136, 138, 139, 149, 218 (n. 43), pl. 4-1; and southeastern market, 98; and financing by customers, 98–101; and network of credit, 100–101; investments by, 101–2, 146, 163; use of steam power, 101–3, 114–15, *115*, 154, 222 (n. 119); guitar-

making factory of, 101–3, *115*, *147*; commitment to craftsmanship, 103, 160, 122, 190; and wholesalers seeking exclusive rights, 107–8; supremacy of, 108, 167; and delayed orders, 109; and Waters, 109–10, *110*, 132; jobbing by, 110, 111, 127, 134, 139, 143; and consignment, 111; and transportation problems, 111; and hand craftsmanship, 113, 134; import costs of, 118; imports tuning machines, 120, pl. 2-15, pl. 5-12; and Firth, Pond, & Company, 124; income of, 124, 146, 148, 217 (n. 29); and requests to use Tilton improvements, 132; rejects experimentation, 134; and Jaques, 136; retains control over naming of guitars, 136; competition for representation of, 137–39, *138*; and Peters, 137–39, 148; marketing network of, 139; market supremacy of, 140; financial success of, 142; income of, 144; and Panic of 1857, 144; and credit, 144, 218 (n. 42); builds workshop in Nazareth, 145; forms C. F. Martin & Company, *145*; and increased involvement with Moravians, 145; shares responsibilities with son, *145*; during Civil War, 145–46, 148–49, *149*; reconciliation with Zoebisch, 148; taxes paid by, 148, 208 (n. 15); and North Main Street property, 150; yields control of business, 150; suffers stroke, 150, 152, 185; funeral of, 150, 185, 186, 215 (n. 3), 229 (n. 7); photograph of, *151*; guitarmaking supplies of, 151, 154–55, *156*; production methods of, 152;

and division of labor, 153; inventory of, 155, pl. 2-5, pl. 2-9, pl. 2-36; use of model numbers by, 156; and Holland, 163–65, *164*, *165*, 167; weathers economic difficulties, 168–69; and deceit by Bruno, 175–77; severs ties with Bruno, 176, *177*; moves into son's home, 185; declining health of, 185, 186; legacy of, 190; children of, 207 (n. 5); and Hartmann, 209 (n. 24); and financial difficulties, 218 (n. 40); and Raddé, 218 (n. 41); sale of Main Street property, 230 (n. 15); and Berwind, 232 (n. 35); and "Knoop" cello, 232 (n. 40); tools used by, pl. 2-12, pl. 2-13. *See also* C. F. Martin & Company; Martin guitars

Martin, Christian Frederick, Jr. (Frederick or Fritz), xii, xiv, xvii, 36, 38, 78, 79, 81, 100, 102, *145*, *146*, 152, 153, 154, 164, 167, 171, 183, 186, 208 (n. 10), 217 (n. 27), 218 (n. 42), 230 (n. 14); growing interest in business, xv; moves to Nazareth, 144, 150; purchases Nazareth property, 145, *147*; daughter of, *165*; assumes father's duties, 185; and Zoebisch, 185, 190; takes over C. F. Martin & Company, 186; death of, 190

Martin, Christian Frederick, IV, xvi

Martin, Clara Emilie, 230 (n. 14)

Martin, Emily Clara, 207 (n. 5)

Martin, Emma Natalie, 230 (n. 14)

Martin, Frank Henry, 183, 190, 230 (n. 14); marketing by, 190

20–21, 55, 211 (n. 67), 215
(n. 8). *See also* O'Kill,
Mary
Music: and middle class, xi,
12, 13; as common cultural
denominator, 9, 11–12; in
the home, 12, 13, 14; and
growth of instrument trade,
13–14; and children, *14*, 19,
23; and social status, 19; as
positive moral influence, 19,
22, *23*; and American culture, 11–13, *14*, *15*, 16, 17, 28,
205 (n. 34), pl. 1-5; orchestral, 74; growing interest in,
114; in European culture,
205 (n. 34), pl. 2-7; popular,
205 (n. 34); classical, pl. 2-4;
African American, pl. 2-7
"Musical fruit," 44
Musical instruments: woodwind, xi, 41, 42, 44, 46, 47,
52, 54, 69, 74, 81; brass, 41,
44, 46, 47, 52, 68, 69, 74,
210 (nn. 35, 43), pl. 2-5,
pl. 2-8; importing of, 41, 65,
74, 214 (n. 110); wholesaling
of, 42, 172, 177, 181; stringed,
44, 51, 69, 74; replacement
parts for, 44, 53, 69; repair
of, 46–47, 50–52, 54, 63, 66,
69, *75*, 76–77, 87, 125, 145,
209 (n. 33), 211 (n. 51), 214
(n. 110), 231 (n. 34); prices
of, 47, 54, 183, 210 (n. 35),
211 (n. 64); rental of, 55;
"Italian style," 64; European, 69, 71, 142; American,
124, 142; composite, 130;
collection of, 160; sales of,
180; mass production of,
183; women associated
with, *186*. *See also specific
instruments*
Musical theater, 12
*Musical World and New York
Musical Times*, 130, 142,
228 (n. 56)
Musicians, 55, 139, pl. 2-5,
pl. 4-1; professional xi, xii,
xiii, 5, 6, 7–8, 9, 12, *15*,

29–30, 40, 41, 47, 68, 76,
85–87, *88*, 89, 94, 111, 130,
133, 161, 163, 215 (n. 15), 217
(n. 30), pl. 2-4, pl. 2-5; amateur, xii, xiii, 8–9, *10*, *11*, 12,
13, *13*, *14*, 16, 17, 22, *22*, 27,
30, 40, 41, 47, 68, 74, 82,
111, 130, 228 (n. 50), pl. 1-5;
European, 56; Spanish, 163;
African American, pl. 1-7;
folk, pl. 2-4
Music instruction, *20–21*, 205
(n. 38), 206 (nn. 47, 58);
cost of, *87*. *See also* Guitar
tutors; Instruction books;
Music instructors
Music instructors, xiii, 12, 17,
25, 26, 40, 42, 46, 50, 53,
55, 56, 59, 74, 76, 79, 82,
85–87, 89, 94, 104, *135*, *137*,
139, 161, *162*, 164, *164*, 173,
185, 206 (n. 49), pl. 2-9,
pl. 2-14, pl. 2-28, pl. 2-35;
referrals to Martin by, 54,
160
Music publishing, 17, 26, 133,
164. *See also* Sheet music
Music trade, 206 (n. 47); consolidation of, 40, 109, 110;
retail, 109; American, 124;
wholesale, 171

Nash, E. P., 53, 96, 98
Nashville, Tenn., 96, 98, 99,
100, 143
Natchez, Miss., 19, 98, pl. 1-7
Nat Turner's Rebellion, 163
Naugatuck Railroad, 114, 224
(n. 12)
Naugatuck River, 113, 114, 118
Nazareth, Pa., xii, xvii, 68, 71,
72, 73, 74, 78, 79, 84, 87, *87*,
90, 93, 94, 99, 142, 144–45,
147, 151, 154, 164, 217 (n. 27),
231 (n. 22), pl. 2-12, pl. 2-37
Nazareth Hall, 74, *75*, 145, 161
Neukirchen, xii, 35, 36, 37,
42, 62, 68, 71, 134, 175, 178,
211 (n. 56), 214 (n. 111), 229
(n. 62)
New and Improved Method for

the Spanish Guitar (Torp),
24, *25*, *32*, 50
Newark, N.J., 73, 215 (n. 12)
*A New Edition of Carcassi's
Celebrated Instructions for
the Guitar* (Meignen), *26*
New England, 14, 74
New Haven, Conn., 53, 61
*New Instruction for the Span-
ish Guitar, Containing a
Variety of Songs and Pieces
by a Professor*, 206 (n. 47)
*New Instructions for the Gui-
tar, to which is added a Col-
lection of Popular Arias, by
M. Carcassi, with French
and English Text*, 206
(n. 47)
*New Instructions for the Span-
ish Guitar...by a Professor*
(Willig), 24
New Jersey, 73
*New Method for the Guitar,
Containing Elementary
Instructions in Music,
Designed for Those Who
Study without a Master*
(Converse), 29–30
New Orleans, La., 81, 86, 96,
97, 98
New York, N.Y., xii, xv, 12, 18,
19, *20–21*, 26, *26*, 31, 33, 38,
45, 46, 47, 54, 55, 63, 68–86
passim, 90, 93, 94, 96, 97,
99, 103, 105, 107–8, 109, 111,
128, 138, 144, 148, 154, 155,
155, *156*, 157, 159, 167, 174,
177, 179, 181, 185, 186, 190,
206 (nn. 49, 58), 215 (n. 12),
217 (n. 27), 218 (n. 43),
224 (n. 9), 231 (n. 29), 233
(n. 87), pl. 2-2, pl. 2-12,
pl. 2-17, pl. 2-21, pl. 2-36,
pl. 3-3, pl. 4-1; music
houses, xiv, 52–53, 82, 83,
107–11, 113, 114, 116, 117, 124,
126–27, 132–34, *135*, *137*,
138, 139, 142, 148, 163, 169,
179; as center of American
music trade, 35, 40–41, 68,
136, 139, 167, 183; neighbor-

H. EUGENE AND LILLIAN YOUNGS LEHMAN SERIES

Lamar Cecil, *Wilhelm II: Prince and Emperor, 1859–1900* (1989).

Carolyn Merchant, *Ecological Revolutions: Nature, Gender, and Science in New England* (1989).

Gladys Engel Lang and Kurt Lang, *Etched in Memory: The Building and Survival of Artistic Reputation* (1990).

Howard Jones, *Union in Peril: The Crisis over British Intervention in the Civil War* (1992).

Robert L. Dorman, *Revolt of the Provinces: The Regionalist Movement in America* (1993).

Peter N. Stearns, *Meaning Over Memory: Recasting the Teaching of Culture and History* (1993).

Thomas Wolfe, *The Good Child's River*, edited with an introduction by Suzanne Stutman (1994).

Warren A. Nord, *Religion and American Education: Rethinking a National Dilemma* (1995).

David E. Whisnant, *Rascally Signs in Sacred Places: The Politics of Culture in Nicaragua* (1995).

Lamar Cecil, *Wilhelm II: Emperor and Exile, 1900–1941* (1996).

Jonathan Hartlyn, *The Struggle for Democratic Politics in the Dominican Republic* (1998).

Louis A. Pérez Jr., *On Becoming Cuban: Identity, Nationality, and Culture* (1999).

Yaakov Ariel, *Evangelizing the Chosen People: Missions to the Jews in America, 1880–2000* (2000).

Philip F. Gura, *C. F. Martin and His Guitars, 1796–1873* (2003).